The Continuing Relevance of Wesleyan Theology

The Continuing Relevance of Wesleyan Theology
Essays in Honor of Laurence W. Wood

Edited by
NATHAN CRAWFORD

With a Foreword by Stanley Hauerwas

☙PICKWICK *Publications* · Eugene, Oregon

THE CONTINUING RELEVANCE OF WESLEYAN THEOLOGY
Essays in Honor of Laurence W. Wood

Copyright © 2011 Wipf and Stock Publishers. All rights reserved. Except for brief quotations in critical publications or reviews, no part of this book may be reproduced in any manner without prior written permission from the publisher. Write: Permissions, Wipf and Stock Publishers, 199 W. 8th Ave., Suite 3, Eugene, OR 97401.

The publisher and editor gratefully acknowledge permission from the Wesley Theological Society to reprint the following articles:

William J. Abraham, "The End of Wesleyan Theology," *Wesleyan Theological Journal* 40.1 (2005) 7–25.

Barry L. Callen, "Heart of a Radical Reform: Christology and the Church of God (Anderson)," *Wesleyan Theological Journal* 44.2 (2009) 168–88.

Pickwick Publications
An Imprint of Wipf and Stock Publishers
199 W. 8th Ave., Suite 3
Eugene, OR 97401

www.wipfandstock.com

ISBN 13: 978-1-60899-538-7

Cataloging-in-Publication data:

The continuing relevance of Wesleyan theology : essays in honor of Laurence W. Wood / edited by Nathan Crawford ; with a foreword by Stanley Hauerwas.

xii + 278 p. ; 23 cm. Includes bibliographical references.

ISBN 13: 978-1-60899-538-7

1. Wood, Laurence W., 1941–. 2. Methodism — History. 3. Theology, Doctrinal. I. Crawford, Nathan. II. Hauerwas, Stanley, 1940–. III. Title.

BR50 .C62 2011

Manufactured in the U.S.A.

Contents

Foreword—Stanley Hauerwas / vii

List of Contributors / ix

Introduction—The Continuing Relevance of Wesleyan Theology: An Introduction and Proposal—*Nathan Crawford* / 1

PART ONE: RETHINKING THE HISTORY

1. Augustine's Interpretation of Romans 7:14–25, His *Ordo Salutis* and His Consistent Belief in a Christian Victory over Sin—*Christopher T. Bounds* / 15

2. Exploring the Background for the Pentecost Connection in Early Methodism—*J. Steven O'Malley* / 28

3. Heart of a Radical Reform: Christology and the Church of God Movement (Anderson)—*Barry L. Callen* / 38

4. John Fletcher's Influence on the Nineteenth-Century American Holiness Movement's Worldview—*D. William Faupel* / 53

5. A Baptism of Divine Love: The Pentecostal Experience of Spirit Baptism —*Kimberly Ervin Alexander* / 68

6. Evangelicalism Examined . . . Again: Continuing the Debate between Donald W. Dayton and George Marsden—*Jonathan Dodrill* / 83

PART TWO: CONTRIBUTION TO CURRENT THEOLOGICAL PROBLEMS

7. The End of Wesleyan Theology—*William J. Abraham* / 97

8. Sketching a Fundamental Wesleyan Theology: Pursuing a Hermeneutic of Love with Augustine's *De Doctrina Christian*—*Nathan Crawford* / 111

9. Pushing the Mystery Button: The Limits of Logic and Language —*Kevin Kinghorn* / 123

Contents

10 Evolution and the Deep Resonances between Science and Theology
—*Michael L. Peterson* / 139

11 Kenosis and Emergence: A Wesleyan Perspective—*Bradford McCall* / 159

12 Revisiting the Day of Atonement—*Graham McFarlane* / 175

13 Bind Us Together?: A Sketch of Shame and Violence in the Day of Atonement and Communion—*Aaron Perry* / 186

14 *Prima Gratia, Prima Fide,* and *Prima Scriptura*: Reforming Protestant Principles—*Don Thorsen* / 201

15 Theological Interpretation and Wesley—*Joel B. Green* / 225

16 Preaching and Practicing Wisdom—*Michael Pasquarello, III* / 237

17 From Suspicion to Synthesis: Toward a Shared Wesleyan and Pentecostal Theology of Spirituality—*Tony Richie* / 252

Afterword: A Response to the Essays—*Laurence W. Wood* / 269

Works by Laurence W. Wood / 277

Foreword

STANLEY HAUERWAS

In 1989 I was privileged to give the Ryan Lectures at Asbury Theological Seminary. As a result of my being at Asbury, I was a witness to a remarkable event. Before my first lecture, Larry Wood was installed in his chair at Asbury. I was not only pleased to see Larry receive this well deserved honor, but I was particularly struck by the fact he was asked to take an oath before he was installed. I do not remember the exact wording of the oath he took, but I do remember he bound himself to grow in holiness.

One of the reasons I found this to be such a remarkable event was because I had recently read Alasdair MacIntyre's Gifford Lectures, *Three Rival Versions of Moral Inquiry: Encyclopedia, Genealogy, and Tradition*. In the last chapter, MacIntyre argues that when the universities of Scotland no longer required those who held chairs in moral philosophy to take oaths to express their loyalty to the precepts of Reformed theology the intellectual life of those universities became incoherent.

According to MacIntyre the oaths were made possible by a high degree of homogeneity in fundamental belief and what counted as rational justification shared by the wider public as well as in the universities and colleges of Scotland. As a result of these fundamental agreements MacIntyre argued that creative rational disagreements were possible in the universities of Scotland because disagreement necessarily takes place against a background of agreements necessary to constitute a community of enquiry. That Asbury would ask Larry to take an oath, that Larry was willing to take the oath, suggested to me that the Wesleyan tradition, at least at Asbury, was still in good working order.

The life and work of Larry Wood has exemplified the oath he took and the service he has provided for the churches that are identified in the Wesleyan tradition. He has not only done fundamental work to help us better understand theological developments in early Methodism, but he has extended the tradition by helping us understand how Wesley and those who followed him are rightly understood only if we read them in light of the great Catholic tradition. He has also put the theology of Wesley and other theologians of early Methodism in conversation with contemporary theology and science in a way that has prevented the Methodist tradition from becoming enclosed on itself.

Larry Wood has kept the promise he made when he took the oath of his office. That he has done so, and one can only hope he will have years left to continue his work, is a gift we desperately need. For if Billy Abraham is right to suggest in his essay for this volume that we may be confronting the exhaustion of the Wesleyan theological tradition then we will continue to need the kind of theological work Larry Wood has exemplified.

Contributors

WILLIAM J. ABRAHAM is Albert Cook Outler Professor of Wesley Studies at Perkins School of Theology, Southern Methodist University. His interests lie in a variety of places, from Wesleyan studies to concerns over canonicity and evangelism to the philosophy of religion. He has published many books and numerous articles in a wide variety of journals, on a wide spectrum of topics. Most recently he has been engaged in the promulgation of what he terms "Canonical Theism."

KIMBERLY ERVIN ALEXANDER is Associate Professor of Historical Theology at the Pentecostal Theological Seminary, Cleveland, Tennessee. Her expertise, shown in her publishing record, lies in the history of the Pentecostal movement.

CHRISTOPHER T. BOUNDS is Associate Professor of Religion and Philosophy at Indiana Wesleyan University. He is concerned with the communication of the Wesleyan distinctive of theology. He is also interested in the doctrine of entire sanctification, especially in its historical development in the early church fathers. He has published in several journals and has a forthcoming monograph (Routledge).

BARRY L. CALLEN is University Professor of Christian Studies at Anderson University, Anderson, Indiana. He has written or edited more than sixteen books and is editor of the Wesleyan Theological Journal. In addition to his teaching and writing, Barry is a popular speaker at churches and conferences in North America and around the world.

NATHAN CRAWFORD is a PhD Candidate at Loyola University of Chicago and is Adjunct Professor of Religion and Philosophy at Wesley Seminary, Indiana Wesleyan University. He has published articles on everyone from Augustine of Hippo to David Tracy, while also seeking to speak theologically in a postmodern world.

JONATHAN DODRILL is a PhD student at Garrett-Evangelical Theological Seminary working in the areas of American religious history and Wesleyan Theology. His current work focuses on the affects of industrialization upon Holiness city missions and Fundamentalism's role in their changing eschatology."

D. WILLIAM FAUPEL is Director of the Library and Professor of the History of Christianity at Wesley Theological Seminary. He is an expert in the history of the holiness movement and the Pentecostal movement. He has done much research and published widely in both of these areas.

Contributors

Joel B. Green is Professor of New Testament and Associate Dean for the Center for Advanced Theological Studies, Fuller Theological Seminary. He is the author or editor of almost thirty books, including *Body, Soul, and Human Life: The Nature of Humanity in the Bible* (2008), *Reading Scripture as Wesleyans* (2010), and *Methods for Luke* (2010). He edits the *Journal of Theological Interpretation*.

Stanley Hauerwas is Gilbert T. Rowe Professor of Theological Ethics at Duke University. He was recognized as "America's Best Theologian" by *Time* in 2001. He has published numerous books, journals, reviews, and chapters.

Kevin Kinghorn is Associate Professor of Philosophy at Asbury Theological Seminary and Tutor for Philosophy and Philosophical Theology at Wycliffe Hall, University of Oxford. He has published articles in philosophy of religion, ethics, and philosophical psychology; and he is the author of *The Decision of Faith: Can Christian Beliefs Be Freely Chosen?* (T. & T. Clark, 2005). His current research interests lie in ethical theory, and he is completing a book on the nature of the Good.

Bradford McCall is a PhD Student at Regent University (Virginia). His current research seeks to bridge the seeming gulf between theology and the natural sciences. He has published numerous reviews and articles in various journals.

Graham McFarlane is Lecturer in Systematic Theology at London School of Theology. He has written two books on the Scottish theologian Edward Irving, *Christ and the Spirit* and *Edward Irving* and has launched the popular *Why Do You Believe?* series with Paternoster Press. He is presently finishing two books: *Forgiveness and Atonement* and *Relational Theology*.

J. Steven O'Malley is John T. Seamands Professor of Methodist Holiness History and Director, The Center for the Study of World Christian Revitalization Movements, at Asbury Theological Seminary. He has served as pastor in the United Methodist Church in Austria, as well as in the US. He has also published six monographs, numerous journal articles and book chapters, edited and co-edited 35 volumes in the Revitalization Studies Series (Scarecrow and Emeth Press).

Michael Pasquarello, III is the Granger E. and Anna A Fisher Professor of Preaching at Asbury Theological Seminary. His teaching and research interests focus on the relationship between the practices of theology, preaching, and pastoral ministry in the life of the church. He has published *Sacred Rhetoric: Preaching as a Theological and Pastoral Practice of the Church* (Eerdmans, 2004); *Christian Preaching: A Trinitarian Theology of Proclamation* (Baker Academic, 2005); *We Speak Because We Have First Been Spoken: A Grammar of the Preaching Life* (Eerdmans, 2009); *John Wesley: A Preaching Life* (Abingdon, 2010); *God's Ploughman: Hugh Latimer, a Preaching Life 1490–1555* (Paternoster Press, 2010) and co-edited with Joel B. Green, *Narrative Reading, Narrative Preaching: Reuniting New Testament Interpretation and Proclamation* (Baker Academic, 2004).

Contributors

AARON PERRY is Pastor of Christian Education at Centennial Road Church in Brockville, Ontario. He is co-author (with Tim Perry) of *He Ascended into Heaven: Learn to Live an Ascension-Shaped Life* (Paraclete Press, forthcoming) and is currently editing *Developing Ears to Hear: Listening in Pastoral Life and Roles* (Emeth Press). He is author of several articles, essays, and reviews.

MICHAEL L. PETERSON is Professor of Philosophy of Religion at Asbury Theological Seminary. Dr. Peterson's interests and publications are in philosophy of religion, philosophy of science, and philosophy of education. He has written or been senior author in a number of books: *Reason and Religious Belief* (Oxford University Press); *God and Evil: An Introduction to the Issues* (HarperCollins/Westview); *With All Your Mind: A Christian Philosophy of Education* (University of Notre Dame Press); *Evil and the Christian God* (Baker Books); and *Philosophy of Education: Issues and Options* (InterVarsity Press).

TONY RICHIE is missionary teacher at SEMISUD (Quito, Ecuador), guest lecturer at the Pentecostal Theological Seminary and Lee University (Cleveland, TN) and adjunct theology professor for Regent University Divinity School (Virginia Beach, VA). Dr Richie is an Ordained Bishop in the Church of God, and Senior Pastor at New Harvest Church Knoxville, TN. He serves the Society for Pentecostal Studies as Ecumenism Interest Group Leader and Liaison to the Inter-Faith Relations Commission of the National Council of Churches (USA) and represents Pentecostals on Inter-religious Dialogue and Cooperation of the World Council of Churches (WCC, in Geneva, SW). He is also an ecumenical representative to the Commission of the Churches on International Affairs (CCIA), a think tank and advisory board to the WCC and the United Nations, the first ever Pentecostal appointed in this capacity. He is widely published in numerous journals.

DON THORSEN is Professor of Theology and Chair of Advanced Studies in the Graduate School of Theology at Azusa Pacific University. He is the author of several books, including *The Wesleyan Quadrilateral, Theological Resources for Ministry, Inclusive Language Handbook*, co-authored with Vickie Becker, *An Exploration of Christian Theology*, and *Everything You Know about Evangelicalism Is Wrong, or Almost Everything*, co-authored with Steve Wilkens. Thorsen also edited *The Holiness Manifesto*, with Kevin Mannoia. He is also an Advisory Editor for the magazine *Christianity Today*, and he does ecumenical work with several organizations, including the Commission on Faith and Order, and Commission on Interfaith Relations, both affiliated with the National Council of Churches.

LAURENCE W. WOOD is the Frank Paul Morris Professor of Systematic Theology and the coordinator for the London School of Theology /Asbury Theological Seminary PhD program. He has been an influential voice in the Wesleyan movement, writing numerous articles and publishing a number of books.

Introduction

The Continuing Relevance of Wesleyan Theology
An Introduction and a Proposal

NATHAN CRAWFORD

THE GOAL OF THIS text is twofold: first, it is an attempt to pay tribute to the Wesleyan theologian Laurence "Larry" Wood. Second, though, it is meant to put forward an argument that Wesleyan theology has a relevant role to play in the current theological discussion, offering different ways of thinking and interesting solutions to complex problems that may not be seen from other traditional viewpoints. Laurence Wood's concern as a theologian has been to not just espouse distinctly Wesleyan doctrines to Wesleyans, but to bring Wesleyan theology into broader dialogue with the orthodox[1] church tradition while also explicating ways the orthodox tradition may change the way that Wesleyan theology is done. All in all, the goal of this text is to continue to carry on the impetus set by Dr. Wood to show the continuing relevance of Wesleyan theology to the broader theological arena.

The concern, then, of both Wood and this collection is to enter what Albert Outler termed "Phase III" of Wesleyan studies.[2] For Outler, "Phase I" was the "Methodist Cocoon" which focused upon the link between John Wesley and Methodism.[3] "Phase II" is a selective interpretation of Wesley, focusing upon his thought and praxis outside of his specific ecclesial context of Methodism.[4] "Phase III" seeks to read Wesley and his theology within the broader historical context while also showing the broader ecumenical relevance of his theology.[5] Outler believes that this phase entails three necessary issues which must

---

1. By orthodox, I do not mean the specific "Eastern Orthodox" church tradition, but the broader, universal Christian tradition that follows in the line of, and gives credence to, the seven ecumenical councils of Christianity.

2. See Albert Outler, "A New Future for Wesley Studies: An Agenda for 'Phase III,'" in *The Wesleyan Theological Heritage: Essays of Albert C. Outler*, ed. Thomas C. Oden and Leicester R. Longden (Grand Rapids: Zondervan, 1991) 125–42.

3. Ibid., 128–30.

4. Ibid., 130–32.

5. Ibid., 132–42. Outler sees "Phase III" as more of a "vision" or a "beginning" than an achievement. This is the ongoing task of Wesleyan theology.

be addressed. First, there is the methodological issue, with Outler advocating that a theologian must deal with the whole Wesley, both thought and practice, instead of picking one specific feature or thought pattern.[6] Second, Wesleyan theology needs to read Wesley in light of his sources, which means there is a necessity to read him in the "ecumenical tradition of historic Christianity," including classics, the patristics, the reformation and counter-reformation, along with thought from his own time period.[7] Third, Wesleyan theology must speak to the larger Christian tradition. This includes the commitments that the tradition has while also pursuing thought in light of one's current situation.[8]

Now, one of the concerns that arises in a program such as Outler's for Wesleyan theology is the idea of the orthodox, Christian tradition. If Wesleyan theology is to do theology in concert with this tradition, both learning from and speaking to it, then we should begin by pursuing what we mean by the orthodox, Christian tradition. The way that most of the authors in the following text—along with Laurence Wood—have thought about orthodox Christianity comes from the work of the Methodist theologian Thomas C. Oden. Oden has worked quite tirelessly to offer an ecumenical approach to theology through a rearticulation of the work of Vincent of Lérins, specifically his *Commonitory*.[9] Oden has shown that for Vincent, there are three general criteria for what can be defined within orthodoxy: first, it is universally assented to in the Christian tradition; second, it is rooted in apostolic antiquity; and, third, it has been consented to within the seven ecumenical councils of Christendom.[10] Wolfhart Pannenberg reinforces this by showing that dogmatic statements within Christianity continue the tradition founded in the early church by speaking to the universality of an experience within the religion.[11] Orthodox Christian theology, then, becomes a unifying center within the tradition. It is those dogmas that Christianity holds to be central and, to a certain extent, nonnegotiable; however, these are not meant to divide, but to offer a place for agreement among a multiplicity of people. Christian theology, then, becomes a "wide circumference" that rethinks this center that is orthodoxy.[12]

Michael Peterson further develops the idea by articulating what he sees as two sides of orthodoxy. First, he shows that there is a cognitive side, which is the set of beliefs

---

6. Ibid., 137.

7. Ibid., 138.

8. Ibid.

9. Vincent of Lérins, *The Commonitory*, in *Nicene and Post-Nicene Fathers* 11 (Peabody: Hendrickson, 1994) 127–57.

10. Thomas C. Oden, *The Rebirth of Orthodoxy* (New York: HarperOne, 2002) 162–63.

11. Pannenberg, *Basic Questions in Theology, Volume I.*, trans. George H. Kehm (Philadelphia: Westminster, 1970) 208.

12. Thomas C. Oden, *After Modernity . . . What?* (Grand Rapids: Zondervan, 1992) 175ff. Many theologians see the event of Jesus Christ as the center of Christian theology. See, for example, Karl Barth, Karl Rahner, David Tracy, Wolfhart Pannenberg, and Robert Jenson, among a multitude of others. What these disparate theologians have in common is that all theological work begins with meditation upon the experience of Jesus Christ within the Christian tradition, with all Christian dogma moving from this center. For this point, see specifically Pannenberg, *Basic Questions in Theology*, 190–95.

developed within the Christian tradition.[13] This set of beliefs is described by Vincent of Lérins as the faith generally shared by all Christians, that set of theological commitments that are intellectually assented to.[14] These would be those dogmas like the belief in the Triune nature of God and the full humanity and full divinity of Jesus. These dogmas act as unifying factors within the tradition as they are a set of beliefs that all Christians can profess as believing. Since the Christians that profess these dogmas extend across multiple times and places, these beliefs give a sense of unification with those that have come before and will come after.[15]

The second side of orthodoxy that Peterson articulates is the personal/ experiential side. This side says that the Christian tradition coalesces around a common experience, which is the experience of Jesus of Nazareth as the Christ, the Son of God.[16] The creeds and beliefs of Christians are predicated upon this experience. The experience is explained and thought through in a way that allows for a dogmatic statement, giving a "right confession" as to what this experience of Jesus: an experience of God.[17] This confession continues the experience of Jesus as the Christ through the action of adoration. The confession is adoration.[18] This experience creates communities of people who all have had similar experience of God's self-disclosure in Jesus.[19] The worship of God recreates this experience, coalescing an entire community around the experience, which results in a unified "body" that allows for moments of meditation upon the nature and person of Christ, giving impetus to the cognitive side. But, there would be no experiential side if there was not an idea of what it was that was being experience.[20] So, the two sides of orthodoxy become inexplicably linked.

Orthodox Christianity, though, is concerned with being able to articulate these doctrines and ways of thinking with the broader culture(s) and world.[21] This concern resides in the very nature of orthodoxy: as Oden says, the orthodox gospel is always declared in a time and place.[22] The gospel's declaration in this time and place refers to orthodoxy's inherent flexibility. Orthodox Christian thinking is not limited to a time or place, which reflects the nature of God. Rather, orthodox thinking, like the Triune God, is revealed and articulated in a time and place.[23] The communication of different dogmatic statements can only occur through a conversation with contemporary culture in a way that

---

13. Michael L. Peterson, *With All Your Mind: A Christian Philosophy of Education* (Notre Dame: University of Notre Dame Press, 2001) 10–11.

14. Oden, *After Modernity . . . What?*, 37.

15. Ibid., 161.

16. Peterson, *With All Your Mind*, 12.

17. Pannenberg, *Basic Questions in Theology*, 202.

18. Ibid., 203.

19. Oden, *After Modernity . . . What?*, 160.

20. Ibid., 181.

21. Robert Jenson, *Systematic Theology, Volume I: The Triune God* (New York: Oxford University Press, 1997) 9.

22. Oden, *Rebirth of Orthodoxy*, 35.

23. Ibid., 41–44.

theology can borrow different idioms and ways of thinking from said culture in order to communicate the thrust of our thinking. The concern, then, is to express the truth of the Triune God to all people, the broader culture included.[24] For Oden, the discipline of theology is a meditation upon the unchanging center of Christian thought within a changing culture.[25]

Thus, Orthodoxy is an attempt to communicate the truths of the Christian faith, as explicated through its tradition, to the broader culture. Christian theology becomes primarily an explication of various Christian dogmas in conversation with the broader culture for not only the culture, but also the church. The thinking that occurs in theology, then, is concerned with openness and having a multiplicity of voices in conversation around this theological center. One such distinct voice comes from the Wesleyan tradition, and especially that part which refers to itself as the holiness tradition. A major voice speaking from this position to not only the broader Wesleyan tradition, but to the whole of Christian theology is Laurence Wood. His work seeks to bring Wesleyan-Holiness theology into conversation with the broader Christian tradition as this tradition attempts to communicate with the whole of culture. He accomplishes this through two methodological choices. First, he wants to rethink the history of the Wesleyan movement by emphasizing the unique contribution of John Fletcher. Second, he has sought to bring a variety of different thinkers—like Kant, Hegel, Kierkegaard, Heidegger, Ricoeur, Pannenberg, and Moltmann—to bear upon the kind of thinking that occurs in Wesleyan theology. This opens his theology up as a place for Wesleyan thinkers to look as an example of Outler's "Phase III." Let's now explore how he does this.

The first area that I want to focus on is Wood's work on the history of the Methodist movement, along with the import of this into an understanding of holiness. His most important contribution here has been his historical work on John Fletcher.[26] Specifically, Wood argues that in early Methodism there was a linking of Pentecost and "baptism in the Spirit" with the doctrine of entire sanctification.[27] He has done this through the historical reconstruction of Fletcher's thought and relationship to John Wesley. Part of the importance of this in Wood's estimation is that this reading lends a certain consistency to the thought of John Wesley. By focusing on Fletcher and how Fletcher constructs a more systematic, Methodist theology, drawing extensively from the work of Wesley, Wood shows that there could be a consistent theological vision in the movement. Much of this need for a consistent theological vision arises from the inconsistencies on the doctrines of justification and sanctification within John Wesley's corpus.[28] Wood shows, however,

---

24. Pannenberg, *Basic Questions in Theology*, 201–2.

25. Oden, *Rebirth of Orthodoxy*, 30.

26. See Laurence Wood, *The Meaning of Pentecost in Early Methodism: Rediscovering John Fletcher as John Wesley's Vindicator and Designated Successor*, Pietist and Wesleyan Studies 15 (Lanham: Scarecrow, 2002).

27. See, for example, Laurence Wood, "Thoughts Upon the Wesleyan Doctrine of Entire Sanctification with Special Reference to Some Similarities with the Roman Catholic Doctrine of Confirmation," *Wesleyan Theological Journal* 15 (1980).

28. Laurence Wood, "The Origin, Development, and Consistency of John Wesley's Theology of Holiness," *Wesleyan Theological Journal* 43.2 (2008) 38ff.

that Fletcher turns to Wesley's sermons and finds a certain consistency on these issues around the notion of "Pentecost." Fletcher notes that this language is not the dominant or most prevalent in Wesley, but that through the theological underpinnings of the event of Pentecost in Acts 2 he can construct a unified theological vision for the Methodist movement.[29] Eventually, after some resistance, Wesley does pick up on this linking of Pentecost and entire sanctification and gives Fletcher's theology his imprimatur.[30]

The most important and difficult (and controversial) aspect of Wood's historical work comes from the place of prominence he gives John Fletcher, as well as his insistence that Fletcher is the "vindicator and designated successor of John Wesley." In order to explicate this double move on Wood's part, let me first show how he interprets Fletcher and then we can see more clearly the historical tensions concerning Fletcher's relationship with Wesley.

In Wood's exposition of Fletcher's work, he sees the two main sources being Scripture and Wesley himself. So, it comes as no surprise for Wood that Fletcher would attempt to give Wesley a theological consistency through a turn to the scriptural place of Pentecost for a site to think through the issues around the nature of sanctification. Wood argues that Fletcher views the "event of Pentecost as a pattern of Christian experience." Fletcher says that there is a series of two events of salvation in Scripture, that of justification and sanctification.[31] For Fletcher, there is a clear biblical position that salvation consists of more than just the forensic nature of justification, but also includes the growth toward God that the doctrine of sanctification explicates. And, these are not just one event, but two in the life of the believer. Fletcher brings this out explicitly in his interpretation of the day of Pentecost in Acts 2. He says that Luke sees the disciples awaiting the restoration of the Kingdom that had not yet come after the ascension of Jesus. Then there is Pentecost, which restores the Kingdom of God.[32] Fletcher argues that with this restoration of the Kingdom of God is the infusion of the pure, perfect love for God and neighbor into each person.[33] Pentecost brings a new reality into our present reality, the inbreaking of the Spirit, leading to the "baptism of the Spirit."[34] This allows Fletcher to develop a theology that uses a "pentecostal" language for entire sanctification/ perfect love. For Fletcher, Pentecost is the event where the possibility of this salvific perfection is made a reality. It is in the event of Pentecost where salvation reaches its full potential.

However, as Wood shows extensively, Wesley believes that there arises a major theological disagreement between him and Fletcher. This disagreement comes from the fact

---

29. Wood, "Origin, Development, and Consistency," 33 and 45ff. See also Laurence Wood, "John Fletcher's Influence on John Wesley's Theology," *Bulletin of the John Rylands University Library of Manchester* 85.2–3 (2003) 391.

30. Wood, *Meaning of Pentecost*, 89.

31. Laurence Wood, "Pentecostal Sanctification in Wesley and Early Methodism," *Wesleyan Theological Journal* 34 (1999) 27.

32. Laurence Wood, "The Biblical Sources of John Fletcher's Pentecostal Theology," *Wesleyan Theological Journal* 42 (2007) 106–7.

33. Ibid., 107–8.

34. Ibid., 111.

that Wesley believes that Fletcher has misrepresented him, saying that a believer cannot have an assurance of salvation if one has not had the Pentecost experience of entire sanctification. Wesley insisted that every believer has "received the Spirit" in justifying faith, and this means every believer has some measure of assurance and initial sanctifying grace. A major reason for the disagreement was that Wesley believed if a believer could not have an assurance of salvation through receiving the Spirit at justification, then there would be a slippage into antinomianism.[35] Due to this disagreement reflected in private letters to Fletcher, there has been a continued move away from Fletcher among some contemporary Wesley scholars because Wesley disavowed his interpretation of Fletcher. However, Wood's work shows that the mistake was on the part of Wesley, as Fletcher did not believe that assurance could only come in the gift of entire sanctification. Thus, the disagreement dissolved, as Wood has shown extensively.[36]

After showing the end of this disagreement between Fletcher and Wesley, Wood goes to great lengths to show how Wesley places his approval upon the theology and exegesis of Fletcher.[37] Wood shows this extensively by turning to the work of Wesley himself, examining how Wesley picks up on the Pentecost theme and motif. We see Wood explicating this through his analysis of Wesley's exegesis. First, he argues that Wesley picks up the idea that the disciples are justified during the earthly ministry of Jesus of Nazareth; however, it is at Pentecost that the disciples receive the gift of sanctification, along with the full assurance of the Holy Spirit.[38] With this motif being presented here by Wesley, Wood goes onto articulate how Wesley picks up this couplet of justification-sanctification in other places of Scripture. One such place that Wood notices Wesley linking entire sanctification with Pentecost is with the Ephesians in Acts 19.[39] In Wood's estimation, Wesley argues, "The Pentecostal experience of perfect love for God is a continuation and confirmation of regenerating and sanctifying grace initiated in the moment of one's justifying experience and these two moments are to be repeated often enough until the life of perfect love becomes a habit in one's life."[40]

Thus, what Wood makes explicit, is that for Wesley the condition of the possibility for the experience of full salvation in perfect love is Pentecost.[41] This motif of Pentecost, then, gives a direction and consistency to Wesley's thought as it articulates the continued process of salvation from justification through sanctification. This continued salvation is, of course, something that Wesley wants to emphasize. This emphasis is brought forth when he articulates the belief that the possibility of being cleansed from sin and being

---

35. Wood, "Pentecostal Sanctification in Wesley and Early Methodism," 39ff.

36. Wood, *Meaning of Pentecost*, 33–57; Wood, "Pentecostal Sanctification in Wesley and Early Methodism," 32.

37. See, for example, Wood, *Meaning of Pentecost*, 35ff.; Wood, "Biblical Sources of John Fletcher's Pentecostal Theology," 110–13; and Wood, "Origin, Development, and Consistency," 45.

38. Wood, "Origin, Development, and Consistency," 36–37.

39. Laurence Wood, "A Contextual Interpretation of Wesley's Sermons—Kenneth Collins or John Fletcher," *Wesleyan Theological Journal*, forthcoming.

40. Wood, *Meaning in Pentecost*, 117.

41. Ibid., 166.

made perfect in love can only occur after the glorification of Jesus in His ascension and the subsequent coming of the Holy Spirit.[42] And, while Wood acknowledges that Wesley "rarely" uses the language of "baptism with the Holy Spirit" in his writings, he describes a Wesley that "makes sense" in that now we can see a certain consistency to the theology of early Methodism.[43]

Ultimately, then, Wood's contribution to the scholarship on the theological thinking of early Methodism adds a different voice and approach. He does this by taking seriously the work of John Fletcher and seeing how Wesley interacted with him as both friend and theologian. The picture Wood paints is one where there is disagreement, but also a consistency to the thought of early Methodism through the use of language drawn from the event of Pentecost in Acts 2. Now let us see how Wood argues for a similar consistency for theology in the postmodern, pluralistic context.

For Wood, following Jürgen Moltmann and Wolfhart Pannenberg (and Martin Heidegger's *Being and Time*),[44] theology must be understood in light of the rise of critical history, as well as taking into account the subsequent loss of the subject-object distinction.[45] In his revised dissertation, *God and History*, Wood works to show the rise of critical history and what implications this may have for theological thinking through an emphasis on the way that history and a person's historical situatedness plays a significant role in how one theologizes. Through this emphasis, Wood shows that all claims to truth arise out of a certain historical vantage point. This does not lead to a relativism, but argues that all truth claims are made in the limitations that being historically situated places upon the person.[46] But, as Wood emphasizes, the God of Christianity works within history, most notably in the Incarnation. This opens the possibility that humanity's historical situatedness is not a problem as much as the place where God encounters us. Thus, history becomes the place for the beginning of theological reflection.

The necessary next step for Wood is to establish the historical impetus behind theological thinking. Here, his argument relies vastly on eschatology, making the argument with Pannenberg and Moltmann that the inbreaking of Jesus Christ in the Incarnation begins the movement of creation towards its ultimate end in the Triune God. The Incarnation gives us the place, then, where God fully enters humanity. Thus, the eschatological nature of God's salvific work in history becomes the key overcoming the impasse between God and human, between nature and the supernatural.[47] This impasse is solved, in Wood's mind, through Pannenberg's idea that God is not "above" or "within" but "ahead

42. Ibid., 163.

43. Wood, "Contextual Interpretation of Wesley's Sermons."

44. Wood's PhD dissertation at Edinburgh University (Scotland) was one of the first attempts by an English-speaking theologian to deal with the implications of Heidegger's work (it was done under John McIntyre). A revised version of his dissertation can be found in Laurence Wood, *God and History: The Dialectical Tension of Faith and History in Modern Thought* (Lexington: Emeth, 2005).

45. See the early essay, Laurence Wood, "History and Hermeneutics: A Pannenbergian Perspective," *Wesleyan Theological Journal* 16 (1981).

46. See Wood, *God and History*.

47. Ibid., 233ff.; See also Laurence Wood, "Above, Within, or Ahead-of? Pannenberg's Eschatologicalism as a Replacement for Supernaturalism," *Asbury Theological Journal* 46.2 (1991).

of" us "as the power of the unbounded future." Wood argues that this way of thinking allows the divine reality to include space-time as God is not wholly separate from the creation, but is merely "ahead-of," out in front pulling the creation toward Godself.[48] Both Pannenberg and Wood root this "eschatologicalism" in Jesus' teaching of the immanent nature of the Kingdom of God, that it is "here and now." If the Kingdom was not here and now, there could not be this eschatologicalism.[49] But, because Jesus establishes the Kingdom here and now, salvation is inaugurated, bringing the Triune God into the very fabric of the historical.[50] The history of salvation becomes the history of the Triune God interacting with creation in history.

Thus, if theology is to be a hermeneutics—as Wood, following Moltmann argues—then it must be predicated upon how one interprets the Trinitarian history of God as God relates to the creation historically.[51] One must negotiate the movement of God in history because, as Trinity, God interacts with creation, showing the explicitly relational and historical nature of God to the world.[52] The work of God in history is seen specifically in the historical events of creation, reconciliation and glorification. These events bring all of creation into the economy of God.[53] The task of the theologian is to interpret the involvement of God in the world through an analysis of the historical revelation of God, specifically through the doctrine of eschatology. The theologian attests to the personal experience of being part of the salvation history that God brings to the world. Since the theologian is part of this salvation history of God, eschatology is the root of theology.[54] With eschatology framing one's hermeneutical vantage point, the theologian sees that God is at work in the real history of the world. However, this is not to limit theology to a strict study of the human condition, but a hermeneutical theology predicated upon eschatology opens theological thinking to a reality beyond that of historical experience: the reality of the Triune God.[55]

The question becomes how it is that we do theology as historically situated. This is the question that Wood probes in his *Theology as History and Hermeneutics*, arguing that theology is primarily a hermeneutical discipline, following the post-critical path set by those like Michael Polanyi.[56] For Wood, the hermeneutical nature of theology carries certain implications. At the forefront of these implications would be that there is a need to

---

48. Ibid., 243–44.

49. Ibid., 246–47.

50. Ibid., 252.

51. Wood, *Theology as History and Hermeneutics*, 197ff.; Laurence Wood, "From Barth's Trinitarian Christology to Moltmann's Trinitarian Pneumatology: A Methodist Perspective," *Asbury Theological Journal* 48 (1993).

52. Ibid., 200.

53. Ibid., 205.

54. It would be prudent to remember that here eschatology is referring to the "now ... and not yet ..." of Paul and not a strict study of the end times. Eschatology, for Wood, deals with the work of God in the sweep of history.

55. Wood, *Theology as History and Hermeneutics*, 200–202.

56. Laurence Wood, *Theology as History and Hermeneutics: A Post-Critical Evangelical Conversation with Contemporary Theology* (Lexington: Emeth, 2004).

rethink ontology. In Wood's estimation, ontology in the postmodern, post-critical world should be historical and relational.[57] Following this rethinking of ontology as historical and relational, Wood argues that theology must reject the subject-object dualism of truth because if existence is primarily historical and relational, there is no way for a subject to be out of relation to the object, meaning that the subject and object cannot be divided. This rejection leads to the acknowledgement on Wood's part that the knower/ observer/ subject is part of the determination of truth through some prior commitment(s).[58] This rejection of the subject-object split also leads to a critique of metaphysics for Wood through an embrace of the pluralistic nature of all thinking, especially that of theology.[59] From this, Wood adopts a theological method that follows Wolfhart Panneberg in arguing for an anti-foundationalist approach to theology that is aware of its own historically contingent nature.[60] Theology becomes a hermeneutical discipline that explores the intimate connection between a text[61]—which could be any and all of the world—and reader.[62] There is, borrowing from Gadamer, two horizons that meet in an interpretive moment which we call theology. Here, the horizon of certain foundational texts, like Scripture, collide with the horizon of the reader to give rise to new interpretive moments. This is theology for Wood.

In Wood's corpus, there are few places this hermeneutical approach to theology is seen more clearly than in his approach to theology's relationship with science. For Wood, theology is inherently disciplinary because all the world is a text. Thus, the theologian's task is to understand as much as possible all parts of the world and bring this understanding to bear upon theology. Wood does this in multiple avenues, arguing for divine foreknowledge through a use of Einsteinian physics and uses relativity and quantum theory of physics to show the openness of the future to new possibilities, displacing the notion of a closed-system universe perpetuated by Kant and Newton;[63] he uses contemporary neuroscience to argue for a unified vision of the human person;[64] as well as arguing against "limited omniscience theories of God" by showing that everything is present in and by God because of the fact that God is not bound by time, which the theory of relativity shows to be possible.[65] There are other examples that could also be pointed to in Wood's corpus, but the thrust here is that Wood not only argues for a hermeneutical theology predicated upon interpreting and understanding the world, but that he gives us an example to follow in our quest.

---

57. Ibid., 71.
58. Ibid., 82–84; 121.
59. Ibid., 85.
60. Ibid., 92.
61. Ibid., 129.
62. Ibid., 143.
63. Wood, *God and History*, 259–309.
64. Laurence Wood, "Recent Brain Research and the Mind-Body Dilemma," *Asbury Theological Journal* 41 (1986) 37–78.
65. Wood, *God and History*, 265.

But, the real question here, in light of the first part of this introduction, is how this is a Wesleyan contribution to rethinking some of the most common problems in contemporary theology. The Wesleyan contribution on the part of Wood comes from his movement away from an epistemological viewpoint or hermeneutics to a soteriological one. Wood moves questions of "belief" and "truth" and "knowledge" and "understanding" outside of a pure epistemology and makes them part of a soteriological viewpoint: one where we believe because we are saved.[66] Theology, then, becomes an extension of one's faith, where the theologian bases his or her thinking upon "the acceptance of God's revelation that comes in the moment of faith."[67] When theology is predicated upon this acceptance of God's revelation, it becomes a "hermeneutical validation of faith."[68] This means that the theologian works out one's faith because one has faith and one's theology is the validation of said faith. The theologian, then, is not examining the faith and God for some new knowledge, but is in the midst of relationship to God through faith and theology becomes the working out of this faith.

Laurence Wood, then, does much work to move Wesleyan theology into Outler's "Phase III." In what I have said so far, this has been done primarily through a rethinking of the Methodist tradition through an exposition of John Fletcher and through a rethinking of how Wesleyan theologians deal with contemporary issues and theologians. What Wood exemplifies is the ability of any theology to bring in multiple conversation partners in order to do theology the best way possible. Wood gives an example to follow, even if one does not always agree with where he ends.

This project finds itself within the spirit of Laurence Wood. Like Wood, the contributors here are interested in rethinking the possibilities of Wesleyan theology by drawing out how Wesleyan theology has relevance for rethinking the Christian tradition and dealing with current theological problems. The rest of the book, then, is divided into two parts. The first is an attempt to rethink the history of the Wesleyan-Methodist movement and the subsequent holiness movement. This section starts with an essay by Christopher T. Bounds, where he roots the Wesleyan belief of overcoming sin in the work of St. Augustine of Hippo. Here, he is rethinking two things: first, that the Wesleyan belief in perfection has a rootedness in the patristics; and, second, it is a reinterpretation of Augustine. The next essay in this section belongs to J. Steven O'Malley, as he also rethinks the background and tradition for the Methodist movement. He looks at the streams of thought that converge in John Wesley and John Fletcher which give rise to their Pentecostal paradigm. In the third essay from this section, Barry Callen sketches a history of the holiness denomination the Church of God (Anderson) in the nineteenth century through an analysis of their Christology. D. William Faupel continues what Callen started through an analysis of the influence of John Fletcher on the worldviews of those in the Wesleyan-Holiness-Methodist movement of the nineteenth century. Much of Faupel's work focuses around Fletcher's idea of "dispensations" and how this is used in

---

66. Wood, *Theology as History and Hermeneutics*, 227.
67. Ibid., 236.
68. Ibid., 237.

nineteenth century Holiness movement's theology. Kimberly Alexander moves the discussion slightly by focusing on the Pentecostal movement and their early understanding of "Spirit baptism" with its associated practice of speaking in tongues. Jonathan Dodrill offers the last essay in this section. He provides an analysis of the debate on the idea of "evangelicalism" between George Marsden and Donald Dayton, arguing that Dayton's approach is ultimately more useful.

The second part of the project looks to examine the contribution that Wesleyan theology makes to current theological problems. This section begins with William J. Abraham's essay "The End of Wesleyan Theology," where he argues that Wesleyan theology, based upon the thought of Wesley, has run its course and it is now time to strictly adopt John Wesley as a spiritual Father. Next is an essay by Nathan Crawford where he implicitly pushes back against Abraham by arguing for a Wesleyan fundamental theology that begins with one's disposition. Crawford, through this, looks to reinvigorate Wesleyan theology by beginning the task with love. Kevin Kinghorn, Michael L. Peterson, and Bradford McCall offer the next three essays all of which analyze the role of the sciences for theology coming from the analytic tradition. Kinghorn critiques the postmodern theological retreat into the idea of mystery as a way of escaping some of its more problematic conundrums. Peterson argues for a coherent worldview that makes sense both to a Wesleyan theological understanding of the world and to a scientific worldview. McCall argues for a theology of creation by combining the emergence theory of Philip Clayton with a pneumatological understanding of kenosis. The next two essays, by Graham McFarlane and Aaron Perry, explore the doctrine of the atonement by going back to an exposition of the biblical sources. McFarlane does this and argues that atonement should be understood as part of a relational worldview while Perry explores the implications of violence that surround the doctrine of atonement, doing this in conversation with psychology. The next two essays explore the role of Scripture, with Joel Green offering an understanding of John Wesley's theological interpretation of Scripture while Don Thorsen critiques the Protestant principles of *sola scriptura*, *sola gratia*, and *sola fide* and offers a unified vision for understanding these. The last two essays of this section deal with practical theological matters, with Michael Pasquarello, III articulating a theology of preaching built from the wisdom displayed by Wesley in his preaching ministry and Tony Richie exploring what a shared Wesleyan and Pentecostal theology of spirituality may look like.

All in all, the goal of this volume is to argue for the continued relevance of Wesleyan theology in the broader theological world. The impetus for this project is the work of Laurence Wood, who has so carefully and graciously shown the way that Wesleyan theology can still hold relevance in contemporary theology. Hopefully, then, this project begins a dialogue on how Wesleyan theology should continue to be relevant.

PART ONE

Rethinking the History

1

Augustine's Interpretation of Romans 7:14–25

His Ordo Salutis *and His Consistent Belief in a Christian's Victory over Sin*

CHRISTOPHER T. BOUNDS

INTRODUCTION

THE APOSTLE PAUL DECLARES in Rom 7:14–15, "We know that the law is spiritual; but I am unspiritual, sold as a slave to sin. I do not understand what I do. For what I want to do I do not do, but what I hate to do."[1]

The history and development of Augustine of Hippo's exegesis of this passage has received significant scholarly attention. In his initial forays into Pauline study in 394/395, *Propositions from the Epistle to the Romans*, Augustine interpreted Rom 7:14–25 as a human being "under the law, prior to grace."[2] The "I" pictured here is the quintessential unregenerate person, who has knowledge of the law of God, senses true guilt for sinfulness, longs for deliverance, but is without the grace of Christ to overcome sin. In contrast, the Christian "under grace," infused with the love of God, is victorious over sin and "ceases to sin."[3] In 396, Augustine reiterates his understanding in *Eighty Three Different Questions* and in his work of 398, *To Simplician on Various Questions*.[4]

There is no hint of change in Augustine's basic interpretive approach to Romans 7 until 411 in his treatise *On the Merits and Remission of Sins, and on the Baptism of Infants*. In his examination of Job's righteousness, Augustine compares Job to the person in Rom 7:19–24 who "delights in the law of God after the inner man, while he sees another law in his members warring against the law of his mind." Job is the type of individual who says, "The good that I would I do not: but the evil which I would not, that I do. Now if I

---

1. Romans 7:14–15 NIV.

2. Augustine, *Propositions from the Epistle to the Romans*, trans. Paula Fredriksen Landes (Chico, CA: Scholars Press, 1982) 44.2.

3. Ibid., 13—18:7–10.

4. Augustine, *Eighty-Three Different Questions*, trans. David L. Mosher, *The Fathers of the Church: A New Translation*, vol. 70 (Washington, DC: Catholic University of America Press, 1982) 66.5; Augustine, *To Simplician on Various Questions*, trans. John H. S. Burleigh, The Library of Christian Classics, vol. VI (Philadelphia: Westminster, 1963) I.1–7.

do that I would not, it is no more I that do it, but sin that dwells in me."[5] At this point, there is no inconsistency with Augustine's earlier teaching. However, later in the treatise he will argue that Christians who live a life of righteousness like Job are worthy of praise, but are not without sin and therefore must pray regularly the Lord's Prayer "forgive us our trespasses."[6] Augustine implicitly connects Christians "under grace" with the person of Romans 7.

What is implied in *On the Merits* becomes explicit by 415 in Augustine's *On Man's Perfection in Righteousness*, which sets forth the key seminal ideas of his new interpretation of Romans 7. The person described by Paul in this passage is one "under grace." The "divided self" pictured so poignantly by the Apostle is the Christian believer.[7] Later, in a series of sermons preached in 417, Augustine clarifies that the "I" in this passage is Paul speaking about himself. Paul is testifying to his present Christian experience and providing a description of every Christian life before the resurrection of the body.[8] By 421 in *Against Two Letters of the Pelagians* and in *Against Julian* Augustine acknowledges and repudiates completely his earliest interpretations of Romans 7.[9] In 327, three years before his death, Augustine, writing his *Retractions*, renounces again his earliest position on Romans 7 as a description of an unconverted person "under law" and reiterates his belief that this is Paul's Christian testimony and the experience of every person "under grace."[10]

Intimately tied to Augustine's exegesis of Roman's 7 is his *ordo salutis* or order of salvation. In his earliest written work on Paul, *Propositions from the Epistle to the Romans*, Augustine uses his comments to articulate a theological understanding of personal salvation in four stages. Indeed, this is the focus of *Propositions*. Interestingly, while Augustine changes his understanding of Romans 7 as he grows older, and for that matter, his reading of Romans 9–11 and the doctrine of election, his *ordo salutis* remains essentially the same throughout his life. He articulates it clearly in his early theological work, uses it as a reference point throughout his ministry as priest and bishop, and gives it significant treatment in his later treatises.[11]

---

5. Augustine, *On the Merits and Remission of Sins, and on the Baptism of Infants*, trans. Peter Holmes and Robert Earnest Wallis, *The Nicene and Post Nicene Fathers*, vol. V (Grand Rapids: Eerdmans, 1956) II.17.

6. Ibid., II.21.

7. Augustine, *Concerning Man's Perfection in Righteousness*, trans. Peter Holmes and Robert Earnest Wallis, *The Nicene and Post Nicene Fathers*, vol. V (Grand Rapids: Eerdmans, 1956) XI.28.

8. Augustine, *Sermon 151–156*, trans. Edmund Hill, *The Works of Saint Augustine: A Translation for the 21st Century*, vol. V: *Sermons 148–183* (Brooklyn, NY: New City, 1992).

9. Augustine, *Against Two Letters of the Pelagians*, in *Nicene and Post-Nicene Fathers*, vol. V, I.13–24, 27–28; Augustine, *Against Julian*, in *Nicene and Post-Nicene Fathers*, vol. V, II.2.5; VI.23.70–73.

10. Augustine, *The Retractions*, trans. Sister Mary Inez Bogan, *The Fathers of the Church: A New Translation*, vol. 60 (Washington, DC: Catholic University of America Press, 1968) 22.1; 23.1; 25.2; 27.

11. For Augustine's early discussion of his *ordo salutis* before 400 see *Propositions from the Epistle to the Romans*, 13—18:2-4; *Augustine's Commentary on Galatians: Introduction, Text, Translation, and Notes (Oxford Early Christian Studies)* by Eric Plummer (New York: Oxford University Press, 2006), 46; *Eighty-Three Different Questions*, 66.3 and *To Simplician on Various Questions*, I.1–7. For Augustine's later treatments after 420, see *The Enchiridion*, trans. J. F. Shaw, *The Nicene and Post-Nicene Fathers*, First Series, vol.

In his *ordo* Augustine consistently maintains that a Christian is empowered to walk in obedience to Christ through the infusion of love by the Holy Spirit. He describes a normative Christian life as one free from outward or willful sin. Even as his interpretation of Romans 7 changes, this basic understanding of a Christian's life "under grace" does not, although it is nuanced differently in his later thought.[12]

The question arises: how can Augustine do this with his complete reversal on Romans 7? If the Apostle Paul is describing his Christian life, and with him all Christians, in verses 14–25, how can Augustine maintain a theology of salvation in which a Christian is free from willful sin? The purpose of our paper is to answer this question. To do so, we will first summarize Augustine's *ordo salutis* and highlight some nuances brought to his understanding in later reflection. Next, we will examine how Augustine reconciles his later interpretation of Romans 7:14–25 with his persistent teaching on a Christian's outward compliance to the law. Then, we will look more specifically at the role of will or consent in the Christian "under grace." Finally, we will conclude with a few summary remarks.

AUGUSTINE'S *ORDO SALUTIS*

Augustine in 394 identifies four basic stages in a person's experience of salvation, subsequently carried throughout his ministry as priest and bishop: a life "prior to the law," "under the law," "under grace," and "in peace."[13] However, he acknowledges that some Christians may not pass through all stages, such as the case of infant baptism in which a child moves from a life "prior to the law" to one "in grace," bypassing the stage "under the law."[14]

He also sees his *ordo salutis* as an outline of the history of the church. First, the church existed "prior to the law," from the moment of the fall in the Garden to God's appointment with the nation of Israel on Mt. Sinai. Second, the church lived "under the law" from the revelation of God's law through Moses to Christ's coming. Now, the church lives "under grace" through the incarnate ministry of Jesus Christ. However, Augustine

---

III (Grand Rapids: Eerdmans, 1956) 118; and *The Retractions*, 22.1; 23.1; 25.2; 27. For Augustine's use of his *ordo* between his early and late writings, see *On Man's Perfection in Righteousness*, III.8; VIII.19; *On the Grace of Christ and on Original Sin*, in *The Nicene and Post-Nicene Fathers*, vol. V (Grand Rapids: Eerdmans, 1956) I.43.

12. Unfortunately, in many recent treatments of Augustine's evolving views of Roman 7, his affirmation and expectation of a Christian's victory over willful sin is ignored or misrepresented. For example, in his chapter, "Interpretations of Paul in the Early Church," in *Reading Paul Together: Protestant and Catholic Perspectives on Justification*, ed. David E. Aune (Grand Rapids: Baker Academic, 2006) 146–68, David M. Rylaarsdam ignores this part of Paul's teaching. Mark Reasoner in *Romans in Full Circle: A History of Interpretation* (Louisville: Westminster John Knox, 2005) 70–73 clearly misrepresents Augustine's teaching on sin by failing to make distinctions in sin. Reasoner portrays all sin as the same and fails to incorporate Augustine's finely nuanced understandings of sin into his treatment. This obscuration of Augustine's teaching on a Christian's victory over sin is greatest in the widely lauded *Augustine Through the Ages: An Encyclopedia*, ed. Allan D. Fitzgerald (Grand Rapids: Eerdmans, 1999), in which not one article on "sanctification" or "holiness" in Augustine is included.

13. Augustine, *Propositions from the Epistle to the Romans*, 13–18.2–4.

14. Augustine, *The Enchiridion*, 119.

maintains that life "under grace" is never absent in history, but is veiled and hidden. Before Christ's incarnation, Old Testament saints had some knowledge of and saving faith in Christ or they would not have been able to make prophecies about him. Finally, the church will be "in peace" when it enters the resurrected state in the eschatological age to come.[15]

Specifically, because of original sin, Augustine believes every human being is born into life "prior to the law." They live in ignorance of sin and follow their carnal desires without the restraint of conscience or established prohibitions.[16] He interprets the Apostle Paul's statement, "And I was alive once without the law," as indicative of Paul's early childhood before he could reason, before he reached an age of accountability.[17]

The second stage is a life "under the law." Here, through an awakened conscience and the revelation of God's law, people recognize their sinfulness. Knowledge of the law produces anxiety over their guilt and prepares them for the grace of salvation. They learn how sinful they really are. They are aware of the condemnation of God upon their lives and want to some extent to live in accordance with the law, but are unable to do so. They are slaves to sin and the fear of God.[18] They want to change, but the power of carnal desire is too strong and they find greater pleasure in committing sin. Sin deceives them continually "with its false sweetness."[19]

Augustine believes a person is defeated at this stage "because he does not yet love righteousness for the sake of God and for the sake of righteousness itself. And so when he sees righteousness on the one hand and temporal comfort on the other, he is drawn to the weight of temporal longing and thus abandons righteousness, which he was trying to hold on to only in order to have the comfort he now sees he will lose if he holds on to righteousness."[20] People "under law" may conform to the law, but only as long as it is beneficial to them. The desires of the flesh may lead to obedience, but only for selfish reasons. When keeping the law is no longer beneficial, a person discards it.

The only way humanity's sinful desires can be defeated is through a true love of God and love of the commanded good. In the absence of real love, carnal desire always triumphs. In the third stage of salvation "under grace," Augustine teaches that God gives the love of God to the human heart through the infusion of the Holy Spirit, empowering the Christian to "delight" in the law of God and walk in accordance to love. While Christians still have desires of the flesh, and the flesh is in conflict with the Spirit, the love of God triumphs over these desires so that believers do not obey them.[21]

At this point, it may be helpful to catalogue chronologically some of Augustine's key statements on life "under grace" to demonstrate his consistent belief in a Christian's vic-

---

15. Ibid., 118.
16. Augustine, *Propositions for the Epistle to the Romans*, 13—18.2-4; *The Enchiridion*, 118.
17. Augustine, *Against Two Letters of the Pelagians*, I.14,16.
18. Augustine, *Propositions from the Epistle to the Romans*, 13—18.2-4; *The Enchiridion*, 118; *To Simplician on Various Questions*, I.2.
19. Augustine, *To Simplician on Various Questions*, I.5.
20. Augustine, *Commentary on Galatians*, 46.
21. Augustine, *The Enchiridion*, 118.

tory over willful sin. Augustine in his description of the third stage clearly states in 395, "When this happens, even though certain fleshly desires fight against our spirit while we are in this life, to lead us into sin, nonetheless our spirit resists them because it is fixed in the grace and love of God, and ceases to sin. For we sin not be having this perverse desire but by consenting to it."[22] In 398 in response to questions raised by his friend Simplicius, he answers, "When grace forgives sin and infuses a spirit of charity, righteousness ceases to be hard and becomes even pleasant."[23] Speaking about the perfection of righteousness possible in the present life and experienced "under grace," he teaches in 415, "But whensoever he suffers not sin to reign in his mortal body to obey it in the lusts thereof, and yields not his members as instruments of unrighteousness unto sin … it does not reign, because its desires are not obeyed."[24] In the heights of the Pelagian debates of 422, Augustine affirms that the Apostles did not consent to the lusts of the flesh and lived "under grace." He declares, "I do say that although they were free from consent to depraved lusts, they nevertheless groaned concerning the concupiscence of the flesh, which they bridled by restraint with such humility and piety, that they desired rather not to have it than to subdue it."[25] Then, in the most systematic account of his mature theology in 422, *The Enchiridion*, Augustine describes the Christian in the third stage of salvation: "But if God has regard to him, and inspires him with faith in God's help, and the Spirit of God begins to work in him, then the mightier power of love strives against the power of the flesh, and although there is still in man's own nature a power that fights against him (for his disease is not completely cured), yet he lives the life of the just by faith, and lives in righteousness so far as he does not yield to evil lust, but conquers it by the love of holiness."[26]

While Augustine remains consistent in his teaching on a Christian "under grace," as a life empowered to walk in love and not consent to sinful desires, he does nuance some of the finer points of his teaching, particularly his conception of sin and his understanding of the intensity of sinful desires. First, Augustine develops his definition of sin. In 395 Augustine acknowledges that a Christian still experiences the lusts of the flesh, but does not sin. At this point in his theology, he defines sin as the consent of the will—to obey, or to act according to sinful desire. Simply having sinful desires is not personal sin. He states, "For we sin not by having this perverse desire but by consenting to it."[27] Elsewhere, he writes that God's condemnation does not rest upon the one, "engaged in battle, but on the one defeated in battle."[28]

---

22. Augustine, *Propositions from the Epistle to the Romans*, 13—18.7–10.
23. Augustine, *To Simplician on Various Questions*, I.7.
24. Augustine, *On Man's Perfection in Righteousness*, XI.28.
25. Augustine, *Against Two Letters of the Pelagians*, I.24.
26. Augustine, *The Enchiridion*, 118. In 427, three years before his death, Augustine in *The Retractions* 89 states about *The Enchiridion*, "In this, in my opinion, I have adequately covered how God is to be worshipped, a worship, which Divine Scripture defines as man's true religion."
27. Augustine, *Propositions from the Epistle to the Romans*, 13—18.7–10.
28. Augustine, *Commentary on Galatians*, 46.

However, by the opening decades of the fifth century, Augustine's hamartiology expands. He begins to see sinful desire itself as personal sin and in need of the absolution brought about through the Lord's Prayer: "Forgive our debts, as we forgive our debtors"; as well as through almsgiving. While he only sees it as venial sin and not mortal, it is still sin that a Christian must bear until the resurrection of the body.[29]

Augustine comes to see sinful desire as sin because it falls short of the perfect love of God and neighbor, which is the ultimate end of the law. A Christian operates out of the love of God; the love of God enables a person's obedience, but because of the desires of the flesh, love is not perfect.[30] Augustine states, "It is not the mere 'doing' of a good thing that is not present to him, but the 'perfecting' of it. For in this, that he yields no consent (to the desires of the flesh), he does good; he does good again, in this, that he hates his own lust ... But how to perfect the good is not present to him; it will be, however, in that final state, when the concupiscence which dwells in his members shall exist no more."[31]

Second, Augustine sees more clearly the intensity of sinful desire in Christian life. Early in his theological thought, Augustine recognizes or acknowledges concupiscence in the third stage, but does not give significance to it. However, while writing *The Confessions* he begins to address the psychological dynamics and intensity of fleshly desires in detail. They command Augustine's attention in ways not seen in his earlier work.[32] Nevertheless, while Augustine paints concupiscence in the third stage with greater intensity, he persistently maintains a Christian's victory over it.

In the fourth and final stage of salvation, a life is "in peace." This will take place when the bodies of Christians are resurrected in the age to come. Then, there will be nothing in humanity that resists the love of God, but every part will work harmoniously together. There will be the perfection of love in which people will love God with all heart, soul, and mind. All human action will embody the perfect love of God and neighbor. Sin and sinful desires will be impossible to humanity, since they will be like God, having true freedom—to do only what is in accordance with love.[33]

AUGUSTINE'S LATER INTERPRETATION OF ROMANS 7:14–25

How does Augustine reconcile his consistent understanding of the Christian "under grace" with his later exegesis of Rom 7:14–25? As we stated earlier, by 417 Augustine sees Romans 7 as the Apostle Paul's personal testimony of Christian experience, as well as

---

29. See James Wetzel, "Sin," in *Augustine Through the Ages: An Encyclopedia*, 800–802 for a more extensive discussion on Augustine's developing view of sin.

30. Augustine, *On Man's Perfection in Righteousness*, VIII.19; *The Enchiridion*, 121.

31. Augustine, *On Man's Perfection in Righteousness*, XI.28.

32. Compare Augustine's treatment of concupiscence or fleshly desires in his earlier theological work in *Propositions from the Epistle to the Romans*, 13–18 and *Commentary on Galatians*, 46 with his mature theological treatments in *Against Two Letters of the Pelagians*, I.13–27, and *Against Julian*, II.2.5, VI.23.70–73. Also see Augustine's introspective examination of concupiscence in *The Confessions*.

33. Augustine, *Propositions from the Epistle to the Romans*, 13–18.2-4; *Commentary on Galatians*, 46; *Eighty-Three Different Questions*, 66.3; *Concerning Man's Perfection in Righteousness*, III.8, VIII.19; *Against Two Letters of the Pelagians*, I. 24; *The Enchiridion*, 118.

every individual in the third stage of salvation. To answer this question, we must examine Augustine's interpretation of this passage. His clearest and most thorough treatments are *Sermons 151–156,* preached in 417 and two treatises written in 422, *On Marriage and Concupiscence* and *Against Two Letters of the Pelagians*.[34]

First, Augustine begins by reviewing Paul's teaching from Rom 3:20, 3:27, 4:13, 5:20, 6:14, and 7:4, establishing the fact that the law brings knowledge of sin, and incites sin, but does not take it away. Because knowledge of the law makes a person more sinful and is not able to deliver a person from sin, Augustine is careful to defend the goodness of the law. The law drives a person to seek God's grace. Only divine grace infusing love in the human heart can set an individual free from sin.[35]

Second, Augustine interprets Rom 7:7–13 as the Apostle's personal witness about his life "prior to the law" and "under the law." Paul's statement, "For I was alive without the law once," refers to Paul's early childhood, before his ability to reason, before an age of accountability. "But when the commandments came, sin revived, but I died," addresses the time in the Apostle's life when he became aware of the law, but was not able to keep it, thereby becoming a transgressor.[36] More specifically, the phrase "sin revived" refers to original sin in the Garden, passed down to all humanity, which remains hidden and undetected, until the human heart recognizes it when it encounters and balks at the law of God. Paul's statements, "For without law sin is dead," and "I had not known sin but by the law, for I had not known lust unless the law had said, 'Thou shalt not covet,'" conveys the profound disruption knowledge of sin brings to life. Once sin revives, it becomes "excessive" through the angst created in confrontation with the law. Continuing to speak on the command not to covet, Paul testifies, "But the occasion being taken, sin wrought in me by the commandment all manner of lust."[37] Concupiscence becomes stronger in it assertion of independence from the law.

Third, Augustine argues that Rom 7:14–23 is Paul's present Christian testimony and all Christians "under grace." Verse 14 states, "For we know that the law is spiritual, but I am carnal, sold as a slave to sin." Here, Augustine notes the use of the present tense, "I am," and not the past, "I was." Paul is speaking for himself and his Christian experience. More specifically, the declaration "I am carnal" refers to Paul's physical body, which has not yet experienced the resurrection. It is the same as saying, "I am mortal." "Sold under sin" further conveys the idea of a physical body not yet redeemed from its corrupted state, a body that creates a "drag" upon the soul. Augustine makes clear though, this is

---

34. Augustine, *On Marriage and Concupiscence*, trans. Peter Holmes and Robert Earnest Willis, *The Nicene and Post Nicene Fathers*, vol. V (Grand Rapids: Eerdmans, 1956) I.27–32; *Against Two Letters of the Pelagians*, I. 13–28; *Sermon 151–156*.

35. Augustine, *Against Two Letters of the Pelagians*, I.13.

36. Ibid., I.13. Augustine also addresses what might be a problematic statement to his interpretation of Paul as one unable to keep the law. Paul testifies in Phil 3:6 that as a Pharisee he was blameless in keeping the law. Augustine reconciles his interpretation in Romans 7 with Paul's statement in Philippians by saying that Paul kept the law with outward conformity, but it was motivated by sinful desire and not love. As such, Paul was a man "under law" as a Pharisee. See *Against Two Letters of the Pelagians*, I.15.

37. Ibid., I.13.

also the description of every Christian. However, with Paul, Christians do not consent or obey the desires arising from the body's corrupted state.[38]

Paul writes in verses 15, "For what I would, that do I not; but what I hate, that do I." Augustine does not understand this statement to involve any external act by the Apostle, rather an internal motion in the heart. In essence, this is Paul's admission to concupiscence. He covets or has sinful desires arising from his corrupted body. However, he does not consent or obey these desires. These are desires that wage inside of him. He despises them, longs to be free from them, but finds them nevertheless in his life. Augustine elaborates, "We shouldn't take what he said, 'It is not what I want to that I do, but what I hate, that is what I do' as meaning that he wanted to be chaste, and was in fact an adulterer; that he wanted to be kind, and was in fact cruel . . . That's not the sense in which we should understand (this passage) . . . but in what sense? 'I want not to covet, and yet I do covet.'"[39]

In verse 16 Paul continues, "If then I do that which I would not, I consent to the law that it is good." Here, Augustine develops further his previous thought. What does Paul do that he "would not"? He has sinful desires. The Apostle then recognizes that the law wills that there be no coveting, no concupiscence and he agrees with the law. He wants what the law wants. Augustine explains, "And yet what I don't want (desire, coveting, concupiscence) occurs in me. What the law doesn't want, I join the law in not wanting; what it doesn't want, I don't want either; so I give my consent to the law."[40]

Because there is concupiscence in his physical body, but Paul does not consent or give into these desires, the Apostle states in verse 17, "Now, then, it is no more I that do it, but sin that dwells in me."[41] His body suffers from concupiscence, but not his actions. He does not obey his sinful desires. Therefore, he does not covet, but his body does. Augustine states, "For 'it is not I that do it,' cannot be better understood than he does not consent to set forth his members as instruments of unrighteousness unto sin. For if he lusts and consents and acts, how can he be said not to do the thing himself?"[42]

For Augustine, verse 18 is the crux to understanding Paul's testimony. This is the "clear" passage, through which the more difficult passages of this section are to be read. Paul declares in verse 18, "For I know that in me (that is, in my flesh) dwells no good thing: for to will is present with me; but how to perform that which is good I find not." Augustine argues that Paul is empowered to do the good. He is able to walk in obedience to God and follow the law of God, but because concupiscence exists in his body, his actions are not perfect. This accounts for the Apostle's precision in words. Paul does not say "to do good" is beyond his will to do, but "how to perfect it" is in the present life.[43]

For Augustine verse 18 holds up the ideal action as a basis for judgment of any act. The ideal is an action performed in perfect love of God without any constraints of sinful

---

38. Ibid., I.17.

39. Augustine, *Sermon 154*, 154.2–3.

40. Augustine, *Sermon 154*, 154.10.

41. Augustine also notes the word "now" as indicative of Rom 7:14–25 being Paul's present Christian testimony.

42. *Against Two Letters of the Pelagians*, I.18; *Sermon 151*, 151.6–7.

43. Augustine, *Against Two Letters of the Pelagians*, I.29.32; *Sermon 152*, 152.2.

desire. Augustine states, "for the good is performed imperfectly when one covets, even if consent to the evil of coveting is withheld." Complete action, "perfect" action is by contrast action uniformly supported by a person's desire to act in the love of God.[44] Not only does Augustine contend that this is the correct reading of the verse in which the infinitive "to perfect" appears, but he assumes the other ways of expressing action in Rom 7:14-25, carry implicitly the sense of acting in conformity to the ideal. So, for example, when Paul states in 7:15 that he does what he hates, Augustine interprets this to mean that Paul performs what the law demands, but not without the presence of fleshly desire. Sinful desire does not interfere with his actions, but with the purity of his intentions.[45]

Augustine believes Paul's declaration in verse 18 is amplified in verses 19-21. The Apostle states "For the good that I would, I do not: but the evil which I would not, that I do. Now, if I do that which I would not, it is no more I that do it, but sin that dwells in me. I find then the law, when I would act, to be good to me; for evil is present with me." Again, Paul finds the law good when he consents to do what the law would have him to do; inasmuch as his consent falls short of its perfect keeping, as a result of concupiscence, evil is present even in his consent.[46]

In the first part of verse 22, Paul testifies, "For I delight in the law of God after the inward man." Augustine confesses that this testimony is key to his transition of seeing Rom 7:14-25 as a Christian "under grace." Only a person "under grace" delights in God's law. A person "prior to the law" is ignorant of it; a person "under the law" fears the consequences of breaking the law and is in servitude to it. However, the Christian "under grace" delights in it. This delight comes from realizing the end of the law—love, made possible by the grace of God through the Holy Spirit. In it is love that cheers and gratifies the believer.[47]

The second part of verse 22 and verse 23 continues, "but I see another law in my members warring against the law of my mind, and bringing me into captivity to the law of sin which is in my members." Augustine again interprets this other "law" to be concupiscence in his fallen body. "Bringing me into captivity" addresses the flesh, the body that has a "morbid carnal affection." Augustine states, "In so far then, as there is now this waiting for the redemption of our body, there is also in some degree still existing something in us which is captive to the law of sin."[48] This captivity is in the flesh and not in the mind, in the emotions, but not in consent.[49]

In verse 24, Paul declares, "O wretched man that I am! Who will deliver me from the body of this death? The grace of God, through Jesus Christ our Lord." Augustine

---

44. Augustine, *On Marriage and Concupiscence*, I.28-32.

45. For this analysis of verse 18, I am indebted to James Wetzel, *Augustine and the Limits of Virtue* (Cambridge: Cambridge University Press, 2008) 165-75.

46. *On Marriage and Concupiscenece*: I.30.34; In *Sermon 155:1* Augustine states, "Now it is no longer I that perform it, but the sin that lives in me;" it was because he wasn't performing it by consenting with the mind, but by lusting with the flesh. He gives the name of sin, you see, to that from which all sins spring, namely to the lust of the flesh."

47. Ibid., I. 30.34—31.35; *Against Two Letters of the Pelagians*, I.20; *Sermon 151*, 151.6.

48. Ibid., I. 30.34—31.35.

49. *Against Two Letters of the Pelagians*: I.20; *Sermon 151*: 151.6.

comments, "What are we to understand by such language, but that our body, which is undergoing corruption, weighs heavily on our souls? In the resurrection there will be full liberation."[50] Although the actual law of sin partly holds the flesh in captivity, still it does not reign in the Christian life because a Christian does not obey its desires.

Finally, in verse 25, Paul concludes, "So then with the mind I myself serve the law of God, but with the flesh the law of sin." Augustine again drives home his point that Paul, and by inference, every Christian, serves the law of God by refusing to obey the law of sin. However, the Apostle serves the law of sin by having the desires of the flesh, from which he is not free entirely, although he does not give in to them.[51] Augustine states, "To wit, with the flesh, the law of sin, by lusting; but with the mind, the law of God, by not consenting to that lust."[52] Augustine states elsewhere, "Both the law of God in the mind, and the law of sin in the flesh. I both take delight in this one (mind), and at the same time I feel lust there (flesh). But I am not overpowered; it tickles my fancy, it lays siege to me, it hammers at the door, it tries to take me away, but not it does not (overpower)."[53]

THE ROLE OF WILL OR CONSENT IN PEOPLE "UNDER GRACE"

As we have now seen, while Augustine's exegesis of Romans 7 shifts from a person "under law" who cannot walk in true righteousness to a Christian "under grace" who can walk in obedience to the law, but cannot perfect it, nevertheless, his later interpretation conforms to his basic *ordo salutis* held throughout his ministry.

Now, the question must be asked: what enables people "under grace" to walk in obedience to God, to serve the law of God in their mind and not consent to the desires of the flesh? Augustine's answer: the love of God shed abroad in the human heart by the Holy Spirit. The love of God enables obedience, empowering true consent to the law of God.

Augustine identifies three factors in the exercise of human will: suggestion, delight, and consent.[54] First, a suggestion is any idea that comes to a person's mind through personal reflection, random thinking, or bodily senses. Therefore, when a person is told she needs to go back to school if she wants to work at a particular company, or an individual has a chance idea to start a new business while talking to his wife about a haircut, or a teenager considers eating an ice cream cone after seeing a Baskin-Robbins advertisement, they have experienced suggestion. More specifically, Augustine sees the law of God as suggestion as it comes to human beings in the law given to Adam in the Garden and to Moses on Mt. Sinai, in the law summarized by Jesus Christ, and in the law of reason and conscience.[55]

---

50. *On Marriage and Concupiscence*, I.31.35.
51. Ibid., I.31.36.
52. *Against Two Letters of the Pelagians*, I.21; *Sermon 151*, 151.8.
53. *Sermons 148–183*, 151.8.
54. Augustine, *Commentary on the Lord's Sermon on the Mount*, trans. Denis J. Kavanagh, *The Fathers of the Church: A New Translation*, vol. 11 (Washington, DC: Catholic University of America Press, 1963) I.12.34.
55. Ibid., I.12.34–36.

Next, Augustine teaches that each suggestion encounters internal desires already existing in the human mind. In response to a suggestion presented to the mind, strong feelings of attraction or aversion may arise, motivating a person to move in one direction or another; or it may meet with indifference, creating little inclination to action; or it may encounter conflicting desires, causing internal division within the mind about what to do.[56] For example, when a person encounters a suggestion to eat an ice cream cone from a Baskin-Robbins commercial, strong feelings of sensual pleasure may arise, or stimulate a deep fear of gaining weight, or cause internal turmoil if pleasure and fear are both persuasive to the mind.

From whence do these desires come? Augustine identifies two places: love and the force of habit.[57] First and most basic, Augustine believes human desires have their origin in love—either the love of God or the love of self.[58] By creating humanity in the divine image, God made people to love God, which then enables them to turn toward their neighbor in self-giving love, and truly love themselves for God's sake. However, because of original sin, love has been corrupted, becoming self-centered, seeking its private interest above all else. In fallen humanity, desire or delight, are all manifestations of a person's egoist love. Augustine calls these "desires of the flesh" and "concupiscence." All human desires or delights have self-love as their basis, rather than the perfect love of God.[59]

Second, Augustine believes some desires are built and fortified by habit. A habit begins when a suggestion arouses pleasure that leads to consent. Then, the experience of gratification fuels the pleasure desire, so that when the same suggestion comes again, even greater desire arises, leading to action. As a person continues to consent to the pleasure inclination, the pleasure desire increases in strength, forcing other competing desires (fear, caution) to recede to the background, forming a habit almost impossible to break.[60]

Finally, Augustine believes a suggestion that arouses the strongest delight leads to consent of the will, which results in action. He believes human beings consent to what they ultimately want. Humanity does whatever is their strongest desire. Human consent follows the desire most aroused by a suggestion.[61] For example, in the suggestion of eating an ice cream cone, Augustine believes a person will consent to whatever the strongest desire is. If the pleasure desire is stronger, she will eat the ice cream; if the fear of gaining

---

56. Ibid., I.12.34.

57. Augustine, *Sermon 151*, 151.4–5.

58. Augustine, *On Free Will*, trans. John H. S. Burleigh, The Library of Christian Classics, vol. VI (Philadelphia: Westminster/John Knox, 1953) I.16. Augustine states here, "We have discovered that there are two kinds of things, eternal and temporal. Two kinds of men, as well, have been clearly and sufficiently distinguished: those who pursue and love eternal things, and those who pursue and love temporal things."

59. Augustine, *On Christian Doctrine*, ed. Philip Schaff, *The Nicene and Post-Nicene Fathers*, vol. II (Grand Rapids: Eerdmans, 1956) I.22–35. For Augustine this is true for aversion as well. Aversion can play a role in the development of habit.

60. Augustine, *The Lord's Sermon on the Mount*, I.12.33–34.

61. Augustine, *On the Spirit and the Letter*, ed. Phillip Schaff, *The Nicene and Post-Nicene Fathers*, vol. V (Grand Rapids: Eerdmans, 1956) V, LX.

weight is stronger, she will abstain; and if both are powerful, she will have some inner turmoil, but will eventually do whatever the strongest desire is.

As such, the key for Augustine in the sequence of suggestion—delight—consent is delight or desire. Accordingly, humanity in the stage "prior to the law" cannot begin to fulfill the law of God. They cannot "delight" in the true love of God and neighbor. Instead, their "delight" is completely self-focused. Because all human desire in this stage is self-focused, defined by "concupiscence," the act arising from willful consent will always be selfish. As such, they do not keep the law of God.[62]

In the stage "under the law," humanity by God's grace begins to recognize a need to keep the law of God. They see the need to love God and neighbor. They may begin to desire to walk in true love.[63] As such, a new desire enters into the mix. However, when the suggestion of God's law comes by instruction or reason, concupiscence rises to the fore, dominating any desire to walk in divine love, so that they are not able to keep the law. Their consent follows their fleshly desires. Even when they act in outward conformity to the law, concupiscence is at the root. In wanting to avoid punishment, earn praise, or gain some personal reward, they act out of egoist love in the outward performance of the law. Only when a person wants God's will out of the love of God alone is the law kept.[64] Thus, in *The Confessions* Augustine testifies of his life before conversion as one "under law" in which he wants to follow God, but is not able to relinquish his fleshly desires that bind him to the world. His fleshly desires are stronger than his desire for God.[65]

In the third stage "under grace," Augustine teaches that God infuses divine love or "delight for the law" by the Holy Spirit into human life. This comes as a gift of God to a person. Therefore, when the suggestion of the law comes, it encounters the internal desire to love God, which subordinates any other contrary desire or inclination, leading to a person's consent. God empowers a person with love, so that this delight, this pleasure, this inclination, "draws" or "leads" human consent. Divine love becomes the strongest desire or delight in a Christian and the human will consents to this love. What the law commands, love seeks and obtains by divine grace.[66]

However, as already been intimated, because concupiscence resists love and consent to the good, the good accomplished by consent is marred. It is not perfect love. Nevertheless, the inclinations against which a person "under the law" struggles are now overcome because a higher inclination, love of God, has subordinated them.

More specifically, in Rom 7:14–25 Augustine sees two conflicting delights. The first, which is the consequence of original sin is concupiscence. Human beings find pleasure or delight in the wrong things. This is the law of sin. The second, which is a result of God's grace infusing the heart with love by the Holy Spirit is delight in the law of God. Augustine makes clear in his interpretation of this passage that a person "under grace" can consent to the good and yet not be free of conflict. Because concupiscence resists

---

62. T. Kermit Scott, *Augustine: His Thought in Context* (New York: Paulist, 1995) 209.
63. Augustine, *On the Spirit and the Letter,* XIV, LVI.
64. Augustine, *Spirit and the Letter,* LVI.
65. Augustine, *The Confessions,* VII.3.
66. Augustine, *On the Spirit and the Letter,* XVI.

love and consent to the good, the good accomplished by consent is marred. It is not perfect love.[67]

Augustine states, "And, without the gift of God—that is, without the Holy Spirit, through whom love is shed abroad in our hearts—the law may bid but it cannot aid. Moreover, it can make of man a transgressor, who cannot then excuse himself by pleading ignorance. For appetite reigns where the love of God does not ... (but) if a man begins to be led by the Spirit of God, then the mightier power of love struggles against the power of the flesh. And although there is still in man a power that fights against him—his infirmity being not yet fully healed—yet the righteous man lives by faith and lives righteously in so far as he does not yield to evil desires, conquering them by his love of righteousness."[68]

CONCLUSION

In conclusion, while Augustine's interpretation of Rom 7:14–25 undergoes revision in his work as priest and bishop, his basic understanding of a person "under law" and Christian "under grace" does not. Augustine consistently maintains that a person "under law" is unable to keep the law, because of "delight" for self-love. The Christian "under grace" is able to consent to the law and be victorious over the desires of the flesh, because of "delight" in God's love.

Augustine's teaching stands in a long historical line of witness to the expectation of a Christian's victory over willful sin and a life defined by the love of God and neighbor. Augustine in his doctrinal treatises believes Christians are able to overcome their sinful desires, because of the love of God shed abroad in their hearts. Because Christians "under grace" have true love, love subdues all other desires, enabling them to walk in love. While it is not perfected love, it nevertheless is love made manifest in heart and life.

---

67. Augustine, *Sermon 151*, 151.6. Speaking of the Apostle Paul, Augustine states, "He was struggling, he was not subdued. But because he did not even want to have this thing to struggle with, that is why he said, "It is not what I want to, that I do." I don't want to covet, but yet I do. So I do something I don't want to; but all the same, I don't consent to this lust."

68. Augustine, *Enchiridion*, 117–18.

2

Exploring the Background for the Pentecost Connection in Early Methodism

J. Steven O'Malley

In the years I have been privileged to teach with Professor Laurence Wood at Asbury Theological Seminary, I have gained immeasurable insight from his probing work in the sources that influenced John Wesley in enunciating a theology of holiness. In particular, his work has done much to correct a one-sided tendency to emphasize the discontinuity rather than the continuity between the theology of Wesley and that of normative, nineteenth century American Methodism and the theology of the Wesleyan holiness movement of that century. Wood has taken head on the revisionist tendency to drive a wedge between John Fletcher and John Wesley, which sees Wesley as a Christocentric evangelist-theologian, with restrained emphasis on pneumatology. This is also an attempt to distance Wesley from his nineteenth-century successors, who supposedly traded Christology for an exaggerated pneumatology. Through meticulous work with sources, Professor Wood has demonstrated the essential continuity that exists between John Wesley's later writings and the work of his designated heir, John Fletcher. In many respects, Fletcher's work, published with Wesley's blessing and support, offered a somewhat more systematic portrayal of the Wesleyan *ordo salutis*, based on the underlying schema of successive dispensations of grace in the unfolding of salvation history.

Fletcher's, and Wesley's, description of the "baptism of the Holy Spirit," identified with the gift of Pentecostal grace which is subsequent to justifying grace, becomes a critical template for primitive Methodism in early England and North America as well. As Wood has reminds us, this theme resonates on the one hand with Wesley's Anglican heritage, especially in relation to the liturgical tradition of confirmation, as found in the Book of Common Prayer, which completes the original unitary act of baptism/chrismation found in the apostolic liturgies of the Eastern Church. On the other hand, it also resonates with the recovery of Pentecost as the motif for Christian revitalization which had been undergoing a major impetus in the decades before the rise of Methodism, within the proto-revivalists emerging from German Pietism.

What we investigate in these pages are the historical precedents for the Wesley-Fletcher tendency to read Christian perfection in view of a renewal of Pentecost. These precedents take us directly to continental Pietist sources, and, indirectly, to apostolic sources to which Pietists and later Methodists appealed. It is known that Wesley and Fletcher were not writing about this theme in a vacuum, but there is room for more extensive and definitive source study that would clarify the extent to which their outlook was fashioned, either implicitly or explicitly, from these continental sources.

At least four streams of influence flowed toward Wesley and Fletcher in the development of their Pentecost-based portrayal of the *ordo salutis*.

First, there was the apostolic influence from the pseudo "Macarius the Egyptian". As a point of illustration, both early Methodists and radical Pietists were taken up with the homilies of the pseudo-Macarius. The English text of these spiritual homilies, upon which Wesley relied, came into print in the same era in which the first German edition of the homilies was produced by the radical Pietist Gottfried Arnold in 1715–1716.[1] This work became the basis for the most influential patristic model for the eremitic life that was reborn within Protestantism.[2] The work found its appeal among radical Protestants who found in the homilies a basis for their flight from the corrupted church of their day. It appealed to them to launch communities of consecrated seekers of the wilderness ideal of a true ascetic community. For Arnold, this work provided evidence that an unpartisan (or unconfessional) true Christianity existed from apostolic times, and that it represented the true Christianity to be recovered by the faithful in his day, as signified in his signature work, *The Unpartisan History of Church and Heresy (Die unparteiische Kirche und Ketzer Historie)*, which appeared in 1699 in preparation for the coming expected year of apocayptic judgment after a century of horrendous religious warfare in Europe. In preparation for this end, true believers were taught a threefold movement of the heart from the dominion of evil, to the inner wilderness struggle between sin and grace, to the ultimate expulsion of sin from the heart by the Holy Spirit, creating a "perfect man in God and an heir and son."[3] Both Fletcher and Wesley made use of the homilies in English translation, which demonstrated to Fletcher apostolic grounding for his own dispensation doctrine.[4] For Arnold, as well as for Fletcher (two generations later), the pneumatology of the homilies was read in light of the federalist theology, that exercised decisive influence on German Pietism in virtually all its branches, as well as in the thought of the Swiss émigré, John William Fletcher, who brings it to the attention and embrace of John Wesley.

---

1. E. Benz, *Die protestantische Thebais: Zur nachwirkung Makarios des Agypters im Protestantismus des 17. und 18. Jahrhunderts* (Wiesbaden: Franz Steiner, 1963).

2. This theme is treated in W. R. Ward, "Mysticism and Revival: The Case of Gerhard Tersteegen," in Jane Garnett and Colin Matthew, eds, *Revival and Religion Since 1700: Essays for John Walsh* (London: Hambledon, n.d.) 51.

3. Pseudo-Macarius, Homily 32.6, in George A. Maloney, *Pseudo-Macarius* (New York: Paulist, 1992) preface, xiii.

4. Laurence Wood, *The Meaning of Pentecost in Early Methodism* (Lanham: Scarecrow, 2002) 349.

Second, it is apparent that the Macarian spirituality was being rediscovered and redeployed within Western Europe in the early eighteenth century within the context of the growing, even pervasive, impact of the writings of Johannes Cocceius (1603–1669), the German covenantal theologian, whose work, published in Holland, did much to redirect Reformed scholastic theology from its fondness for Aristotelian scholasticism to a framework steeped in a biblical theology of salvation history (*Heilsgeschichte*). This new direction for theology would offer a new and historically progressive biblical hermeneutic that anticipated and helped to shape the German *Aufklärung* of the eighteenth century. It was Friedrich A. Lampe, Cocceius' most celebrated disciple among German Reformed pastor theologians of the early eighteenth century, who articulated the paradigmatic force of this theme. In his *Secret of the Covenant of Grace*, Lampe wrote,

> Since new discoveries are daily being made within the natural world, what is it to wonder that new discoveries are also taking place through an increasing diligence in the use of the divine Word of God, [whereby] the promised growth in knowledge in the last times (Daniel 12:4, ex. 47:4) is always being enhanced toward its complete fulfillment.[5]

Later Pietism was identified as an opponent of the Enlightenment, but not so this earlier voice. In fact, the Coccean prophetic reading of history, both biblical and universal history, provided the milieu in which the early Methodist theme of a coming Pentecost was grounded.

Cocceius and his followers, like Lampe, placed more attention on the past unfolding of the *Heilsgeshichte* in the periodization of church history. However, it would be left to the radicals, like Arnold and others, to shift its focus to the future, and to the age of the Spirit which was emerging. It was this expectation that offered them a platform on which to read and identify with the forward looking spiritual homilies of the pseudo Macarius. Here, the eschatological theme from primitive Christian liturgy was being recovered through more radical or socially marginal voices, whose witness appears amid a dispirited eighteenth-century German Protestantism.

Third, Wesley encountered the eremitic ideal of Macarius in the course of his translation of two key hymns of Gerhard Tersteegen (1697–1769), which he found during his Georgia ministry (1735–1738), after receiving a copy of German devotional hymns from the Moravians. At a formative stage in his personal life, Wesley encountered there the expectant piety of Tersteegen's "Thou Hidden Love of God," which served as an influence upon his subsequent Aldersgate experience.[6] Tersteegen's verse represents the epitome of those produced in the entire Pietist movement. His work as a proto-evangelist throughout the lower Rhineland and the Netherlands involved an extensive network of conventicles which he shepherded, and his huge correspondence with religious seekers across Europe and North America was the outcome of a life widely perceived by his

---

5. Friedrich A. Lampe, *Geheimnis des Gnadenbundes* (Bremen: Nathanael Saurman, 1748) IV, 124 (author's translation).

6. See. J. Steven O'Malley, *Gerhard Tersteegen und John Wesley in Zusammenhang Ihrer Welt,"* in Dietrich Meyer and Üdo Strater, *Zur Rezeption Mystischer Traditionen im Protestantismus des 16. bis 19. Jahrhunderts* (Cologne: Rheinland, 2002) 305–12.

contemporaries to be one lived as a vibrant "friend of God." In later revival addresses delivered in the Netherlands, he articulated his call to salvation within the categories of Pentecost, especially in his "Outpouring of the Holy Spirit."[7]

His work was centered in the city of Mulheim an der Ruhr, where Tersteegen emerged as the most spiritually-authentic revivalist on the Continent by 1750. He appropriated themes from the French Quietists, reading them with the salvation history template grounded in his indigenous Heidelberg Catechism, which was itself the base for Cocceius' early spiritual formation, and in the homilies of the Cocceian Pietists. From this base Tersteegen moved to apostolic sources, and to a prolonged study of the history of Christian spirituality, relying almost exclusively on Roman Catholic mystics like St. John of the Cross in an anti-Catholic polemical age. His immediate influences in early adolescence were the revivals of a group of radical Pietists known as the Inspirationists, and he adopts their language of Canaan without picking up their propensity for ecstatic excesses. It was in that form that he ventured forth as the most successful revivalist in the Rhine Valley and as far as Amsterdam, where his revival addresses result in the conversion of hundreds from all religious backgrounds. I offer as a specimen his revival address of 1753, delivered in Amsterdam on the theme of The Outpouring of the Holy Spirit. It could easily have been a Methodist homily, reflecting the Wesleyan-Fletcher trajectory of the coming General Spread of the Gospel. Tersteegen brins together the themes of apostolic unity under Pentecostal grace amid the sectarian strife of his day:

> O let us study to be unanimous! Let us incessantly and unweariedly strive after it! . . . am certain that, according to Zephaniah 3:10, the Lord will bring souls together more and more from all places and corners of the earth, from all the different religious sects, and lead and guide them to the one thing needful . . . the baptism with the Spirit and the heavenly unction to the conversion and renewal into the image of God which entirely depends on it. . . .[8]

Tersteegen used the language of Pentecost he learned from the so-called New Prophets of his day, devoid of their ecstatic religious baggage, since his achievement was to make room for a solid work of regeneration in the heart that would be a life of holy discipline leading to Christian perfection. He was sought out by Zinzendorf, the Moravian leader, but declined due to the Count's focus on flamboyant conversion, preferring instead the steady inner work of "Jesus Immanuel" through the Holy Spirit, leading to the baptism in the Spirit unto sanctification. Ward observed that "Tersteegen made Wesley's call for Christian perfection without Wesley's abrasiveness."[9]

Fourth, when Wesley, after 1770, found himself drawn to the Pentecostal account of sanctification presented by John Fletcher, he was revisiting a theme to which he had earlier been exposed in his encounter with Christian David at Herrhnut, after Wesley's

---

7. Gerhard Tersteegen, "Outpouring of the Holy Spirit," (1753), published in English translation in Harvey and Tait, eds, *Gerhard Tersteegen: Sermons and Hymns* II (Shoals, IN: Old Paths Tract Society, 1999) 39–65.

8. Tersteegen, "The Ourpouring of the Spirit," in *Sermons and Hymns*, 53.

9. W. R. Ward, *Christianity under the Ancient Regime, 1648–1789* (Cambridge: Cambridge University Press, 1999) 130.

Aldersgate conversion. In August, 1738 Wesley traveled to Halle and also to Herrnhut, the Moravian community led by Zinzendorf. Wesley's contentious conversation with his host, in which they disagreed sharply over whether justifying and sanctifying grace are imputed only (Zinzendorf) or also imparted (Wesley), is well known. What is less known is the positive contact Wesley had with Christian David (1691–1751) at Herrnhut, who helped Zinzendorf create the first settlement of the proto-Moravian community near Berthelsdorf and who became the chief itinerant evangelist for the Moravians across Europe and into North America.

Wesley reports that on four occasions he heard sermons from Christian David who was the "first planter" of the "private bands," akin to the one that Wesley had joined in England, founded by Peter Böhler.[10] Three times David chose the subject of those who are "weak in the faith," that is, justified in Christ but without the "indwelling of the holy Ghost". He described the state in which the apostles were living from the crucifixion of their Lord until the descent of the Holy Spirit at Pentecost as a time when they "had faith" but "were not properly converted" and "had not new hearts nor received the gift of the Holy Ghost."[11] It was the fourth sermon, "concerning the ground of our faith," which made the deepest impression on the newly-converted Wesley. Speaking against the "penitential struggle" (*Busskampf*) which Francke of Halle had required as a condition for justification, David insists that "the right foundation is not *your* contrition, . . . not *your* righteousness, . . . nothing that is wrought *in you* by the Holy Ghost; but it is something without you, viz., the righteousness and blood of Christ." "So shall you be cleansed from all sin . . . being renewed day by day in righteousness and all true holiness."[12]

Two days later Wesley spent several hours with Christian David, whose preaching was having great influence on the Moravian Brethren as well as Wesley, with its emphasis on the great objective work of Christ combined, notes Ward, with a "pietistic sense of his indwelling," through the gift of the Holy Ghost (Acts 2:38).[13] In conversation with Wesley, David related how he (David) had been a seeker in Moravia, and, after leaving his Roman Catholic and Lutheran roots, he began to search for evidence that the New Testament prophecies had been fulfilled. He began to realize that "'being justified' is widely different from the having the 'full assurance of faith.'" David had come to experience the power of the gospel of Christ while being visited in illness by Pastor Johann Christian Schwedler of Niederwiesa, a Lutheran church in Upper Silesia on the Silesian border, that was being swept by revival among the Silesian refugees there, fleeing imperial persecution in their homeland. Following this conversion, David reported that he continued to struggle with moving from "being justified" to "having the full assurance of faith."[14]

It was not until David the carpenter had built the first house for the Moravians at Berthelsdorf (before Herrnhut was developed), that he came to understand and appropri-

---

10. W. R. Ward and Richard P. Heitzenrater, *The Bicentennial Edition of the Works of John Wesley*, vol. 1: *Journal and Diaries (1735–1738)* (Nashvillle: Abingdon, 1984) 270.

11. Ward and Heitzenrater, *Journal and Diaries*, 1:271.

12. Ibid., 1:272.

13. Ibid., 1:273 n. 98; also 271 n. 90.

14. Ibid., *Journal and Diaries*, 1:274.

ate the whole economy of God with regard to salvation, from justification to the sealing of the Spirit in entire sanctification, as a gift available not just to a few (as the Calvinists held) but to all persons. He was confirmed in this faith by Johann David Steinmetz, the Lutheran Pietist pastor at Teschen, Silesia. Steinmetz was a follower of Spener's writings, and his remarkable congregation had been started by Francke as an outpost of the extensive ministry the latter had founded at Halle. This was a megachurch consisting of Czech, Slovakian, and Polish (as well as German) refugees of Jesuit opposition against the Protestants of that province. Steinmetz was a close confidant to Zinzendorf, who had sent David to him for this counsel.[15] Indeed, the revival at Teschen among these refugees became the basis for the success of the Herrnhut project, when that revival was transferred there, through the leadership of Christian David.

The present author's research has brought to light an important link between the Pentecostal theology of David, conveyed to Wesley, and that of Steinmetz, David's spiritual mentor, in the form of a volume of addresses delivered by Steinmetz at Teschen on "The Sealing of Believers with the Holy Spirit, in some edificatory Pentecost meetings based on Ephesians 4:30."[16] Steinmetz had also been the revival preacher who first stirred the awakening in Moravia, leading to the exodus of David and others to their centers of refuge in Upper Lusatia (where Zinzendorf was working). This evidence substantiates the claim made by Martin Schmidt that "it was this preaching that prepared John Wesley for conversion and that he owed more to David than to anyone, Peter Böhler only excepted."[17]

Fifth, it is the contention of this study that there are common sources for Wesley's use of the Pentecost motif in relation to sanctification, that occurred through his contacts with the Silesian revival via Christian David, and his later attraction to the recovery of Pentecost in the dispensational theology of John Fletcher. Hence, let us probe the possible influences that had been operative on Fletcher before his arrival in England from his native Switzerland. In order to understand the Pietist milieu in Switzerland, we need to acquaint ourselves with two influential spiritual (or radical Pietist) groups not often acknowledged in the annals of the birth of Methodism. These are the Philadelphians and their successors in the eighteenth century, the Inspirationists. Some background discussion will be helpful at this point.

We have noted that it was under the influence of Steinmetz' revival preaching at Teschen in Silesia (from 1725) that the first awakenings erupted in Moravia, leading to the exodus of those refugees (including David) to Upper Lusatia and to the lap of Zinzendorf at Herrnhut. Revival was the only way to safeguard the interests of Protestants in Silesia since that province lay outside the imperial boundaries where protection to Protestants was guaranteed by the Peace of Westphalia. This was the treaty which granted religious

---

15. This information was related to Wesley by David in personal conversation on August 10, 1738, as found in Wesley, *Journal and Diaries*, 1:275.

16. Johann Adam Steinmetz, *von der Versiegelung der Glaubigen mit dem heiligen Geist. In einigen Pfingst-Erbauungsstunden aus Epheser 4, 30* (Frankfurt/Main: Brönner, 1857, third edition), 131 pages; first published ca. 1720 while pastor at Teschen.

17. Martin Schmidt, *John Wesley*, cited in Ward and Heitzenrater, *Journal and Diaries*, 1:273.

toleration to Protestants in the lands of the German Empire after the close of the Thirty Years War. When that same revival moved into Herrnhut, it changed the character of that community, putting David on a counter course from that of Zinzendorf with regard to soteriology. The former stressesd a progressive view of the order of salvation, moving from justifying to the experience of sanctifying grace in the language of Pentecost, while the latter, following Lutheran monergism, stressed the immediate, imputed nature of saving grace in the cross of Christ.

However, in terms of ecclesiology, Zinzendorf was influenced to establish a Philadelphian-style community at Herrnhut, based on the model attempted at his wife's estate at Ebersdorf. At Ebersdorf, revivalists had been invited to preach and to fill the court with officials who were nonsectarian Christians guided by their common "Philadelphian" love of the Savior.[18] This experiment was an expression of Jane Leade's "Philadelphian Society" in England (from the 1670s), which was finding numerous daughter communities in Germany. Their intent was to gather a pure congregation of unpartisan love for Christ (reflecting Revelation 3:7–13) out of all branches of Christendom. This was the goal which Zinzendorf hoped to realize when he formed his community at Herrnhut.[19] Zinzendorf fixed his hope of realizing this ideal to restarting the old Unity of the Brethren (rooted in the followers of John Hus in the early fifteenth century), now linked to the local Lutheran parish in Upper Lusatia. However, David formed a Reformed-leaning separatist group that moved out of Herrnhut, which was soon won over to revivalism. Unfortunately for Zinzendorf, he found that his attachment to the Philadelphian vision conflicted with traditional Moravians' adherence to their ancient traditions. By the time Wesley had arrived, these divisions and points of tension within the Herrnhut community were being overcome by a new wave of revival, initiated by Steinmetz and his preachers in collaboration with Zinzendorf. However, this surge of revival also brought down on Zinzendorf the conservative Saxon government, who stopped Zinzendorf's revivalist agenda and forced him into exile to the Wetterau district in the Rhineland (where Tersteegen's ministry was also based), and from there Zinzendorf's Moravian movement spread to Holland and England. In his absence, the Moravians remaining at Herrnhut swung over toward Lutheran Orthodoxy in their soteriology.

Zinzendorf now focused on the worldwide diaspora of his missionaries, with Moravian missionaries traveling throughout Europe and to North America. It seems that his larger strategy was to connect with revival wherever it was to be found in the hopes of engaging or even co-opting it for his plans to extend the Moravian world mission, according to his Philadelphian interests.

The Moravian leader now found the most current expression of revitalization near his relocated center at Herrnhaag in the Wetterau. It was the awakening led by the New Prophets, who have already been identified as the Inspirationists. They were descendants of the French prophets of Cevennes, who had been driven into exile after brutal suppression in their apocalyptic-driven uprising against Louis XIV. The Inspirationists

---

18. Ward, *Christianity under the Ancient Regime*, 91.
19. Ibid., 113.

inherited the mantle of the earlier generation of Philadelphians, with their vision of a universal spiritual community of brotherly/sisterly love love, unfettered by confessional divisions. This meant the New Prophets, now cut off from their French roots, had resurfaced after 1700 as revivalists, since they no longer were part of any church or nation to renew. They were clearly operating from a Cocceian framework of salvation history, anticipating an imminent general manifestation of Pentecost that would herald a coming age of the Spirit.

Disparate separatist groups, now living in refuge under the protection of minor German counts in the Wetterau, were won to the Inspirationists' unitive vision, and their leaders, E. L. Gruber (1665–1728) and later, J. F. Rock (1678–1749), proposed to extend the reign of Pentecost, with the baptism of the Spirit bringing sanctification and a disciplined life to all who were bound in legalism to divisive church confessions. Somewhat akin to the revivalist methods of Steinmetz' Silesian Lutheran preachers (though the extraordinary gifts of the Spirit were not encouraged by the latter), the New Prophets made use of fervent and unpartisan evangelistic camp meetings and voluntary prayer meetings; although outside the structures of the state churches, their intent was to draw together all the children of God in a spiritual church, including the masses of dislocated religious seekers within and without the established religious structures of the day.

Zinzendorf attended a large Inspirationist love feast near Frankfurt, where he was swayed by Rock's Spirit-driven revivalism. Zinzendorf hoped to enlist Rock for the Moravians. To Zinzendorf's disappointment, Rock found the strictures of Moravian community life oppressive to the free work of the Spirit, and chose not to associate with the Moravians. Rock held Inspirationist revivals in Saxony, within proximity to the earlier revival centers opened by Steinmetz. Ward notes that the goal of their jubilant hymn singing, love feasts, and public evangelistic meetings was to form a network from the "children of the prophets and from all sects and peoples."[20]

Meanwhile, back in the Wetterau, Zinzendorf's new Moravian community of Herrnhaag was caught up with overly enthusiastic piety revolving around the adoration of Christ's wounds in the eucharist, known as the celebratory "time of sifting (1745–1750). This phase, supported by Zinzendorf, was a reaction against the discipline of the main party of Pietists at Halle, and those at Herrnhut as well. Zinzendorf had chafed under what he regarded as legalism and scrupulousness which he had found objectionable among both Pietists and Orthodox Lutherans. However, the enthusiastic excesses at Herrnhaag, which came on the heels of his abortive attempt to jump start Philadelphian communities in such distant locations as Pennsylvania, resulted in bankruptcy for Herrnhaag as its financial supporters withdrew under the weight of extravagant expenses incurred during the time of its excesses. Herrnhaag now became a center for the Inspirationists.

Having placed the Philadelphians and the Inspirationists in their larger context, we can now give focus to their operations in Switzerland. Although Fletcher hailed from the western French-speaking canton of Vaud (born at Nyon near Lausanne), the prevailing influence from Pietism in the central canton of Bern had permeated beyond that

20. Ibid., 124.

canton. Rational Reformed Orthodoxy did survive into eighteenth century Switzerland, and more in the German than the French speaking cantons. It was based in the Formula Consensus, signed at Bern in 1675, and took root in Vaud as well. The Formula forbade all deviations from high Calvinism, including Quietists like Antoinette Bourignon and Pierre Poiret (Tersteegen's mentor), as well as the Cartesians.[21] These restrictive policies were strongly resisted in the Vaud.[22] The Consensus was especially intended to keep Huguenots from evading the high Calvinist tenet of limited atonement. Fletcher was born into just such a Huguenot family. Pietists represented the cosmopolitan spirit, since they were connected with intellectual and spiritual currents abroad, whereas Orthodoxy was provincial and isolationist. The most repressive measure of Orthodoxy in Switzerland was the Association Oath of 1699, passed by the Bern council, which forbade discussions of the millennial kingdom, conventicles, and reading mystical writings.[23] As a consequence, many Pietists went abroad, or moved into separatism and found primal influence from the English Philadelphians like Jane Leade.[24] When Pietism returned in the next century, it came in the explosive form of revivalism, concentrating in the Bernese Oberland.

The great name associated with Swiss Pietism in the years of Fletcher's youth in the Vaud was Samuel Lutz (1674–1750), whom Ward notes was "pushed out of the way into the French-speaking Vaud," and he "made his base [Vaud] the Pietist centre for the whole area."[25] Furthermore, Lutz was closely connected with the Steinmetz circle in Germany, and he impressed Christian David who visited him, and he also entertained Rock, the leader of the Inspired, but he succeeded in drawing Rock's followers back into the church.[26] So, it appears that a greatly influential figure in Fletcher's home area was the key to the main channels of Coccseian dispensational (*heilsgeschichtlich*) thinking of that day, as well as to German proto-Pentecostalism, and this is precisely the system that Fletcher develops in his *Checks to Antinomianism* after his later association with John Wesley and the Methodists in England. Ward also notes that this kind of prophecy was not new in Switzerland, since "the Swiss had been exposed direct to the Cevennes [French] prophets and highly exposed to the hybrid variety, Inspiration."[27] Goebel also documents the extent to which this part of Switzerland was drawn into the Inspired mission field, since "numerous Swiss religious refugees had fled to the Wetterau" using the routes that the Inspired had taken south into Württemberg."[28] Further, the community

---

21. Ibid., 87.
22. Ward, *supra*.
23. Ward, *Christianity under the Ancient Regime*, 88.
24. Ward, *supra*.
25. Ward, *Christianity under the Ancient Regime*, 125.
26. These incredibly direct connections between Pietist Pentecostal thinking in Germany and Fletcher are described by Ward in *Christianity under the Ancient Regime*, 125.
27. Ward, *Christianity under the Ancien Regime*, 126.
28. Max Goebel, *Geschichte der wahren Inspirations-Gemeinden von 1688 bis 1850, III; Zeitschrift zur historische Theologie* 19 (1854–1855) 129–31.

of the Inspired in the Wetterau "continued to exercise pastoral oversight over the Swiss brethren for the rest of the [eighteenth] century."[29]

To say that Fletcher could have escaped such pervasive influence in his home canton, which was the center for Lutz's revival ministry, is not plausible. Fletcher corresponded with Lutz during his second return trip to his birthplace in Nyon (1778–1781), a convalescence trip due to physical illness, late in his ministry.[30] While there, a pastor invited him to preach, until the local authorities forbade the pastor from allowing him to hold meetings in the parish house, since this was the property of the state. For that reason, he held his meeting in the home of his brother, Henri Louis, where he preached on the "power to become sons of God" through the love of Jesus Emmanuel. Streiff notes that, during this time of ministry at Nyon, Fletcher read "with contentment" the apology of Samuel Lutz, and became convinced that he [Fletcher] "needed to focus on corresponding with the local population in written correspondence (concerning the great themes these men were advancing), since he such little opportunity to preach."[31]

As a consequence of this study, it is apparent that Wesley's Pentecostal language, and most likely Fletcher's as well, owes a profound debt to the streams of radical Pietism that fed the earliest expressions of revivalism on the European continent.

---

29. Ward, *supra*.

30. Patrick Philipp Streiff, *Jean Guillaume de la Flechere John William Fletcher, 1729–1785* (Frankfurt/Main: Peter Lang, 1984) 401–9.

31. Ibid., 404.

3

Heart of a Radical Reform

Christology and the Church of God Movement (Anderson)

Barry L. Callen

The Church of God movement (Anderson) is both a holiness-rooted and free-church tradition that emerged in the midst of the American Holiness Movement of the last quarter of the nineteenth century. The dual sources of this movement's heritage are the Wesleyan and the "Radical" or Believers Church traditions.[1] The primary pioneer, Daniel S. Warner (1842–1895), had been influenced theologically by the earlier reforming work of John Winebrenner.[2] Once Warner became separated from the Winebrennerians, mostly because of his embracing and vigorous preaching of Christian holiness, he and others who gravitated to the same theological and ecclesial concerns became "come-outers," even from the formal expressions of the Holiness Movement.[3]

The separatist impulse came from a perception of what should be the natural results of the embracing of Christian holiness. Daniel Warner, "after being challenged by his respective church [Winebrennerian] on the issue of holiness evangelism, sought to apply the logic of Christian perfectionism, with all the ultraistic inclinations of the perfectionist mentality, to the church question."[4] Warner became convinced that both believers and the church itself should be holy—meaning for Warner that it must be purified from sin, that is, released from human control and united with all Christ-believers by the cleansing power of God's Spirit. The result was Warner and many others separating from all existing church structures in order to stand free in the one and only church of God. The clear intention was whole-church reformation and not the founding of another "denomination." The very existence of denominations was judged the sad result of compromising

---

1. See Barry L. Callen, *Radical Christianity: The Believers Church Tradition in Christianity's History and Future* (Nappanee, IN: Evangel, 1999).

2. See Richard Kern, *John Winebrenner: 19th-Century Reformer* (Harrisburg, PA: Central, 1974).

3. See Barry L. Callen, *It's God's Church! The Life and Legacy of Daniel Sidney Warner* (Anderson, IN: Warner, 1995).

4. Melvin Easterday Dieter, *The Holiness Revival of the Nineteenth Century* (Metuchen, NJ: Scarecrow, 1980) 246.

the true life of holiness in God's Spirit. Instead, the movement was toward a recovery of the Pentecostal dynamic of the "apostolic church."[5]

When considering such a radical reformationist tradition, the status of formalized Christian theology becomes an obvious question area. What happens to theology in the midst of radical reformers who are reacting to the unholy, abusive use of church structures, with their "humanized" creeds and practices? In particular, what about Christology—key to Christian faith, the subject of many "heresies" among earlier church reformers, and thus the stimulation of numerous creedal statements and church divisions? What have the radical reformers of the Church of God movement done theologically in this regard?

In brief, the answer is that these reformers, especially in the movement's earliest generations, determined to be loyal both to the classic Christian tradition of theological teaching (assuming it to be essentially biblical) and to the vision of necessary separation from all the institutionalized disobedience of the church, including mandatory submission to formalized creedal statements that often have functioned as tools of divisive denominationalism. Even so, Christology, as classically defined by the leading church councils, quickly became central to the movement's teaching tradition.

CHRISTOLOGY IN THE CONTEXT OF RADICAL REFORM

The holiness-oriented reform movement of the late nineteenth century, coming to be known as the Church of God movement (Anderson) in the twentieth century, initially was comprised of numerous ex-Methodists, Winebrennerians, Mennonites, and others. They were sincere Christians reacting to perceived abuses of church life, affirming a fresh vision of God's intention, a holy and undivided church, and separating from all that was seen as less than the divine ideal. There was a strong anti-organizational bias. In fact, this bias against "man-rule" in the church led Daniel Warner to separate even from the Holiness Movement itself—which affirmed or at least tolerated denominationalism. Its focus was more on personal holiness and not also on the corporate holiness of the church evidenced by a challenging of the legitimacy of church structures as such.

In the name of Christian holiness and its divinely-intended implications, the new reform movement challenged all traditional church structures, including formalized creedal statements, viewing them as inappropriate tools of denominational identity and control and causes of ungodly (unholy) division in the body of Christ. The Church of God movement, accordingly, was and still is an unusually "open" fellowship, one with a strong focus on biblical authority, Christian experience, and the present work of the Holy Spirit (without being "pentecostal" in the tounges-speaking sense). The Spirit's work is relied upon to enable newly-sanctified persons to move in the Spirit's flow toward a newly-united church with fresh integrity that can spawn authentic and credible mission.

It is assumed in the Church of God movement that an obvious integrity of faith, life change, and the resulting Christ-like, united community of faith will be able to present Jesus Christ more effectively to the world. After all, insist these holiness reformers, the

---

5. Charles E. Brown, *The Apostolic Church* (Anderson, IN: Gospel Trumpet, 1947).

PART ONE: RETHINKING THE HISTORY

Christian faith is *about Jesus Christ*, and the church is to be in the business of radical change into Christ's image, being the distinctive Christ community, and being on the mission of spreading the good news of Jesus Christ to all the world. Regardless of its strong resistance to institutionalized creedal systems, then, it is important to note that the reform movement of the Church of God has always been deeply committed to the person, work, community, and mission of Jesus the Christ. All of this is to be biblically defined, life-changing, world-engaging, and Christ-centered.

With a disdain for humanly devised creeds and ecclesiastical organizations, becoming systematically theological, or at least formally honoring the systematic theological work of others, has hardly been a preoccupation of the Church of God movement. Even so, movement leaders have always been very convictional, preaching oriented, and evangelistically persuasive. No one has claimed to be a "prophet" in the sense of bringing from God any dramatic new revelation outside of biblical teaching. There has been nothing "heretical" being announced, not even anything tangential to the historic faith of Christians.

What, then, has there been? This movement has centered on Jesus Christ, believed to be the core of Christian faith. It has championed a new commission understood to be from God, one involving primary focus on (1) "all truth" [not just denominational pieces of truth], (2) a reintroduction of the Spirit-born and Spirit-led "apostolic church," and (3) unity of the contemporary church, primarily through the proclamation and power of commonly experienced holiness. Daniel Warner's personal journal for March 7, 1878, reads:

> On the 31st of last January the Lord showed me that holiness could never prosper upon sectarian soil encumbered by human creeds and party names, and he gave me a new commission to join holiness and all truth together and build up the apostolic church of the living God. Praise his name! I will obey him.

The heritage of the Church of God movement (Anderson) has been the quest to find the best ways of embracing and implementing such a "radical" holiness vision. As the title of historian John W. V. Smith's book has it, the movement has been "The Quest for Holiness and Unity."[6] Both holiness and unity must be Christ oriented and inspired by the Spirit of the Christ.

In the light of this vision, the persistent and potentially "denominationalizing" question keeps emerging. How is the belief life of the church to be governed if the usual tools of theological control (a key aspect of "denominationalism") are disdained as human intrusions on legitimate church life? According to Daniel Warner and other "come-out" reformers, the answer is clear, even if impractical in the eyes of many others. The church is to be the community of God's Spirit, who alone chooses the members, grants the gifts, directs in mission, and instructs in proper belief. The church is the gathering of the saints who are to rejoice in their Spirit-life and find unity with each other because of the sharing of the sanctified life being enabled by God's unmerited graciousness. As believers

---

6. John W. V. Smith, *The Quest for Holiness and Unity* (Anderson, IN: Warner, 1980/2009).

gather together in the study of the biblical revelation, which centers in Jesus Christ, the Spirit of Christ will instruct, protect, enliven, order, and send.

What, then, is the church to believe, and how can it protect against false belief? The prevailing assumption of the Church of God movement has been that Christian truth consists in going back to "the blessed old Bible" and believing everything that it teaches—and not insisting on anything not clearly taught. Since no Christian ever fully understands biblical truth, the life of the church involves an ongoing searching of the Scriptures together for growing understanding. With no legislated creed to restrict or prematurely abort this process, the Spirit is free to teach all things about and in Jesus Christ. Accordingly, the teaching focus of the Church of God movement has been a conscious return to the "apostolic church" where, it is believed, Jesus Christ reigned in immediacy through the Spirit—who inspired the composition of the Bible for the understanding of all generations of believers.

The center of Christian faith is viewed as the work of God in Jesus Christ as now mediated by Christ's Spirit. John Winebrenner, Daniel Warner's theological mentor, had included the following in his 1844 list of "avowed principles" about the church: "She believes in one Supreme God, consisting of Father, Son, and Holy Spirit, and that these three are co-equal and co-eternal."[7] Charles E. Brown, later theologian and historian of the Church of God movement (Anderson), fully agreed, writing a book that he titled *We Preach Christ*. It is organized around the classic roles of Christ as prophet, priest, and king, with subsections covering the full range of theological subjects. Brown assumed that "there is no clear revelation of God except in Jesus Christ" (see Matt 11:27).[8] Christology is forever crucial.

This, then, is the vision, the idealism, the perceived commission, and the general Christ-centered theological focus of the Church of God movement (Anderson). There are questions that naturally now arise after 130 years of a reform movement's life. Recognizing the movement's earliest years of protest and attempts at radical reform of church life, and given its anti-organizational and anti-creedal attitudes, we focus here on how Christology has functioned over the decades in this reforming tradition. How analytical, articulate, and "orthodox" has it been? How has it functioned in practical ways to help govern the church's life? Given the experience-oriented nature of the movement in general, how important have been the details of formal Christology, details that most Christians have judged extremely important to avoid heresy?

TWO "REFORMATION PRINCIPLES"

The Church of God movement has been very cautious about introducing organization in church life, resisting what it has called "man-rule." Even so, a limited amount of organization has evolved over the decades to consolidate, order, and expand the life and witness of the movement. All such organization has been created only as judged essential, with

---

7. Kern, *John Winebrenner*, 48.

8. Charles E. Brown, *We Preach Christ: A Handbook of Christian Doctrine* (Anderson, IN: Gospel Trumpet, 1957) 15.

all of it kept from controlling local churches in any way (other than moral persuasion). Cooperative ministries are strictly voluntary. Many that have arisen in North America and involve the movement in general are coordinated by Church of God Ministries, a body responsible to the General Assembly that first was organized in 1917. To avoid being an "ecclesiastical" body, this Assembly is self-defined as follows (select words italicized for emphasis):

> The purpose of this Assembly shall be to function as a *temporary* presbytery in the conduct of (1) the general business of the Church of God in the United States and [in certain regards] Canada and (2) its annual North American Convention. . . . This Assembly shall be regarded as a *voluntary* association. It shall *not* exercise ecclesiastical jurisdiction or authority over the Church of God in general or over individual congregations in particular. It shall, however, retain the right of a voluntary association to define its own membership and to declare, on occasion, when individual ministers or congregations are not recognized by the Assembly as adhering to the general reformation principles to which the Assembly itself is committed. (Articles II and III of the *Constitution and Bylaws of the General Assembly of the Church of God*).

What are these "general reformation principles" that can regulate Assembly membership? No "creed" exists or likely will be created any time soon. No such principles have been formally stated by the Assembly over the years, but various ones have been regularly assumed in light of the general teaching tradition of the movement. However, arising out of two contentious issues handled by the Assembly in the 1980s, two such principles became more clearly recognized—although still only relating to the membership of the Assembly itself and to the Assembly's expectation of the governing boards and elected officials charged with oversight of the operational policies of ministry agencies and the credentials of ministers related to the Assembly. These principles essentially repeat what has been celebrated in a movement song for decades, namely, "the Bible is our rule of faith and Christ alone is Lord." Christology is central, and is to be defined biblically.

The first general reformation principle, then, is *biblical authority*. In June, 1981, the Assembly resisted a move on the part of some ministers who were reflecting the "battle for the Bible" context of the time (spearheaded by Harold Lindsell and other evangelical "fundamentalists"). These ministers had hoped to make "inerrancy" the official Church of God expectation of how the meaning of biblical inspiration should be understood (which, in effect, would be a creedal statement, something traditionally unacceptable in the movement). Historian of the Church of God, John W. V. Smith, offered this perspective, his way of deflecting the inerrancy push by some. Among thought leaders of the Church of God who wrote during the early twentieth century, when the fundamentalist controversy over biblical inerrancy was splitting churches apart, "there is practically no evidence that any of them, with the possible exception of C. E. Brown, felt that their high view of the Bible needed to be supported by legalist definitions applied to the text such as 'inerrancy' and 'verbal inspiration.' They simply saw no need to enter into that debate."[9]

---

9. John W. V. Smith, "The Bible in the Church of God Reformation Movement: A Historical Perspective," in *Centering on Ministry* 6.3 (1981) 6.

After considerable debate, what the 1981 Assembly finally affirmed, instead of the call for "inerrancy," was this: "The Bible truly is the divinely inspired and infallible Word of God. The Bible is without error in all that it affirms, in accordance with its own purpose, namely that it is 'profitable for teaching, for reproof, for correction, for training in righteousness, that the man of God may be adequate, equipped for every good work' (2 Tim 3:16–17, NAS), and it therefore is fully trustworthy and authoritative as the infallible guide for understanding the Christian faith and living the Christian life." Here was the principle of appropriate authority in church life, stated in principle more than in creedal or technical terms. Truth is to be biblically defined. The Bible is trustworthy because the Spirit of God superintended its composition and also its current interpretation.

Then in 1985 came the identification of the second reformation principle, one necessarily drawn from the authoritative biblical source. The concern at this time was that some cooperative national ministries of the Church of God had developed limited working relationships with units of the National Council of Churches (U.S.A.)—although the movement itself was not a member of the Council. Recent media news stories had highlighted particular positions and actions of this ecumenical body that offended some ministers, who then called for a full disassociation of the movement from National Council work at any and all levels. Some leaders of the movement strongly disagreed, thinking this an overreaction that would be hurtful to certain Christian relationships and cooperative Christian ministries of the movement.

After some heated discussion on the Assembly floor and then a period of careful study launched by the Assembly, this body, the most representative voice of the Church of God movement, adopted a statement that focused on Christology. Ecumenical ministry partnerships were said to be appropriate in principle, but only if the partner is clearly committed to the full divinity and lordship of Jesus Christ (meant to exclude some bodies using the name "Christian" but clearly unorthodox in Christology). Said the Assembly: "Any inter-church body involved in a relationship [with national ministry bodies of the Church of God] should be committed publicly to the divinity and lordship of Jesus Christ. He is central to the meaning and the mission of the church!"

Therefore, two reformation principles were identified by the General Assembly during the 1981–1985 period, with their contexts and details reported by Barry L. Callen.[10] The Assembly had not set out to establish such principles, even though its own legal documents presumed their existence. It had backed into them in times of crisis. Even so, the two "principles" now existed in a more public way, at least in relation to the Assembly's own membership. They have always been basic to the teaching tradition of this movement and were justified by the Assembly as not "ecclesiastical" actions, not involving unacceptable creed-making. Nonetheless, they did draw two important theological lines in the sand, essentially restating the movement's historic approach to Christian theology as summarized by the Anderson University School of Theology faculty in a 1979 booklet titled *We Believe*:

---

10. Barry L. Callen, *Following the Light: Teachings, Testimonies, Trials, and Triumphs of the Church of God Movement, Anderson* (Anderson, IN: Warner, 2000) 198–204.

We are privileged to have received the basic *truth of Christ* in the biblical revelation, but we realize that our understanding and application of that truth are always subject to the continuing ministry of the Holy Spirit in our midst.... It is our conviction that God increasingly is leading all Christians to the challenge of *holiness* and *unity*. We feel ourselves especially called to proclaim these essentials of church life, to pray for them, to work toward them, and, most of all, to model them so that the church which is seen by the world will be an effective representative of Christ.[11]

That is, Jesus Christ is the heart of Christian faith. Belief must focus on him, but with a humility of understanding open to the ongoing teaching ministry of the Spirit of Christ. The church's mission is to represent Christ in the world. It is in him, and in him alone, that the Spirit of Christ can bring to believers a personal holiness and a corporate togetherness that will allow the unity necessary to represent Christ effectively in this divided world. It all centers in Jesus Christ, yesterday in a cradle and on a cross, and today, through his Spirit, to be in control of all dimensions of church life.

As with the Church of God movement in general, its General Assembly in North America is not in the creed-making business. Its two "reformation principles" are not intended to define a particular "brand" of Christianity, but rather to state what it means to be Christian at all. The Bible is the authoritative guide to the person and story of God in Jesus Christ. That person and story combine to constitute the core of Christian faith. To insist on additional details of belief introduces divisive denominational distinctives; to believe less is to be something other than Christian.

With the Bible accepted as the authoritative base, and with its revelation that Jesus Christ is our divine Lord and Savior, God actually with us for our salvation, what further needs to be said about the many details and theological traditions related directly to Christology? This question is very important, although it has not been handled often and in detail in the teaching life of the Church of God movement.

SINGULARITY IN A PLURALISTIC WORLD

It is hardly surprising that the appearance of systematic theologians has been a relatively rare occurrence in the history of the Church of God movement. The first was Frederick G. Smith (*What the Bible Teaches*, 1914), followed by Russell R. Byrum (*Christian Theology*, 1925), and Albert F. Gray (*Christian Theology*, 1944/46). Three substantial books of theology appeared in the 1990s by a new generation of movement theologians. They were Kenneth E. Jones (*Theology of Holiness and Love*, 1995), Barry L. Callen (*God as Loving Grace*, 1996), and Gilbert W. Stafford (*Theology for Disciples*, 1996). Detailed discussions of Christology have been limited and rarely on center stage. When they have occurred, they have tended to appear in the work of these writers and to affirm the "orthodox" Christological tradition of Western Christianity.

Since the original reforming concerns of the Church of God movement related mostly to the nature of the church and the Christian life, not to the doctrine of God, the movement's early theologians—Smith, Byrum, and Gray—tended to follow traditional or

---

11. See Anderson University School of Theology, *WE BELIEVE* (Anderson, IN: Warner, 1979).

orthodox Protestant positions on God, Trinity, and Christology. The more recent of the movement's theologians—Jones, Callen, Stafford—have done the same, exhibiting a tendency to highlight relational motifs that incline toward emphases now common among "open" theologians like Stanley J. Grenz,[12] Henry H. Knight III,[13] Clark H. Pinnock,[14] and Roger E. Olson.[15] In fact, Barry L. Callen is the intellectual biographer of Pinnock.[16] At no point, however, does this "open" or more relational (pietistic) tendency depart from the basic soil of traditional Christian theology concerning God as Father, Son, and Spirit.

Callen organizes his *God as Loving Grace* around the Trinitarian scheme of God the Sovereign (Father), God the Savior (Son), and God the Sustainer (Spirit).[17] Stafford places particular stress on the cruciality of the "orthodox" view of the "Trinitarian God." He speaks of the "three-personed God" and stands with the Nicene Creed in affirming oneness in plurality and plurality in oneness.[18] The Trinity, he insists, is "ontological" and "immanent," revealing "the eternal lover." The Trinitarian God is "the ongoing, outgoing God of history . . . the pilgrim God . . . the here, there, and everywhere God . . . the God of the whole Bible—the God of the Old Testament, the God revealed in Jesus Christ, the God poured out at Pentecost."[19]

None of these theological books has been an "official" statement of the movement's theological stance (nothing is); they, however, have been the expressions of especially respected leaders whose views have been referenced most and considered faithful reflections of biblical teaching. These theologians have stood together on several "orthodox" Christian understandings of the doctrine of God. One such understanding is the doctrine of the Trinity. The prominence of Islam in today's religious and political arenas forces this forward. Jews, Muslims, and Christians believe in the one sovereign God, but "Trinity" teaching clearly brings separation among the three monotheistic faith traditions. For instance, Adam W. Miller of the Church of God once insisted:

> We are confronted today with a revival of that teaching which would remove Christ from his absolute position as sovereign Lord of history and the world's only hope of redemption. It would make Christ and all he represents but a single contribution in the world's quest for religious truth. It is an attempt to strip Christ of his claim to be *the* truth. . . . But the Christian church cannot and must not accept such an

---

12. Stanley J. Grenz, *Revisioning Evangelical Theology: A Fresh Agenda for the 21st Century* (Downers Grove, IL: InterVarsity, 1993).

13. Henry H. Knight, III, *A Future for Truth: Evangelical Theology in a Postmodern World* (Nashville: Abingdon, 1997).

14. Clark H. Pinnock, *Tracking the Maze: Finding Our Way through Modern Theology from an Evangelical Perspective* (New York: Harper & Row, 1990); *Flame of Love: A Theology of the Holy Spirit* (Downers Grove, IL: InterVarsity, 1996); Clark H. Pinnock with Barry L. Callen, *The Scripture Principle: Reclaiming Full Authority of the Bible*, 3rd ed. (Grand Rapids: Baker, 2009).

15. Roger E. Olson, *Reformed and Always Reforming: The Postconservative Approach to Evangelical Theology* (Grand Rapids: Baker, 2007).

16. Barry L. Callen, *Clark H. Pinnock: Journey Toward Renewal* (Nappanee, IN: Evangel, 2000).

17. Barry L. Callen, *God as Loving Grace* (Nappanee, IN: Evangel, 1996).

18. Gilbert W. Stafford, *Theology for Disciples* (Anderson, IN: Warner, 1996) 176.

19. Ibid., 189.

evaluation or concept of Christ or his gospel. To do so would mean that the church would become merely the dispenser of some important truth and not the witness to nor proclaimer of *the* truth.[20]

Stafford tied this insistence on singularity to the traditional Christian doctrine of the Trinity:

> The foundational question is whether we view Christian claims that God is Trinity and that Christ Jesus is the only divine savior as being merely options among many equally (or unequally) acceptable conceptions of God or whether we view them as being ultimately true. The watershed issue that decisively influences one's approach to people of other faiths is whether we are convinced that the Trinitarian God is the only eternal God.[21]

Callen agreed with Miller and Stafford, but with a little irenic commentary. A witness to Jesus Christ as the full and final truth does not mean that other religious traditions are totally lacking in truth, and therefore are to be denounced. In fact, "Since God is not without a witness among the nations (Acts 14:16–17), one should expect to encounter echoes of God's activity in the maze of the world's religions.... [Even so], anything true anywhere is already in Christ, is best understood in light of Christ, and finally will be consummated with Christ."[22]

These representative and influential theologians of the Church of God movement have agreed with another consistent aspect of this movement's teaching tradition. Emphasis should be on the historic coming of God in Jesus and the present meaningfulness of that historic coming because of the present work of Christ's Spirit. Eschatological teachings should not detract from the present lordship of Jesus Christ by relegating hope to some future "millennium" on earth after the return of the Christ. Nor should they depart from the obvious emphasis of Jesus by insisting that a millennium will come that features a political dominance of Christ back on earth, an earthly kingdom like is typical among humans and that Jesus refused to establish, despite pressure from some of his followers. An "amillennial" eschatology is to be affirmed as biblical teaching, in part because it honors the work of Jesus in his first coming and highlights the work of Christ's Spirit in and through the church prior to Christ's return to conclude history and initiate the final judgment. Barry L. Callen's 1997 book *Faithful in the Meantime* is a good example of the amillennial focus.[23] It addresses the subjects of "final things" in the context of the present possibilities for and responsibilities of Christians. The wonderful news is not merely that Jesus is Lord of tomorrow; it is that he also is Lord of today!

MINISTERIAL EDUCATION AND CREDENTIALING

What does the North American seminary of the Church of God affirm about Christology? What is required of Church of God ministerial ordination candidates when the move-

---

20. Adam W. Miller in *The Gospel Trumpet* (February 2, 1957) 1–2.
21. Stafford, *Theology for Disciples*, 330.
22. Callen, *God as Loving Grace*, 159–60.
23. See Barry L. Callen, *Faithful in the Meantime* (Nappanee, IN: Evangel, 1997).

ment is "orthodox" by theological tradition, clearly convictional and preaching oriented, but has no uniform creed as a common and mandatory basis of group belief? Answers to these questions can have very practical implications.

The movement leans on the "reformation principles" of its General Assembly (see above) and tends to follow the thinking of its most respected theological writers (see above). The various state assemblies and their credentialing committees set the particulars of their own ordination standards and practices. What prevails is the Bible as the accepted authoritative base, with the ministers in charge of the credentialing process functioning as the Bible's local interpreters (in light of the general teaching heritage of the Church of God movement as an honored backdrop). This brings general uniformity, along with some inevitable and occasionally awkward difference.

Recent years have seen the development of a national credentials manual intended as a guide to increased uniformity of policy and procedure among the national credentialing units. The manual, of course, is in effect only as given assemblies choose to adopt it as their own (as presented or in some modified form). What does this manual, now relied upon in many places, have to say about the necessary theological commitments of ministerial candidates? The key statement is that credentialing is "for those who possess a well-developed and scripturally valid belief system and whose lives give indication of the assimilation of that belief system" (24). The manual goes on to say that "theology ultimately arises out of one's own encounter with the loving embrace of God. True theologizing cannot be done by the unspiritual person, since such a person lacks the insight provided by the presence and wisdom of the Holy Spirit."

Reflecting the pietist and evangelistic heritages of the Church of God movement, it is clear that "spiritual experience" is valued highly. A movement slogan is that "Christian experience makes you a member" of a congregation. Reads the credentials manual: "Theological understanding can never rest on intellectual investigation alone. By its very nature, it must be experiential as well as academic." The present transforming work of the Holy Spirit is judged crucial. Even so, candidates are asked to prepare a written statement of their beliefs, including direct comment on fourteen subjects listed in the manual. The first three are: "The nature and revealing activity of God; The nature and saving mission of Jesus Christ; and The Holy Spirit's cleansing and gifting work in the believer's life."

Formal educational requirements are not fixed for all ordination candidates—the work of the Holy Spirit cannot be so restricted. Even so, the highest level of ministerial education available to candidates is expected (given their differing abilities, ages when called to ministry, etc.). A seminary education is said to be the ideal, although most candidates have not achieved this educational level in the past. The life of the mind is appreciated generally, but spiritual giftedness and vitality have been even more highly regarded.

A stated assumption in the ministerial manual is that, despite the theological freedom prevailing in this movement, a ministerial candidate's commitments should be "within the bounds of biblically based belief" and should be "in general agreement with the teaching tradition of the Church of God movement" (25). To help identify this particular teaching tradition, listed are fourteen books of theology by respected Church of God authors. They are required or strongly recommended for reading. Once books are consulted and a personal belief statement is written, dialogue occurs between the candidate and credentialing committee. Some subjectivity of committee members is inevitable. This introduces variance among committees regarding the nature and detail of theological expectations and probings that are experienced by ministerial candidates. The variance is usually not dramatic in its dimension, although there are stories of individuals avoiding certain states because of their theological reputations.

At least one element of the occasional variance has been perceived as a problem, particularly by the late movement theologian Gilbert W. Stafford. He expressed deep concern that "it is altogether possible for a [Church of God] congregation to call a minister who, although ordained, does not believe in the faith of the historic Christian church."[24] For Stafford, Christology was a special concern. He noted one ordination service where the question put to the candidate was, "Do you believe in the one God?" To Stafford, that was not a distinctively Christian question—"Jehovah's Witnesses, Unitarians, Jews, and Muslims all could have said yes to that question."[25] The more distinctively Christian question would be about the *Trinitarian* God—Father, Son, and Holy Spirit. To be sure, insisted Stafford, "Christians believe in one God, but that is not what sets us apart as Christians. That which sets us apart is that we are convinced the Scriptures teach *the Trinitarian view* of this one God."[26] The likelihood is that no credentialing unit would disagree with Stafford; the situation is just that some are not as thoughtful and intentional theologically as they might and probably should be, particularly on the central issue of the nature of God in Christ.

A significant and sometimes awkward tension exists in a Christian reform movement that intends to be both thoroughly biblical and staunchly anti-creedal. Leaders of the Church of God movement have resisted any reducing of Christianity to a series of belief statements. The real essence of the faith has been judged to include *experiencing* the truth. Reflecting what Roger E. Olson calls "post-conservative evangelical theology," a style growing out of the more pietistic side of evangelicalism, the Church of God movement has vigorously affirmed the reality of divine revelation and biblical authority, but has avoided the "inerrancy" approach to biblical inspiration as too rationalistic, considering the purpose of revelation to be more *transformational* than merely *informational*.[27]

It is important to be clear that the intent of Church of God leaders has *not* been to minimize the importance of the theological content of faith; rather, it has been to highlight the necessity of being involved personally in life-changing obedience to the forgiveness and sanctifying grace of God—who is the source, focus, substance, and end of all true doctrine. Beyond right words lies the divine power to illumine the mind and alter life itself. To "know" God is to be related rightly to God *through Jesus Christ* and to be engaged rightly in God's present purposes in this world. Faith is always a pilgrimage, a journey guided by the Spirit toward more and more light. Faith's focus should be less

---

24. Gilbert W. Stafford, *Church of God at the Crossroads* (Anderson, IN: Warner, 2000) 31.
25. Ibid.
26. Ibid.
27. Olson, *Reformed and Always Reforming*, 53.

on philosophic and creedal statements about the Christ and more on *the living person of Jesus* who is himself the truth (John 14:6) and who, through the Spirit, now reigns in the church.

There is to be no isolated, merely intellectual, or routinely repeated confessional formulations of doctrine. Christianity, in the usual view of Church of God teachers, already has endured too much use of theological creeds as protectors of historic church institutions and dividers among believers. Early historians of this reform movement tended to read church history as a sad trail of compromises with "the world." Thus, the goal was to return to the "early morning light" (apostolic church and Bible). It was believed that God intended to have this pure light of Jesus Christ shining again in the "evening time" of the church's troubled history. Granted, the early creed-making centuries of the church had sought to protect the church from heresies by careful definitions of the person and work of Jesus. However, it is also true that the immersion of the church into the Greek-Roman-European cultural stream brought an inevitable infusion of humanity into the reasons for, styles of, and uses of the creeds being produced.

The classic Christian creeds are viewed in the Church of God as valuable, of course, but with limitations. They are milestone attempts to define biblical teaching in other than biblical times, languages, and philosophies. Thus, they are instructional, but not themselves biblical. This movement, highlighting Christian "experience" and reacting against organizational paralysis in church life, naturally has de-emphasized any formal status for "systematic" theologies and formalized creedal statements. It has shared to a point the argument of J. Denny Weaver.[28] Especially in our "postmodern" time, credibility for Christians is hardly won merely by making claims to universal philosophic truth. It comes more from demonstrating what differences Christian faith can make in the laboratory of human history. The witness must be to the "way of Jesus," and it must be made with lives that actually reflect Jesus.

Thus, Barry L. Callen included in his autobiography an original essay that he titled "Please Don't Call Me 'Christian'!" He says that "the center of the Christian faith is Jesus Christ, not a full identifying with all of the history, structures, and creeds that have carried the name 'Christian.'"[29] The preference is being known as a "follower of Jesus." Callen also wrote a commentary on the biblical book of Colossians,[30] dealing at length and fully agreeing with the great biblical affirmation of the unlimited scope of the supremacy of Jesus Christ (Col 1:15–23). Earlier, however, he also had written a book on the history, theology, and ethics of the "Believers Church" tradition (important for the Church of God movement), in which he said:

> The Christian confession concerning the Christ initially was derived from historical narrative, autobiographical testimony, the story of divine reality as experienced in the life, teachings, death, and resurrection of Jesus. Explaining this incarnation

---

28. See J. Denny Weaver, *Anabaptist Theology in the Face of Postmodernity* (Telford, PA: Pandora, 2000).

29. Barry L. Callen, *A Pilgrim's Progress: The Autobiography of Barry L. Callen* (Anderson, IN: Anderson University Press: Emeth, 2008) 398.

30. Barry L. Callen et al., *Galatians, Philippians, Colossians* (Indianapolis: Wesleyan, 2007).

reality philosophically and theologically would come later in the process of struggle with competing claims and the challenges involved in engaging in world mission. But first came the foundational witness of the New Testament to the joy of the living reality of Jesus the Christ. The conviction of the Believers Church tradition is that *all Christological formulating should remain in close touch with the biblical witness to and the living reality of Jesus Christ.*[31]

While never denying the foundational truths about Jesus Christ contained in the classic Christian creeds, the Church of God movement has expressed limited interest in the theological detail of it all. On the one hand, Christology is not to become captive to spiritual experience and thus be whatever an enthusiastic believer says it is; on the other hand, there has been general discomfort with putting a spotlight on complex theological details that traditionally have hardened into divisive creeds and competing denominations. Thinking of the Wesleyan and Pietistic streams that have influenced the Church of God heritage, the movement has reflected John Wesley's characteristic of not being quite a "systematic" theologian—orthodox, clearly, but also deeply pietistic intentionally.

CONTEMPORARY TRENDS: A GENEROUS ORTHODOXY

Two contemporary trends are pulling vigorously on pastors of Church of God congregations. One is the growing diversity of church backgrounds from which the people are coming. Congregations hope to be constructively related to their immediate environments, sharing the gospel with whomever is nearby and will hear. Once drawn to the congregation, the pastor is often inclined to avoid being perceived as theologically restrictive or narrowly denominational—which the Church of God has not wished to be anyway. The alternative, now being called "post-conservative evangelical theology" by a few prominent "evangelical" theologians, is well described with the adjectives *critical, generous, progressive,* and *dispositional.*[32] The freedom, freshness, and yet faithfulness of such theology is seen in books like *The Flame of Love* by Clark H. Pinnock. It is a merging of rationalism and pietism, a version of the "Wesleyan Quadralateral" where the Bible base and interpretative triad of reason, experience, and tradition are surrounded by the work of God's Spirit.[33]

Pastoral wisdom and the heritage of the Church of God movement both support a hesitation to be theologically detailed or demanding. The principle of biblical authority is not to be compromised. Even so, the increasingly wide range of biblical understandings in the pews is obvious, and a circumstance that pastors must manage carefully. The challenge is still to go "back to the blessed old Bible" and be wary of arrogance about absolutizing interpretative traditions (creedalism). As Alister McGrath says, "Evangelicalism is principally about being biblical and not the uncritical repetition of past evangelical beliefs."[34]

---

31. Callen, *Radical Christianity*, 90.

32. Olson, *Reformed and Always Reforming*, 193–208.

33. Callen et al., *Galatians, Philippians, Colossians*, 351.

34. Alister McGrath, "Evangelical Theological Method: The State of the Art," in *Evangelical Futures*, ed. John G. Stackhouse Jr. (Grand Rapids: Baker, 2000) 32.

The second contemporary trend, related to the first and sounding almost counter to it, sends today's pastor in another direction. It is a move toward being very clear theologically about what is most distinctively Christian. Apart from the things that constitute the many "brands" of Christianity, the question now is: What constitutes Christianity as a distinct faith in a world of competing faith communities? Biblical teaching points to the historic fact and cosmic significance of Jesus the Christ. This central fact is stated clearly by Barry L. Callen in his commentary on Col 1:15–18:

> The strict monotheism of Jewish tradition is not to be violated: even so, a dramatic new reality has come about, one that soon would have Christian theologians talking seriously about the "Trinity" of God—a *multiplicity* in relation to the *one* God. Speaking adequately about God necessarily involves reference to divine revelation *in the Son* as now illumined for us by the Spirit. . . . Salvation hinges on the Son, both on who He is by nature and by what He has done for us in His earthly life, death, and resurrection.[35]

The trend to deal openly and gently with multiple Christian traditions in the same congregation is limited at least by a strong belief in the classic claim that Jesus Christ is the *one* Son of God and the *only* Savior of humankind. Reflective of the two "reformation principles" discussed above, the essential foundation of a distinctive Christian faith is (1) biblical authority, which yields a necessary belief in (2) Jesus Christ as Lord and Savior of all.

Both of these two contemporary trends, a flexible pastoral approach to theological diversity and a fixed Christology made necessary because of biblical revelation, are seen in the 2003 theological statement of the North American seminary of the Church of God, Anderson University School of Theology. On the one hand, the seminary did not attempt to set or even claim to represent officially the theological stance of the Church of God movement, as no person or group does or can. It was made clear that this statement represents only this particular faculty and staff, and only at that point in time. On the other hand, the seminary was aware that being Christian means something distinctive in today's marketplace of religious claims. The distinction rests on a particular understanding of God as biblically presented, the Triune One revealed in the Son, Jesus Christ. The seminary also wanted to better define itself theologically in the eyes of its constituencies. Its 2003 statement concludes:

> In devotion to Christ as the head of the church, we desire to be a biblical people, a people who worship the triune God, a people transformed by the grace of God, a people of the kingdom of God, a people committed to building up the one, universal church of God, and a people who, in God's love, care for the whole world.[36]

This statement of theological identity represents well the general teaching heritage of the Church of God movement. It does not seek to introduce any new teaching outside the received "orthodox" tradition, and certainly it does not seek to establish a particular

---

35. Callen et al., *Galatians, Philippians, Colossians*, 290–91.

36. See Anderson University School of Theology, *WE BELIEVE* (Anderson, IN: Anderson University Press, 2003).

denominational stance on any doctrine. It seeks only to affirm clearly what is thought to define Christianity as a distinctive faith tradition in a pluralistic world. The focus is on Jesus Christ, who brings God to us and who, through his Spirit, should head the current Body of Christ, the church, wherein people are privileged to worship the Triune God. Instead of abstract explorations of this great mystery of incarnation, the spotlight is on people being transformed by God's amazing grace, celebrating the united body into which the Spirit of Christ ushers them, and joining together in the mission of Christ in today's world.

The fact and significance of the divine Christ, the center of Christian faith, were stated classically by a Quaker philosopher and theologian who was a good friend of the Church of God movement and shared much of its "radical" reforming. Wrote David Elton Trueblood:

> A Christian is a person who . . . becomes convinced that the fact of Jesus Christ is the most trustworthy that he knows in his entire universe of discourse. Christ thus becomes both his central postulate and the Archimedean fulcrum which, because it is really firm, enables him to operate with confidence in other areas. . . . To say that Christ is the fulcrum is not merely to say that He was the greatest figure of history or the finest moral teacher. It is, instead, to see Him as the genuine revelation of the mystery of existence, the one clear light among the many shadows. Commitment is thus vastly more than mere admiration. It means passionate involvement in His life, teachings, death, and resurrection.[37]

Accordingly, the Church of God movement agrees with the title of a 1957 book authored by Charles E. Brown, one of its loved teachers and theologians. The title is *We Preach Christ!* The movement also echoes the title of a popular booklet by Laura and Oral Withrow written about the movement. That title is *Meet Us at the Cross*.[38] The core attitude of the movement was stated well by another of its deeply loved leaders, R. Eugene Sterner. Often saying, "We do not ask you to come to us. We invite you to meet us at the foot of the cross," Sterner made clear that this movement has never wanted to start another denomination, but rather has intended "to take a position of openness on the Godward side to all the truth . . . and an openness on the manward side to fellowship with all of God's people everywhere."[39] To do that as true Christians, Christology must be central both in theological belief and, through the power of Christ's Spirit, in life and church transformation.

---

37. David E. Trueblood, *A Place to Stand* (New York: Harper & Row, 1969) 38–39.
38. Laura and Oral Withrow, *Meet Us at the Cross* (Anderson, IN: Warner, 1999).
39. Eugene R. Sterner, *We Reach Our Hands in Fellowship* (Anderson, IN: Warner, 1960) 19.

4

John Fletcher's Influence on the Nineteenth-Century American Holiness Movement's Worldview

D. William Faupel

Laurence W. Wood has greatly advanced our knowledge of John Fletcher's impact on nineteenth-century American Wesleyanism and early-twentieth-century Pentecostalism. In his early work *Pentecostal Grace*, Wood identified two aspects of Fletcher's theology that gave shape to Wesleyan theology, especially as it developed within the American Holiness Movement and in the subsequent emergence of Pentecostalism. These two interrelated themes were his "Doctrine of Dispensations," and the identification of Wesley's doctrine of "Christian Perfection" with "The Baptism of the Holy Spirit."[1] In his more recent writings, Wood has broadened his thesis to argue that Fletcher's "doctrine of dispensations" also caused John Wesley to rethink his understanding. He seeks to show that that during the last third of his life he tended to express this doctrine of Christian Perfection in Luke-Acts categories of Spirit Baptism.[2] This later claim has been hotly contested[3] and undoubtedly another generation of Wesley scholars will be needed before consensus is reached.

A TRANSFORMATION OF WORLDVIEW

Although the focus of Wood's work on Fletcher and the subsequent discussion has focused on Christian Perfection/Baptism of the Holy Spirit equation, in this article I will attempt to show that Fletcher's doctrine of dispensations enabled a second shift in

---

1. Laurence W. Wood, "John Fletcher's Concept of Christian Perfection," *Pentecostal Grace* (Wilmore, KY: Francis Asbury, 1980) 177–239.

2. Laurence W. Wood, *The Meaning of Pentecostal in Early Methodism: Rediscovering John Fletcher as John Wesley's Vindicator and Designated Successor* (Lanham, MD: Scarecrow, 2002).

3. See for example, Donald Dayton's review in *Pneuma* 26 (2004) 355–61 and the series of rejoinders: Laurence W. Wood, "An Appreciative Reply," *Pneuma* 27 (2005) 163–72; Donald W. Dayton, "Rejoinder to Laurence Wood," *Pneuma* 27 (2005) 367–75; Laurence W. Wood, "Can Pentecostals Be Wesleyan," *Pneuma* 28 (2006) 120–30; and Donald W. Dayton, "A Final Round with Larry Wood," *Pneuma* 28 (2006) 265–70. See also Kenneth J. Collins, "The State of Wesley Studies in North America," *Wesleyan Theological Journal* 44 (2009) 28–36.

Wesleyan theology. In his work, *The Theological Roots of Pentecostalism,* Don Dayton argued that there was a gestalt of five doctrines that, over time, transformed Wesleyan theology into Pentecostal categories: justification, entire sanctification, divine healing and the second coming of Christ.[4] He contended that a paradigm shift took place within the Holiness Movement in the mid-nineteenth century, in which the Christian perfection, Baptism of the Holy Spirit identification made by Fletcher eighty years earlier was finally embraced by the Holiness Movement.[5] Dayton further argued that this shift was quickly followed by a widespread conversion from a postmillennial eschatology to premillennialism.[6] On the surface this change appeared to be minor. In many ways premillennialism looked forward to a thousand-year period that was similar in character to that which was expected by postmillennialists. The one apparent difference was that Premillennialists believed that Christ's Second Advent would take place before the inauguration of the millennium, whereas the postmillennialist position was that Christ would appear at the end of this period. As Dayton would demonstrate, however, despite the apparent similarities, much more was at stake than a simple change of timetable. The new chronology disclosed a transformation in world-view.[7]

Although Wesley held to a premillennial eschatology it was inconsequential in shaping his world-view.[8] His understanding was rooted in soteriology. For him, the devastating clutches of sin must give way to the power of the cross. Salvation must be the restoration of that which was lost in the fall. Otherwise, he reasoned, the curse was greater than the cure. In that event, God's redemption was ineffectual. Wesley's view of soteriology had obvious social as well as personal implications. While his message had been taught in one form or another throughout the history of the Church, especially by the monastic movement and mystics, it had been directed primarily toward Christian elite. Wesley, on the other had, sought to aim his message toward the masses, especially to the disenfranchised. To reach and restore them to a pre-fallen state entailed a radical reordering of society.[9] Such a message lent itself readily to the mood for moral reform and personal piety that characterized the American scene at the dawn of the nineteenth century. As a result, as Wesleyan theology grounded itself in the American context it quickly developed a postmillennial world-view,[10] that would dominate antebellum America.

---

4. Donald W. Dayton *Theological Roots of Pentecostalism* (Metuchen, NJ: Scarecrow, 1987) 21–23.

5. This of course, is the heart of the dispute between Dayton and Wood. Wood argues that the late Wesley and the subsequent Wesleyan movement accepted this identification prior to the turn of the 19th century. In this view both sets of categories and biblical texts were used interchangeably. Wood would agree with Dayton that following the American Civil war, the Spirit Baptism terminology and the Luke-Acts supporting texts would become the predominate mode of expressing the doctrine.

6. Dayton, *Theological Roots of Pentecostalism,* 165–67.

7. Ibid. 165.

8. The best articulation of Wesley's eschatology remains Clarence L. Bence, "Progressive Eschatology: A Wesleyan Alternative," *Wesleyan Theological Journal* 14 (1979) 45–59.

9. For an assessment of Wesley's impact on social reform, see Maldwyn Edwards, *John Wesley and the Eighteenth Century: A Study of His Social and Political Influence* (London: Epworth, 1955).

10. This was so pervasive most nineteenth-century Methodists could not conceive of Wesley being a premillenialist. This conviction was most forcefully argued in H. Rall *John Wesley, A Postmillennialist* (New York: Methodist Book House, 1921).

On the other hand, premillennialism which was always a minority position in North America through the first half of the nineteenth century seemed totally discredited when the Second Advent failed to happen in 1844 as predicted by William Miller and others.[11] The 1857–1858 revival seemed to confirm expectations that the work of the church was about to bring about the transformation of society and usher in the millennium.[12] This consensus was shattered by the Civil War. Those that would remain within Methodism would tend to follow the lead of Bishop Jesse Peck who argued that the nation, brought into existence by God had been judged for its sin of slavery. Now released from the restraint once imposed "by a powerful internal despotism," the Church, "the life force and organizing power of liberty," must redouble its efforts to transform society.[13] The Holiness Movement, on the other hand, gravitated toward refocusing its message to appeal exclusively to the individual. Revivalistic efforts at structural reform were restricted to a number of rescue operations.[14] This trajectory would ultimately lead adherents to adopt a new form of premillennialism propagated by John Nelson Darby [15]

Darby argued that all of human history is divided into seven dispensations. Each dispensation was marked by a change in God's method of dealing with His creation, especially with respect to sin and human responsibility. Each age offered a new test for natural man; each age ended in failure and judgment. On this point Darby stood in agreement with *Historic Premillennialism*. What marked a new development were two underlying presuppositions. First, he believed in the absolute separation of Israel and the Church as distinct peoples of God. As a result, he contended that the unfulfilled prophecies of the Old Testament applied only to the Jewish nation. Israel, God's *earthly* people, by rejecting Christ as their promised Messiah, was cut off for a season, while the Church, God's *heavenly* people, was called forth from the Gentile nations to be prepared as Christ's waiting bride. Second, since many of the Old Testament prophecies remained unfulfilled, he taught that at end of the Church age there would be a period when the Jewish nation would be restored, the divided kingdom would be united, and the Messiah accepted.[16] Darby further argued that God would not resume the prophetic time-clock until the true church had been taken into heaven. This would occur through a secret rapture. St. Paul provided the biblical evidence.

> For the Lord himself shall descend from heave with a shout, with the voice of the archangel and the trump of God; and the dead in Christ shall rise first, then we

---

11. An excellent account of William Miller is David L. Rowe, *Thunder and Trumpets: The Millerite Movement and Apocalyptic Thought in Upstate New York* (Chico, CA: Scholars, 1985).

12. Perry Miller, *The Life of the Mind in America: From the Revolution to the Civil War* (New York: Harcourt, Brace and World, 1965) 90–91.

13. Jesse T. Peck, *The History of the Great Republic: Considered from a Christian Standpoint* (New York: W. C. Palmer Jr., 1868) cited by P. Miller, *Life of the Mind*, 91.

14. Donald W. Dayton, *Discovering an Evangelical Heritage* (New York: Harper & Row, 1976) 100.

15. John Nelson Darby was an Irish Calvinist Anglican Priest who broke with the state church to help form the Plymouth Brethren in the 1820s. A good introduction to his eschatology is Larry V. Crutchfield: *The Origins of Dispensationalism: The Darby Factor* (Lanham, MD: University Press of America, 1992).

16. Timothy P. Weber, *Living in the Shadow of the Second Coming: American Premillennialism, 1875–1925* (New York, NY: Oxford University Press, 1979) 16–17.

which are alive and remain shall be caught up together with them in the clouds, to meet the Lord in the air and so shall we ever be with the Lord.[17]

At the time of the rapture, Darby contended, Christ would come invisibly *for* the Church. Seven years later, at the time of the Second Advent, He would appear visibly *with* the Church. Between these two events, Israel would be restored as a nation, the anti-Christ would be unveiled, and the great tribulation would occur.

The secret rapture, Darby's most distinctive teaching, proved to resolve neatly the most perplexing problem faced by the millenarians. The secret event would restart God's prophetic time-clock. No longer would proponents have to struggle, trying to correlate biblical prophecy with history. They could hold that Christ may come at any moment without the embarrassment of subsequent disconfirmation.[18]

Following the Civil War, Darby's view of premillennialism began a relentless and successful penetration of American Evangelicalism. Darby himself was extremely successful in putting this assault into motion. Energetic and magnetic, he made seven visitations to the United States between 1862 and 1877. His greatest impact came at such urban centers as St. Louis, Missouri; Detroit, Michigan; Chicago, Illinois; Boston, Massachusetts; Philadelphia, Pennsylvania; and New York, New York. In each city, several prominent clergymen were converted to his eschatological views.[19]

A monthly periodical, *The Prophetic Times,* was established in 1863 to champion the futuristic premillennial cause. Edited by Joseph A. Seiss,[20] *The Prophetic Times* provided an ecumenical forum to enable millenarians from the Lutheran, Anglican, Presbyterian, Baptist, Moravian, and Dutch Reformed traditions to articulate their views. It proved to be a major mechanism by which American Evangelicals were molded along Darby's dispensationalist lines.[21]

Dispensationalism gained still another forum in 1875 with the advent of the Bible Prophecy Conferences. The Niagara Bible Conference, held annually until 1900, became the mother of this movement. During the twenty-five year period, some 120 Protestant leaders addressed this annual event. Dwight L. Moody, who adopted Darby's views in 1877, instituted the annual Northfield Prophecy Conference in 1880. Its first group of

---

17. 1 Thess 4:17. Prior to Darby's exposition, all futurists interpreted this passage as relating to Christ's second coming. Weber, *Living in the Shadow of the Second Coming,* 21.

18. Ernest Sandeen, *The Roots of Fundamentalism: British and American Millenarianism, 1800–1930* (Chicago: University of Chicago Press, 1970) 64.

19. Among those who acknowledged their indebtedness to Darby were Dwight L. Moody, evangelist from Chicago; James H. Brooks, pastor of Walnut Street Presbyterian Church in St. Louis; Adoniran J. Gordon, pastor of the Clarendon Baptist Church in Boston and founder of Gordon College and Seminary. Sandeen, *Roots of Fundamentalism,* 70–80, 134.

20. Seiss edited *The Prophetic Times* for twelve years, resigning in 1875. He was a powerful voice for the millenarian cause until his death in 1904. In addition, to his work on behalf of the millenarian cause, he was an active and loyal Lutheran churchman. He pastored St. John's Church in Philadelphia, the largest English-speaking Lutheran church in the United States from 1858–1874. He served as President of the Board of Directors of the Philadelphia Lutheran Theological Seminary from 1865–1904. He edited *The Lutheran* from 1867–1879 and authored over two dozen book. Dumas Malone, ed., *Dictionary of American Biography,* Vol. 16 (New York: Scribner's, 1943) 564.

21. Sandeen, *Roots of Fundamentalism,* 94–97.

speakers was all veteran leaders from the Niagara conference. Northfield also attracted people from a variety of theological traditions. By the mid-80's regional conferences were being held throughout the United States and Canada.[22]

The initial American converts to the *futurist premillennial* position came primarily from within the Reformed and Baptist traditions.[23] In many ways their theological instincts fit closely with Darby's who had grounded his dispensational theology in ultra-Calvinistic presuppositions, emphasizing the sovereignty of God, limited atonement and imputed righteousness. When translated to the American context, however, Darby's theology quickly adapted to the prevailing perfectionist surroundings. From the outset, Darby found his converts in the United States to be tainted by perfectionism. "Work, not truth," he once lamented, "is the American line of things." On his trip to the States in 1875, he complained, "a notion of perfectionism accompanied by a wild looking for the Spirit is one thing one has to contend with."[24]

The perfectionist impulse in the form of Keswick holiness teaching[25] penetrated Millenarianism by way of the Northfield Conference.[26] Initially, millenarian leaders were alarmed. They felt that by inviting Keswick leaders to Northfield, Moody was introduc-

22. Ibid.,. 132–45, 173–75; and Weber, *Living in the Shadow of the Second Coming*, 28.

23. Sandeen, *Roots of Fundamentalism*, 151–52.

24. John Nelson Darby, *Letters*, vol. 2, 2nd ed. (London: Morrish, 1914) 255, 396.

25. Keswick is named for a small village in the Lake District in Northern England, which was the site of an annual convention focusing on teaching the "Higher Christian Life" beginning in 1875. James Orr correctly traces the roots of Keswick to the 1857–1858 revival that arrived in England n 1859. However, it was the arrival of the husband and wife team, Robert and Hannah Pearsall Smith, in 1873 that the Holiness movement really blossomed in Britain. The Smiths, from Presbyterian and Quaker backgrounds respectively, had been swept into the Holiness movement during the 1857–1858 revival. They became friends with Phoebe and Walter Palmer and were fully indoctrinated into holiness teachings by the leaders of the National Camp Meeting Association. After active work in the movement for many years on the American scene, they went to England for rest and recuperation. Soon they introduced a circle of new friends to the Holiness teachings. Lord and Lady Mount Temple offered their Broadlands estate for a conference in July 1874. Approximately 100 guests attended. The meeting was so successful that a second larger meeting was planned to be held at Oxford the following month. Over 1,000 pastors and church leaders responded to the call including several from the Continent. At the conclusion of the Oxford meeting, plans were laid to hold a larger convention at Brighton in May 1875. Smith in the meantime traveled through the continent where he enjoyed huge success. He returned to Brighton a conquering hero to address crowds of over 8,000. Charles Finney and Asa Mahan from Oberlin, were also main speakers. Canon Hartford-Battersby offered Keswick as the site for the next convention, which met later that autumn. It has met at this site annually ever since. As this "Higher Christian Life" penetrated Reformed circles, the substantive language of "sinful nature" was replaced by relational categories. Keswick theology taught that by "yielding" to the Holy Spirit and "abiding" in Christ, a person could live an "overcoming" life freed from the power of sin. The best articulation of Keswick's history and theology remains: Steven Barabas, *So Great Salvation: the History and Message of the Keswick Convention* (London: Marshall, Morgan and Scott, 1952).

26. Moody had been conducting an evangelistic crusade in London when the Brighton Convention for the Promotion of Scriptural Holiness, the precursor of Keswick, convened in May, 1875. Moody sent a telegram to Robert Pearsall Smith on the opening day, stating he had offered a prayer at his meeting: "Let us lift up our hearts to seek earnestly a blessing on the great Convention that is now being held at Brighton, perhaps the most important meeting ever gathered together." *Record of the Convention for the Promotion of Scriptural Holiness Held at Brighton, May 29th to June 7th, 1875* (Brighton: W. J. Smith, 1875) 47. Moody followed the development of the Keswick doctrine with interest and saw it fitting to introduce it to his American following.

ing theological heresy into the conferences. Such leaders as F. B. Meyer and Andrew Murray, however, soon convinced them that this brand of holiness was compatible with the Reformed tradition. Most soon embraced the teaching as their own. By the mid-90's, almost all the prophecy conferences included a message on the Keswick doctrine of holiness.[27]

While the prophecy conferences were the vehicle for spreading the Keswick view of sanctification throughout America, Darby's dispensationalist views had more difficulty penetrating the Wesleyan Wing of the Holiness Movement. Of the 122 persons who signed the "call" for the First International Prophecy Conference held in New York City in 1878, for example, only six were of Methodist background. Of these, two were German Methodists and two others had already severed their Methodist connections. Since Methodism was the largest Protestant denomination at the time, claiming over three million adherents, they were grossly under-represented at this self-consciously ecumenical conference. Presbyterianism, on the other hand, with fewer than a million constituents had forty six representatives who signed this call.[28] Daniel Steele, Professor of Systematic Theology at Boston University and long-time leader in the National Holiness Camp meeting Association, took quiet delight in this discrepancy.

> This is not a matter which we are disposed to cry over. It indicates that Methodists are in too close a grapple with the present wicked world to sit down and waste time in speculation upon the future. It indicates that as a Church we are by no means so discouraged with the progress of the Gospel as to pronounce the dispensation of the Holy Spirit as inadequate to the conquest of the world for Christ ... there are theological reasons for cold shoulder of Methodism.[29]

Steele and others such as G. W. Wilson[30] consistently argued against the doctrine. The National Holiness Camp meeting Association banned the teaching from being preached in their meetings until well into the twentieth century.[31] Despite this resistance however, as Wesleyan groups left the Methodist church in the last half of the nineteenth century over the doctrine of entire sanctification most quickly converted to premillennialism.[32]

THIS TRANSFORMATION MODIFIED BY FLETCHER'S DOCTRINE OF DISPENSATIONS

However a closer examination reveals that the Holiness Movement did not adopt Darby's understanding without significant modifications that were more compatible

---

27. Sandeen, *Roots of Fundamentalism*, 176–77.

28. Ibid., 96.

29. Daniel Steele, *Antinomianism Revived: or, the Theology of the So Called Plymouth Brethren Examined and Refuted* (Boston: McDonald Gill, 1887) 193.

30. George W. Wilson, *The Sign of Thy Coming, or, Premillennialism, Unscriptural and Unreasonable* (Boston: Christian Witness, 1899).

31. Donald Dayton, *Theological Roots of Pentecostalism*, 133.

32. Ibid., 165–67.

with a Wesleyan world-view. In so doing, it is clear that they were following John Fletcher's lead.

Dayton's analysis, for example, provides interesting clues. He contends that this transformation of world-view was made possible when *Pentecostal* categories replaced *Perfectionist* categories in describing entire sanctification. In John Wesley's understanding, the Cross of Christ stood at the focal point of history. On the other hand, John Fletcher saw two foci: The Cross and Pentecost. Once Spirit-Baptism became the paradigm by which entire sanctification was understood, it tended to be identified with Pentecost rather than with Calvary. This shifted focus to Lucan texts where Pentecost is linked with eschatological themes and where a strong theology of the cross is lacking. Thus, when Luke-Acts became the hermeneutical key by which the rest of Scripture was interpreted, Pentecost became identified with the forward look to the Second Advent.[33]

Although Darby's theology had a strong Christology, it, too, tied Pneumatology to eschatology. It is important to note, for example, that his term for the *great parenthesis* or church age, was *the dispensation of the Holy Spirit*. Although he vigorously resisted all perfectionist tendencies, he stressed the work of the Spirit in the present age and linked it directly to the Second Advent.[34] It was on the axis of Pneumatology/Eschatology reflected in Fletcher and Darby that the Holiness Movement could develop a new synthesis.

The theology of Arthur Tappan Pierson, a Keswick proponent, illustrates this development. Pierson, a prominent Presbyterian pastor, is best known for his interest in foreign missions. His publication *The Crisis of Missions*, which appeared in 1886, became a classic and did much to arouse missionary activity and stimulate interest in local churches. In 1890, he became editor of *The Missionary Review of the World*, a post he retained until his death in 1911.[35]

In 1878, under the influence of George Muller, the Plymouth Brethren leader who pioneered the "faith work" concept in Bristol, England, Pierson was converted to premillennialism and adopted Darby's dispensationalism.[36] He embraced the Keswick teaching of sanctification in 1895 while attending a Northfield Prophecy Conference.[37] An analysis of four of his books, published in the last decade of the nineteenth century reveals *how* the emerging synthesis of premillennialism and perfectionism took place.

In *The Coming of the Lord* (1896), Pierson spells out his philosophy of history. History, he maintained, has two foci:

> We have been accustomed to think of a circle as the most perfect form, but, for the illustrations of many truths, it serves imperfectly, for a circle allows of but one center, where an ellipse allows of a twin center.... this serves to illustrate the rela-

---

33. Dayton, *Theological Roots of Pentecostalism*, 151.

34. Harold Rowden, *The Origins of the Brethren, 1825–1850* (London: Pickering & Ingles, 1967) 48–49.

35. Dumas Malone, ed. *Dictionary of American Biography*, vol. 14 (New York: Scribner's, 1943) 589–90.

36. Delavan L. Pierson, *Arthur T. Pierson: A Spiritual Warrior, Mighty in the Scriptures; A Leader in the Modern Missionary Crusade* (New York: Revell, 1912) 142–43.

37. J. Kennedy Maclean, ed., *Dr. Pierson and His Message: A Sketch of the Life and Work of a Great Preacher Together with a Varied Selection from His Unpublished Manuscripts* (London: Marshall, n.d.) 35.

tion which the whole scheme of redemption bears to the two great events—Christ's first and second coming.[38]

In this scheme, Pierson sees the history of redemption divided into three major periods: the period of the Jew; the period of the Church; and the period of the millennial kingdom. On the negative side, each age, including the millennial kingdom, ends in failure. Humankind rejects God's plan for redemption. On the positive side, each age ends with a remnant who responds to God's plan. In addition, each age foreshadows and anticipates the next, disclosing more of God's plan for the ages. "Never," Pierson declared, "is there one backward or halting step."[39]

The implications of this philosophy of history are explicated in three other works: *The Acts of the Holy Spirit* (1895),[40] *The New Acts of the Apostles* (1894),[41] and *Forward Movements of the Last Half Century* (1900).[42] In *The Acts of the Holy Spirit*, he states that Luke's mission is an unfinished task, and that the Acts of the Apostles is an unfinished book. The Acts sets forth, at the beginning of church history, what the Holy Spirit "continues to do and teach." The Holy Spirit falls on a few believers at Pentecost. They, in turn, endued with His power, set the world ablaze. One sees in the Acts, a foreshadowing of what life will be like in the millennial kingdom when the Holy Spirit is poured out upon all flesh. However, even in Luke's lifetime, there was evidence that Christians were falling away from this Pentecostal fullness. Repentance and new infusions of God's power were needed, both then and throughout the history of the Church.[43]

In *The New Acts of the Holy Spirit*, Pierson looked for and found evidence of effusions of the Spirit in the history of missions, especially during the nineteenth century.

> If within forty years there were four distinct and separate outpourings in the Apostolic age, who is competent to say that in the centuries succeeding there, have been no other Pentecostal effusions, … May there not be modern saints upon whom the Spirit has not yet fallen in the Pentecostal sense, but would come in power in answer to believing prayer?[44]

Based upon the positive response of the modern missionary movement, he urges his readers to respond in faith for ever greater outpourings of God's power and grace. These manifestations in recent history lead him to the conclusion that the end of the age is very near.[45]

38. Arthur T. Pierson, *The Coming of the Lord* (New York: Revell, 1896) 9–10.

39. Ibid., 13–14, 28.

40. Arthur T. Pierson, *The Acts of the Holy Spirit: Being an Examination of the Active Mission and Ministry of the Spirit of God, the Divine Paraclete, as Set Forth in the Acts of the Apostles* (London: Morgan & Scott, 1895).

41. Arthur T. Pierson, *The New Acts of the Apostles, or the Marvels of Modern Missions* (New York: Baker & Taylor, 1894).

42. Arthur T. Pierson, *Forward Movements of the Last Half Century* (New York: Funk & Wagnalls, 1900).

43. Arthur T. Pierson, *Acts of the Holy Spirit*, 8, 34, 88–89, 134.

44. Arthur T. Pierson, *New Acts of the Holy Spirit*, 16.

45. Ibid., 416.

In *Forward Movements* this thrust is intensified. Pierson surveyed some thirty movements that had emerged in the past fifty years. All held to a premillennial view and all equated entire sanctification with the Baptism of the Holy Spirit. He identified this understanding of holiness in these movements as signifying the Church was entering the last days.

> All real advance finds its starting-point, as also its goal, in more conformity to God. Character lies back of conduct; what we *are* ultimately shapes what we *do*. Hence the stress of the whole word of God lies upon the transformation of the man himself.... Like a bold headland at sea, with its lighthouse to guide the mariner, stand, in the survey of the past fifty years, the singularly varied attempts to raise the standard of practical godliness, sometimes called Holiness Movements.... In this union of all disciples in common prayer and self-surrender to God for holy living and serving, is to be found the most significant sign of the times.[46]

He ends this survey of *Forward Movements* with an analysis of the study of the last things. "There is," he concludes, "a general consensus of opinion that we are now on the threshold of that crisis, unparalleled in the history of the Church ... concerning which Christ would have us pray." Pierson believed this crisis would take place before 1920.[47]

In this brief survey it becomes clear how Darby's premillennialism was combined with Perfectionism to develop a new synthesis. By pinpointing two foci in his philosophy of history, Pierson was able to translate Darby's dispensational scheme into Pentecostal categories. Once that was accomplished, the pneumatological and eschatological themes found in the book of Acts could easily be combined. Darby's understanding of the end of the age could thus be integrated with the Keswick understanding of sanctification. Further more Darby's seven dispensations were collapsed into Fletcher's three.

The Wesleyan wing of the Holiness movement followed a similar pattern, which can be illustrated in the thought of George Watson. Watson became a Christian following a terrifying battle in the Civil War. Upon being discharged at the end of the war, he prepared for pastoral ministry. He was ordained a Methodist in 1867. In 1876 he sought and received the experience of Spirit-baptism. Four years later he left the pastorate to enter full time evangelistic work. For twelve years he held countless revival meetings mainly in southern United States. Often he shared the platform with such leaders in the National Holiness Association as John Inskip and William MacDonald. Despite his close association with prominent leaders within the Methodist Church, he felt the need to withdraw in 1892. Four years later he adopted the premillennial view.[48]

Watson was a prolific writer. A survey of his books reveals a clear development in his thought. In 1882 he published his first work, *A Holiness Manual*. Although he included a chapter entitled "The Baptism of the Holy Spirit," the work is controlled by texts and themes that dominated the discussion of Christian Perfection of the pre-Civil

---

46. Arthur T. Pierson, *Forward Movements of the Last Half Century*, x, 1.

47. Ibid., 409, 411.

48. Eva M. Watson, *Glimpses of the Life and Work of George Douglas Watson* (Cincinnati: God's Bible School and Revivalist, 1929) 30, 53, 67–68, 114; and George D. Watson, *Steps to the Throne and Holiness Manual* (Cincinnati: God's Revivalist, 1898) 5.

War period.⁴⁹ The following year he published *White Robes*. The same hermeneutic and understanding of sanctification prevailed, but a new theme emerged. The sanctified are set forth as the Bride of Christ who have put on their wedding garments. This theme is entirely spiritualized and there is no hint of an imminent return of Christ.⁵⁰

By 1889, the Bride of Christ dominates his thinking. In *The Seven Overcomeths*, he writes an exposition of the Revelation of St. John. He interprets John's imagery as allegory, calling the "Bride" to a life of entire sanctification. Spirit-baptism language is more pronounced throughout the book.⁵¹ In 1891, when *Love Abounding* appeared, the transformation to Pentecostal categories was complete. Reference to the work of the Holy Spirit appears on almost every page. Repeated allusions are made to such themes as "the tongue of fire," "the day of Pentecost," "Spirit-baptism," and "gifts of the spirit," throughout the text. He makes reference to John Fletcher's doctrine of dispensations for the first time. Once again, full discussion of The Sanctified as "The White Robed Company" is fully discussed. Although he still articulates this in a "spiritual" dimension, one senses that Watson's conversion to premillennial thought is imminent.⁵²

For the next seven years, Watson's prolific pen was silent as he struggled with the transformation taking place within his thinking. In the preface to his next work *Steps to the Throne*, he reveals the transformation that took place:

> For twenty five or thirty years of my life I accepted the ... notion, which is accepted by most Protestants, that the Second Coming of Jesus would be after the millennium, and at the time of the general judgment. Then for a few years, I was unsettled in my views on the subject for I saw so many portions of Scripture that could not have any reasonable interpretation in harmony with that old theory. Early in 1896 I began to pray very earnestly for the Holy Spirit to open the Scriptures to me clearly on that subject. In two or three weeks afterwards the Spirit began unfolding in my mind in a remarkable way ... the premillennial coming of Christ.⁵³

In the years that followed, Watson felt the need to rewrite much of what he had previously published to set forth his work in a manner consistent with his new understanding of God's operation within human history. His work, *The Bridehood Saints*, appearing in 1913 reflects his mature view. The book pulsates with the expectation of Christ's imminent return and gives a clarion call for the Church to put on her Bridal garments in preparation for the Marriage Supper of the Lamb. Only those who have been sealed with the Baptism of the Holy Spirit will be part of this Bridal party. Most significant is his discussion of his view of history. Like Pierson, he speaks of three dispensations, each initiated by a Pentecost of the Spirit.

> There are to be three great Pentecosts in the history of our world. The first was at the beginning of the Jewish age, the second was at the beginning of the Church

---

49. George D. Watson, *A Holiness Manual* (Chicago: Christian Witness, 1882).

50. George D. Watson, *White Robes: or, Garments of Salvation* (Cincinnati: Author, 1883).

51. George D. Watson, *The Seven Overcomeths* (Boston: MacDonald, Gill & Company, 1889).

52. George D. Watson, *Love Abounding, and Other Expositions on the Spiritual Life* (Boston: MacDonald, Gill and Co., 1891).

53. George D. Watson, *Steps to the Throne*, 5.

age, and the third will be at the beginning of the Kingdom age, or the Millennium. The Scriptures tell us of three dark days, days of supernatural darkness that are to mark the history of our world, and these dark days are days of judgment, and are connected with Pentecost, as they form the prelude to Pentecost.[54]

Watson saw the first day of judgment as the Passover at which time Egypt was judged. The second came at Calvary when the Jews were cut off from Salvation history. The third will come at the time the Bride is raptured when the whole world will go through the time of tribulation. The first Pentecost came at Sinai when the law of God was written on tablets of stone. The second came on Pentecost when God's law was established in the hearts of the believers. The final Pentecost will result in God's law penetrating all nature.[55]

Watson's mature view of salvation-history is identical to Pierson's. His focus is on three dispensations rather than two covenants. Each dispensation is inaugurated by a Pentecost. Each anticipates the next and is more expansive than the last. The routes traveled by Pierson and Watson typify the experience of Reformed and Wesleyan adherents who embraced the doctrine of holiness. Those in the Reformed tradition experienced a transformation of world-view in the 1870's and 1880's. The emergence of eschatological themes in their new theological understanding brought into focus a new understanding of Pneumatology which preconditioned them for a ready acceptance of the Keswick view of holiness.

The Wesleyans, on the other hand, first experienced a transformation of categories in their view of Christian Perfection, from a soteriological to pneumatological understanding. This process, which started in the 1860's, was complete by the 1880's. Once pneumatological themes became the exemplars for articulating entire sanctification, the Wesleyan Holiness adherents were preconditioned to accept the new understanding of eschatology. This was *how* it happened. The question yet to be addressed is: *Why*?

WHY THE TRANSFORMATION OF WORLDVIEW TOOK PLACE

George Watson noted that for several years before he adopted the premillennial position, he had been struggling with the realization that much of Scripture could not be adequately interpreted in light of his postmillennial world view. This confession corresponds to the development of thought evident in his writings. In *Love Abounding*, which he wrote in 1891, he expounded the Classical view of entire sanctification in terms of cleansing and power. He traced these negative/positive aspects through both the Old and New Testaments. It was then only a short step for him to translate this *negative/positive* dynamic which he applied to personal experience into historical categories: the three judgments and the three Pentecosts of salvation history. Having taken that step, Scriptures that he had interpreted only in spiritual categories, then took on literal meaning. The prophets, the Gospels, and the Revelation of John came to be understood in

---

54. George D. Watson, *The Bridehood Saints: Treating of the Saints Who Are the "Selection from the Selection" . . . Those Saints Who Are to Make Up the Bride of Christ* (Cincinnati, OH: Office of God's Revivalist, 1913) 82–83.

55. Ibid.

a new light. Dayton is correct when he suggests that the logic inherent in the shift of Christian Perfection to Spirit-Baptism thrust the Holiness adherents toward a premillennial position.[56]

However, this was true only for the Wesleyan wing of the Holiness Movement. The Reformed Wing, as has been shown, accepted the premillennial world-view before they embraced the Keswick doctrine of sanctification. The logic in this instance was working in reverse. Dayton recognized that this internal logic was not alone sufficient to effect the change. Events in the external world were having disconcerting effects upon the Movement's psyche.[57]

Underlying the "end-times" issue was a far more profound concern. The basic assumptions upon which the Evangelical/Perfectionist synthesis had rested in the first half of the nineteenth century came under relentless assault in the second half of the century. Naturalistic explanations of historical development which were embodied in Darwinism and higher criticism led to conclusions that threatened the very foundations of Christian belief.[58] The dominant Protestant response was to "sanctify" the resultant secularization with Christian symbolism.[59] Postmillennialism provided the framework on which this reformulation could be constructed. Progress in history was retained. But God's working in history was now perceived as coming primarily through *natural* rather than *supernatural* means. Scientific investigation and education were the principal tools to be employed in future development.[60]

An excellent example of this trend can be seen in the experience of William Newton Clarke, a prominent liberal Baptist theologian. Looking back on the course of his life, he recalled that in the 1870's the battle had raged between the postmillennial and premillennial positions. Clarke, a postmillennialist, none-the-less came to the conclusion through the results of higher criticism, that the Bible taught both views. Furthermore, he noted that both Jesus and His disciples fully expected Christ's Second Advent to occur in their generation. History proved them wrong. Sound scientific exposition of "the facts" led him to abandon both his belief in the supernatural origin of the formulation of the Scripture, and his conviction that Scripture was without error. Clarke came to believe that he must be free to judge which aspects of Scripture were true. History and scientific investigation, a sort of progressive revelation through natural means, provided the answer. On this basis, he declared that Christ's kingdom is not other-worldly or in the future, it is here and now. It is not external, but rather is an internal ethic based on the ideals of Jesus.

Those who would abandon the postmillennial view of history did so in part as an attempt to shore up the foundation for the traditional understanding of the Christian Faith and the accuracy of the Biblical account upon which that belief had been grounded. They

56. Donald Dayton, *Theological Roots of Pentecostalism,* 152, 165.

57. Ibid., 160–61.

58. George Marsden, *Fundamentalism and American Culture; The Shaping of Twentieth-century Evangelicalism 1870-1925* (New York: Oxford University Press) 48.

59. Martin Marty, *The Modern Schism: Three Paths to the Secular* (New York: Harper & Row, 1969) 95.

60. George Marsden, *Fundamentalism and American Culture*, 51.

were faced with the same issues as emerging liberalism. They used the same assumptions of empirical scientific investigation for their method of approach. They sought to show that the "facts" of Scripture correlated with the "facts" of history and of the natural order. Darby's doctrine of dispensations provided the framework upon which they could build their case.

This assertion can easily be demonstrated in the thought of A. T. Pierson. In his perception, most systematic theology started with a preconceived theory of reorganization to which the "facts" of Scripture were forced to fit. In contrast, he stated his view:

> One likes a *Biblical* theology; not a system that follows the Aristotelian method of reasoning, beginning with some hypothesis, and then warping the facts and the philosophy to fit the crook of a preconceived dogma or theory; but a theology framed on the Baconian system first gathering the teachings of the Word of God, and then seeking to induce some general law under which those facts can be classified and arranged.[61]

Pierson argued that theology is a science, and like all science, its facts are organized around a center. Making a comparison with the natural sciences, Pierson noted that Botany is arranged "about the cellular law of growth; Zoology, about a type of structure; Geology, about an order of strata." When he came to astronomy, he observed that the laws of planetary motion could not be discovered until Keller recognized that an ellipse, with two focal points was the organizing principle. It was the ellipse with the two foci—Christ's first and second advents—which became Pierson's organizing principle around which he would organize the facts of Scripture. These dual foci enabled him to "rightly divide the word of truth." The discrepancies which Clarke had found to be so distressing could be separated by chronology. References to a present internal kingdom, where the law of God is written on the heart, relate to the present age. References to a future external kingdom, where the law of God is written in the design of the universe, refers to the Millennium. Granted Pierson's dual foci, a perfect pattern, where all the facts fit, emerged. The system was consistent with the scientific method and preserved the supernatural origins of Scripture and the Christian Faith.[62] Darby's system of premillennial thought provided the theological framework.

This effort to stave off the critical assault on the supernatural understanding for the origins of Christian Faith and Scripture was but one reason for the paradigm shift. As Dayton correctly notes, the Oberlin postmillennial vision began to show cracks and flaws "almost as soon as it was articulated." Oberlin's commitment to abolitionism came into direct conflict with her position of non-violence. During the Civil War, she had to choose between commitment to anti-slavery and commitment to peace.[63]

---

61. Arthur T. Pierson, *Coming Lord*, 7. For an excellent analysis of the impact that the Baconian ideal of the inductive method has upon American religious thinking see Theodore Dwight Bozeman, *Protestants in an Age of Science: The Baconian Ideal and Antebellum American Religious Thought* (Chapel Hill: The University of North Carolina Press, 1977). Bozeman argues convincingly that Bacon's method was mediated to the American scene through the Scottish Realism of Thomas Reid, 4–8.

62. A. T. Pierson, *The Coming of the Lord*, 7–11.

63. Donald Dayton, *Theological Roots of Pentecostalism*, 160.

Following the war, the debate between the two positions centered on the question "Is the world getting perceptively better, or is it growing markedly worse?" In response to this question, postmillennialists noted advances in science and technology; the spread of western culture through the colonialization of the third world; and the renewed activity of mission work. Premillennialists readily conceded these issues. However, they seriously questioned whether the moral climate was improving. Conservatives, especially, had problems reconciling their postmillennial world-view with the pervasive onslaught of secularization. One can sense this dilemma in the thought of William Jones, a prominent holiness evangelist. Writing in 1885, he acknowledged that "the turbid stream of immigration which is emptying its ever-increasing flood upon the national shores"; "the millions of illiterate and imbruted ex-slaves"; "the fetid Indians that still linger in squalor and filth upon our Western borders"; and "the degenerate spiritual inclinations in the life of the churches" posed a real problem for his world-view. He was able to retain his postmillennial vision because of his faith in the Holiness Movement which God had raised up for these last days.

> God is tunneling the world and packing it with His truth. When the Church gets ready, when the world is filled with pure Christian thought, when the ministry shall believe in the Holy Ghost, and accept His fiery baptism . . . the Father will let slip one spark of Pentecostal fire . . . and the whole earth will become the Kingdom of God.[64]

As the "evil" onslaught continued to persist and with the Holiness Movement splitting into three factions, the vision could not be sustained. A. T. Pierson spoke for all who abandoned the postmillennial world-view in light of these historical realities of the time.

> What is the real character of our civilization? We may as well face the facts. It is gigantic in invention, discovery and enterprise, achievement, but its gigantically worldly, sometimes and somewhere monstrous, God-denying and God-defying . . . Philosophy now blooms into a refined and poetic pantheism or a gross, blank materialism, or a subtle rationalism or an absurd agnosticism. Science constructs its systems of evolution and leaves out a personal God . . . We have the ripest form of worldly civilization, but the RIPENESS BORDERS ON ROTTENNESS. . . . Our golden age is far from unfolding even the promise of a millennium.[65]

CONCLUSION

By the turn of the twentieth century the conversion to premillennialism within the Holiness Movement was virtually complete.[66] When Pentecostalism emerged from the

---

64. William Jones, *From Elim to Carmel* (Boston: Christian Witness, 1885) 78–81.

65. Arthur T. Pierson, "World-Wide Evangelism," *Prophetic Studies of the International Prophecy Conference, Chicago, 1886* (Chicago: Revell, 1886) 31.

66. The major exception to the prevailing trend was the emerging Church of God (Anderson). The founder, Daniel S. Warner, held an amillennial view of eschatology to which this church still subscribes. In many respects, this understanding is similar to the postmillennial view. It teaches that most of the Old Testament prophecy has been fulfilled and that the Hebrew Bible, as well as the Gospels, applies to the

Holiness Movement, it continued to hold Fletcher's three dispensations view.[67] Aimee Semple McPherson is typical:

> Just as there are three in the Godhead: Father, Son and Holy Ghost, so there have been three separate and distinct dispensations or periods of time. First came the dispensation of the Father as recorded in God's Word throughout the Old Testament from Genesis to Malachi ... Secondly, came the dispensation of the Son as recorded in the four Gospels ... Thirdly, came the dispensation of the Holy Spirit which opened on the day of Pentecost ... until Jesus comes for His waiting bride.[68]

However, following World War I, Fletcher's understanding of dispensation gave way to Darby's in both the Holiness and Pentecostal Movements. The popular use of the Scofield Bible by both traditions; and the fall out of the Modernist-Fundamentalist controversy that reached its height in the Scopes trial moved both the Holiness and Pentecostal groups in the direction embracing Darby's understanding more fully. In 1946 Frank M. Boyd, an Assemblies of God professor sought to combine Fletcher's and Darby's views in a book entitled *Ages and Dispensations*, which the threefold understanding of Fletcher was now entitled "ages."[69]

Church. Like postmillennialism, it holds that the kingdom of God will triumph through the process of history. However, it maintains that the 1,000 year period mentioned in Revelation is a symbolic representation of the church age. For analysis of this church's position see C. E. Brown, *The Hope of His Coming* (Anderson, IN: Gospel Trumpet, 1927).

67. See David. W. Faupel, "The Function of Models in the Interpretation of Pentecostal Thought," *Pneuma* 2 (1980) 55.

68. Aimee Semple McPherson, *Lost and Restored, or the Dispensation of the Holy Spirit from the Ascension of the Lord Jesus to His Coming Descension* (Montwait, MA: The Author, 1921) 8–9. Although not realizing the dependence on Fletcher, Larry McQueen recognized that early Pentecostal eschatology broke significantly from Darby's dispensationalism. In examining all of the issues of the *Apostolic Faith* magazine published at Azusa Street in Los Angles, he found no dependence on Darby's form of dispensationalism. Larry McQueen, "Early Pentecostal Eschatology," Unpublished paper presented at the 38th Annual Meeting of the Society for Pentecostal Studies, Eugene, Oregon (March 26–28, 2009).

69. Frank M. Boyd *Ages and Dispensations* (Springfield, MO: Gospel Publishing, 1946).

5

A Baptism of Divine Love
The Pentecostal Experience of Spirit Baptism[1]

KIMBERLY ERVIN ALEXANDER

Author's Note: I first came in contact with the work of Larry Wood as a young scholar, working on a PhD thesis and teaching undergraduate classes at two institutions, one from a Pentecostal tradition, the other a Methodist college. In addition to assigning as required reading his very fine work on Wesleyan spirituality, it was at this time that I first heard Larry enthusiastically present his research on John Fletcher. I was overwhelmed by both the strength of his research but also by his passion for the work as he re-evaluated the contributions of both Fletcher and Wesley with regard to their interpretation of Pentecost. Later, I was equally moved as he preached a sermon at a morning service at the Pentecostal church where my husband served as pastor. Larry provided for me a model for my own work: a theologian who is both a thorough and passionate scholar. This is, I believe, a truly Wesleyan and Pentecostal model. I am grateful for his friendship and encouragement, but also for his model.

THERE HAS BEEN LITTLE argument from the onset of the Pentecostal revival that the experience of Spirit baptism, with its accompanying manifestation of speaking in tongues, has been the most notable of the distinguishing characteristics of the movement. This is not to suggest that Spirit baptism and *glossolalia* are the *only* distinguishing features;[2] neither is it meant to suggest that this experience can or should be isolated

---

1. An earlier version of this paper appears in Stephen J. Land, Rickie D. Moore & John Christopher Thomas, eds., *Passover, Pentecost, and Parousia: Studies in Celebration of the Life and Ministry of R. Hollis Gause*. JPTS 36 (Dorset, England: Deo, 2010) under the title: "Boundless Love Divine: A Re-Evaluation of Early Understandings of the Experience of Spirit Baptism."

2. Don Dayton argues, "Perhaps even more characteristic of Pentecostalism than the doctrine of the baptism of the Spirit is its celebration of miracles of divine healing as part of God's salvation and as evidence of divine power in the church" (Donald Dayton, *Theological Roots of Pentecostalism* [Peabody, MA: Hendrickson, 1987] 115). It might also be argued that Pentecostal churches were known as much for their adherence to the doctrines of sanctification and holiness as a standard of living as they were for Pentecostal manifestations. In fact, holiness and Pentecostal experience were synonymous in the view of both insiders

from other experiences and doctrines central to the spirituality of the movement. The Pentecostal doctrine of Spirit baptism is not an "add-on" to Evangelical theology, nor is the experience simply an ecstatic episode. As Steven J. Land writes, "Thus, the point of Pentecostal spirituality was not to have an experience or several experiences, though they spoke of discrete experiences. The point was to experience life as part of a biblical drama of participation in God's history."[3] What it does suggest is that a new understanding of baptism in the Spirit, and the accompanying manifestation, did distinguish these believers from their contemporaries and from the churches from which they came. Although this distinction was viewed by many as divisive and sectarian, for those who had experienced Spirit baptism it served as a marker signaling that they were now a part of a Last-Days move of God. Land writes, "It was this fifth motif ['The baptism in the Holy Spirit evidenced by speaking in tongues'] that, more than anything else, served as a "sign" that the "evening light" was shining before the darkness when no one could work."[4]

Classical Pentecostals, in differentiating themselves early on from Holiness groups and later from Charismatic groups, have maintained that Spirit baptism is subsequent to initial salvation and that the purpose is power for witness, evangelism and fulfilling the Great Commission. Drawing from Acts 1:8, Pentecostal preachers, leaders and theologians have often limited the function to be a vocational one *only*.[5] The result of this vocational view is that the experience has been regarded as utilitarian. In its simplest translation, "power for witness" has been translated into boldness, contrasted with intimidation or introversion.

However, though extroversion may be a perceived result of Spirit baptism, the verb in Acts 1:8 is a verb of being, not doing. As Land says, "The point is to walk in and live out of the fullness of God, to exist in radical openness, meek yieldedness and passionate zeal for the things of God." He continues, "Being filled with the Spirit is being yielded to, directed and empowered by God to give a witness more consistent with his Spirit to Jesus Christ."[6] Spirit-filled believers *bear* witness to Jesus. The witness that was received on the Day of Pentecost was a witness that the Resurrected Jesus had ascended and had poured out the Spirit.

---

and outsiders. See R. Hollis Gause, "The Historical Development of the Doctrine of Holiness in the Church of God" (unpublished paper) and "A Pentecostal Theology: Perils and Prospects" (unpublished paper). See also R. Hollis Gause, "Issues in Pentecostalism" in *Perspectives on the New Pentecostalism*, ed. Russell Spittler (Grand Rapids: Baker, 1976) 106–16.

3. Steven J. Land, *Pentecostal Spirituality: A Passion for the Kingdom* (Sheffield, UK:Sheffield Academic Press, 1993) 74–75. Land argues for an integrated core (the fivefold gospel), which correlates with religious affections (gratitude, compassion and courage). He says, "My thesis is that the righteousness, holiness and power of God are correlated with distinctive apocalyptic affections which are the integrating core of Pentecostal spirituality. This spirituality is Christocentric precisely because it is pneumatic; its "fivefold gospel" is focused on Christ because of its starting point in the Holy Spirit" (23).

4. Land, *Pentecostal Spirituality*, 18.

5. See Peter Hocken, "The Meaning and Purpose of "Baptism in the Spirit," *Pneuma* 7:2 (1985) 125–33. Hocken argues that the *meaning* of Spirit Baptism can be spoken of differently than one speaks of the *purpose* of the experience. Purpose may be linked to service, but meaning lies in the transformational nature of the experience and in the believer's new relationship to the persons of the Trinity.

6. Land, *Pentecostal Spirituality*, 170.

PART ONE: Rethinking the History

This paper will attempt to re-assess the early understanding of Spirit baptism through the voices of those testifying to the experience, particularly those in the Wesleyan-Pentecostal tradition.[7] It is believed that hearing these voices will shed light on how early Pentecostals viewed their transformation. The examination will pay close attention to manifestations (visions, sensations, prophetic messages) that accompanied the experience as well as any interpretation offered by the witness(es).

A THIRD EXPERIENCE

The Pentecostal movement first identified itself as the "Apostolic Faith" movement, a term inherited from Charles Fox Parham.[8] The revival in North America, by most accounts, actually began as a "self-aware" movement in Los Angeles in 1906. That is, those gathered at the home of Richard and Ruth Asberry on Bonnie Brae Street, who later moved to Azusa Street and opened a mission to house the growing revival, were actively seeking the experience of Spirit baptism with the "Bible evidence" of speaking in tongues.[9]

Though most early Pentecostals considered themselves to be non-creedal, many did adopt "Statements of Faith," identifying the commonly held doctrinal tenets of the Pentecostal Movement, or their branch of it. The statement, found in the inaugural issue of *The Apostolic Faith*, the monthly publication of the Apostolic Faith Mission at 312 Azusa Street, is typical. This statement includes a tenet on Spirit baptism, identifying "speaking in new tongues" as evidentiary. It reads,

---

7. The Classical Pentecostal tradition can be divided into two streams: the Wesleyan-Pentecostal and the Finished Work streams. Donald Dayton, William Faupel, and others have shown that the movement clearly had Wesleyan roots but a fissure erupted in 1910–1911 when William H. Durham formalized what was called Finished Work Pentecostalism, a re-organization of Pentecostal soteriology that disclaimed sanctification as a second definite work of grace, seeing justification and sanctification as occurring at the moment of conversion. He based his theology on what he termed the Finished Work of Christ on the cross. This move, in effect, collapsed the three stages into two by combining initial conversion and sanctification into one work. See Dayton and Faupel, *The Everlasting Gospel: The Significance of Eschatology in the Development of Pentecostal Thought*, JPTS 10 (Sheffield: Sheffield Academic, 1996) and Kimberly Ervin Alexander, *Pentecostal Healing: Models of Theology and Practice*, JPTS 29 (Dorset, England: Deo, 2003) for elaboration on this fissure and its theological implications.

8. This paper will not attempt to rehearse the story of the origins of the movement. For the most recent treatment of the historical account, see Cecil M. Robeck Jr., *The Azusa Street Mission and Revival: The Birth of the Global Pentecostal Movement* (Nashville: Nelson, 2006). See also Vinson Synan, *The Holiness-Pentecostal Tradition: Charismatic Movements in the Twentieth Century* (Grand Rapids: Eerdmans, 1997) for a history of the movement as it spread beyond Los Angeles. For a more recent study of the growth of the movement beyond Azusa Street see Allan Anderson, *Spreading Fires: The Missionary Nature of Early Pentcostalism* (Maryknoll, NY: Orbis, 2007).

9. Clearly, those leading and attending this revival were not the first to have this experience. There had been sporadic outpourings as well as expectations of this type of outpouring for decades in other parts of the world, but those other revivals were not catalytic in the way that Azusa was, nor did they necessarily see the experience as normative. Agnes Ozman had sought for and experienced Spirit baptism with the outward manifestation of tongues in Kansas City on January 1, 1901. Accounts of other revivals, including the Shearer Schoolhouse revival in North Carolina (1896), where around 100 people reportedly spoke in tongues, detail this same type of outpouring. However, there is little evidence that most of these understood tongues as evidentiary in the way that the adherents at Azusa understood it.

> The Baptism with the Holy Ghost is a gift of power upon the sanctified life; so when we get it we have the same evidence as the Disciples received on the Day of Pentecost (Acts 2:3, 4), in speaking in new tongues. [*sic*] See also Acts 10:45, 46; Acts 19:6; 1 Cor. 14:21. "For I will work a work in your days which ye will not believe though it be told you" (Hab. 1:5).[10]

This statement is telling theologically. First, it states that the experience is a baptism "with the Holy Ghost." This hallmark experience of the revival has been correlated with the language used by John the Baptist (Matt 3:11; Mark 1:8; Luke 3:16; John 1:33), by Jesus (Acts 1:5) and by Peter (Acts 11:16). Secondly, the experience is understood to be a gift consisting of power. There is here neither an explanation of the kind of power received nor one of its purpose. Thirdly, the gift is subsequent to the experience of sanctification. Fourthly, it is evidenced by "speaking in new tongues" in the same way that it was evidenced in the experience of the disciples on the Day of Pentecost. Scriptures referenced in addition to Acts 2:3–4 reveal that the Azusa leaders understood the accounts in Acts 10 (Cornelius' family) and Acts 19 (Ephesian believers) to be recurring incidents of the experience of the disciples in Acts 2. Finally, the citation of the Habakkuk text reveals that they understood this to be a "new work" of God.

Although the statement is by itself theologically significant, its real significance is found contextually. An examination of the full doctrinal statement is telling of the movement's polemic. The Holiness churches, from which many of these leaders had come, had identified sanctification with Baptism in the Holy Spirit.[11] It was incumbent upon the leadership of the movement that they both differentiate the two experiences and show the biblical support for the validity of Spirit baptism and speaking in tongues.

The initial sentence states, "The Apostolic Faith Movement stands for the restoration of the faith once delivered unto the saints—the old time religion, camp meetings, revivals, missions, street and prison work and Christian Unity everywhere."[12] The claim of this statement is that everything that follows (ten tenets) is consistent with the "faith once delivered unto the saints." The first eight tenets deal with aspects of initial conversion: repentance, godly sorrow, confession, "forsaking sinful ways," restitution and faith. The next statement identifies justification as the "first work." The "second work" is sanctification. The statement reads, "Sanctification is the second work of grace and the last work of grace."[13] Following this claim is a lengthy explanation and definition of sanctification followed by scriptural warrant. The point of the explanation is that sanctification "makes us holy" and is an act of cleansing. The polemic increases with the following:

> The Disciples were sanctified before the Day of Pentecost. By a careful study of Scripture you will find it is so. "Ye are clean through the word which I have spoken unto you" (John 15:3; 13:10); and Jesus had breathed on them the Holy Ghost (John

---

10. *The Apostolic Faith*, vol. 1 (September 1906) 2.
11. See Robeck, *Azusa Street Mission and Revival*, 51–58 for a discussion of this schism.
12. *The Apostolic Faith*, vol. 1 (September 1906) 2.
13. Ibid., 2.

20:21, 22). You know, that they could not receive the Spirit if they were not clean. Jesus cleansed and got all doubt out of His Church before he went back to glory.[14]

What follows is the statement regarding Spirit baptism discussed above. It seems that the extreme position, which implies that Spirit baptism is not a work of grace, is a reaction to those in the Holiness churches and tradition who had previously identified sanctification as Spirit baptism. Other early statements and explanations are similar, carefully making distinctions between this new experience and previous ones. However, an examination of the testimonies of those experiencing Spirit baptism in the context of the Pentecostal revival reveals a more carefully nuanced and less reactionary explanation of the "third blessing."

EXPERIENCES IN THE SPIRIT

Walter Hollenweger, in identifying the African roots of Pentecostalism, delineated five characteristics common to both black spirituality and Pentecostal spirituality:

> 1) "orality of liturgy"; 2) "narrativity of theology and witness"; 3) "maximum participation at the levels of reflection, prayer and decision-making and therefore a form of community that is reconciliatory"; 4) "inclusions of dreams and visions into personal and public forms of worship"; 5) "an understanding of the body/mind relationship that is informed by experiences of correspondence between body and mind,"[15] Land has lifted Hollenweger's work to the forefront and views Pentecostal spirituality as a "confluence" of this black spirituality and Wesleyan spirituality—a confluence that is essentially "transformationalist."[16]

There is no better way to view this spirituality than by reading the testimonies recorded in the periodicals and journals produced by the revival. Because of the movement's evangelistic orientation there were many of these publications, which now allow readers a century later to view the revival as it occurred. These periodicals were published with frequency and with a sense of urgency that is reflected in the formatting. *The Apostolic Faith*, published at the Apostolic Faith Mission at 312 Azusa Street, is replete with testimonies of those receiving "their Pentecost," either at the Mission or in some other Pentecostal outpost around the world. Other periodicals, such as *The Bridegroom's Messenger, The Pentecostal Testimony*, and *The Church of God Evangel*, give us a similar view.

Another valuable source for this "inside look" may be found in personal journals and diaries kept by itinerant ministers within the movement. In these journals, one may read the ministers' own testimonies as well as reports of the revival or camp meeting services in which he/she ministered. These primary witnesses, along with the primary witness found in the periodicals, will be utilized as a way of hearing these voices testify of their experiences of being baptized in the Spirit.

---

14. Ibid.
15. Land, *Pentecostal Spirituality*, 52.
16. Ibid., 51.

The inaugural issue of *The Apostolic Faith* (September 1906) announced that "Pentecost Has Come." In order to demonstrate that this was a restoration of what was "recorded in the book of Acts," the editors printed numerous testimonies, along with their own observations of what had been happening since the movement's beginning in April of the same year. One of the most remarkable of those testimonies, and especially relevant to this study, is found on page one. It reads,

> A Nazarene brother who received the baptism with the Holy Ghost in his own home in family worship, in trying to tell about it said, "It was a baptism of love. Such abounding love! Such compassion seemed to almost kill me with its sweetness! People do not know what they are doing when they stand against it. The devil never gave me a sweet thing, he was always trying to get me to censuring people. This baptism fills us with divine love."[17]

Given the context, and especially the opposition by Nazarene leaders and preachers, this testimony is quite telling. Notice the descriptions of his change in disposition: "abounding love," "compassion," "sweetness," "divine love." In opposition to what others were doing (standing "against it," "censuring people") this man describes being baptized and filled with the love of God.

Similarly, a report in the same issue describes a preacher who was baptized in the Holy Spirit and began speaking "Zulu and many other tongues more fluently than English and interprets as he speaks." The account goes on to say that he was used by the Lord to "stir a whole city." The writer concludes, "He is filled with divine love. His family were first afraid to see him speaking in tongues, thinking he had lost his mind, but when his wife and children felt the sympathy and divine love which the Holy Ghost puts in people's hearts, they said, 'Papa was never as sane in his life.'"[18] Again, there is a juxtaposition of the "before and after" dispositions and affections in the one experiencing Spirit baptism.

In another observation of Azusa, a participant reports that, while some are "opposing and arguing," others are "falling down under the power of God" at the altar, "feasting on the good things of God."[19] This description, too, denotes a disposition that is to be contrasted with those who argue and oppose. Those who are at the altar, under the power of God, are "feasting." Again, there is an intimacy or union with God experienced in this nourishment.

J. H. King, a leader in the Holiness movement, was, at first, one of those who opposed and fought the revival. In 1885 he had experienced sanctification and describes that transformation as a "marvelous change." He explains, "I found my ear was filled with light, love, and glory. . . . I seemingly was taken out of myself and thought I was within a few feet of the gates of heaven." To King, however, the Pentecostal message, which had been quickly disseminated to the Southeast by G. B. Cashwell, appeared fanatical.[20] After

---

17. *The Apostolic Faith*, vol. 1 (September 1906) 1.

18. Ibid.

19. Ibid.

20. It should be noted that King's caution was undoubtedly conditioned by his previous experiences in the Fire Baptized Holiness Association, under the leadership of B. H. Irwin. Irwin's movement was marked

a careful study of the Acts accounts, King became convinced that those baptized in the Holy Spirit would speak in tongues. He testifies of his own experience of February 15, 1907:

> As I was seeking, the Scripture recorded in John 7:37–39 seemed to be applied to my heart, and I was persuaded to rest unreservedly upon this promise. There was a joy in my heart, and I began uttering praise with my lips. There came into my heart something new, though the manifestation was not great. There was a moving of my tongue, though I cannot say that I was speaking a definite language. I only know that there was some moving of my tongue as I had never experienced before. I had some assurance that the Comforter had come into my heart. There was a peace that permeated my spirit, and I was resting in the Lord in a very blessed manner. Soon the Word began to be opened to me in a new way, and it seemed as if I had a different Bible . . . during all the remaining months of that year I preached with such inspiration and power as I had never before experienced.[21]

King's testimony also reveals a transformation, and it is noteworthy that he does not mention a resulting inclination toward foreign missions, though the experience has clearly affected his vocation. His transformation resulted in a new way of seeing Scripture and more Spirit-anointed preaching. It is especially noteworthy that King uses the Wesleyan language of "assurance" with regard to *glossolalia*. This assurance resulted in peace and "resting in the Lord."

The testimony of another prominent leader, Charles Harrison Mason, of the Church of God in Christ, is published in *The Apostolic Faith*.[22] Mason confesses that he had struggled over the new doctrine and over the interpretation of Mark 16:17–18. He reveals that he had been given a vision before coming to Los Angeles. Then, in Los Angeles, he was given a "parable." He explains,

> I went to the altar and the Lord put a parable before me. If you were going to marry, would you be sad? I said, no, when I was going to be married, I was glad. He then showed me this was wedlock to Christ. If there was anything imperfect about me, He would make it right and marry me anyway. Then my faith was settled and laid firmly hold on the promise.[23]

---

by openness to further works or baptisms in the Spirit beyond sanctification and what often resulted in excess. After Irwin's confession of immorality, King succeeded him as General Overseer. See Synan, *Holiness-Pentecostal Tradition*, 59. In the latter years of the 1940s King published a history of the Pentecostal Holiness Church that included a history of the Fire Baptized Holiness Association. He reflects upon the excesses of that movement: "Where the Holy Ghost is mightily working and multitudes are under His control, or are the subjects of His powerful operations, in convicting, converting, saving, sanctifying and filling souls, of all classes, ages and temperaments, there will be the working of 'wicked spirits in high places' producing strange, wild, abnormal manifestations in order to counteract by counterfeiting the work of the Holy Ghost. The Holy Ghost is never the author of insane religious manifestations, but it is the product of satanic demonry, working through man's insane religious nature to offset the influence and effect of the Spirit's glorious work" (Joseph Hillery King, "History of the Pentecostal Holiness Church," unpublished, 14–15).

21. J. H. King quoted in B. E. Underwood, *Christ—God's Love Gift: Selected Writings of Joseph Hillery King*, vol. 1 (Franklin Springs, GA: Advocate, 1969) 13.

22. *The Apostolic Faith*, vol. 1.6 (February–March 1907), 7.

23. Ibid.

An unsigned exhortation in an earlier edition of *The Apostolic Faith* emphasizes this union or marriage resulting between Jesus and the one baptized in the Spirit. Commenting on Matt 11:29, the author writes, "The Lord showed me that this yoke was the covenant of the New Testament in His blood, and we put this yoke on when we are baptized with the Holy Ghost. This covenant is a marriage covenant. We are married, not for one day or year or life, but eternally married." The writer concludes the analogy with praise, "Hallelujah! Jesus and I are united. He baptized me with love."[24] This testimony and interpretation of the experience describe its result as "covenant" and "union," both of which are biblical metaphors of salvation (see Rom 6:5; Phil 2:1).[25]

Four testimonies describing reception of the Spirit are remarkably similar. These detailed accounts provide valuable insight into how the recipients interpreted the work of the Spirit at the time of the experience. It has already been noted that C. H. Mason had received a visionary confirmation before going to Azusa. He describes what occurred at Azusa as he returned to his seat and began to focus on Jesus. At this point,

> the Holy Ghost took charge of me. I surrendered perfectly to Him and consented to Him. Then I began singing a song in unknown tongues, and it was the sweetest thing to have Him sing that song through me. He had complete charge of me. I let Him have my mouth and everything. After that it seemed I was standing at the cross and heard Him as He groaned, the dying groans of Jesus, and I groaned. It was not my voice but the voice of my Beloved that I heard in me. When He got through with that, He started the singing again in unknown tongues. When the singing stopped, I felt that complete death. It was my life going out, but it was a complete death to me. When He had finished this, I let Him hold my hands up, and they rested just as easily up as down. Then He turned on the joy of it. He began to lift me up. I was passive in His hands. I was not going to do a thing. I could hear the people but did not let anything bother me. It came to me, "I charge thee, O daughters of Jerusalem, that ye stir not up nor awake my Beloved until He please." S. S. 8. 4. He lifted me to my feet and then the light of heaven fell upon me and burst into me filling me. Then God took charge of my tongue and I went to preaching in tongues. I could not change my tongue. The glory of God filled the temple. The gestures of my hands and movements of my body were His. O it was marvelous and I thank God for giving it to me in His way. Such an indescribable peace and quietness went all through my flesh and into my very brain and has been there ever since.[26]

In September 1908 *The Pentecost* published an extended testimony of Ruth Angstead, composed on November 24, 1907. She begins, "I have a precious story to tell, for I too plunged into that 'fountain opened in the house of David for all sin and uncleanness' and found all the horrible bondage of my spirit, soul and body go like darkness before day." She continues, "Our union, so sweetly begun, grew to such preciousness and glory as the months and years sped by, with panting hunger that He should manifest His 'never failing' love and almighty power in the vessel He had washed in His own life blood."[27]

---

24. *The Apostolic Faith*, vol. 1.2 (October 1906) 3.
25. Seymour develops this marriage analogy in *The Apostolic Faith*, vol. 2.13 (May 1908) 4.
26. *The Apostolic Faith*, vol. 1.6 (February–March 1907) 7.
27. *The Pentecost*, vol. 1.2 (September 1908) 1.

Angstead describes a visionary experience in which she not only saw but also felt the pains of the crucifixion and the agony of Gethsemane, much as Mason has described. She narrates the experience,

> I tasted of the cup of His suffering. It seemed my very heart would break and the blood oozed from the pores of my body. I then had a glimpse of the Celestial City of Glory. A stream pure as crystal flowed from under the throne, winding about, with trees of life on either side. Oh such wonderful flowers and mansions. No tongue or pen could describe these or the wonderful glory from His radiant countenance which lighted the whole, no, not through the ceaseless ages of eternity. [sic] Then I saw the ascension and His glorious return in the clouds with ten thousand of His angels. Beloved of earth He cometh soon.[28]

Her vision transported her to hell and to the judgment of nations. She states, "A remnant I could not see were ever reached by His love." After telling of a struggle with Satan, whom she says tried to stop her communion with God, Angstead describes hearing God speak, "I was determined God should accomplish his pleasure in this and He said 'Do not leave the room till I sing through you in tongues.'"[29] She then describes the result of the visionary experience:

> Then I sank out of self in such glorious worship before the Father, far too deep for any utterance. There seemed to be many waters surging through my being, then the Holy Spirit sang through me four songs, such beautiful words and music. I never could sing much. I was a spell-bound listener to the songs just bursting forth from the glorified Jesus through His Holy Spirit. The first three, as I sang them each time—often in English—were new to me, but the fourth was that glorious old song "All glory and praise to the Lamb that was slain:" [sic] Then I spoke in tongues, each time interpreting, magnifying Father, Son and the precious blood.[30]

This testimony of a mystical vision and journey in the Spirit reveals the depth of the experience for Ruth Angstead. This account is particularly illustrative of R. Hollis Gause's explication of Pentecostal theology as a "Theology of Worship," in which he delineates three elements: *rapture*, *rapport* and *proleptic*.[31] Angstead is caught up in ecstatic experience or *rapture* in which Gause contends "the emotions are transported to the level of worshipping in the Holy Spirit, both in song and prayer."[32] *Rapport* can be noted in her intimate communion with God, going so far as to identify with and share in the sufferings of Jesus. The third element, *proleptic*, or "anticipation of the worship to be enjoyed when believers will fall before the thrones of the Father and of the Lamb in the consummation of the kingdom of God" is experienced as she participates in heavenly worship through song.[33]

28. Ibid.
29. Ibid.
30. Ibid., 1–2.
31. R. Hollis Gause, "Distinctives of a Pentecostal Theology," unpublished paper.
32. Ibid., 36.
33. Ibid., 21.

Church of God General Overseer Tomlinson testifies of his own experience of Spirit baptism, which occurred January 12, 1908. He describes his experience in *The Last Great Conflict*:

> He [G. B. Cashwell] preached on Saturday night, and on Sunday morning, January 12, while he was preaching, a peculiar sensation took hold of me, and almost unconsciously I slipped off my chair in a heap on the rostrum at Brother Cashwell's feet. I did not know what such an experience meant. My mind was clear, but a peculiar power so enveloped and thrilled my whole being that I concluded to yield myself up to God and await the results. I was soon lost to my surroundings as I lay there on the floor, occupied only with God and eternal things. Soon one of my feet began to shake and clatter against the wall. I could not hold it still. When it got quiet the other one acted the same way. Then my arms and head were operated. My jaws seemed to be set, my lips were moved and twisted about as if a physician was making a special examination. My tongue and eyes were operated on in like manner. Several examinations seemed to be taken, and every limb and my whole body examined.
>
> My body was rolled and tossed about beyond my control, and finally while lying on my back, my feet were raised up several times, and my tongue would stick out of my mouth in spite of my efforts to keep it inside my mouth.
>
> At one time, while lying flat on my back, I seemed to see a great sheet let down, and as it came to me I felt it as it enveloped me in its folds, and I really felt myself literally lifted up and off the floor several inches, and carried in that sheet several feet in the direction my feet pointed, and then let down on the floor again. As I lay there great joy flooded on my soul. The happiest moments I had ever known up to that time. I never knew what real joy was before. My hands clasped together with no effort on my part. Oh, such floods and billows of glory ran through my whole being for several minutes! There were times that I suffered the most excruciating pain and agony, but my spirit always said "yes" to God.[34]

Curiously, Tomlinson's extensive description at first centers on the physical aspects of this experience and he describes the Spirit's work as that of a doctor performing an examination.[35] From this physical description, Tomlinson moves to describe the visionary aspects of his Spirit-baptism experience. Tomlinson journeys in the Spirit:

> In vision I was carried to Central America, and was shown the awful condition of the people there. A paroxysm of suffering came over me as I seemed to be in soul travail for their salvation. Then I spoke in tongues as the Spirit gave utterance, and in the vision I seemed to be speaking the very same language of the Indian tribes with whom I was surrounded.[36]

Tomlinson continues to describe his "travels" to South America and Africa. When seeing Jerusalem he writes that while he was there, "... I endured the most intense suffering, as

---

34. Tomlinson, *Last Great Conflict*, 234.

35. This is especially curious for someone who is adamantly opposed to the use of doctors and medicine! It is consistent, however, with his understanding of Jesus as the Great Physician. Apparently, the other *Paraclete*, the Holy Spirit, is a physician as well. See Alexander for a discussion of Tomlinson's views on the use of medicine and physicians (108–11).

36. Tomlinson, *Last Great Conflict*, 234.

if I might have been suffering similar to that of my Savior on Mount Calvary. I never can describe the awful agony that I felt in my body."[37] From Jerusalem he was transported to Northern Russia, France, Japan and "North" among the Eskimos. In each place he speaks the language of the people—an experience that is preceded by a "paroxysm of suffering."

In addition Tomlinson describes "terrible conflict" with the devil. He claims,

> I came into direct contact with him. While in this state came the most awful struggle of all. While talking in an unknown tongue the Spirit seemed to envelope me, and I was taken through a course of casting out devils. A real experience in the vision, and the last verses of Mark sixteen came very vividly before my mind.[38]

His vision concluded with a scene of "multitudes of people awakened and coming this way. Among them were Mrs. Tomlinson and my children."[39]

Tomlinson interprets his vision as one in which he is shown his mission: he sees his whole family on mission together; he says that he was able to speak ten different languages in the vision; in each place, "multitudes" came to the light. He concludes, "I do not know whether God wants me to go to these places or not, but I am certainly willing to go as He leads."[40]

One may observe in this description the transformative nature of the experience. Tomlinson apparently saw this experience as a kind of therapeutic change, going so far as to use the language of medical procedure. The result is a new focus and a new way of seeing. The similarities with the experience of Angstead are striking. Both experienced visions involving transport, suffering the agony of the crucifixion and spiritual warfare. These mystical experiences are in keeping with the tradition of mysticism where one identifies with the suffering Christ and communes intimately with him. The difference, for Tomlinson at least, is that the result is a vision for the lost.

The testimony of Marie Burgess Brown, founder of Glad Tidings Hall (later Glad Tidings Tabernacle) in New York City, recorded in *The Midnight Cry*, is similar to that of Tomlinson. In 1906, after a period of tarrying for several days at a Pentecostal mission, Brown is baptized in the Spirit and is transported by the Spirit. She writes,

> In searching the word of God I found I had not what the disciples had when they received their baptism and it created a deeper hunger in my heart for all he had for me. And on the third day of waiting (tarrying) He came just as He came to them in that upper room. He did not make me a Peter or a John, but just a witness, and for five hours He filled and flooded my whole being.
>
> Then He opened my eyes to see the great need of this dark world. It seemed as if I went from one foreign field to another and in each field He would pray through me in the language of that people. I knew it not—but He did. There seemed to be great stone walls about each field and I could hear them cry for Jesus and as the

---

37. Ibid., 235.
38. Ibid., 235–36.
39. Ibid., 236.
40. Ibid.

Holy Spirit would begin to pray in the language of each field, I could see the walls begin to crumble and fall.

How this cry touched my heart, as every cry of the Holy Spirit will and I said, "Lord, send me, send me," that those who want Jesus may find Him.[41]

This experience allowed Brown to both see and hear the need and cries of those who were lost. She exhorts that the devil wants to "blind your eyes" so that you do not see the "Lamb of God." She warns, "And while you are looking at other things and what others have done and are doing—Behold He cometh!" For Brown, Tomlinson and others the experience of Spirit baptism is about being given new eyes and ears to hear the cries of the lost and the voice of God.[42]

A SALVIFIC VIEW OF BAPTISM IN THE SPIRIT

Without question, early Pentecostals "officially" viewed Spirit baptism in a category other than a soteriological one. The earliest statements of faith, or creeds, attempted to separate the experience from the realm of a work of grace. There are at least two reasons for this compartmentalization. First, preparatory instruction by proto-Pentecostals like Frank Sandford and Charles Parham had proclaimed that there would be a restoration of apostolic Christianity that would commence with the outpouring of the Spirit as on the day of Pentecost (Acts 2). Those on whom the Spirit was poured out would speak with the tongues of the nations; the Bible evidence or sign was missionary tongues.[43] Secondly, the revival and its accompanying doctrine and practice caused a serious rift in the Holiness churches that, for the most part, had taught that the second experience, sanctification, was an experience of baptism in the Holy Spirit.[44] Early Pentecostals were put on the defensive and were forced to write apologetically and sometimes polemically. The result was a sharp differentiation between the two experiences. This rigid approach produced definitions and doctrinal tenets that stated unequivocally that "sanctification was the second and last work of grace" and that Spirit baptism was not a work of grace. The end result of this has been a vocational view that sees Spirit baptism as "equipment for service." This has developed into a diminishment in thought regarding the necessity of Spirit baptism for other than those with a special call to evangelism and has resulted in a decline in numbers of experiences in classical Pentecostal churches.

In reading the more thoughtful reflections of Pentecostals, especially those receiving the experience, even in the earliest months of the revival, one is made aware that this

---

41. Marie Burgess Brown, "A Testimony By Mrs. Marie Burgess Brown" in *The Midnight Cry*, vol. 1, 2nd ed., No. 1 (March–April 1911) 1–2.

42. Brown, "Testimony," 2.

43. This background is explored in depth by Faupel in *The Everlasting Gospel*. It has not been within the scope of this paper to explore early understandings of tongues and the shift from *xenolalia* to *glossolalia*. This is, however, a much-needed study.

44. See Dayton. For more recent and comprehensive scholarship examining this terminology and how it was used by John Wesley and John Fletcher, see Laurence W. Wood, *The Meaning of Pentecost in Early Methodism: Rediscovering John Fletcher as John Fletcher's Vindicator and Designated Successor* (Lanham, MD: Scarecrow, 2002).

experience did more than just "equip." These testimonies, and the theological reflection written in light of the experience, reveal that this was a transformative crisis experience. Much of the description utilizes the language of soteriology: union with Christ, marriage, covenant. The typological interpretations presuppose process or progress, either through the Holy Place to the Holy of Holies or through the Hebrew calendar, from one feast to the next. These places, furnishings or feasts were connected, each dependent on the former and anticipating the next. This implies, though not always stated directly, that Spirit baptism is an experience in the *via salutis*, or to use the phrase early Pentecostals would have employed, *the way*.

Most recently, Gause's work *Living in the Spirit* has explicitly stated that Spirit baptism "has a place in the redemptive order and experience because of its relationship to and dependence on the cross, resurrection and ascension of Jesus. As a redemptive experience it is transformational in the cultivation of righteousness and its anointing for the pursuit of holiness."[45] As a part of the way, it "is the climax of all preceding experiences in salvation."[46]

Even those who have a sense of calling at the time of the experience describe the process therapeutically: new vision, being "operated on" by the Spirit. This language is linked to the idea of becoming a "new creation" or to healing and restoration, all soteriological language.

What is most striking is the mystical experience described by several in which they are transported through visions by the Spirit. This "vision quest" gives them solidarity with the suffering Christ, resulting in their pain and groaning. In mystical traditions, these visions are a part of the ladder-like pursuit of holiness, anticipating the beatific vision, when one sees God and is made like him. It seems that this visionary means by which those being baptized in the Spirit see Jesus in his passion gives credence to Blaine Charette's recent offering that sees *glossolalia* as a sign of the recovery of the *imago dei*. Charette writes,

> It is noted in scripture that one cannot see God's face and live. We are not at present prepared for such a face to face encounter. And yet the goal of redemption is that we will one day see his face. In the meantime the Spirit of God is active in our lives transforming us ever more into his likeness. It has been the argument of this paper that, as an essential element in this process of moving us towards our own true face, the Spirit causes us to speak with a genuine voice. It is a voice that gives expression to the truth of God's purpose for his creation and to our actual longings as his people. Glossolalia is the true voice given us today that helps form the true image of tomorrow.[47]

Common to all of the early testimonies, and stated most clearly by Myland, is the view that Spirit baptism is related to worship. It is received in worship and produces what Myland calls "true worship." While none of the earliest doctrinal statements and little of

---

45. R. Hollis Gause, *Living in the Spirit* (Cleveland: R. Hollis Gause, 2007) 13.

46. Ibid., 13.

47. Blaine Charette, "Reflective Speech: Glossolalia and the Image of God," 28.2 *Pneuma* (September 2006) 201.

the earliest exposition recognized this fact, outsiders would have made that observation immediately! Pentecostal worship has always been demonstrative, in the sense that it demonstrates the reality of the presence of God. There is always response to the entry of God's Spirit, whether by weeping, shouting, dancing, jerking, singing, clapping or leaping. Gause would concur on this connection to worship, noting, "We can expect the coming of the Holy Spirit where believers join together in praising and blessing God."[48] In fact, he explains the "normalcy" of the manifestation of tongues in Spirit baptism in terms of worship:

> This experience represents a profound rapport between two persons: the divine person, the Holy Spirit, and the human person, the believer. These two persons meet together through kinship and affection in such intimacy that the believer becomes fully responsive to the Holy Spirit. As He acts, wills, and communicates, the responding believer speaks and acts. This act of submission and responsiveness is essential to other acts of submission and responsiveness to the Holy Spirit.[49]

First and foremost, however, this experience transformed the affections. Joy and peace are experienced. Others testify that they are "baptized in Divine Love:" love for God, neighbor and the world. These testimonies anticipate the recent work of Margaret Poloma, Matthew Lee and Stephen Post in which they build on the work of Sorokin where showing "Unlimited Love" is described: "to affectively affirm as well as to unselfishly delight in the well-being of others, and to engage in acts of care and service on their behalf; unlimited love extends this love to all others without exception in a manner that is enduring and constant." They go on to define "Godly Love" as "the dynamic interaction between divine love and human love that enlivens benevolence."[50]

A Wesleyan-Pentecostal model of Spirit baptism places the experience on the *via salutis*, indicating that it is a salvific work, by grace, through faith. This model sees the experience as a part of a life of worship and witness, whereby one worships in Spirit and in truth; where the Spirit of God is imparted; where one groans as the Spirit groans; where one sits in heavenly places, both participating in and anticipating the glory to come; where one is baptized in Divine Love, receiving a new vision of those who are lost and begins to see them as God the Father sees them, as Jesus who died for them sees them and as the Spirit who is always drawing and wooing sees them. This model views Christ who has sent this that the world now sees and hears in the believer's life of worship and witness.

This integrated model is illustrated in one further testimony.

---

48. Gause, *Living in the Spirit*, 210.

49. Ibid., 209.

50. Matthew T. Lee, Margaret M. Poloma, and Stephen G. Post, "Researching Godly Love in the Pentecostal Tradition: A White Paper for the Flame of Love Project," 3. Online: http://www3.uakron.edu/sociology/flameweb/rfp.html.

PART ONE: RETHINKING THE HISTORY

"LIVING IN THE PRESENCE"

On Thursday, March 30, 1911, while in the Bahamas, Rev. Carl M. Padgett made this entry in his diary:

> Today one year ago I received the baptism of the Holy Ghost. It seems to me such a short year. The year has had its attendant trials, but I believe I can say that it has been the best year of my life. How near the Lord has been to me. All the black deeds of my life, all my mistakes, for I have been so unworthy of his love, are all under the blood of Jesus. And now I want to live for the glory of my Lord, do I think that I will be good, do I think that I will live holy, No, I have tried it and proved a failure, in my nature was vileness, but the Lord took it out and by His grace and power I do live holy, by His power I can over come. [sic] May the words of my mouth and the meditations of my heart be acceptable in His sight. Living in the presence of my Lord, in his holy sanctuary, where the cloud of His glory rests, there is where I want to dwell.
>
> Preach on the street tonight about the second coming of Jesus.[51]

---

51. Carl M. Padgett, unpublished diary, March 30, 1911.

6

Evangelicalism Examined... Again

Continuing the Debate between Donald W. Dayton and George Marsden

JONATHAN DODRILL

"Defining evangelicalism has become one of the biggest problems in American religious historiography"[1] —Timothy Weber

EVANGELICALISM HAS, FOR A very long time, been a troublesome category for historical research. This is especially true for historians of the Wesleyan/holiness movement as well as of the Pentecostal and charismatic movements. The histories of the Wesleyan/holiness and Pentecostal movements have been significantly skewed and researched under an inappropriate historical framework: that of generic evangelicalism. The dominant voices in the histories of evangelicalism have misconstrued the stories of holiness and Pentecostal folks while the dominant narratives of American religious history have largely left them out. Thus, it is vital to come to terms with what/who constitute evangelicalism, what/who constitutes fundamentalism, where Wesleyans fit in these categories and what is missing in the accepted narrative of American evangelicalism.

In much of the modern academy, evangelicalism is taken at face value—the definition is clear. However, the generally accepted working definition of evangelicalism is very narrow. The story of evangelicalism is often told taking firm root in the Reformation, working its way through the radical splits of the Reformation, sailing to America via George Whitfield and finding intellectual prowess in Jonathan Edwards, establishing itself in the Old School Presbyterianism of Princeton in order to ward off liberalism, transforming via fundamentalism and moving to Westminster Theological Seminary in the midst of controversy at Princeton Theological Seminary, and finally taking proper form in the intellectual new evangelicalism as espoused by the major figures at Fuller Seminary and *Christianity Today*. In light of the birth of fundamentalism, evangelicalism, though preceding fundamentalism, is somehow coalesced to it and thus we have

---

1. Donald W. Dayton and Robert K. Johnston, eds., *The Variety of American Evangelicalism* (Knoxville: University of Tennessee Press, 1991) 1.

a framework of evangelicalism in the middle of the twentieth-century that cannot be separated from fundamentalism.

Much of this framework relies on the centrality of educational institutions: Princeton Seminary in particular but also Westminster and Fuller Seminaries. This narrow framework has caused problems for many scholars—theologians as well as historians of religion. Randall Balmer's influential book and video series *Mine Eyes have Seen the Glory*[2] focuses on the diversity of evangelicalism, as does the book *The Variety of American Evangelicalism*, edited by Donald Dayton and Robert K. Johnston (which includes a chapter written by Marsden). However, such attempts are rare, and their success is even rarer. Some scholars have given up on any type of "diversity model" of evangelicalism. Donald Dayton is very clear that he is not advocating for a diversity model of evangelicalism; for a "diversity model" ultimately will still be grounded in one particular tradition though making room for "others."

Therefore, the task of this essay is to examine the diverse meanings of evangelicalism and its relationship with fundamentalism in the scholarship of Donald W. Dayton and George Marsden. Marsden has put forth a theory/definition of evangelicalism that is widely accepted (often times unquestionably). Consequently, Dayton has constantly challenged this generally accepted paradigm and offers an example of how Pentecostalism[3] is just as much a foundational point for evangelicalism as is fundamentalism. For this project I have engaged various articles and books from both scholars while relying heavily on their interpretation of the evangelical movement.

Since both scholars are responsible with their work, each scholar has sought to put his biases on the table (they have even aided one another in pointing out the others' biases!). George Marsden comes from the Reformed tradition, received a degree from Westminster Theological Seminary and has taught at one of the major Reformed colleges in America, Calvin College. Donald Dayton was raised in The Wesleyan Church, earned a degree from Houghton College (a Wesleyan school), and has taught/worked at various Wesleyan schools such as Drew and Azusa Pacific universities as well as Asbury Theological Seminary. Marsden has been content to expound in great detail the story of evangelicalism as the forerunner and remnant of the warriors against liberalism. Dayton, alternatively, has pointed to other stories of evangelicalism (notably the holiness and Pentecostal movements) which do not seem so bent to ward off liberalism.

The first task will be to examine Marsden's work on evangelicalism and fundamentalism. It is necessary to observe how he frames the story, who he offers as the exemplars of evangelicalism and how the general flow of evangelicalism is interpreted in his paradigm. This will be followed by Donald Dayton's critique to which will be added supplementary critiques of Marsden's work. The supplementary critiques will focus mainly on the relationship between orthodoxy and evangelicalism, the centrality of elite educational institutions in Marsden's historiography, and the terminology of "fundamentalist" and "evangelical" used to label particular groups/individuals. Finally, there will be

---

2. Randall Balmer, *Mine Eyes Have Seen the Glory: a Journey into the Evangelical Subculture in America* (New York: Oxford University Press, 2006).

3. Donald W. Dayton, *Theological Roots of Pentecostalism* (Grand Rapids: Francis Asbury, 1987).

a consideration of selected proposals put forth by Dayton. What will be concluded is that while Marsden's paradigm of evangelicalism is suitable for understanding the history of Presbyterian, various Baptist, and other Reformed groups, it is nonetheless inappropriate to use as the archetypal paradigm for all of evangelicalism. There are numerous fringe groups who claim to be evangelical (or are labeled as such) that do not benefit from such a paradigm. Additionally, to study such communities (Pentecostals, Wesleyans, Restorationists, etc.) with the Marsden paradigm creates a skewed history of the various groups as well as a skewed history of American Christianity in general.

EVANGELICALISM ACCORDING TO GEORGE MARSDEN

For George Marsden, evangelicalism is explicitly tied to fundamentalism. In the twentieth-century, evangelicalism is a form of restructured fundamentalism and expressed most accurately in the new evangelicalism of Fuller Theological Seminary.[4] Therefore, if we are to understand what evangelicalism is according to George Marsden, then we must understand what fundamentalism is according to George Marsden.

"A Fundamentalist is an Evangelical who is angry about something."[5] This is the plain understanding of fundamentalism. It is also what modern American media has portrayed as the typification of evangelicalism. The late Jerry Falwell is the great example of an angry fundamentalist. More specifically, though, Marsden states that "an American Fundamentalist is an evangelical who is militant in opposition to liberal theology in the churches or to changes in cultural values or mores, such as those associated with 'secular humanism.'"[6] This characteristic is what sets fundamentalism apart from other related Christian communities.[7] This does appear to be an appropriate defining characteristic of a fundamentalist. But the problem comes when evangelicalism is filter through this fundamentalist movement. Marsden understands evangelicalism in light of fundamentalism before and after fundamentalism became manifest.

He does this by placing orthodoxy and the resistance to liberalism at the center of late nineteenth-century evangelicalism as *the* unifying characteristic of the movement. While he gives a very general definition of evangelical as one who participates in the "proclamation of Christ's saving work through his death on the cross and the necessity of personally trusting him for salvation,"[8] he largely ignores this definition in his work. This given definition would best describe what a "Christian" in general is.[9] Instead of using

---

4. Hence his book, George Marsden, *Reforming Fundamentalism: Fuller Seminary and the New Evangelicalism* (Grand Rapids: Eerdmans, 1987).

5. George Marsden, *Understanding Fundamentalism and Evangelicalism* (Grand Rapids: Eerdmans, 1991) 1.

6. Ibid.

7. George Marsden, *Fundamentalism and American Culture: The Shaping of Twentieth-Century Evangelicalism, 1870–1925* (New York: Oxford University Press, 1980) 4.

8. Marsden, *Understanding Fundamentalism and Evangelicalism*, 2.

9. This definition is faulty for two reasons. First it is much too general for the term "evangelical" and Marsden shows this by how he engages in the history of evangelicalism. Secondly, to ascribe such a definition to evangelicalism makes evangelicalism a pointless category: what Protestant would not subscribe to such a definition?

this definition which would allow for diversity within nineteenth-century evangelicalism, Marsden introduces a conservative/liberal construct to support his overarching thesis that evangelicalism during this time period was concerned chiefly with preserving orthodoxy.

The "liberals" that Marsden portrays are academics who sought to maintain credibility in the eyes of the more academic communities (European universities) by "modifying some central evangelical doctrines."[10] These doctrines usually center on biblical authority and atonement theory. In exemplifying these doctrines, we can see how Marsden is funneling nineteenth-century evangelicalism into the fundamentalist debates of the twentieth-century. "Biblical authority" is vague enough of a definition but what is central to this is the doctrine of inerrancy. To say that liberals were compromising Biblical authority can be misleading. Many liberal leaders of the nineteenth-century saw themselves as saving Biblical authority by modifying it. Marsden's framing of liberalism's compromise equates Biblical authority with inerrancy and thus starts to amalgamate evangelicalism (in all its "diversity") to a sort of proto-fundamentalism.

He establishes evangelicalism as those who "continued to believe the traditionally essential evangelical doctrines."[11] Again, this is centered on biblical authority and is set up against liberalism. The question then arises, "what are these essential evangelical doctrines?" Did we not just see evangelicalism defined as those who proclaim the "saving work of Christ" and the "necessity of personally trusting him for salvation?" What then does biblical authority have to do with this? In this way, Marsden situates evangelicalism within the "conservative" camp rounding out his conservative/liberal construction. To reiterate, at this point in Marsden's scholarship, evangelicalism is against "liberalism" and adheres to a "conservative" belief system that is "traditional."

In this system, such a person described as a "liberal evangelical" cannot exist. Yet it is paradoxical that Marsden includes Henry Ward Beecher as one of the "Stars" of "When Evangelicalism Reigned."[12] Beecher was brought up on heresy charges because he "sidestepped" traditional doctrines claiming that Christianity is more of a heart matter than an orthodox matter.[13] This sounds strikingly similar to parts of John Wesley's theological discourses, specifically his insistence on "heart religion" and his trifling of orthodoxy. If Marsden's liberal/conservative construct is to be kept intact, then Beecher cannot be labeled an evangelical because of his unorthodox views.

In Marsden's narrative, nineteenth-century evangelicalism kept liberalism at bay until an impasse occurred at Princeton Theological Seminary. Here, the heir of Old Princeton Theology (equated with evangelical orthodoxy), J. Gresham Machen, sought to defend orthodoxy from the liberalism seeping into the halls of Princeton. Though Machen was not fond of the term "fundamentalist" he still fit the mold. Many (including Machen) thought fundamentalism was a backward, anti-intellectual movement. This is a

10. Marsden, *Understanding Fundamentalism and Evangelicalism*, 3.

11. Ibid.

12. "Stars" and "When Evangelicalism Reigned" are subtitles to the first chapter in *Understanding Fundamentalism and Evangelicalism*.

13. Marsden, *Understanding Fundamentalism and Evangelicalism*, 17–18.

muddy issue, but it seems that there was a fundamentalism of the people (characterized by an anti-evolutionary stance and a Dispensationalist worldview) and a more academic fundamentalist theology.[14] However Machen is to be characterized, it is widely documented that Machen's biggest problem was not his orthodoxy but his attitude. Marsden points out that he was investigated by a committee for his "divisiveness."[15] If Marsden's landmark characterization of fundamentalism is to be upheld—that of a militant attitude in defending orthodoxy from liberalism—then Machen can be seen as nothing but a fundamentalist.

After the great Princeton split, where did evangelicalism reside? Did it reside in Princeton which was purged of "fundamentalist leaning" evangelicals? Or did it make the trip to Glenside, Pennsylvania, establishing itself in Westminster Theological Seminary under J. Gresham Machen? Or was it somewhere else altogether?

Continuing his narrative after the Princeton split, Marsden speaks of a bastion of light which came out of the "academic dark age of conservative evangelicalism,"[16] Fuller Seminary. In his book, *Reforming Fundamentalism: Fuller Seminary and the New Evangelicalism*, Marsden states that Fuller is an "evangelical institution."[17] This is seemingly ironic because Fuller sought to reform fundamentalism, so how is it an "evangelical" institution? This question lies at the heart of the matter in Marsden's interpretive paradigm: fundamentalism is evangelicalism. Though he takes care, at points, to distinguish fundamentalism from evangelicalism,[18] he nonetheless intertwines the two at numerous points. This is not necessarily because he has an agenda to promote, but it does mirror what happened at Fuller where there was an abandonment of pejorative terminology (fundamentalist) in order to establish a more acceptable terminology (evangelical or new evangelical). Marsden states that in the 1940's "'evangelical' and 'fundamentalist' were not then separate entities."[19] This is a difficult notion to accept considering the embarrassment caused to fundamentalism by the Scopes Trial just fifteen years earlier. It seems that religious groups loosely defined as evangelical would want to disassociate themselves from the connotations coupled with fundamentalism. In essence, this is precisely what Fuller Seminary sought to do. Their goal, according to Marsden, was to uphold the orthodoxy of fundamentalism while reinventing the public image of fundamentalism.[20]

According to Marsden's narrative, the Fuller scholars adopted the name "new evangelical" clearly though they espoused the exact same theological essentials as the fundamentalists. Marsden even states that these new evangelicals were fundamentalists.[21] Again, if we stick to Marsden's definition of fundamentalist—centered on a militant defense of orthodoxy against liberalism—then how can the Fuller scholars be called anything but

14. This would include the series, *The Fundamentals* which drew various renowned scholars.
15. Marsden, *Understanding Fundamentalism and Evangelicalism*, 182–83.
16. Ibid., 183.
17. Marsden, *Reforming Fundamentalism*, 2.
18. See for example *Fundamentalism and American Culture*, 4.
19. Marsden, *Reforming Fundamentalism*, 3.
20. Ibid., 10.
21. Marsden, *Understanding Fundamentalism and Evangelicalism*, 150.

fundamentalists? Marsden here opts to use the new evangelicals self-description stating that, "[Ockenga] and others at the [Fuller] seminary and in the NAE had long preferred to use 'evangelical' as a self-description to escape the stigma of 'fundamentalist.'"[22] Part of this stigma was the lack social involvement/concern attributed to fundamentalism. Carl Henry, one of the Fuller Scholars, advocated for a dual emphasis on orthodoxy and social responsibility. However, the latter failed to happen unless an official institutional statement condemning racism in the 1960's (the extent of their social responsibility through this time period) qualifies as being socially responsible. While calling attention to racism is commendable, the seminary had yet to admit an African American student and also disallowed women from participating in the same coursework as men. Despite their institutional statement, the student body remained vastly politically and socially conservative.[23]

Beyond Fuller Seminary, Marsden situates evangelicalism strongly in the leadership of the National Association of Evangelicals (NAE) and in the Christian publication, *Christianity Today*. According to Marsden, the NAE was "an agency founded in 1942, primarily to foster intrafundamentalist unity."[24] Furthermore, he exemplifies Carl Henry's voice as saying that the term "evangelical" is tied to the NAE which sought to bring back "Reformed and evangelical roots."[25] For many, Reformed theology is equated with evangelical orthodoxy. This raises all sorts of problems for definitions of evangelicalism which is so seemingly "diverse."

In the present era, Marsden reserves the term "fundamentalist" for those who are separatist, Dispensationalist Baptists. He also states that it has become a "self-designation."[26] Conversely, he sees evangelicalism in the mid to late twentieth century as diverse, stating that, "evangelicalism describes a much more diverse coalition ... evangelicalism today includes any Christians traditional enough to affirm the basic beliefs of the old nineteenth-century evangelical consensus."[27]

THE PROBLEM OF "EVANGELICALISM" ACCORDING TO DONALD DAYTON

Dayton views evangelicalism quite differently than Marsden. Specifically, his major critique is that Marsden uses a "Presbyterian paradigm" to interpret evangelicalism (which often manifests in a central role of fundamentalism). Dayton sees an incoherence in evangelicalism that his counterparts (Marsden as well as numerous other scholars) often try to ignore.[28]

22. Marsden, *Reforming Fundamentalism*, 146.
23. Ibid., 146, 254–55.
24. Marsden, *Understanding Fundamentalism and Evangelicalism*, 150.
25. Marsden, *Reforming Fundamentalism*, 10.
26. Marsden, *Understanding Fundamentalism and Evangelicalism*, 4.
27. Ibid. This description will be taken up below.
28. Dayton and Johnston, *The Variety of American Evangelicalism* (Knoxville: University of Tennessee Press, 1991) 2. Though many scholars, including Marsden, promote the idea of diversity within evangelicalism, very few proceed with historical narratives to include such diversity. Randall Balmer is a rare exception to this hoard of scholars as he promotes the idea of evangelicalism's diversity *and* explores the various

Dayton's critique of Marsden, found in its most explicit form, is in his review of Marsden's book, *Reforming Fundamentalism*.[29] Through this essay, Dayton traces Marsden's terminology associated with evangelicalism and follows it through to its logical conclusions. He also offers his own historiographical interpretation as a substitute for Marsden's.[30] While Marsden is content to work with a Presbyterian paradigm, Dayton suggests that a more generic Methodist paradigm (to account for the "Age of Methodism") be employed when studying evangelicalism in America. Furthermore, he understands fundamentalism not as the transformation of evangelicalism, but rather as the corruption of "classical evangelicalism."[31] By "classical evangelicalism," Dayton refers to the line of Christianity that came through Pietism, the Great Awakening(s), the British evangelical revivals, and nineteenth-century revivalism.

Where Marsden sees classical evangelicalism as falling in line with Reformation principles, Dayton sees classical evangelicalism as attempting to correct Reformation principles (by emphasizing sanctification).[32] Here we come to one of the major components of the debate: the role of orthodoxy. On the one hand, Marsden understands evangelicalism as a great defender of orthodoxy, which is why he can draw such close similarities between evangelicalism and fundamentalism. Dayton, on the other hand, understands evangelicalism and orthodoxy as two separate entities. Dayton's version of evangelicalism is rooted in promoting human will and sanctification. Thus, when the two are seen together, they result in social involvement. This would explain why the Evangelical United Front was more concerned with social issues (slavery, temperance, women's rights) rather than orthodoxy (biblical authority, substitutionary atonement, etc). Dayton goes so far as to state that there is a dimension of anti-orthodoxy in evangelicalism.[33]

Furthermore, Dayton points out that equating evangelicalism with orthodoxy blinds scholars to the various religious communities who are theologically outside of the Reformed tradition. It also demands the sort of conservative/liberal construct that Marsden presents.[34] This construct leaves out multiple groups that identify with the evangelical movement. Are holiness churches liberal or conservative? Are Dispensationalists liberal or conservative? Is the African Methodist Episcopal Church liberal or conservative? While each group has symptoms of conservativism, from a demand for holy living to a literalist hermeneutic, none fit into either category of the conservative/liberal construct. Included in this construct is the idea of "splitting." This is seen in Marsden's

---

groups he sees as the components of that diversity. See especially his, *Mine Eyes have Seen the Glory*.

29. Donald W. Dayton, "'The Search for the Historical Evangelicalism': George Marsden's History of Fuller Seminary as a Case Study" reprinted in Christian T. Collins Winn, ed., *From the Margins: A Celebration of the Theological Work of Donald W. Dayton* (Eugene, OR: Pickwick, 2007).

30. Ibid., 257.

31. Ibid., 258.

32. Ibid., 259.

33. Ibid., 259–60. Considering the privileged place of Calvinism as "orthodox" in the nineteenth century, it is easy to see socially conscious Arminians and Wesleyans as "unorthodox."

34. Ibid., 261.

centralization of the Princeton split. Dayton prefers a type of radicalization over and against the idea of "splitting." Therefore we can see holiness churches as the radicalization of Methodism rather than a split from Methodism.[35]

Beyond the overarching liberal/conservative construct, Dayton also takes issue with Marsden's definition of fundamentalism. Where Marsden takes Ernest Sandeen's central thesis[36] lightly, Dayton wishes to uplift it as foundational. Sandeen's central thesis is that Dispensationalists and inerrantants coalesced to form fundamentalism. This intertwining of doctrines shows how a fundamentalism of the academy (inerrancy) joined together with a fundamentalism of the people (Dispensationalism) to form a militant opposition to new theological movements. This is troubling for Marsden because his central question in historical analysis is "what has stayed the same in evangelicalism?" Dayton's central question is "what has changed in evangelicalism?" This leads Marsden to point to orthodoxy (thus narrowing the definition of evangelicalism) while Dayton points to moments of radicalization within established denominations.[37]

In describing fundamentalism, Dayton agrees with Barr that "fundamentalism distorts and betrays the basic true religious concerns of evangelical Christianity."[38] If it is thus used to explain the origins of such a movement as Pentecostalism, then it only provides a distorted view. While it may be tempting for some Pentecostals to self-define along the lines of fundamentalism as they move from sect to institution, they may not be drawing on their true lineage.[39]

What is at stake for Donald Dayton is the potentiality for fringe movements to be lumped into a bland evangelicalism that is dominated by Reformed orthodoxy under a Presbyterian paradigm. Hence, when David Wells lamented evangelicalism's disunity, he was assuming that there was one general theological strand that bound evangelicalism together.[40] This is the mundane symptom of situating evangelicalism within a narrow Presbyterian paradigm.

ADDITIONAL CRITIQUES OF MARSDEN'S HISTORIOGRAPHY

While Dayton's critique of Marsden is landmark and vastly important, there are some additional critiques that could be made of Marsden's work. First and foremost is his exclusive research of elite educational institutions. Marsden situates the split at Princeton Theological Seminary as the catalyst movement that shook evangelicalism to its core. It was thus saved by the "conservatives" at Westminster Seminary and finally reformed into a new, more intellectual evangelicalism at Fuller Seminary. While the events at these institutions and the scholars who shaped them are very important, they are not completely

---

35. Ibid., 261–62.
36. Ernest Sandeen, *Roots of Fundamentalism: British and American Milleniarianism 1800–1930*.
37. Dayton, "Search for Historic Evangelicalism," 265.
38. Dayton, "Evangelicalism without Fundamentalism."
39. Dayton and Johnson, *Variety of Evangelicalism*, 48–49.
40. Ibid., 1.

representative of the vast majority of evangelicalism. Marsden, being a responsible scholar, even acknowledges this. However, he still focuses on "top-down" religious history.

Donald Dayton has called for a "people's history" of evangelicalism,[41] something Marsden has not accomplished. The emerging genre of "people's history" is often avoided due to its complex nature (or an unwillingness to learn new methodologies), which asks central historical figures (often academic theologians) to abdicate their privileged place in historical research. Yet, the genre can help create meaningful histories for social and religious groups that do not have a central "thinker." Researching grass-roots, revivalist movements through conventional historical research (the top-down approach) simply does not work. Expounding on the academic journals of B. B. Warfield may provide us with a good idea of what he thought, but it does not tell us what the revivalists in Kentucky were putting into practice. Instead of exploring the theological work of scholars with limited influence, it may be beneficial to explore the theological work of evangelists, revivalists, Sunday school teachers and circuit riders. Instead of focusing on scholarly theology, why not focus on folk theology?

Folk theology works with a hermeneutics of suspicion, essentially deconstructing institutionalized theology in relation to lived theology. The masses of laity obtained their theological framework (in a pick-and-choose manner) through Sunday school material, popular books, revival leaders, and a host of other sources. Furthermore, if one takes into consideration geographical location, s/he will be confronted with the fact that the institutions Marsden explores are on either side of the country's coasts. What happens to the people in the middle? Are their lives and theological understandings dominated by these coastal seminaries? As it currently stands, a history of evangelicals in southern Illinois in the 1950's is subject to interpretation through a coastal Presbyterian paradigm. Assuming that scholarly theology is handed down directly from scholar to laity is quite dim. The transformation of scholarly theology to laity goes through a fourfold (at least) transformation from idea to parish: scholar's thought to scholar's pedagogy to students/pastors reception to students/pastors presentation to the laity's reception. Hence what starts as the "orthodox theology" of an "orthodox scholar" is transformed into the folk theology of the people.

Additionally, if we are to take Nathan O. Hatch's thesis[42] seriously, Princeton's, as well as Fuller's, influence on twentieth-century evangelicalism comes into question. If Christianity, or more specifically evangelicalism, was being formed from the ground up, what role do elite educational institutions have in American religious historiography?

Another major critique of Marsden is his situating orthodoxy as the crux of evangelicalism. Dayton does a fine job of pointing out how this sets up very narrow parameters around evangelicalism. Yet Marsden tries to strike a balance between the orthodoxy and diversity of evangelicalism stating, "evangelicalism describes a much more diverse coalition [as compared to fundamentalism] . . . evangelicalism today includes any Christians

---

41. Dayton, "Ecumenical Riff Raft," 94, reprinted in Christian T. Collins Winn, ed., *From the Margins: A Celebration of the Theological Work of Donald W. Dayton* (Eugene, OR: Pickwick, 2007).

42. Nathan O. Hatch, *The Democratization of American Christianity* (New Haven: Yale University Press, 1989).

traditional enough to affirm the basic beliefs of the old nineteenth-century evangelical consensus."[43] Marsden goes on to define this "nineteenth-century consensus" as including the Reformation doctrine of the final authority of the Bible, the real historical character of God's saving work recorded in Scripture, salvation as the redemptive work of Christ, the stress of evangelism and missions, and the pursuit of a spiritually transformed life.[44] While these seem general enough, the mention of the Reformation as the foundation of doctrinal belief excludes those who sought to correct Reformation doctrine instead of upholding it. Likewise, the emphasis on scriptural authority seems to point indirectly to a semi-inerrantist view of scripture. Moreover, in this definition, what makes a person an evangelical is found solely in what s/he *believes*.

Orthodoxy is, and has been throughout Christian history, an exclusionary tool used by those in power (those who are privileged to spell out orthodoxy) to weed out competing or alternative theologies (such as revivalism, healing, glossilia, etc.). Furthermore, in addition to Hatch's thesis should be added E. Brooks Holifield's thesis on the decline of Calvinism in American theology.[45] If there was both a decline in traditional Calvinism and a flowering of democratized evangelicalism, how can there be such a thing as "traditional nineteenth-century evangelical *consensus*?"[46]

The final critique to be added is that of defining terminology. Marsden provides us with a terrific definition of fundamentalism yet he shifts this definition when it becomes pejorative. If a militant defense of traditional beliefs against liberalism is the hallmark of fundamentalism in the 1920's–1940's, why does it change from the 1950's onward? If the definition stayed the same, would not Harold Lindsell's militant demand for widespread acceptance of biblical inerrancy[47] qualify him to be labeled a fundamentalist? Rather, he is labeled an evangelical. This is because at this point, according to Marsden, "fundamentalist" becomes a self-designation which is typically reserved for separatist, Dispensationalist Baptists.

There are many things wrong with this switch. First and foremost is the current description. Marsden states that fundamentalism *became* separatist gradually. Yet the birth of institutional fundamentalism came through a separation from Princeton Theological Seminary in 1929. Secondly, Sandeen has offered a very plausible (yet underappreciated) thesis about the coalescence of Dispensationalism and fundamentalism in the early twentieth century. Finally comes the role of self-designation, which has disastrous potentiality.

---

43. Marsden, *Understanding Fundamentalism and Evangelicalism*, 4.

44. Ibid., 4–5.

45. E. Brooks Holifield, *Theology in America: Christian Thought from the Age of the Puritans to the Civil War* (New Haven: Yale University Press, 2003).

46. Emphasis is mine.

47. Harold Lindsell, *The Battle for the Bible* (Grand Rapids: Zondervan, 1978). For an excellent assessment of Lindsell's negative impact on evangelicalism, see Dayton's essay on religion-online.org. Donald W. Dayton, "The Battle for the Bible: Renewing the Inerrancy Debate." Online: http://www.religion-online.org/showarticle.asp?title=1823.

The "new evangelicals" sought to defend the exact same orthodoxy that fundamentalists defended a generation before. However, these militant defenders of orthodoxy avoided the stigma of the term by coining a new term. Yet this new term eventually overtakes an older term, "evangelical." This is a highjacking of sorts for the "new evangelicals" redefined evangelicalism through their fundamentalist roots thus skewing the histories of any group previously associated with evangelicalism.

Marsden is correct in stating that fundamentalism has taken on a pejorative connotation. However, if historians allow each group to self-describe then there would be no need for a historian. Therefore, the "new evangelicalism" as it came to be known, should have been labeled the "new fundamentalism" for that is what it was. Currently the diversity of evangelicalism is a conglomeration of Pentecostals, Pietists, Wesleyans, Calvinists, and others. But why has the definition of fundamentalism fallen away? Why is a militant defense of traditional beliefs no longer labeled "fundamentalism?"

The answer is that no group wants to be labeled as "fundamentalist" in our current culture. Jerry Falwell was probably the last Christian willing to publicly declare his fundamentalist title on national television. With the additional media coverage and demonization of fundamentalist Islam, it can be safely assumed that very few Christians feel comfortable adopting the title "fundamentalist Christian." But if we take Marsden's main point in *Fundamentalism and American Culture* seriously, we can label many Christians as fundamentalist. Yet, evangelicalism has replaced fundamentalism in much of the public sector as evangelicals are portrayed as being militantly opposed to evolution, and other humanist beliefs.

SCHOLARSHIP TO EMPLOY

Though Marsden's historical analysis on fundamentalism is invaluable to American religious history, a new framework for evangelicalism as put forth by Donald Dayton is the best possible paradigm for future scholarship. There are four aspects in particular that would aid in future scholarship.

The first tool stems from Dayton's observation that the term "evangelical" is highly limited in the English language. He thus uses German to expound on the diverse meanings of "evangelicalism." The first is *"Evangelisch"* which describes those communities relating to the continental Reformation (Lutherans, Calvinists, etc). The themes exemplified in *Evangelisch* include an Augustinian anthropology, stressing God's sovereignty, and an aversion to Catholicism.[48]

The second German term is *"Erweckungsbewegung."* This refers to "classical evangelicalism" as defined by Dayton. This would include those who stressed "convertive piety" such as the Puritans, eighteenth-century British revivalism and nineteenth-century American revivalism. A central focus for this community is the emphasis on social amelioration (which distinguishes it from fundamentalism).[49]

---

48. Dayton and Johnston, *Variety of Evangelicalism*, 47–48.
49. Ibid., 48.

The final German term is "*Evangelikal*," which for all intensive purposes describes American fundamentalism and new evangelicalism. The central concern of the *Evangelikal* is the affirmation of orthodoxy and conservativism over and against liberalism.[50]

The second component of Dayton's scholarship which will aid in future research is the role of *embourgeoisement*.[51] *Embourgeoisement* takes into consideration the role of class in establishing new sectarian movements and the following generations' upward mobility from the lower to the middle class.[52] Focusing on such sectarian groups with this in mind can enlighten how social, political, and economic factors contribute to the changing religious landscape of evangelicalism. As a part of this, Dayton wishes to establish a difference between a pre-critical reading of Scripture from an anti-critical reading of Scripture.[53] The latter describes an established fundamentalist hermeneutic while the former describes the typical hermeneutic of a lower class sectarian group.

Finally, in conjunction with Holifield's thesis, Dayton calls for an acknowledgement of the "Age of Methodism."[54] The dying Calvinist doctrine in nineteenth century America was subject to the circuit riders of Methodism who promoted an Arminian/Wesleyan theology that harmonized with typical American notions of "freedom" and "self-determination."

CONCLUSION

The thesis of this paper was that while Marsden's paradigm of evangelicalism is suitable for understanding the history of Presbyterian, various Baptist, and other Reformed groups, it is nonetheless inappropriate to use as the archetypical paradigm for all of evangelicalism. By looking at Dayton's critique and additional critiques it can be seen that the widely accepted Presbyterian paradigm which stresses the liberal/conservative construct and is most manifest in fundamentalism and new evangelicalism is not an appropriate model for interpreting groups that did not stress a radical defense of orthodoxy.

Unless current scholars can seriously consider a total revision of twentieth-century evangelical historiography then Donald Dayton's call for a moratorium on the use of "evangelicalism" is the only responsible option. This could be avoided by taking into consideration Dayton's distinctions drawn from the German language. The historians of Christianity in general are the subject of massive critiques as many fail to take seriously the history of diverse groups within a time period opting rather to expound upon a central theological figure. American evangelicalism is no exception. If scholars continue to frame the story in light of elite institutions and intellectuals, the diverse nature of evangelicalism will continue to lie dormant. Yet, if we take seriously the call for a "people's history" of evangelicalism, such a travesty can be avoided.

---

50. Ibid., 48–49.
51. Even Marsden finds this to be a highly important interpretive tool.
52. Dayton, "Search for the Historical Evangelicalism," 264.
53. Dayton and Johnston, *Variety of Evangelicalism*, 247.
54. Dayton, "Search for the Historical Evangelicalism," 258.

PART TWO

Contribution to Current Theological Problems

7

The End of Wesleyan Theology

WILLIAM J. ABRAHAM

CONTEMPORARY WESLEYAN THEOLOGY IS now slowly but surely being laid to rest. In the nineteen sixties this was not the case. At that time those interested in Wesley saw the dawn of a new day. At least in mainline Methodist circles where Wesley had been hidden away in the closet or shunted far back in the attic, the euphoria was palpable.[1] A new generation of brilliant historians arose to bring John Wesley on to the world stage. Giants stalked the land. Of the many we could take into account, I mention but two.[2] Consider Frank Baker, the meticulous antiquarian buried in the details. Here was a quiet Englishman with the mind of a fox, hunting down every nook and cranny of the material. Consider Albert Outler, the swashbuckling, hang-glider researcher, nervously scanning the horizon to stay in touch with the most recent trend across the whole encyclopedia of knowledge. Here was a Southern Gentleman with the mind of a hedgehog looking for that one big idea that would save the world. The service rendered by these giants was extraordinary. The labor continues, most notably in the work of Richard Heitzenrater, perhaps without peer in his knowledge of the details, the sources, and the historical issues to be pursued.[3]

---

1. I want to pay tribute at this point to the great work done to keep the name and work of Wesley alive in the Holiness tradition. Especially within that tradition the scholars of the Church of the Nazarene, the Jesuits of our heritage, deserve our deepest gratitude for their tenacity. Consider, for example, George Turner, William Arnett, Delbert Rose, Claude Thompson, Timothy Smith, Mildred Bangs Wynkoop, William Greathouse, Carl Bangs, Paul Merritt Basset, H. Ray Dunning, J. Kenneth Grider, and many others.

2. In what follows I cannot begin to do justice to a galaxy of scholars, including Robert Cushman, Thomas Langford, William R. Cannon, David Shipley, Horton Davies, Franz Hildebrandt, John Lawson, Colin Williams, John Deschner, Bernard Semmel, and many others. I leave aside the important work done outside North America. I also give special attention in what follows to the work of Albert Outler; I trust that the reasons for this will be obvious.

3. We still await a full-scale biography of Wesley from his hands. Should it appear, we would have much cause for rejoicing.

PART TWO: CONTRIBUTION TO CURRENT THEOLOGICAL PROBLEMS

It is worth retelling how Outler came to be involved in the prodigious effort to make available a new edition of Wesley's works.[4] He was a member of an Oxford University Press panel in the New York offices working on a library of Protestant thought. After the standard names were identified (Luther, Calvin, Schleiermacher, et al.), Outler suggested the name of John Wesley. The other members of the committee collapsed into titters of laughter. One colleague gently but firmly reminded Outler that they were working on a projected library of Protestant *thought*. Naturally he won the argument that ensued and was assigned the volume on Wesley.[5] That day, surely a great day in the history of scholarship, Outler vowed that by the time he was finished there would be more non-Wesleyans reading Wesley than Wesleyans. He more than accomplished his goal. The sales of his Wesley volume have exceeded the total sales of the other member volumes in the series. One reason for his involvement in the Wesley Works project was his dissatisfaction with the standard editions.

As Outler's work and legacy reveals, the recovery of Wesley was (and is) as much an ideological exercise as it was (and is) a work of intentionally pure historical scholarship. His fastidious editorial efforts and his brilliant essays functioned ideologically at three levels.[6] First, they were a way to legitimize Methodism as a player on the world ecumenical stage. They served to make it clear that the heirs of Wesley could hold their own in the world of theological scholarship, even though their elder brothers and sisters in the faith were constantly tempted to dismiss them as talkative intellectual midgets poisoned by pietism.[7] Second, they were a rallying cry to scattered sheep and wolves scurrying and prowling in and around the Methodist Episcopal fold. They provided a way to gather up the disorderly bands of Methodists that could agree about next to nothing other than that they had inherited a tradition initiated by John Wesley and that they ought somehow to hang together as freshly minted ecumenists.[8] Third, they were a creative personal agenda. They constituted a new method in theology that would fix the doctrine of scripture once and for all and breathe new life into a tradition long on theological smugness and apathy and short on intellectual virtue.

Outler's Wesley was an invented Wesley, a Wesley at once Catholic, Reformed, Evangelical, Enlightened, Ecumenical, non-dogmatic, pragmatic, pious, relative to his

---

4. I am relying at this point on my own conversations with Outler. Outler tells the story with characteristic panache in "A New Future for Wesley Studies: An Agenda for Phase III," in Thomas C. Oden and Leicester R. Longden, eds., *The Wesleyan Theological Heritage: Essays of Albert Outler* (Grand Rapids: Zondervan, 1991) 125–42.

5. It appeared as Albert C. Outler, ed., *John Wesley* (New York: Oxford University Press, 1964). I was given a copy on my ordination to the Irish Methodist ministry that I still treasure.

6. I have long been convinced that Outler is at his best as an essay writer; at his best, he is among the best of the best as an essay writer. For my appreciation of Outler see my preface to William J. Abraham, ed., *Evangelism: Essays by Albert Outler* (Wilmore: Bristol, 1998) 8–11.

7. Recently one veteran ecumenist summed this sentiment up for me abruptly by noting that talking to a Methodist theologian was like trying to have a theological conversation with one's thirteen year-old daughter.

8. Once we add in the folk from the Evangelical United Brethren then the diversity multiplies. My sense is that for Outler the Holiness tradition was a planet in outer space which it took him time to recognize and acknowledge.

place and time, pluralist in ecclesiology, and always open to the future. Despite the savvy work on the historiography of Wesley, this was a Wesley carefully constructed to fill a network of needs.[9] This is not in any way a cheap shot at Outler as a historian. Nor it is a lapse into a vulgar form of postmodernism that has no place for old-fashioned critical, historical scholarship. Ernst Troeltsch was right to insist that our interest in historical data is intertwined with our other interests, that interests of the first degree mesh with interests of the second degree. My aim is simply to highlight the secondary interests that are clearly visible in the Outlerian historical agenda.[10]

In a host of ways, Outler's work was a resounding success, even though he died a bitterly disappointed scholar and churchman.[11] Consider the following laundry list. First, he and the others who worked in the team managed to get the works of Wesley published, despite the early withdrawal of Oxford University Press. I was with him on the day that the news came through from Oxford University Press that his edition of the sermons (twenty years of amazing labor) was in jeopardy. Even though I had more than a suspicion that he already had Abingdon Press in the bag as an alternative, there was a clear note of disappointment in his demeanor. In the end Abingdon came through, and we have a magnificent critical edition of the works in the making.

Second, Outler's theological vision was canonized in his own brand of Methodism. He chaired the crucial doctrinal commission that brought its deliberations to the General Conference of The United Methodist Church in 1972 and the report he effectively wrote was passed with next to no dissenting votes.[12] All this happened despite the fact that the adoption of his theology was carried through in the form of unconstitutional developments implemented in a church too weak to deal with its own juridical waywardness and too intimidated to stand up to Outler's deft political maneuverings.[13] He deeply opposed and regretted the updating of his proposals in the nineteen eighties, when the primacy of scripture was inserted, and when the language of diversity ousted the language of pluralism.[14] In the end he bowed to the inevitable, and so he should, for he had won the war on three critical fronts. The relativist and thoroughly historicist reading of the tradition he championed remained in place. Wesley's *Sermons* and *Explanatory Notes on*

---

9. For a very important historiographical essay, see his "A New Future for Wesley Studies: An Agenda for Phase III."

10. I find the common tendency to dismiss Troeltsch's illuminating comments on the nature of historical investigation as positivistic superficial and uncritical. I stand by my analysis of Troeltsch to be found in *Divine Revelation and Limits of Historical Criticism* (Oxford: Oxford University Press, 1981) chap. 5.

11. Outler reported to some that if he had it do over again he would never have done the work on the sermons of Wesley. I owe this observation to my colleague James Kirby.

12. Bishop Cannon's comment on Outler during the work of commission is fascinating. "Whatever Outler proposed John Cobb opposed. There was constant friction between the two. Outler was of a nervous temperament. He had been accustomed to having his own way in most theological discussions. I was fearful that John Cobb would give him a nervous breakdown. At the end of a day's meeting, I would have to walk with Outler for long periods of time to calm him down enough for him fall asleep." See William Ragsdale Cannon, *A Magnificent Obsession* (Nashville: Abingdon, 1999) 252.

13. This side of Outler is well brought out by Bob W. Parrot, *Albert C. Outler, The Gifted Dilettante* (Wilmore: Bristol, 1999).

14. This observation comes in part from personal conversations with Outler.

PART TWO: CONTRIBUTION TO CURRENT THEOLOGICAL PROBLEMS

the New Testament were inserted in the list of original doctrines purportedly adopted in 1808.[15] Outler's vision was systematically internalized in a whole generation of Wesleyan scholars and church leaders.[16]

Third, Outler's one big idea, the "Quadrilateral," lingers on like a case of the flu, migrating outward through evangelical circles eager to fend off the attractions of fundamentalism and keen to solve the perennial problem of the authority of scripture. Commitment to the "Quadrilateral" is so deep that even objections to it are read as presupposing its validity.[17] To attack the "Quadrilateral," it is now repeatedly said, is to use the "Quadrilateral"; even Immanuel Kant failed to find a transcendental argument as quick and easy as this one. For the record, my own deepest objections to the Quadrilateral have been epistemological.[18] If we want to use the infelicitous language of the past, my

---

15. Both these innovations remain in the current *Book of Discipline* of The United Methodist Church.

16. Consider the following splendid summary of the Outlerian orthodoxy provided by a current candidate for the episcopacy from the Texas Conference of The United Methodist Church. "Pluralism in its finest form is the offering of diverse and varied opinions, giving credence to the assumption that 'our differences enrich us.' I feel that because there are legitimate ideas, opinions and voices of a theological nature which are different from our own creates full participation in the body of Christ known as The Church. However, if The United Methodist Church makes an effort to 'be all things to all people,' we would soon realize that the tapestry on which our faith is woven would soon be ripped apart and irreparably damaged. This is where the genius of Wesley comes to the forefront. The boundaries that determine theological pluralism were defined 200 years ago by John Wesley, and are distinctly laid out for us through his understanding of scripture. tradition, reason, and experience. Our Doctrinal Standards and Theological Task which are included in *The Book of Discipline* say to me that we can be open to different theological points of view, but they must be 'filtered through' and 'framed' within the context of Wesley's quadrilateral." See "Responses to the Questionnaire for Episcopal Candidates South Central Jurisdiction," by Dr. Robert E. "Bob" Hayes Jr., Texas Annual Conference, privately circulated (Feb. 19, 2004) 6.

17. Outler's ambitious project had at least four elements, beginning with his proposals about the "Quadrilateral." I do not think it is too much to say that the whole of the Outler project stands or falls by the "Quadrilateral." He made the significance of the "Quadrilateral" abundantly clear in his "A New Future for Wesley Studies: An Agenda for Phase III." That bet has failed. Outler's whole project also depended, secondly, on a utopian historical agenda that expected far too much from historical investigation in the resolution of theological questions. I think that that bet fails because theological problems simply cannot be resolved by historical investigation. The third bet (and this time the issue is material rather than methodological or formal) Outler made was his deployment of Wesley's vision of the Christian life (his "resolution" of the grace/works debate) as somehow pivotal in resolving longstanding log-jams between East and West. Clearly this bet has been lost as well. This theologically material take on Wesley is well brought out in his "The Place of Wesley in the Christian Tradition," in Kenneth E. Rowe, ed., *The Place of Wesley in the Christian Tradition* (Metuchen, NJ: Scarecrow, 1976) 11–38. The fourth and final bet was on the ecumenical movement. That bet is now also in serious trouble. It needs to be clearly recognized how comprehensive the Outler agenda was. He had a persistent passion to turn the tide of modernity and to secure a future for the Christian faith in the face of the towering challenges it faced. One can see his boldness and depth in part by comparing his comprehensive theological agenda with that of his colleague at Perkins School of Theology, Schubert Ogden. Outler opted for an historical agenda centered on Wesley; Ogden opted for a philosophical agenda centered on Whitehead and Hartshorne. There is a fascinating story to be told at this point, but it cannot be pursued here. I consider it a great privilege to share the same faculty as these remarkable theologians.

18. See, for instance, my *Waking From Doctrinal Amnesia* (Nashville: Abingdon, 1996). My objections to the "Quadrilateral" are manifold and bear repeating here. 1) It involves a serious misreading of Wesley's complex and incomplete epistemology of theology. 2) It sets an impossible standard, in that nobody can seriously execute the tasks involved. Only God could use the "Quadrilateral," and presumably God does not

objections are derived from reason and experience; they do not at all presuppose a commitment to the "Quadrilateral."

Fourth, though Outler had very few graduate students, he managed to inspire a generation of assiduous scholars, who have benefited from his prodigious and insightful labors, and who have sometimes all too readily picked up his ideological bad habits. One of his former students repeatedly shared the joke that made the rounds after Vatican II that Outler had come back from Rome with a bad dose of creeping infallibility. Certainly, he was rarely lacking in self-confidence in public, a feature of his character that always made it a joy to hear him speak. I was once in a question and answer session with him at a meeting of the Oxford Institute of Methodist Theological Studies in which he kept questions at bay for ninety minutes by the simple trick of drawing breath in the middle of a sentence. Even then, we were given an extraordinary display of rhetoric and learning that made us readily ignore or forgive his refusal to hear contrary voices. He was an inspiration to most who heard him. We are all in his debt, albeit in radically different ways, as befits the impact of a very complex person and scholar.

Consider now the wealth of material that had emerged from the post-Outler and post-Baker era. I am going to assume at this point that most of us are familiar with the texts behind the names. I am further going to assume that I will offend someone by an omission here or there.[19] The really interesting stuff lies on the other side of the typology that follows. Of course, any typology we propose at this point will be controversial, but we can make progress initially by using Outler's practice of playing off the extremes against the center.

Think of the playing field like this. On the far right we can place the work of Allan Coppedge; on the far left we can place the work of Theodore W. Jennings Jr.. For Coppedge Wesley is best seen as a fundamentalist holiness preacher and leader; for Jennings he is a wobbly Liberation theologian. Right of center we can locate the portrait of Laurence Wood; left of center we can place the portrait of Ted Runyon. For Wood Wesley is a proto-Pentecostal theologian; for Runyon he is a proto-Liberation theologian. Coming in further towards the center from the right we have Kenneth Collins; and coming in

---

need it. 3) It provides for quick and easy proofs of critical Christian doctrine. The doctrine of the Trinity is easily proved, for example, given its secure place in the tradition of the Church. If it is contained in tradition, then it is contained in a combination of scripture, tradition, reason, and experience. 4) It treats scripture and tradition as epistemic concepts on a par with reason and experience, an obvious category mistake. 5) When push comes to shove, as it inevitably will, reason and experience will be privileged over scripture and tradition because the former are logically prior to the latter. 6) Epistemologically it is severely underdeveloped, assuming that we know what to make of reason and experience. 7) It omits the critical concept of special revelation from any serious place in the epistemology of theology. 8) Given that the primary warrant for the "Quadrilateral" is that it is constitutive of Wesley historically, what we really have on offer is a cult of John Wesley disguised as a scholarly project. 9) My relentless opposition to the "Quadrilateral" is fuelled not by my fighting Irish temperament but by my sense of shame that Wesleyan theologians have been so smug in the arena of epistemology and so ignorant of the revolutionary work done in the field over the last forty years. Using (and abusing) the "Quadrilateral" has become an excuse for various intellectual vices that Wesley would have excoriated.

19. I make no claim to being comprehensive. Adding or subtracting a name will not alter the argument I am about to make.

further towards the center from the left we have Donald Dayton. For Collins Wesley is a revivalist Anglican; for Dayton he is a soft Liberation theologian with Pentecostal temptations. And then there are all those folk who lay claim to the center: Randy Maddox, Ted Campbell, Robert Tuttle, Stephen Gunter, Henry H. Knight III, Gregory Clapper, Scott Jones, Rebecca Miles, Rex Matthews, Philip Meadows, David Hempton, Thomas Oden, David Watson, Douglas Meeks, Theodore R. Weber, John Cobb, Robert Monk, Thomas Langford, Ann Taves, and Geoffrey Wainwright. Taken together we might say that the portraits of Wesley that emerge in the center are not far from that of a liberal evangelical, or of a catholic evangelical, or of an evangelical liberal, but these hackneyed labels cannot do justice to the diversity exhibited. However we draw up the typology, one conclusion is clear: there are as many Wesleys as there are Wesley scholars. Once we add, as we must, that there is an early, middle, and late Wesley, the number multiplies by three.[20] The quest for the historical Wesley has morphed into a discovery of the Wesleys of faith, with Wesley turning out to be very much like the mirror images of the historians under review.[21] This accounts for the degree of polemic and passion that we currently see, say, between Kenneth Collins and Randy Maddox,[22] between Donald Dayton and Laurence Wood,[23] between Joerg Rieger and Scott Jones,[24] and between William Abraham and Gregory Clapper.[25]

Expressed slightly differently, we have seen over time how Wesley has been brought into play in the rival theologies on offer in the tradition that bears his name across the centuries since he died. His legacy is a contested one that has been claimed by Revivalists and Institutionalists, by Social Gospellers and Personalists, by Fundamentalists and Modernists, by Liberals and Conservatives, by Liberationists and Pietists, by Radicals and Moderates, by Revisionists and Traditionalists, by Marginalists and Centrists, by Systematicians and Occasionalists, by Inclusivists and Exclusivists, by Feminists and Patriarchialists, by Holiness Advocates and Pentecostals, by Conventionalists and Charismatics, and by Confessionalists and Pluralists.

For my part I see this development as a cause for celebration. Gilbert Murray once insisted that the best traditions produce the best rebels. By this criterion Wesley has had a terrific run for his money, even though the rebels have found ingenious ways to mask their rebellion as forms of loyalty. More charitably, we might say that historical theology, that is, the deployment of a great figure of the past as a platform for contemporary theological

---

20. I leave aside what secular historians have made of Wesley of late.

21. For a little gem of a paper that made a similar point some thirty years ago, see Kenneth E. Rowe, "The Quest for the Historical Wesley," in Kenneth E. Rowe, ed., *The Place of Wesley in the Christian Tradition*, 1–7. Rowe suggests that a the great variety of labels he noted might be due to faults in the editions used; perhaps he hoped that the new critical edition of the Wesley corpus would narrow the range of options available; if he did, he was clearly mistaken.

22. One critical issue between them is the understanding of sanctification.

23. The central issue revolves around the place and significance of baptism in the Holy Spirit in Wesley and in Pentecostalism.

24. The primary issue in this case is whether we should see Wesley as a centrist or at the margins.

25. The fundamental dispute here is how to read the significance of affections in our evaluation of Wesley's theology.

commitment, has flourished in the Wesleyan tradition. Wesley has proved to be a fecund source of inspiration; he let loose a torrent of ideas and practices that have flowed well beyond the banks of the Methodist mainstream and formed their own rivers and lakes. His legacy has also furnished a point of entry to radically different forms of Christian thought and practice and a fertile field for inventive borrowing and creative innovation. Much as Wesley may not have wanted it, he created and let loose a tradition that from the beginning was unstable. Like it or not, he inspired a network of ecclesial communities that fostered a latitudinarianism that he himself vehemently rejected. The continued use and abuse of his sermon, "Catholic Spirit," is ample testimony to his inability to prevent the development of incoherent forms of ecclesial pluralism. His followers have scattered like sheep to a thousand hills to find pasture. They have migrated to Evangelicalism, to Feminism, to Narrative theology, to Liberation theology, to Process theology, to Karl Barth, to John Howard Yoder, to Michael Foucault, to Rosemary Ruether, to anything and everything under the theological sun.

What is cause for celebration is also cause for stocktaking. Three points emerge immediately.

First, what the Roman Catholic Church did to Thomas Aquinas in the eighteen seventies, Wesleyans did to Wesley in the nineteen sixties. Effectively, despite our Protestant commitments, we tried to canonize Wesley as a Doctor of the Church. The originating causes were analogous. Like Pope Leo XIII, we were in search of theory of authority that would meet the challenges of the day. More specifically, we were looking for one more way to fix once and for all the problem of the authority of scripture. The outcome in both cases was the same. The quest for the historical Wesley has proved to be as elusive as the quest for the historical Aquinas. Within forty years there were so many different visions of Aquinas theology emerging that even Karl Rahner and Joseph Ratzinger were able to make it past the gatekeepers with their idiosyncratic updates of Thomas in hand, even though in their cases it was a close call. The Wesleyans have their gatekeepers (they are located in the editorial boards of publishing houses), but they have not been able to secure an agreed vision of Wesley. Wesley, like Aquinas, has become the site of rival contemporary theological proposals that were presented or masked as historical investigation. In the end Roman Catholic scholarship came to terms with the diversity of Aquinas. As I have argued above, this is precisely the stage we have reached in Wesley studies: we are immersed in a sea of competing portraits. In our case there will be no Vatican II to sort things through; it will all be a matter of the contingencies of our scholarship.[26]

Second, the crucial problem that the quest for the historical Wesley was meant to resolve remains as thorny as ever. The problem of the authority of scripture is as big a problem as ever in contemporary Protestantism. Outler's attempt to salvage Wesley's vision of scripture by arguing that he offers us a unique theological method enshrined in the "Quadrilateral" is neither true to the historical Wesley, nor will it work as a normative epistemological agenda. The shift from modernity to postmodernity may have taken the passion out of the issue, but the underlying epistemological issues remain as unresolved

---

26. If things proceed as they have with Thomas Aquinas we are in for a bumper crop of work over the next thirty years.

as before. They cannot be resolved by historical investigation; they are inescapably philosophical and normative in nature; the very idea of solving them by appeal to Wesley is a category mistake.[27] In my judgment the very idea of the authority of scripture, crucial as it was in the recovery of the Bible at the Reformation, has outlived its usefulness. As I shall note below, claims about the authority of scripture have killed Protestantism from within.[28]

Third, effectively this plethora of historical Wesleys signals the end of Wesleyan theology.[29] As a specific, determinate experiment in the history of Western theology, Methodism is now over. This does not mean that the institutions and ecclesial bodies invented by Wesley and his followers have ceased to exist; these will continue to wind their way through the course of history as best they can.[30] The historical investigation of the last thirty years constitutes a very long obituary notice. In an earlier address to this body, I argued that the critical missiological agenda of Wesley together with the practices that were constitutive of it have been abandoned.[31] At that time I also noted that the acids of criticism from within have eaten away the background theological assumptions on which Wesley critically depended, so that there is now in place a pluralism of background assumptions that do the theological heavy lifting. The material theologies that result, and that are now clearly visible, are only secondarily Wesleyan. Their deep inspiration and their core commitments are derived from non-Wesleyan sources. So in that paper my argument was more indirect.

My argument here is more direct. It is not just Methodism as a determinate experiment that is over and gone; so too is Wesleyan theology in any meaningful or robust sense of that term. Wesley has become a historical cipher for our diverse and competing contemporary commitments. Where there was once a time when there existed a relatively coherent set of ideas and correlative practices, these have now collapsed and been replaced by competing alternatives. What is gone is a coherent experiment in theology that bears any kind of robust continuity with Wesley. The great hymns are no longer sung; the

---

27. It is perhaps this mistake more than any other that bedeviled the Outler agenda. Outler was well aware of the constant dangers of eisegesis in the study of Wesley, but he never faced up to this as a live option in his own work. Perhaps we should also take much more seriously the possibility that he really was a dilettante when it came to crucial sectors of work in theology.

28. This does not mean that the issues that the idea of biblical authority was designed to resolve disappear. On the contrary, we now have to reformulate the issues in a more appropriate manner and then set about finding appropriate solutions. For me the debate about the authority of scripture needs to be reformulated as a quest for an adequate vision of canon and as a quest for a really compelling epistemology of theology.

29. On at least one occasion it is interesting to note that Wesley worried that reading history would come to supplant the cause of God's work in the priorities of his preachers. "I fear there is altogether a fault in this matter, and that few of us are clear. Which of you spends as many hours a day in God's work as you did formerly in man's work? We talk,—or read history, or what comes next to hand. We must, absolutely must, cure this evil, or betray the cause of God." See *Minutes of Several Conversations* in *Works*, vol. 8, 314–15. It is clear that Wesley himself loved reading history and derived much spiritual benefit from it.

30. They do so committed *de facto* to a congregationalist ecclesiology where local clergy and their congregations effectively go their own ways.

31. See "Saving Souls: A Missiological Midrash on John Wesley," in *WTJ*.

fervent sacramentalism has been eroded; the robust orthodoxy has been undermined; the commitment to the poor has become a normative ideology; the evangelistic fervor has been sidelined; the biblical literacy has been lost; the official, canonical doctrines of the tradition are despised or are idling; and the specific doctrines of new birth, assurance, perfection, and predestination are unknown or received with consternation.[32] What we have are bits and pieces of the tradition grafted into theological visions that have their roots elsewhere. As a serious experiment in theology, Wesleyanism is over. The wake may have been a long one, but the funeral is now upon us. To be sure some are in denial, and others are wrangling over the reading of the will and the ownership of the last legacy, but the reality is that Wesleyans have moved on and found new lives and lovers.

On my own theological reading of Wesley, I think that this quest for new lovers was inevitable. Think of it this way. Wesley at his core was a staunch Protestant Biblicist. Drawing on a medieval vision of divine revelation, he was convinced that all proper theology had to be grounded in scripture. Whatever bells and whistles we want to add either epistemologically or hermeneutically to this thesis, the ultimate test of truth in theology for Wesley was scripture.[33] This immediately undercuts any idea of appeal to Wesley as a warrant in theology; on pain of inconsistency the warrant simply has to be scripture not Wesley. Thus from the beginning, the idea of accepting anything because it is Wesleyan involves introducing a warrant that is not available to a Wesleyan. At best, appeal to Wesley can operate as a criterion of identity; it cannot operate as a criterion of credibility or truth. Furthermore, given that there is no agreed theology in scripture, or given that scripture provides a license for a plethora of competing theologies, it was inevitable that over time Wesley's own reading of scripture would collapse and be replaced by other readings by his own followers. Thus, unless we are doomed to settle into an incoherent Wesleyan scholasticism, instability and disagreement were inescapable and inevitable over time.

In turn such instability and disagreement led some to develop a revisionist construal of biblical authority or to look for other foundations of theology outside of scripture. These moves simply added to the instability and disagreement.[34] We were furnished with another network of theological options and systems derived from suitably revised epistemological visions. Sooner or later the results of such work was bound to appear at odds with the original Wesleyan construal of scriptural teaching; the dissonance between the two has now become plain to discerning observers. To face up to this yawning gap as reality is to stare death in the face. The quest for the historical Wesley over the last generation was, in these circumstances, a loyalist strategy to keep the truth at bay. It was a playing for time; it was a clear sign that the tradition is the final stages of decline and decay. What we were promised was a compelling portrait intended to breathe new life into the tradition; what we got was a round of obituary notices that signify that we have just laid the body to rest.

32. I have found that the last two are simply non-starters among contemporary United Methodists.

33. Wesley even sought to ground his epistemological proposals on scripture.

34. Robert E. Chiles, *Theological Transition in American Methodism, 1790–1935* (New York: University Press of America, 1983) remains the classic rendering of this thesis.

PART TWO: CONTRIBUTION TO CURRENT THEOLOGICAL PROBLEMS

So the Wesleyan tradition, like the earlier traditions spawned by the great Reformers before him, has gone the way of all flesh. Yet one more noble Protestant experiment has run its course. One of the lesser tribes of Israel has expired. He who has been regarded as the least of the theologians in the line of the Reformation has been brought to his final resting place. One more noble and wonderful experiment within Protestantism has failed. The deadly virus of *sola scriptura* and the epistemologies it has spawned has once more killed its followers. Once more the faith of the Church has been splintered in pieces and scattered to the winds. Once more, it has been a case of death by our own hands. Once more, we have participated in and witnessed yet another grand funeral within Protestantism.

Funerals are usually solemn and sad occasions. They can be celebrations of lives well lived. They are also a time of freedom, when those left behind are released into a new future, however painful that future may be. In this instance, insofar as we accept the core of my argument, we will have our own way of laying hold of our freedom. For my part I suggest the following tasks as having some purchase upon us as scholars of Wesley. The first two are historical in nature and the third is metatheological.

First, the historical work will and should continue unabated. Here I remained committed to the ideals of "classical" historical investigation. Oliver O'Donovan captures the matter nicely. Speaking of the study of the Thirty Nine Articles, he writes: "In conducting a study the scholar puts his intellectual powers completely at the service of the text, and makes it his only business to enable the text to speak clearly. It is a weakness in his work if his own concerns and the fashions of his time intrude."[35] The necessary transposition to Wesley is obvious. Our primary object of attention is Wesley, his life and work in his time and context, and the chief business of the historian is to enable Wesley to speak clearly, whatever we may think of what he did or said. Of course, historians and philosophers will take issue with this historiographical vision, but such disagreement is secondary. However we conceive of historical investigation, we all agree that Wesley should be studied historically with all the creativity and rigor we can muster. As I see it, we need to renegotiate how best to read his background in seventeenth and eighteenth century Anglicanism and then relocate Wesley very firmly within this world. In short, we have got to reconsider and rework the background music of the Enlightenment that has had such a grip on our imaginations and hear a quite different set of tunes. We have to come to terms with the radically confessional nature of the state and church to which Wesley belonged. Once we do this, we will have to recalibrate much of what we say about Wesley. The portrait of Wesley, when we do so, will be quite different from of the options currently on offer.[36]

This suggestion is, of course, a point about the macro-narrative in which we locate Wesley. My second is in the neighborhood. We also need to ferret out those neglected elements in the micro-narrative of Wesley that are hard to hear today. Take for instance his vision of double predestination. This was more than a polemical aside in his debates

---

35. Oliver O'Donovon, *On the Thirty Nine Articles: A Conversation with Tudor Christianity* (Exeter: Paternoster, 1986) 7.

36. I plan to explore this option in a short, introductory volume on Wesley in the near future.

with the Calvinists. I suspect that it was pivotal in his deep sense of the sovereignty of a God of unconditional goodness that was bedrock in his theology as a whole and crucial to his self-confident leadership of Methodism. Or consider his thoroughgoing supernaturalism. His feisty reply to Conyers Middleton was not just a skirmish about miracles. Wesley, like John Henry Newman a century later, saw that a principled attack on the miracles of the church could not be halted at the doors of the canon of scripture. As the subsequent history shows, far more was at stake for our general understanding of the world, for our conception of critical investigation, and for our expectations in ministry in the present. Or consider his doctrine of assurance enshrined in the witness of the Holy Spirit. It is remarkable how well Wesley is truer to Paul on this topic than the whole history of Protestantism, yet it remains an enigma in modern Wesleyan circles.[37] Or consider his vision of Christian perfection. This is really the mad theological aunt in the basement of Wesley's theology. She deserves a fresh, sympathetic visit now that we have had a spirited revision of what happened to the doctrine of the baptism of the Holy Spirit after Fletcher of Madeley initiated by the controversial work of Laurence Wood and now that we know that the effort to assimilate Wesley's perfectionist vision to a generic vision of *theosis* in Eastern Orthodoxy has limited hermeneutical value.

Neither of these suggestions comes close to registering the magnitude of the theological crisis that faces us within the Wesleyan tradition. Indeed, as I have already intimated, the turn to history is often a strategy of denial, so burying ourselves in the historical agendas I have just enumerated may well be a sophisticated evasion. We have surely a problem on our hands that cannot be resolved by more historical excavation. We have to find a whole new way do theology beyond Wesley and even beyond the Protestantism of which he is a paradigm instantiation. As I see the landscape, and as I have argued on a larger canvas elsewhere, the death of our own tradition is simply a microcosm of the death of Protestantism itself.[38] We are at the end of the line where Protestant theology is concerned; five hundred magnificent years of theology have come to an end. Epistemology has destroyed us from within.[39] We can no longer dress up our contemporary theological commitments in Wesleyan garb. The shroud of Wesley has been shredded by our historical work; it is no longer available for rent. We have to go home from the funeral in peace; and we must openly, explicitly, and self-consciously find a new theological future. Of course we can expect that all sorts of insights from Wesley will have a place in that future. However, Wesley's contribution is strictly limited; we can no longer ignore his severe limitations or hide behind his skirts. We must now speak in our own voice and take full responsibility before God and before each other for what we say and how we say it.

---

37. For Wesley, as for Paul, the inner witness of the Holy Spirit spoke to the issue of our relationship of sonship to God; it did not speak to the issue of what books belong in the canon of scripture.

38. This is the upshot of my *Canon and Criterion in Christian Theology: From the Fathers to Feminism* (Oxford: Clarendon, 1998).

39. In these circumstances, postmodernity is not medicine; unless radically relativized, it is likely to be another dose of poison that will simply kill those who look to it for salvation. Nor can we be saved by turning to Roman Catholicism, for Roman Catholicism, as we know it today, is simply one more effort to fix the Protestantism it inevitably spawned.

PART TWO: CONTRIBUTION TO CURRENT THEOLOGICAL PROBLEMS

In the meantime what shall we do with our beloved Wesley? I finish with a hint that dovetails nicely with the theme of death and funerals. When they came to bury John Wesley in City Road, London, the liturgist made a fascinating and unrehearsed change in the wording of the Anglican service. Coming to that point in the service where they committed his body to the ground, earth to earth, ashes to ashes, the liturgist could not use the designation "our brother." Instead, by a spontaneous and extraordinary shift, he designated Wesley as "our Father." Consider now the amazing report of Tyerman of another event, this time after the funeral. "The notice to his friends was short; but hundreds attended; and to each was given a biscuit, in an envelope, engraved with a beautifully executed portrait of the departed, dressed in full canonicals, *surmounted by a halo and a crown.*"[40]

What we see here is the natural and entirely apt recognition of Wesley as an evangelist, spiritual Father, and saint. This designation of Wesley as a evangelist, saint, and spiritual Father in God is, of course, pastoral and religious; to see it as sexist is to reveal our bondage to the shibboleths of our own day. It means that Wesley, as an agent of the Holy Spirit, had operated in his day first and foremost as a spiritual midwife who brought thousands of people to birth in the womb of the Gospel. In an inimitable and wonderful way he helped people find God in conversion, became a model for them of the spiritual life, and provided a network of resources to nourish genuine holiness.[41]

The liturgist at the funeral was not the first to recognize the proper status of Wesley in our tradition. There is a wonderful witness to Wesley along these lines in the remarkable description of Wesley penned by a total outsider to Methodism in 1769. The author is Professor Johan Henrik Liden of the University of Uppsala in Sweden. Note in what follows how Wesley is identified as a spiritual Father and compared to the apostle John.

> Today I learned for the first time to know Mr. John Wesley, so well known here in England, and called the *spiritual Father of the so-called Methodists*. He arrived home from his summer journey to Ireland, where he visited his people. He preached today at the forenoon service in the Methodist Chapel in Spitafield for an audience of more than 4,000 people. His text was Luke 1:68. The sermon was short but eminently evangelical. He has not great oratorical gifts, no outward appearance, but he speaks clear and pleasant. After the Holy Communion, which in all English Churches is held with closed doors at the end of the preaching service, when none but the Communicants are usually present, and which here was celebrated very orderly and pathetic. I went forward to shake hands with Mr. Wesley, who already . . . knew my name, and was received by him in his usual amiable and friendly way. He is a small, thin old man, with his own and long and strait hair, and looks as the worst country curate in Sweden, but has learning as a Bishop and zeal for the glory of God which is quite extraordinary. His talk is very agreeable, and his mild face and pious manner secure him the love of all rightminded men. He is the personification

---

40. See L. Tyerman, *The Life and Times of the Rev. John Wesley* (New York: Harper, 1872) 3:656. Emphasis added.

41. It is worth remembering here that Wesley clearly saw himself as a Father in God to Francis Asbury, as is clear from his correspondence. I am grateful to my colleague James Kirby for drawing this to my attention.

of piety, and he seems to me as *a living representation of the loving Apostle John.* The old man Wesley is already 66 years, but very lively and exceedingly industrious.[42]

Canonical status in the wider Christian world has always been developed from the bottom up rather than from the top down; Wesley is no exception to this rule; and it is what we see happening in this description and in the events at his funeral. The aftermath of Wesley more than amply bears witness to the drive to perceive Wesley as a saint, evangelist, and as a spiritual Father in God. The vast iconography spawned by Wesley bears extraordinary testimony to his spiritual impact across the generations. Wesley was (and) is so important spiritually that he deserves to be painted larger than life and hung on the walls of our offices and church halls. Spiritually speaking, it is a deep mistake to restrict ourselves to the hard and fast rules of good historical scholarship in its quest for the real physical portrait of Wesley. We should also mention in this regard the wonderful hagiography that persists despite the labor of historians and critics. Wesley cannot be contained within the boundaries of our critical, clinical, historical scholarship; the spiritual treasure that he is by grace deserves the creative hand of pious exaggeration and romantic hyperbole.[43] The spiritual jewel that he is also shows up in the setting aside of sacred sites at City Road, London, at the New Rooms in Bristol, and in Lincoln College, Oxford. It is equally manifest in the ineradicable drive to engage in pilgrimage to those sites. It is, moreover, visible in the long-lasting tendency to name children after Wesley. Perhaps even more important is the formal canonization of a set of standard sermons in British and Irish Methodism. His sermons became in time so valuable in The United Methodist Church that they were unconstitutionally shoehorned into the canonical material of that church in 1972.[44] This was juridically wrong but spiritually correct. Happily, neither the staunch formal Protestantism of the Methodist movement nor the scoldings of the historians have been unable to keep the informal canonization of Wesley at bay. Wesley as an evangelist, spiritual Father, and saint simply outstrips our narrow, secularist strictures; he bursts through the boundaries of our inventive theological projections and still finds a way into the hearts of folk desperate to find food for their souls.[45]

It is here, with Wesley as our spiritual Father in God, that we can still find solace. John Wesley is not some norm of truth; nor is he a folk theologian waiting to be organized into a systematic theologian; nor is he merely our brother in the faith; nor is he a

---

42. See Richard Heitzenrater, *The Elusive Mr. Wesley* (Nashville: Abingdon, 1984) 2:87–88. Emphasis added.

43. I can still recall as a teenager after my conversion reading my first great piece of Wesleyan hagiography, John Wesley Bready's *England: Before and After Wesley* (New York: Harper, 1938). It nurtured my soul in the midst of backbreaking, soul-destroying work in East Anglia in England.

44. It is a great pity that we do not have a handy and attractive copy of the standard forty-four sermons that are available in Britain. It is one thing to have a set of sermons selected for historical investigation in the seminary or university; it is another to have a set clearly designed as Wesley designed them for spiritual nourishment.

45. John M. Todd makes some tantalizing but perhaps exaggerated comparisons between Wesley and St. John of the Cross and St. Francis. See his *John Wesley and the Catholic Church* (London: Hodder & Stoughton, 1958). Todd reported that he prayed privately to Wesley, a practice permitted to him within his Roman Catholic tradition.

doctor of the church; nor is he a prince of the church. He was and continues to be for many a spiritual Father in God. He was and is a minister of the gospel who has birthed us indirectly in the faith. He is a thinker and spiritual guide who has gone on to Glory and whose work, with all its shortsightedness and shortcomings, can still bring us to God and foster holiness of life and thought. In short, he belongs in the canon of spiritual Fathers and saints.[46] While we have no ecclesial mechanism for formally making this move, this is where he belongs: in the list of spiritual Fathers and saints of the Church. Thereby he brings us into a wholly different way of thinking about the wider canonical heritage of the Church. It is within the bosom of that wider canonical heritage of the Church that we will find the full salvation of our souls. It is also within that canonical heritage that we will find the charter for a whole new way of doing theology. That last claim is not a claim I can explore today, but it is one I will gladly make good on in the future.[47]

So then I bring before you bad news and good news, one piece of bad news and two pieces of good news. The bad news is that half a century of splendid historical investigation has unwittingly become a worthy obituary notice for the death of the Wesleyan theological tradition. The good news is that we are now free to stop pretending that Wesley is a great theologian (or even a theologian) and to receive him for what he is, an extraordinary evangelist, great saint, and a remarkable spiritual Father in God. The other good news is that the funeral of Wesleyan theology is a clarion call for a radically fresh start in theology for all those who acknowledge John Wesley as a spiritual Father in God and as a saint of modern Protestantism.

---

46. It may seem farfetched to deploy this sort of language within Protestantism, but in fact it crops up *de facto* all the time at a popular level. There is a very definite though informal canon of Protestant heroes and heroines floating around. One encounters it explicitly from time to time. See, for example, Ernest Gordon, *A Book of Protestant Saints* (Chicago: Moody, 1946). Gordon uses the criteria of biblical commitment, the presence of miracle (understood broadly), and appropriate deathbed scenes. Clearly Wesley fits these criteria without difficulty.

47. For a more extended promissory note, see the last chapter of *The Logic of Renewal* (Grand Rapids: Eerdmans, 2003).

8

Sketching a Fundamental Wesleyan Theology
Pursuing a Hermeneutic of Love with Augustine's De Doctrina Christiana

NATHAN CRAWFORD

AFTER READING HIS WORK as an undergraduate, I first encountered Laurence Wood the person as a student at Asbury Theological Seminary. Here, I was drawn to Dr. Wood as he and I shared similar influences and concerns. Specifically, what drew me to Dr. Wood was the fact that he was working out a Wesleyan theology in conversation with sources that were not typically Wesleyan. He also thought extensively through the philosophical tradition, especially as it stemmed from Kant and running through Hegel, Nietzsche, Heidegger, and Ricoeur. As a student, he helped me to open myself to the questions that these thinkers were asking and how this may change the way that we did theology, specifically Wesleyan theology. Not only this, but as a person Dr. Wood was able to display a way of being that exhibited his theology was not merely of the head, but overflowed from the heart.

In the midst of my time being associated with Dr. Wood, I have noticed a relatively large hole in the project of Wesleyan theology: the failure to work out a fundamental theology that is distinctively Wesleyan. It is this hole that the following argument seeks to fill. I do not propose to offer a complete solution, but to sketch a way forward. The way I do this is to argue that what makes a Wesleyan theology distinctive is that the starting point is not a specific doctrine or method, but a disposition and way of being. This disposition is one of love, both love of God and love of neighbor. So, in what follows, I pursue a hermeneutic of love that begins from the place of both loving and being loved; this becomes the beginning point of any theology that marks itself as Wesleyan.

In order to accomplish my task, I will take three steps. First, I will articulate what makes a fundamental theology Wesleyan by pursuing the place of disposition in theology. Next, in order to more fully articulate the way this disposition is one of love, I will turn to St. Augustine's *De Doctrina Christiana*,[1] which articulates his account of how to best

---

1. Augustine, *Teaching Christianity*, The Works of St. Augustine: A Translation for the 21st Century I/11, trans. Edmund Hill, O.P. (Hyde Park, NY: New City, 1996). All references to *De Doctrina Christiana* will be

be an interpreter of Scripture through a hermeneutic of love that comes through a way of life and in a rhetoric. Third, I show that this way of life and rhetoric is dependent upon the event of love in the incarnation of God in the person of Jesus. This results in a transformation of the person, which gives the disposition to be in such a way as to be able to do theology. The result of my exposition will be a sketch of what a fundamental Wesleyan theology may look like. This will also serve as a beginning point for those theologians who come from the Wesleyan tradition to go beyond some of the typical Wesleyan constructs.

PURSUING A FUNDAMENTAL WESLEYAN THEOLOGY

In order to begin sketching a fundamental Wesleyan theology, we must first ask what makes Wesleyan theology distinctive. By pursuing the Wesleyan distinctive, we will see the way to be open to the beginning of theology in the Wesleyan strain. This will also propel us into the rest of the argument, as I believe that it is the pursuit of perfect love that is the distinctively Wesleyan move in theology. By putting love at the center of the theological endeavor, Wesleyans do theology in a more originary way, beginning from the experience of love found both in God and neighbor.

We see the Wesleyan impetus for this beginning in John Wesley himself. In his "A Plain Account of The People Called Methodists," Wesley writes what could be described as both a description and apology for the Methodist movement. One of the first things he does in the treatise is to lay out the main four points upon which Methodism insists. The first is that religion is not merely orthodoxy or orthopraxy, but the pursuing of "the mind that was in Christ" leading to righteousness. Second, Methodists insisted upon the fact that the only way to attain righteousness was through repentance and the placing of faith in Jesus Christ. Third, faith in Jesus Christ is what leads to being justified by God's grace alone, opening the path for redemption. And, fourth, this justification is not merely the cleansing of sin, but is the making of a person who is "holy and happy," abandoning sin to dwell with Christ.[2] As Wesley goes on to describe the way the Methodists have helped people attain the life of holiness and happiness, we see the consistent move on his part to not talk of getting them to believe rightly, but *be* rightly. In fact, the entire goal of the movement is to make sure that the people are built up in their faith, rejoicing in God and living the abundant life of love, strengthened to do good works.[3] We see, then, through this treatise on the very foundations of the Methodist movement that for Wesleyans the goal is not just to believe rightly or parse theology correctly, but to exist in such a way as to pursue God through love. The goal of the movement was to create people who had the correct way of being, and this lead to a people who were able to do theology and minister to others.

---

to this translation, with the letters "DDC," and refer to the book and paragraph per this translation.

2 John Wesley, "A Plain Account of the People Called Methodists," in *The Works of John Wesley*, volume 8 (Grand Rapids: Baker, 2002) 249.

3. Ibid., 259.

If the goal of the Methodist movement is to create people who pursued a certain way of life, this was due to the fact that central to the Wesleyan understanding of Christianity was the fact that transformation could occur. Wesleyan theology embraces a theology that begins from the disposition of love due to the belief that transformation of the theologian occurs, that one goes from "bondage to adoption."[4] Wesley says that as a person encounters God, "there is a total change" where one's eyes are opened to see, one's ears opened to hear, one's entire being changed to feel the presence of God. The goal of this is not just to be justified, but to move to perfect love, to holiness, where love of world is displaced due to one's continued growth in love of God.[5] We see, then, the transformation of the person to being a person of love due to the encounter one has with God through the redeeming work of Jesus Christ.

As we have seen, then, a distinctively Wesleyan theology must begin from the place of pursuing love. This is not about a right belief or action, but an entire way of life. For the Wesleyan, theology begins from the very existence of a person who has been changed through an encounter with Jesus Christ. Thus, part of any Wesleyan theology must also take into account the nature of transformation. Thus, a fundamental Wesleyan theology must articulate what it means to have a disposition of love, how this comes about through transformation, and how this enacts the beginning of theology. In what follows, I will articulate this through a discussion of Augustine's *De Doctrina Christiana*. It is my contention that here Augustine pursues a fundamental theology predicated upon a hermeneutic of love. This will help us to be able to sketch a more thoroughly Wesleyan fundamental theology.

LOVE: THE BEGINNING OF THEOLOGY

In order to begin to sketch this hermeneutic of love, I begin with the last book of *De Doctrina Christiana*. We begin here because this is where Augustine shows that the outcome of the previous three books is the formation of a rhetoric for the Christian theologian and minister. The goal, then, of the entire treatise is not to develop the hermeneutical tools that would allow one to interpret rightly, but to develop the person in such a way as to allow them to learn to exist in love so that they may be able to be a proper interpreter of Scripture: the way to this is through the life of love. Augustine will show that it is only in the pursuing of a life of love that one can be rightly disposed to God so as to interpret rightly.

So, we see that the main goal of *De Doctrina Christiana* is not a right method. Augustine is not concerned with performing a correct technique, but developing the person in the right way. This right way is to be properly ordered in love. In Book I, Augustine had already explicated what it would mean to have this proper ordering in love. Following the greatest commandment of Jesus in Matthew, he says that there are

---

4. See John Wesley, "The Spirit of Bondage and Adoption," in *The Works of John Wesley*, volume 5 (Grand Rapids: Baker, 2002) 98–110.

5. John Wesley, "The New Birth," in *The Works of John Wesley*, volume 6 (Grand Rapids: Baker, 2002) 70–71.

two primary loves: love of God and love of neighbor. Under love of neighbor, he also includes love of self, since we are to "love our neighbors as ourselves," per Jesus. Augustine, thus, sees the rightly ordered life of love to be one where a person loves self, loves the neighbor(s), and also loves God; however, the order for this is reversed. Augustine ultimately believes that love of God is most important, with love of neighbor and love of self following. This is because we ultimately love our neighbor and love our self on account of our love of God; but, by loving neighbor and self, we also learn to love God more. We find ourselves wrapped up in the process and movement of love, always with the goal of pursuing love more, thus pursuing God more.[6]

The reason that we can love is because we have first been loved. As we will see in more depth below, the event of Jesus Christ in the Incarnation is the movement of God to humanity in love.[7] We are taught that God does not seek our love first before loving us; rather, God first loves us. God turns Godself to us, attuning Godself to humanity so that humanity may in turn be in tune with God. There is no movement without the first movement of love, which is always God reaching toward humanity and creation in such a way that the creation can in turn reach toward God. This is a double movement of love, where God's love makes possible our love, but, in turn, our love allows more reception of the love of God through God's grace.[8] Thus, love as self-giving, both on the part of God and creation, becomes the center of reflection on the interaction of God and humanity. It becomes the beginning point of any attempt to think through theology. Thus, love becomes the ultimate hermeneutic by which Augustine interprets Scripture and, also, by which one lives life.[9]

The issue for theology, then, is what to do with this double movement of love. We must pursue a mode of interpretation/ understanding for how it is we approach the theological endeavor of thinking about God. But, as Augustine shows us, the goal is not so much the manner or way of doing theology as much as the place from which one goes about beginning the theological endeavor. To begin theology from a place that does not begin with love of God which leads to love of neighbor is to automatically step incorrectly. And, a theology that does not seek to lead us into the movement of love of God and love of neighbor becomes a failure. Rather, the theological endeavor becomes one that begins from the site of love, from the disposition of love necessitate through the double movement of love first initiated by God. So, for Augustine, it does not matter how one interprets or the words one uses of God if one's life does not reflect the transformation that has occurred because of one's encounter with God.[10]

---

6. Augustine, *DDC*, I.27–33.

7. Of course, this is not to say that this is God's only movement toward humanity, just the most explicit.

8. This logic is made explicit in Nicholas of Cusa's *De Visione Dei*, where he articulates that it is first the movement of God in God's looking at humanity that then allows humanity to have a vision of God. The vision of God allows the vision of God. See Nicholas of Cusa, *On the Vision of God*, in *Nicholas of Cusa: Selected Spiritual Writings*, ed. and trans. H. Lawrence Bond (Mahwah: Paulist, 1997) 233–90.

9. See, for example, Augustine, *DDC*, I.39.

10. Ibid., IV.59.

The result of the placing of the double movement of love at the center of theology is a way of life. This way of life, for Augustine, does not result in a right method, but in a rhetoric.[11] The rhetoric that Augustine articulates is not about a right way of speaking from a pulpit either. It is a way of speaking with one's entire existence, showing how one lives in tune with God. The goal of the articulation of Augustine's rhetoric, then, is not a system. He does not want to put together a system for how we are to speak about God. Rather, if God is the one that we love and the one we pursue in love (because God has first pursued us), then theology becomes a way of chasing God in this love. The impetus, then, to try and systematize, totalize, or create hegemony in our thinking on God is a fundamental mistake in Augustine's view. Rather, theology is not a systematic endeavor, but one that seeks to move with God, always breaking the ways that we have "boxed" God. This theology flows out of one's life, where the impetus is to follow God in love, learning to love God more deeply with one's heart, mind, soul, and strength. This love is not an attempt to control, but to be-with. Life, then, becomes the place to begin theological thinking.

The goal of this life does not come from a correct ethical system or right articulation of God's laws. Rather, Augustine places prayer at the center of this life, which leads to a right rhetoric.[12] Prayer is not so much a correct belief system as a crying out to God, a way of being open to God in such a way that we can then hear God, not only in the prayer, but throughout the music of God played in creation. Prayer does not set the right form for speaking and thinking of God, but opens the theologian to the movement of God, making sure that the theologian does not place some idol in the place of God. The resulting language used for God is not a systematic treatise. Rather, the rhetoric the theologian must use is that of praise, due to love.[13] The prayer that attunes the theologian to God results in a theology that praises God when thinking of God. It is a theology that does not seek to determine God, only to follow this God and lead others in the same. It is a theology that seeks to praise God, as well, not only in one's speaking, but also in the life of the theologian through love. This becomes not just the basis for the proper Christian rhetoric, but the rhetoric itself.

In Book I, we see the basis for this rhetoric is the incarnation of the Second Person of the Trinity in the human person of Jesus of Nazareth. Augustine turns to the Christ event—in being born, crucified, resurrected, and ascending—as the basis for the rhetorical life that he develops. The event of Jesus Christ is the basis for the rhetoric because of the way in which the embrace of the incarnation is a cleansing event for the person which results in a removal of those things that keep one from loving God.[14] We are able to develop a way of life from this belief because Jesus shows us the way of life that we must undertake. Jesus' life is a journey that the believer must follow because it is here that we are given not only the power to live, but also the example for the type of life to live.[15]

11. See *DDC*, Book IV, for an exposition of Augustine's pursuit of a Christian rhetoric as way of life.
12. Ibid., IV.32.
13. Ibid., IV.38.
14. Ibid., I.12–18.
15. Ibid., I.11.

The life that Jesus advocates is one that embraces the love of God and looks to spread this love through the embrace of one's neighbor. One's life, following the example of Jesus, becomes the "speaking" of love, the rhetoric upon which one goes about communicating the Gospel. And, the living of this way of life results in the ability to not only "speak" love with one's actions, but to "speak" love through one's theology.[16]

It is important to note, here, thought that Book I does not set the content or system for which this rhetoric must speak. Rather, it opens the way in which the theologian can be formed and attuned—or, the right disposition—in such a way as to be able to "speak" this rhetoric through the way of life exemplified by Jesus. Book I shows the impetus for the hermeneutic of love as the incarnation which thus becomes the basis for Augustine's rhetoric.

Again, though, this rhetoric of love does not set the content or systematize the way that theology must be done. The type of theological thinking that Augustine lays out for us is not a totalizing, hegemonic system. Augustine does not want to show the way that God works; rather, Augustine follows the working of God on the road of love, deeper into the contemplation of God as love.[17] Theological thinking, then, when embracing a hermeneutic of love, is not concerned with the construction of a coherent system that explains everything. The God revealed as love is not like this. Neither God nor love can be explained fully, wrapped up, etc. God and love are embraced, moved with, given over to, chased. So, then, the theology that this hermeneutic of love opens up becomes a (de)centered, unstructured form that learns to hear and move with God, following God in the love that God shows for all.

THE EVENT OF LOVE

Now, after describing how love becomes the foundation for theology in Augustine's view, we must now describe why it is that love attains this foundation. In what follows, instead of describing love as a "thing" or "object," we will take love to be an event, an occurrence that changes everything. As we have seen, the event of the incarnation opens theology up to a hermeneutic of love. Now, we must retread the ground of the incarnation, except this time we will describe the incarnation as an event of love, as an event of the rhetoric that God "speaks" to humanity. Theology, then, must embrace this event in the moment of transformation, which will then open the ability to not only think about love, but to practice love, enabling theology to fulfill its desired role.

As we have seen, the example for the rhetoric of love is the Incarnation, where Jesus Christ, as Wisdom adopts human form and communicates itself to humanity without losing the essence of God.[18] Since God has come into the world through the Incarnation, the world has been "baptized" by God in a way that all things resonate with the divine image/ vestige that, when rightly disposed, can be seen and heard by the believer. The

---

16. Ibid., I.39.

17. This can be seen explicitly in the journey Augustine describes (and takes his readers on) in *Confessions*.

18. Ibid., I.12–13.

importance, though, comes from the fact that the believer and the community are also one of these things endowed with the resonation of God, where God "rings" through the universe through them. The problem that occurs is when one does not recognize the image of God. Rather, there is a dis-attunement that occurs, where one cannot hear or see God. The necessity, then, results in the fact that there must be a moment of transformation of the person, a conversion which allows him or her to embrace this image of God as it resonates throughout the whole cosmos.

This leads us to a brief detour into contemporary philosophy. There has been a continued concern on the part of contemporary phenomenological philosophy to elaborate the nature of transformation.[19] I start with Hans-Georg Gadamer. In his classic study *Truth and Method* he turns to the idea of transformation as part of the necessity of the hermeneutical process.[20] In this discussion, there is a moment when Gadamer looks to explicate the difference between alteration and transformation. He says that alteration is a change in a thing/ person, but in such a way that it remains the same and maintained. Transformation, on the other hand, "means that something is suddenly and as a whole something else ... When we find someone transformed we mean precisely this, that he has become another person, as it were."[21] Here, Gadamer is showing that transformation is not concerned with a change, but with the creation of something different. And, for Gadamer, this transformation leads one deeper into the truth of one's being: one does not transform into falsity, but towards the grasping for truth. Thus, transformation becomes a becoming-different/ other in such a way as to dive deeper into the truth of one's being.[22]

Two other thinkers explicitly take this notion of transformation up with a view towards the idea of God/ Wholly Other. First, Jean-Louis Chrétien elucidates the idea of transformation in his *The Call and the Response*.[23] In this text, Chrétien looks to develop a phenomenology of what it means to call and be responded to, often times turning on the idea of the call that comes from the Wholly Other (or God). At the point of my interest, he is articulating what it means to respond to the other voice. He says, "To answer the voice of events is to speak, but also to act, by letting ourselves be transformed by it."[24] Here, Chrétien pushes Gadamer's conception further, arguing that not only is transformation a change of becoming-different, but that this becoming-different is not a passive receptivity of something different, but is an active change in our movement toward the true and beautiful through the Other's voice that prods us. Transformation is an active moment. Jacques Derrida continues Chrétien's line of thinking by using the example of the confession. The confession, for Derrida, is not in telling God what God may already know, but is the active movement on my part to transform my relationship with God

---

19. This stems from Marx's emphasis on transformation to move from capitalism to communism.

20. See Hans-Georg Gadamer, *Truth and Method*, 2nd revised ed., trans. Joel Weinsheimer and Donald G. Marshall (New York: Continuum, 1989) 110–21.

21. Ibid., 111. We see resonances here of Paul's theology of the "new creation."

22. Ibid., 116.

23. Jean-Louis Chrétien, *The Call and the Response*, trans. Anne A. Davenport (New York: Fordham University Press, 2004).

24. Ibid., 69.

through transformation of myself through the admission of guilt.²⁵ For Derrida, the confession is a decisive moment of active transformation in that I go to the other and declare myself guilty, transforming myself in the eyes of the other and, perhaps, in my own.²⁶ So, then, transformation is not just about a change or decision, but is an active engagement in such a way that one becomes different—other—not only in one's own eyes, but in the eyes of others.

It is imperative, then, to see how this idea of transformation is at work in Augustine in order to continue moving in the direction of the cultivation of a disposition that allows one to practice a hermeneutic of love. Here I turn to Augustine's *Confessions*²⁷ where he articulates the love that God has for him, as well as how he comes to love God. The event of love as a moment of transformation is central to Augustine's narrative. The ground upon which Augustine explicates his thinking in *The Confessions* is the love of God, specifically the love that God has for Augustine. Throughout Augustine's autobiographical narrative, he learns to see God as an active agent in helping through his different predicaments. He sees God leading him back to God, that with every movement away from God, God is actually bringing Augustine back to God. The (non)ground of Augustine's theology, then, becomes the imperative to follow the movement of God, learning to embrace God in love because God has first loved.

Augustine narrates his movement to the place where he actually learns to love God. We see him move from ideology and worldview to ideology and worldview. He goes from astrology to Manicheism to Neo-Platonism and, finally, to being a Christian. Each movement is guided by God and further brings Augustine into the event of love that is the Triune God. Each of these ideologies and worldviews move Augustine closer to the place of the encounter with God. However, none fulfill him until he comes to be a Christian through his encounter with God in the garden while reading Paul.²⁸ In Book VII we see the intellectual movement of Augustine to God through Neo-Platonism, but this ultimately does not result in "knowing" God. Rather, it is Book VIII where we see the encounter with God in the garden, which leads to transformation. This encounter finally opens Augustine up to the love of God and allows him to embrace this love while also reciprocating the love. The whole confession is a movement to this embrace with God in love. This is what finally fully tunes Augustine into the Triune God.

However, Augustine still goes onto write five more books in *The Confessions*. The text and narrative, then, are not over. Yet, after Book VIII he makes a fundamental change, no longer articulating his move toward Christianity and the attunement to God in love that comes with this. Rather, now the move is toward a deeper love of God aroused through

25. Jacques Derrida, "A Certain Impossible Possibility of Saying the Event," trans. Gila Walker in *Critical Inquiry* 33.2 (Winter 2007) 448.

26. Here, one could say that Dostoyevsky's novel *Crime and Punishment* is a moment of transformation for the main character in that he moves from being guilty in his own eyes to confessing his guilt to all he knows, transforming himself in the others' eyes. This moment of transformation has great affects on his loved ones, especially his mother who can barely cope with the confession, throwing her world into freefall. This is the transformation Derrida is articulating.

27. St. Augustine, *The Confessions*, trans. Maria Boulding, O.S.B. (Hyde Park, NY: New City, 1997).

28. Ibid., Book VIII.

a meditation upon God's creation. The result is no longer a theology that systematizes the creation story or draws out multiple doctrinal statements. Here, Augustine looks to follow God's movement by thinking about creation and playing upon the words "In the beginning God created heaven and earth." He does not get past this line. The theology, then, that Augustine practices is one that does not close the narrative of God, but seeks to reorient oneself through the transformative encounter with God so that theological thinking always remains open, willing to follow God and never seek closure.

As was said, the new move that Augustine makes is to meditate upon God and God's work in creation. This is not meant to be a doctrinal and systematic endeavor but is to arouse Augustine to a deeper love of God.[29] It is this desire to love God more and follow God in God's work through this love that opens theology in a way so as to be able to be uncentered and able to move to God. The center no longer becomes a doctrine or system, but a love of God, which moves with God, never closing in around God.

In *De Doctrina Christiana*, Augustine makes a similar move with the doctrine of the Incarnation. The Incarnation of the Word/ Wisdom leaves the trace of God in all of creation so that the one attuned rightly to God can hear this trace and use these things as signs that point to God. The Incarnation acts, then, as the nongrounding ground upon which Augustine will build his rhetoric. The Incarnation sets the way in which theology is done, being a mediator and opening others up to God because one is rightly disposed to God. And, the Incarnation is the reason that one can be attuned to God in this right disposition of love, as it is here that God's ultimate revelation takes place. Theology, then, becomes a practice of following God by being rightly disposed, which ultimately occurs through the right ordering of love, loving God above all else and loving all other things because they bring one closer to God.[30]

Thus, love becomes the key to a right interpretation so that only one rightly attuned to God through the Incarnation is able to interpret Scripture correctly. This correct interpretation results in a hermeneutic of love, where all interpretations must point to love of God and love of neighbor.[31] Love, then, is the form for theological thinking within Augustine's rhetoric. This is important because love does not seek to dominate the other, but allow this other to exist and disrupt one's life. It is the love of God that leads to love of neighbor, but the love of neighbor is just as important, opening the theologian to remember all those others who are not accounted for. Augustine's rhetoric of love, then, opens the way for theology to be constantly shifting, rightly disposed to God, but not seeking to dominate this God with some foreign concepts. Rather, love seeks to follow God in God's love for neighbor, to follow God in God's desire for a rightly ordered creation, and to follow God in God's overall movement.

What we have seen, then, in our reading of Augustine's *De Doctrina Christiana* is that theology must not begin with a set of first principles, but with a rightly ordered love, loving God and neighbor. From this place, one can begin to do theology, but all theology

---

29. Ibid., XI.1.
30. *DDC*, I.34.
31. Ibid., I.39–40.

must come back to this place of transformative love that occurs in the event of encountering the Triune God. This event of love shows us what it means to love, that we are loved, and gives the grace and power necessary to love back. Thus, theology is predicated from the start on being rightly disposed, in-line, attuned to God. If this does not occur, then theology cannot "speak" the rhetoric that is necessary to it. The "speaking" of theology comes not just through the doctrines taught or words said, but through the entire way of life, and that life is a life of love. Thus, as Augustine has shown us, theology concerns the whole person, the whole life, that one may live in such a way as to pursue God.

CONCLUSION: THE LIFE OF LOVE AND WESLEYAN THEOLOGY

In concluding, I want to show how Augustine's thought informs a fundamental Wesleyan theology. I find this occurring in two places. First, Augustine helps a Wesleyan theology with his focus on theology only being able to begin properly when one is rightly disposed toward God. Second, he pushes a Wesleyan theology by placing the event of love at the center of theology, where all interpretive decisions and all content comes back to the necessity of the promotion of love, both of God and neighbor. This leads to a third moment, which neither Augustine nor Wesleyans have made explicit, but which is implicit: the non-closure of theology.

First, I turn to the necessity of theology to be rightly disposed. Of course, as we have seen, both Wesley and Augustine were very concerned with the disposition of the person, and that the person doing theology be transformed into a person of love. This is the central part of theology for both Wesleyans and Augustinians. However, Augustine pushes Wesleyan theology further by necessitating a hermeneutic of love that interprets everything through the necessity to make people grow in love.[32] Wesleyans have always talked of love, of attaining perfect love, but this has not always been our hermeneutic. At times we have been trapped into the "game" of laying out our theology in such a way as to first get our theology right, and then get our love right.[33] Augustine shows, however, that if our love is rightly ordered, then our theology will follow.

Following this, Augustine also helps Wesleyan theology through his focus on the center of theology as being the event of love which leads to transformation. Wesleyans have always been interested, and promulgated, the idea of transformation through our doctrine of entire sanctification. However, at times, the impetus has been on the event of sanctification instead of the on the transformative event that is the encounter with God. Of course, these two should go hand-in-hand, but do not always.[34] Augustine helps Wesleyans in two ways. First, by making the event of love—in the encounter of God—as central for theology, Augustine opens the place of our encounter with the God who is love as occurring always, in all places, even before the works of grace in justification and sanctification. *The Confessions* show the movement of God with the sinner to the

---

32. Ibid., I.39–44.

33. As representative, I think of H. Ray Dunning, *Grace, Faith and Holiness: A Wesleyan Systematic Theology* (Kansas City: Beacon Hill, 1988).

34. I think of ordination boards I have been questioned by or educated pastors I have talked to. There seems to be a gulf here that should not exist.

place where the sinner can encounter God in the transformative event of love. Second, Augustine helps Wesleyans through his focus on the event of love by showing that a hermeneutic of love is a lived experience. Wesley was very concerned with the living of the Christian life (as only a cursory glance at this writings shows). Augustine makes this explicit through his suggestion that only by living the life of love through transformation may the Christian/ theologian "speak" about God.

Thirdly, I want to briefly point in a direction that theology, as predicated upon the event of love, may go. My reasoning goes as such: if theology is predicated upon love, upon the cultivation of a disposition of love for God and neighbor, then how do we construct a theology that gives coherence to Christian belief? It seems that love is a nebulous center, an a-centered center, where the focus is always shifting or moving. This, of course, reflects the nature of God as infinite, ineffable, etc. By placing love at the center of theology, then we are dealing with an object that is analogous to God. What is analogous is that neither is able to be contained in a closed system. Both God and love are never "caught," but always expand our horizons; they cannot be closed within an explanation, no matter how good the explanation. So, with the pursuit of God as love as the center of theology, a task that seems to be impossible from the beginning, what allows us to go about doing theology? How do we theologize?

If theology is pursuing something that cannot be contained, then we must have a way of theologizing that breaks all containments for our object. Here, I turn to the idea of the fragment.[35] Theology predicated upon love is necessarily fragmented; it is never whole, never complete, but strives for the perfection that is only found in the Triune God. If theology is at the center about pursuing God in love, then all our categories and systems will fall short, being broken by God. If these systems break, it is necessary to pick up on the fragments, those pieces that cannot close a system around God, but which point us toward the God who breaks these totalizing attempts. The question becomes how we bring these fragments together to give coherence.

Here, I turn to the idea of "the gathering" which David Tracy brings out in his most recent articles. Tracy turns to the idea of "gathering" for a way of collecting the fragments and giving them coherence. He argues that theology must gather and order the fragments, but that this is not a way of totalizing them into a system: there is not way to have a full system of symbols.[36] Rather, Tracy is aware of the fact that this gathering can turn into a totalizing. So, he argues that there must be a constant remembering of the fact

---

35. Here, I am quite reliant upon the recent work of David Tracy. For a few representative articles, see David Tracy, "Literary Theory and Return of the Forms for Naming and Thinking God in Theology," *Journal of Religion* 74.3 (July 1994) 302–19; "Theology and the Many Faces of Postmodernity," *Theology Today* 51 (1994) 104–14; "Fragments: The Spiritual Situation of our Times," in *God, the Gift, and Postmodernism*, ed. John D. Caputo and Michael J. Scanlon (Bloomington: Indiana University Press, 1999) 170–84; "Form and Fragment: Recovery of the Hidden and Incomprehensible God," *Center of Theological Inquiry* (1999). (http://www.ctinquiry.org/publications/reflections_volume_3/tracy.htm; accessed November 3, 2008); Lois Malcolm, "The Impossible God: An Interview with David Tracy," *Christian Century* (February 13–20, 2002) 24–30.

36. Malcolm, "Impossible God," 28.

that these religious expressions are in fact fragments, meant to break the whole.[37] The fragments themselves offer a constant interruption. The gathering brings together the fragments and lets them critique each other, where theology may play on a name for God and then turn to another name, playing on this, critiquing the first while enhancing the theology. The gathering offers a way of constantly calling into question the very "system" that attempts to give coherence to the fragments. The coherence is always shaky because the fragments are unsettling, disrupting, and, thus, quite problematic for systematizing.

For Wesleyans, the turn to fragments and gathering should be a breath of fresh air. This way of doing theology seeks to follow God, to love God, and to pursue God where God goes. This is not a systematic theology, but a way of thinking that brings together various strands of thought at various times to give coherence to an idea, but not in a way that totalizes. Rather, the God who loves us and transforms us, also constantly transforms our paradigms and thought patterns about God, breaking the tendency to idolatry that forms in much systematic theology. Theology becomes a pursuit of God in love, to become transformed so that God can be God and we can reflect that God through our loving of God and loving of neighbor.

---

37. Ibid.

9

Pushing the Mystery Button

The Limits of Logic and Language

KEVIN KINGHORN

WHENEVER THE CHRISTIAN TRADITION has sought to describe the nature of God and God's interaction with our world, it has always been with the caveat that God remains mysterious in various ways. But in what ways exactly? And, relatedly, when is it appropriate to appeal to the "mysteries of God" in defending our own affirmations about God from possible objections?

We find a useful avenue for exploring these questions in Larry Wood's discussion of God's relationship to time. In his articles, "Does God Know the Future? Can God Be Mistaken?: A Reply to Richard Swinburne"[1] and "Reply to Alan Padgett,"[2] Wood defends Boethius's claim that the eternal nature of God amounts to "the whole, perfect, and simultaneous possession of endless life."[3] Boethius went on to explain that God is "eternal[ly] present" in all instances of time.[4] Wood defends Boethius from the general objection that God could not act in human history if all events in history were really 'eternally present' to him.

Indeed, Wood offers a number of *kinds* of defenses, which I wish to explore. After arguing that modern physics renders Boethius's claims entirely coherent, Wood notes that both modern physics and our claims about God may seem incoherent "from the standpoint of our common sense."[5] Wood even warns about being "trapped by common sense"[6] and about the "limits of deductive logic."[7] He touches on the limitations of human language, claiming that we should not "insist that theological language must corre-

---

1. In *Asbury Theological Journal* 56.2 (2002) 5–47.
2. In *Asbury Theological Journal* 60 (2005) 9–21.
3. Boethius, *The Consolation of Philosophy*, trans. Richard Green (New York: Bobbs-Merrill, 1962) 116.
4. Ibid., 64.
5. Wood, "Does God Know the Future?" 28.
6. Ibid., 31.
7. Wood, "Reply to Padgett," 6.

spond to the intuitive logic of ordinary human experience."[8] He also talks about a "larger meaning of truth," warning that we may become "confused if we are locked within a modernist notion of truth."[9] Finally, Wood makes use of terms that seem openly ambiguous, asserting that God "embraces all space-time reference frames"; that God "synthesizes everything simultaneously"; and that God is the "unbounded power of the future."[10] In response to the objection that these terms are too suggestive to help in clarifying God's relationship to time, Wood falls back on the Christian's need to employ "dialectical ways of speaking."[11] And we should not forget that "Christian theology has always maintained the mystery" that God created the world—with God's relationship to space-time thus remaining a subject we cannot fully capture with human concepts."[12]

Within Wood's defense of Boethius, there again seem to me to be a number of different lines of response. In what follows I shall attempt to distinguish and clarify some of the key issues at stake when we appeal to the limits of human language and logic. In the process, we shall get a better idea of when it is (and is not) appropriate to appeal to divine "mystery" in explaining the ways of God.

CHALLENGING THE LAWS OF LOGIC

In interpreting Boethius's description of God's eternity, Wood defends the idea that God experiences "all different time-frames simultaneously in his eternal life."[13] While the various events in human history stand in relation to us right now as past, present, or future, all events are present to God. Alan Padgett, however, has challenged the idea of the "eternally present" on the grounds that it is inconsistent with the Christian claim that God acts within the developing timeline of human history. He says,

> the belief that past, present and future are real ontological differences, and the belief that all of the past, present and future are present to God in eternity, along with the belief that God acts in history: these three beliefs cannot all be true. They are logically inconsistent.[14]

The idea is that, if we affirm that there is a real difference between the past and the future (as there obviously is), and if we affirm that all events in history are 'present' to God, then we cannot go on to affirm that God acts *in* history. At best, God could perform acts from all eternity, with the *effects* being felt in time. For, an action within time seems to require a temporal sequence—i.e., a time when the action has not yet been performed, followed by a time when the action is initiated, followed by a time when the action is completed.

---

8. Ibid., 12.
9. Ibid.
10. Wood, "Does God Know the Future?" 30.
11. Wood, "Reply to Padgett," 15.
12. Wood, "Does God Know the Future?" 24.
13. Ibid., 30.
14. Alan Padgett, "Is God Timeless? A Reply to Laurence Wood," *Asbury Theological Journal* 60 (2005) 6.

Hence, it seems that God could not act within human history if God truly experiences all events in history in an "instant."[15]

The charge of logical inconsistency is a serious one. While a minority within the Christian tradition have wanted to insist that God is somehow "above" the laws of logic, the majority within the tradition have affirmed that logical consistency marks all things secular and divine.[16] After all, our ability to affirm *anything* depends on the assumption that the negation of what we affirm cannot *also* be the case. Admittedly, there may be some debate among logicians as to which more complex principles do and do not follow from the so-called Law of Non-Contradiction—i.e., that something cannot *be* the case and also *not be* the case at the same time and in the same way. But if we do not assume this first principle of logic, then we seemingly have no way of identifying heresy, stating the uniqueness of Christianity, or, again, affirming anything positive at all about God. The claim that Jesus singularly atoned for our sins automatically rules out the idea that Jesus *did not* singularly atone for our sins. It also rules out an infinite number of other logically incompatible claims: e.g., that Buddha singularly atoned for our sins, that Napolean singularly atoned for our sins, and so forth. So, we rightly rely on the laws of logic in our descriptions about anything.

John Wesley insisted in his *Address to Clergy* that the competent interpreter of scripture must rely on logic. Wesley took for granted that a knowledge of scripture is impossible without it, saying

> May we not say, that the knowledge of one [of the sciences], although now quite unfashionable, is even necessary next, and in order, to the knowledge of the Scripture itself? I mean logic. For what is this, if rightly understood, but the art of good sense? of apprehending things clearly, judging truly, and reasoning conclusively?[17]

Wesley rightly saw that, in order to reach one conclusion about God at the expense of other possible conclusions, some sort of logical reasoning will be required.

Wood is intentionally Wesleyan in his appreciation of the need for logical coherence in our statements about God. In response to Padgett's charge of logical inconsistency, Wood is adamant that the Boethian view of eternity is entirely consistent. Wood emphasizes through a series of examples that, on an Einsteinian—as opposed to Newtonian—understanding of our physical universe, the temporal relation that an event bears to any person will depend on factors such as the speed the person is traveling. The faster a person travels, the slower time moves relative to other persons whose slower speed remains constant. Thus, "Time may go at different rates for different observers." A ten minute span for a person in a rocket ship approaching the speed of light will run concurrently with the events a person on earth will experience over a much greater length of

---

15. Wood, "Does God Know the Future?" 7.

16. To allay the concern that nothing—not even logic—should be placed "above" God such that God is "bound by" logic, we might wish to view the laws of logic as principles we discover about the nature of God, whom the Bible describes as a God of order. The sense in which God is "bound by" logic would then merely be the sense in which it is incoherent to describe God as acting contrary to his essential nature.

17. John Wesley, "An Address to the Clergy," in *The Works of John Wesley*, vol. 10, ed. T. Jackson (Nashville: Abingdon, 2005) 483.

time. What this points up is that "simultaneity" is determined by one's frame of reference. And while Einsteinian physics does not prove that Boethius's view of divine eternity is correct, Wood does see "the breakdown of simultaneity" as showing how "a Boethian view is intelligible."[18] On the other hand, Wood sees Padgett's affirmations about time as inconsistent with the current scientific consensus about time relativity.

Since Wood's conclusion is that the Boethian view of divine eternity is logically consistent with our current understanding of space-time, it may strike us as odd to read Wood referring to the "paradoxical reality" of Einstein's relativity theory.[19] Wood also comments that quantum theory "contradicts commonsense logic."[20] Again, though, Wood is very much committed to the idea that the laws of logic operate without exception in our world. On closer analysis of his position, his point is simply that some things in our world may *seem* contradictory to us, given certain (mistaken) assumptions. Thus, Wood notes that the "paradoxical nature" of the simultaneity breakdown between two people's frames of reference "is incoherent only if one absolutizes one's own 'reference frame.'"[21] Wood's general position is perhaps not always clear when we look at the wording he uses in some of his arguments. For instance, he states at one point that, if the idea of an "eternal present" seems incoherent to us, it is because we are "trapped by common sense."[22] But, again, the real issue in the end is not one of logic, but rather one of starting premises.

It is certainly common within the Christian tradition to note that various affirmations about God may *seem* improbable, or indeed impossible, from a certain set of background assumptions. For example, the occurrence of a miracle may always seem improbable, if not impossible, from a Humean understanding of how the evidence of experience is to be weighed against the evidence of testimony. But this point is very different than the claim that logical inferences do not always hold. Wood does not attempt to make this (problematic) latter claim. He notes that "the really substantive difference between Padgett's view and my own" is that "we have a different understanding of contemporary physics." Wood nowhere makes the claim that science has somehow revealed violations of the Law of Non-Contradiction;. Rather, his claim is that Padgett's charge of incoherence stems from the (legitimate) application of logical principles to mistaken premises about the nature of space-time.

Interestingly, some scientists seem to go further than Wood, interpreting certain experiments in physics as counterinstances to the laws of logic. With respect to the well-known finding that light behaves both like a wave and like a stream of particles, one conclusion is that light simply *is* both a wave and a particle. Experiments in quantum

---

18. Wood, "Reply to Padgett," 18.
19. Wood, "Does God Know the Future?" 29.
20. Wood, "Reply to Padgett," 13.
21. Wood, "Does God Know the Future?" 30. Cf. Stephen Hawking on the "twins paradox," where one twin travels through space nearing the speed of light, only to return to earth and find that his twin has aged much more rapidly than he has: "The twins paradox is a paradox only if one has the idea of absolute time at the back of one's mind" (*A Brief History of Time* [London: Bantom, 1988] 30).
22. Wood, "Does God Know the Future?" 31.

physics also regularly yield unexpected results. For example, a subatomic particle can be fired manually so that it ends up in one field *and* in another field at the same time. Such experiments led Werner Heisenberg to claim that, if we were to insist on "complete logical clarity" for our experiments, then we "would make science impossible."[23]

At times, Wood might seem close to endorsing the view that science has uncovered instances where the Law of Non-Contradiction is violated. He states in one passage that "Postmodern science has come to recognize the limits of deductive logic."[24] Yet, in the same passage he notes that, in quantum theory, "experimental results contradict classical physics and have forced a new way of understanding the world."[25] This last sentence returns us to the point that it is our *understanding of the physical world* that counterintuitive experimental results force us to reconsider. We are not forced to reconsider the universal application of the Law of Non-Contradiction. And this really is the response to scientists who might claim that an experiment generates a result that is "illogical." To show that the laws of logic have been violated, a scientist would need to establish two things. First, she would need to identify the precise logical principle that has been violated. Presumably, in the case of light behaving both like a wave and like a stream of particles, the logical problem centers on identity. But can we be definite that waves and streams of particles are mutually exclusive, such that, if light is a wave, it could not logically also be a stream of particles? And is the presence of a subatomic particle in one field really logically inconsistent with its presence in another field? I myself do not know the answers to these questions. But if one is to establish logical inconsistency, one would need to identify the logical principle in question and to establish that, given our categories in describing the physical world, a violation of this logical principle really has occurred.

The second thing a scientist would need to establish is that her categories in describing the world are the correct categories. That is, the scientist would need to demonstrate that her ontological taxonomy really does contain the most fundamental things that can be said about the world. If so, then a logical conflict among these categories would show that the world does not always operate with logical consistency.

This double burden of the scientist strikes me as exceedingly difficult to achieve, especially the latter one. Can we really be confident, e.g., that waves and particles capture the nature of light at its most fundamental level? And do we know enough about matter to be confident that the behavior of photons and electrons does not supervene on the activity of more ontologically fundamental physical substances? Do we know enough about space-time to be confident that two different fields within four-dimensional space-time never overlap in some way? Again, as a non-scientist I am not well placed to guide discussions on these matters. However, the current work on such topics as wormholes, dark matter, and further dimensions is rather seminal in nature. And it strikes me as virtually inevitable that our understanding of the physical universe will change substantially over the coming centuries. Certainly, I do not think we can have the kind of confidence in our

---

23. Werner Heisenberg, *Physics and Philosophy: The Revolution in Modern Physics* (London: George Allen and Unwin, 1959) 86. Wood cites Heisenberg in "Reply to Padgett," 14.

24. Wood, "Reply to Padgett," 12.

25. Ibid.

current understanding of final, physical categories that should outweigh our confidence in the universal application of the Law of Non-Contradiction.

When scientists talk about experimental results being counterinstances to "logic," this term may be being used in a colloquial sense, synonymous with "counterintuitive." Wood himself occasionally seems to use the term in this sense. He mentions that experimental evidence in science "often contradicts the intuitive logic of commonsense."[26] This phrasing is a bit unfortunate from the standpoint of the analytic philosopher, who seeks to define terms carefully. "Common sense" obviously does not have its own set of logical principles. But if the point is simply that science will often generate unexpected and counterintuitive results, then the point is well taken.

Wood's phrase can also be taken as suggesting that experimental results really will on occasion generate logical contradictions, given the physical categories scientists use. This suggestion is stronger than the point about general counterintuitiveness. Perhaps some scientists do mean to emphasize that genuine contradictions persist as we investigate certain aspects of the world. But this simply returns us to the question of how confident scientists can be that they are working with a complete understanding of the final ontological categories needed to describe fully the workings of our physical world. And again, it seems very implausible to suggest that scientists today are in such a position.

In this section we have seen little reason to think that we should appeal to violations of the laws of logic as final and accurate descriptions of things—a point that applies equally to scientists and to theologians. A natural question also arises from our discussion: What positive claims *can* we make, given the recognition that our categories may not (will not?) fully capture reality? We shall explore this question in section III. But first, let us observe how Christians may need to acknowledge tensions and paradoxes in what they affirm, even if they do not resort to affirming genuine, logical contradictions.

TENSIONS, PARADOXES, AND MYSTERIES

While the majority of theologians within the Christian tradition have affirmed that accurate descriptions of God will always be logically consistent, this does not mean that there are never tensions in what Christians affirm. Let us define "tension" as a general term where the truth of one affirmation seems to come at the expense of another affirmation. For instance, I might state, "A lot of people do not know this, but my Ph.D. supervisor happens to be very famous." On the surface, these two affirmations come at the expense of one another. The more we establish the fact that lots of people do not know about my supervisor's work, the more difficult it becomes to go on to affirm that he is very famous. Strictly speaking, there is nothing contradictory in the conjoining of these two affirmations. We might make sense of it by further explaining, e.g., that my supervisor is very famous within academic circles or that the reference to "a lot" of people still leaves room for billions of people worldwide. Still, the affirmations are in tension with one another— the truth of one tending to come at the expense of the truth of the other.

---

26. Ibid., 12.

There are of course many such tensions that may characterize the affirmations Christians wish to make. The Biblical witness is that King David was a man after God's own heart. And yet, we read of David's apparent acknowledgement in response to Shimei that he had been a man of blood.[27] Seemingly, these two affirmations are in tension, although we might seek to reconcile them in various ways—e.g., by noting that God prizes humility and that David consistently admitted his mistakes and shortcomings.

Christians affirm that God is all-powerful and perfectly loving; yet they also affirm the reality of evil in our world. They affirm that God seeks to draw us into a relationship with him; yet they also affirm that God "hides himself" from us in the sense that he does not make his existence as obviously clear to us as he could. While theologians have provided plausible ways to reconcile these sets of affirmations, it remains true that one affirmation will tend to come at the expense of the other affirmation.

These kinds of general tensions are surely numerous in almost any person's set of beliefs. And the theologian is as entitled as anyone to affirm statements that may generate tensions. Admittedly, if one affirmation is in tension with enough other affirmations one wants to make, it may become irrational to continue to hold the original affirmation (provided there are not further things that tend to *confirm* the original affirmation). For instance, if the Christian affirms enough facts that tend to undermine God's goodness, then, in the absence of data that tend to confirm God's goodness, it will become more and more difficult to affirm it. Still, the mere fact that two statements generate the kind of general tension we have been discussing is itself not a strong reason to think both statements cannot be true.

Moving from the issue of tension, Christians have always appealed to a second category, *mystery*, in affirming certain things about God. This fact seems inevitable, given our position relative to God. Irenaeus explained: "we, inasmuch as we are inferior to, and later in existence than, the Word of God and His Spirit, are on that very account destitute of the knowledge of His mysteries."[28] The sense of "mystery" here seems to involve our inability fully to understand the workings of God. For instance, although there is no hint of contradiction in the idea that an immaterial God created our physical world, we cannot hope to provide a full, causal explanation of how God's 'speaking the world into existence' brought about the formation of physical matter. Thus, Wood rightly notes that "Christian theology has always maintained the mystery that God created the world out of nothing."[29] And it is surely plausible for Wood to maintain that certain aspects of God's relationship to time will remain a mystery to us.

At the same time, in his discussion of mystery Wood's choice of phrasing is perhaps unfortunate when he talks about our need "to acknowledge that God as Creator transcends our finite logical abilities."[30] In matters of the kind of mystery at issue, it is not our inability to clarify controversial theorems of *logic* that is in question (i.e., whether

---

27. 2 Samuel 16. See also David's appalling actions toward Bathsheba and Uriah in 2 Samuel 11.

28. Irenaeus, "Against Heresies," *Ante-Nicene Fathers*, ed. A. Roberts and J. Donaldson, (Grand Rapids: Eerdmans, 1981) 1:399.

29. Wood, "Does God Know the Future?" 24–25.

30. Ibid., 20.

some theorem does or does not follow from the Law of Non-Contradiction). Rather, it is simply that we cannot offer a complete explanation of God's nature, necessary being and workings. The appeal to mystery in offering certain descriptions of God is entirely legitimate; but we should not conflate this point with questions about our incomplete understanding of the complexities of formal logic.

Having looked briefly at the categories of tension and mystery, let us consider a third category: "paradox." While this term has been defined differently by various writers, let us stipulate here that 'paradox' refers to an *apparent* contradiction. On this definition, Jesus's statement, "whoever loses his life for me will find it,"[31] is a paradox. Other examples include the Trinitarian doctrine that God is both three and one. On the surface these are contradictions (and not merely statements that are in tension with each other). Of course, these (apparent) contradictions are resolved in the end. True contradictions involve the claim that something both is and is not the case, at the same time and in the same way. But upon further examination, we find that the meaning of "life" is not the same in Jesus's statements about gaining life and losing it. We "lose" our lives in the sense of offering control of our lives to God, serving others, deferring to others' interests, and so forth. We "gain" life in the sense of finding ultimate joy and fulfilling our divinely-given vocation. Similarly, a Trinitarian theology does not claim that God is 'three' in the same sense that he is "one." God is said to have one essence and to be one, unified being; he is said to be three persons. The claim that God is both one person and three persons *would* be a genuine contradiction. But the claim that God is one being and three persons is not a contradiction. The surface claim that Jesus is both three and one is a paradox. Admittedly, it remains a mystery how there could be an eternal, self-sustaining, tri-personal being in the first place. But there is nothing internally inconsistent either about the concept of God or the concept of a God who is a tri-personal being.

It is easy enough for Christians to affirm paradoxes when we know how the paradox is to be resolved on closer analysis. The more difficult issue is whether we should continue to affirm paradoxes even when we do not know how they are to be resolved. It seems legitimate to affirm paradoxes when we can at least offer plausible ways in which the paradox *might* be resolved. For example, in affirming that Jesus Christ was both fully human and fully divine, we might appeal to the so-called "kenotic theory" whereby Christ is understood to have "emptied himself" of his divine attributes while incarnate here on earth. Or, we might explain how Jesus Christ could have *two natures*—a divine one and human one—and yet remain *one person* by arguing that there is nothing essential about a human nature that precludes one from also having a divine nature. To be sure, there are possible objections to both theories. One might question whether it is possible for God to empty himself of, for example, omniscience and still retain the properties essential to God. And one might question whether any 'two natures' account of Jesus Christ actually leads to the problematic conclusion that Jesus was *two persons* in *one body*. Still, each approach seems at least a plausible way of responding to the objection that Jesus could not have been both fully human and fully divine. With no compelling reason to think that

---

31. Matt 16:25.

these two affirmations *cannot* therefore be resolved, it seems legitimate for the Christian to make both affirmations (given, of course, that the Christian thinks there is good reason to arrive at each conclusion individually).

But what if we can see no plausible way of resolving the paradox? Should we still maintain that a given set of affirmations *is* a paradox that can be resolved? One might be very tempted to say "no" here. After all, if we can see no plausible way of resolving two or more affirmations, then, as far as we know, we have an actual contradiction. And if we adopt the pattern of accepting new statements even if they seem, as best we can tell, to contradict other beliefs we hold, then we return to the troubles we noted at the beginning of section I regarding how we identify heresy or state the uniqueness of Christianity.

Perhaps many Christians will want to say that, in some cases, God's revelation to us in scripture may lead us to affirm two statements that, as far as we can tell, seem contradictory. To be sure, this suggestion prompts the immediate rejoinder that we rely heavily on the idea of logical consistency to arrive at an interpretation of a passage of scripture. And here we can think back here to Wesley's comments on the need to employ logic if we are to have any knowledge of scripture. A given passage of scripture will have any number of possible interpretations; and we eliminate alternative interpretations primarily on the basis of how they (fail to) cohere with other affirmations we interpret scripture as making. So, we seemingly face the daunting task of identifying the criteria which the Christian will use in eliminating some interpretations due to apparent logical inconsistency while affirming some other interpretations despite apparent logical inconsistency.

Still, let us suppose that the Christian comes to the conclusion that, on the basis of revelation, our best attempts to describe God simply must include two affirmations that, as far as we can tell, are logically inconsistent. At this point, instead of positing that the laws of logic might somehow be suspended within the heavenly realm, we would do better to consider the extent to which the categories we have been using to speak about God are adequate. And this leads us to the subject of models.

THE USE OF MODELS

In defending Boethius's description of an "eternal present," Wood joins authors such as Norman Kretzmann and Elenore Stump in emphasizing the relativity of "simultaneity." Put briefly, the question of whether someone is "simultaneous" with some event will depend on particulars of that person. For instance, a person traveling near the speed of light will be simultaneous with a different set of events than a person traveling at a slower speed. And a three-dimensional figure will view simultaneously all the points on a one-dimensional line, while an imaginary one-dimensional person on that line will understand all but one point on the line to be either past or future. Building on this idea that the notion of "simultaneity" is person-relative, these authors then propose that God is simultaneous with all events in human history, while a human is of course simultaneous with only those events occurring at one particular slice of time.

Richard Swinburne has objected to this appeal to simultaneity as being too suggestive to shed any real light on God's relationship to time. He first notes the "inner incoherence" of the surface claim that God is "simultaneously present" at what I did yesterday, today, and tomorrow. If God is simultaneous with these events in the same sense that I am simultaneous with any event, then clearly "yesterday would be the same day as today and as tomorrow—which is clearly nonsense."[32] To avoid this consequence, "we would have to understand 'simultaneously' in a somewhat special stretched sense."[33] Yet Swinburne questions whether this stretched sense of the term (which its advocates have yet to define precisely and to distinguish from our normal understanding of the term) can be used to defend the idea of "eternal-temporal" simultaneity. He says,

> to call the notion "ET-simultaneity" suggests that what has been defined has some analogy to normal simultaneity, and no reason has been given for supposing that it does. Hence no reason has been given for supposing that if God has an existence outside (our) time, he can have any relation to the events of time which would be in any way analogous to "causing" or "observing" them.[34]

In short, the proposal that an eternal God can be "simultaneous" to all earthly events merely suggests some sort of analogy to the sense in which we are present to various events. But without specifying the sense in which eternal-temporal simultaneity is (and is not) like two temporal events being simultaneous, we gain no more insight into God's relationship to time than is suggested by the term "simultaneous," which is simply chosen as a description of how God relates to time.

As discussed in section I, Wood wants to emphasize that Einsteinian physics *does* give us real insight into the way in which God can be temporally present to events that, from our perspective, will be either past or future. We can take his repeated appeals to the scientific literature emphasizing the relative aspects of "simultaneity" as a response to the charge that this term is merely suggestive of the sense in which an eternal God can be present to all events of human history. Yet, Wood offers a further kind of response when engaging with the arguments of Richard Swinburne and Alan Padgett. He wonders at times whether these analytic philosophers are open to the kinds of themes to which we will invariably need to appeal as we describe God. These themes stem from our inability to understand fully—let along capture in public language—God's nature and his relationship to our world. Wood discusses Church Fathers like Origen, who "spoke of the stretching of language in the Bible when it attempts to speak of God as a personal reality who is involved in time."[35] And indeed there are ample quotes from the Fathers along the lines of Clement of Alexandria's general statement:

> Wherefore let no one imagine that hands, and feet, and mouth, and eyes, and going in and coming out, and resentments and threats, are said by the Hebrews to be at-

---

32. Richard Swinburne, *The Coherence of Theism*, rev. ed. (Oxford: Clarendon, 1993) 228.

33. Ibid., 228.

34. Richard Swinburne, "God and Time," in *Reasoned Faith*, ed. E. Stump and N. Kretzmann (Ithaca, NY: Cornell University Press, 1993).

35. Wood, "Does God Know the Future?" 17.

tributes of God. By no means; but that certain of these appellations are used more sacredly in an allegorical sense.[36]

Wood presses at times this theme in Christian theology that we must use language to describe God, fully aware that our language is at best an approximation of the full truth about God.

With an appreciation of this point, we can perhaps see why Wood's choice of language is not as unambiguous as an analytic philosopher might prefer. He remarks that, "Even as the speed of light transcends every reference frame, it can be thought that God embraces all space-time reference frames."[37] And again, that "God transcends time and yet time is real to the essence of God."[38] He quotes with approval Gregory of Nyssa's statement that the Trinity "is not in time, but time flows from it."[39] Wood's commentary is that, "Just as postmodern science must use dialectical ways of speaking, so the Early Greek Church Fathers and Boethius were forced to speak in dialectical ways as well."[40] This appeal to "dialectical" speaking is Wood's way of emphasizing that our language is always an approximation when we use it to speak of God. We recognize the limitations of old descriptions, as well as the limitations of any new descriptions we might use as replacements.

Wood is certainly correct in noting that scientists and theologians alike rely heavily on approximate, analogical language, which indicates the use of models. As a best attempt at understanding certain physical phenomena, scientists often appeal to other, better known physical phenomena. For example, in understanding the behavior of molecules, scientists may offer the model of billiard balls, which we can readily observe bouncing off each other and off the billiard table cushions. Thus, in describing a rise in air pressure within a container, a scientist may talk about the molecules within the container "bouncing" more frequently off the walls of the container and off each other. This increased activity is used to explain, e.g., why the temperature in the container rises. Of course, a molecule does not behave *exactly* like a billiard ball. Rather, the model of a billiard ball allows us to understand and predict the behavior of molecules.

Theologians of course rely on models as well. The descriptions of God as father, shepherd, and king are examples. Typically, Christians are quick to emphasize that God is best described using the conjunction of multiple models. Thus, the combination of father, shepherd and king more accurately reflects God's full character and interaction with us than any of those models in isolation. Even so, Wood wants (rightly) to note that all our models—as we juxtapose them in what Wood calls "dialectical" ways of speaking—will at most give us partial knowledge of God.

---

36. Clement of Alexandria, "The Stromata, or Miscellanies," *Ante-Nicene Fathers*, ed. A. Roberts and J. Donaldson, (Grand Rapids: Eerdmans, 1989) 2:460.

37. Wood, "Does God Know the Future?" 30.

38. Wood, "Reply to Padgett," 12.

39. Gregory of Nyssa, "Against Eunomius," *Nicene and Post-Nicene Fathers*, ed. P. Shaff and H. Wace, (Grand Rapids: Eerdmans, 1976) 5:69.

40. Wood, "Reply to Padgett," 15.

PART TWO: Contribution to Current Theological Problems

Wood's way of making this point is perhaps not always as clear as it might be. After noting that writers like Stump and Kretzman have shown that Boethius's view of divine eternity is coherent, he comments on Alan Padgett's charge of incoherence.

> Padgett does not agree with this logic, but I believe his either/or thinking does not allow him to appreciate the nature of dialectical thinking. To insist that theological language must correspond to the intuitive logic of ordinary human experience seems too anthropomorphic to me.[41]

There are seemingly a number of potential issues raised here, but among them is our current issue of whether language about God remains analogical. If so, then the categories and terms we use in constructing models for God may sometimes lead us to conclusions which we cannot logically reconcile. But this should not surprise us, given that our categories are not final, ontological categories—but rather our best attempts to describe God given our limited taxonomy of categories.

A natural question arises at this point: What should we do when we find that two claims we make about God are, as best we can tell, logically inconsistent. If we believe these claims are fully accurate, ontological descriptions of God, then we face the problems discussed in section I if we affirm them both. But what if we believe them to be models of God and thus *not* to be fully accurate descriptions of God using final ontological categories?

This question is not unknown to the scientific community. Niels Bohr developed his "principle of complementarity" in response to the manner in which light behaves both as waves and as particles. Although these two categories are thought to be mutually exclusive, scientists have wanted to affirm both of them as models for light. Otherwise, we cannot account for the full range of behavior we observe from light. Importantly, though, scientists need not be committed to saying that light both *is* a wave and *is* a particle. Rather, we are led to *explain* or *describe* the behavior of light using both models; we are led to *think of* light in terms of both waves and particles.

The "principle of complementarity" opens the door for the theologian to insist that we might indeed come to mutually exclusive conclusions about God. A commitment to each of these conclusions might constitute our best description of God—"best" in the sense that it accounts for the full range of information we have about God, based on God's interaction in human history. As a preliminary point, if we find ourselves in such a position, we will need to acknowledge that our descriptions of God are indeed models and not final ontological descriptions about God as God really is. Otherwise, we revisit the problems discussed in section I that come with affirming final contradictions. Having noted this point, the theologian now faces a number of questions that arise from an appeal to the principle of complementarity. I shall mention three.

First, given that models rely on some sort of analogy, the task remains to specify the respective senses in which the analogy does and does not hold. Sometimes this task is fairly straightforward. In affirming God as our heavenly "father," one of the obvious ways in which the analogy to an earthly father breaks down is that God is sexless. One

---

41. Wood, "Reply to Padgett," 11.

of the obvious ways in which the analogy *holds* is that both God and one's earthly father causally contribute to our existence by some means of generation. Still, for many models we might use in describing God and God's relationship to our world, the implications of the model remain disputed by Christians. For instance, in affirming that God is a "loving Father," God's dispositions and actions must bear at least *some* clear resemblance to our best examples of a loving, earthly father. Is Calvin's affirmation of double election at odds with the affirmation that God is a loving father? Our answer will depend on whether double election is decisively at odds with the set of examples through which we understand the meaning of term "loving father." If so, then we cannot affirm that "God is a loving father" without that affirmation losing all meaning for us. The affirmation "God is a loving father" would simply amount to the affirmation "God is God," whatever that involves (i.e., whatever the set of examples with which that affirmation is consistent). In short, the question of whether two affirmations about God are mutually exclusive will sometimes hinge on the way we spell out the analogy involved in these affirmations.

Second, theologians face the question of whether the models themselves can be reformulated. Within science, advancements often take the form of new and improved models—i.e., models which better account for all the data that needs explaining. Thus, astronomers studying our solar system shifted from a geocentric model to a heliocentric model; and physicists studying combustion shifted from models involving phlogiston to models involving oxygen and nitrogen. However, the Christian tradition has affirmed historically that many of the models we use in talking about God have been *given* to us by God. Of course, we may need to make judgments about whether certain models in scripture (e.g., God as "father") and in the Creeds (e.g., that Jesus Christ was one person with two natures) are in fact unique in their divine inspiration and divinely-sanctioned use among confessing Christians. If so, then such models arguably are not open to revision. Unlike in science, usefulness would not be the crucial criterion as to when it is appropriate to adopt a new model.

Third, questions remain as to whether, and in what ways, we are committed to final, ontological claims about God when we make use of models. The early Church settled on the description of Jesus Christ as one person with both a divine and human nature because this description was needed to account for the full range of information it had pertaining to the words and work of Jesus Christ. Remembering our example from science of light as both wave and particle, we noted that scientists need not be committed to saying that light both *is* a wave and *is* a particle. Rather, the point of holding the two models was that it allowed scientists to explain the *behavior* of light. Is it sufficient for the theologian to affirm that Jesus Christ *behaved* as one with both a divine and human nature? Or are corresponding ontological claims needed in order for the Creeds about Jesus Christ to serve a genuine professions of Christian faith?

The three general issues I have raised related to the use of models—how we specify the limits to our analogies, whether models can appropriately be reformulated, and whether models commit us to ontological claims—are by no means exhaustive. Still, they seem to be key questions. I do not attempt here to give definitive answers to the questions, even where definitive answers might be sought. Rather, I raise the questions simply to note them as issues with which we are faced when we use models in our descriptions of God.

ASPECTS OF TRUTH AND KNOWLEDGE

We have noted that some of Wood's references to our limited, "anthropomorphic" language raise issues related to the use of models when speaking about God. Other references to human language seem to raise still further issues having to do with human limitations and even with the limitations of logic. Consider one of the reasons Wood cites as to why we might be tempted to reject Boethius's view of eternity: "I also believe that our understanding of this issue is confused if we are locked within a modernist notion of truth—as if the intent of language and propositions is to mirror reality literally based on the intuitive logic of ordinary human experience."[42] At this point Wood appeals to the work of philosophers such as Richard Rorty, who argues that "the idea that words must mirror reality in a literalist sense truncates the larger meaning of truth."[43] Instead of thinking that our language about God must "mirror" real, objective facts about God, Wood finds promise in the ideas of philosophers such as Paul Ricoeur that we should "appreciate the nature of figurative and poetic language as a valid means of understanding the nature of things and God."[44]

It is unclear, though, just what all this has to do with the nature of *truth*. It seems more natural to think of the kinds of language limitations Wood mentions as indicating the kinds of *knowledge* we might have outside of propositional knowledge, which has been the standard kind of knowledge discussed by early modern philosophers and their commentators. Consider Wood's reference to the sort of scientific knowledge Roger Penrose has sought to identify, saying that

> [Penrose] argues that the mind is capable of engaging in non-computational understanding that transcends mathematics and logic.... Mathematics and the principles of logic are indispensable tools for explaining things and cannot be dismissed as irrelevant, but they have their limitations because there is a dimension of truth that can be derived only from the non-mathematical activity of conscious thinking in general.[45]

Again, I suppose it is possible to spell out this issue in terms of "dimensions of truth." However, I think a much more natural way to explore this issue is to bring out the different kinds of knowledge we can have.

Philosophers and theologians alike have recognized that some kinds of knowledge do not seem readily reducible to propositional knowledge. The example of *knowing someone* is arguably not reducible simply to knowing propositions *about* that person. Theologians have long made use of this point in talking about the kind of knowledge gained by those who have a personal relationship with God. Also, *knowledge how* to do

42. Wood, "Reply to Padgett," 12.
43. Ibid.
44. Ibid.
45. Ibid., 14.

something seems difficult to reduce simply to knowing propositions. For someone who had never ridden a bicycle, reading a long list of instructions about "how to ride a bicycle" hardly allows the person to say that she 'knows how' to ride a bicycle.

In criticizing the idea that we should think of our language about God as simply "mirroring" God, perhaps Woods is seeking to bring out the point that the kind of knowledge we can have of God is not simply reducible to propositional statements which correspond to facts about God. If so, then I will agree. However, I think we would do well to set aside references to different "dimensions of truth." I think we find various issues conflated within most attempts to challenge the traditional correspondence model of truth. And I myself am dubious that a decisive objection to the model will—indeed can—be raised. At any rate, I do not think that Wood needs to appeal to notions of truth to make his general point that our knowledge of God, sometimes gained through personal encounter and sometimes best captured though poetry, will escape reduction to propositional statements. And since we apply logic to the relations between propositional statements, our knowledge of God will sometimes therefore escape logical analysis.

Perhaps the time is right for theologians to recapture the medieval emphasis on contemplation. The rise of the so-called scientific method over the past 400 years has led to theological discussions often taking the form of scientific inquiries. Specific questions are identified, and answers are then sought by investigating the information available to us. To be sure, this method can lead us to deeper understandings in both science and in theology. Wood's discussion of time and divine eternity highlights this fact. However, it is worth asking why much of the Christian tradition historically has commended as part of one's spiritual formation the practice of contemplation, where one allows oneself to be shaped by experiences with God. This is in contrast to the scientific method of identifying specific questions at the outset and then seeking answers to them—with the answers only amounting to genuine answers if they correspond to the pre-arranged categories that give the original questions their content.

The practice of contemplation might be one conclusion suggested by Wood's assertions that out language about God should not become too "anthropomorphic" and should not be always be analyzed in terms of logical relations. Admittedly, Wood's discussion of divine eternity is not in the mode of contemplation. In fact, his discussion assumes that scientists and theologians are engaged in largely the same project, even sharing largely the same methodology. At the same time, he may be (rightly) hinting at the limits of the theologian's adaptation of the scientist's method.

CONCLUSION

In this essay I have tried to show why we should, and ultimately must, rely on logic in making affirmations about God. I have sought to distinguish genuine logical contradictions from tensions, paradoxes, and mysteries, of which the Christian tradition has always made use in describing God and God's interaction with our world. I have discussed the use of models, to which theologians will inevitably need to appeal in describing the God who transcends our world. And I have noted different kinds of knowledge we might have of God, where logical analysis may not always be applicable. All these issues are introduced at various points within Wood's discussion of divine eternity. I have simply sought to disentangle some of these issues. My goal has not so much been to settle these issues, but rather to identify the issues with which we will need to wrestle as we seek coherent descriptions of this God whom we will be seeking to understand more fully for all eternity.

10

Evolution and the Deep Resonances Between Science and Theology

MICHAEL L. PETERSON

EVOLUTION IS AT THE heart of dramatic tensions between science and religion in contemporary American culture. The lines of division are sharply drawn. The New Atheism—advanced by Richard Dawkins, Daniel Dennett, E. O. Wilson, and others—maintains that science, and in particular evolutionary science, answers all important human questions while invalidating religion. Creation Science—developed by Henry Morris and Duane Gish, and currently defended by Ken Ham and his Answers in Genesis organization—insists on a literal interpretation of Genesis, an alternative science of origins, and the fallacies of evolution. Intelligent Design (or ID)—based on writings by Michael Behe and William Dembski, promoted by the Discovery Institute, and recommended to the faithful by Chuck Colson, Rick Warren, and James Dobson—argues that a transcendent intelligence, not evolution, is the explanation of certain complex biological structures.

The controversy over the scientific theory of evolution, of course, raises the more general issue of the relationship of science and religion, a controversy dating back to the dawn of the modern age, when the Galileo affair foreshadowed the coming clashes between these two important human activities. The challenge then, as it is now, is that of relating the theories and findings of science to specifically Christian theological knowledge. In the Galileo affair, the new heliocentric astronomy did not conflict with Christian belief per se but with the ecclesiastical authority which insisted that both the biblical record and theological teaching support a geocentric view. Christian reflections on this event have concluded that there is no inherent conflict between Christianity and science, and that indeed science is a means of discovering the empirical details of God's creation. But then what about evolution as described by science? The Christian community generally has come to embrace the breath-taking sweep of cosmic evolution—the Big Bang 13.7 billion years ago, the nuclear activity of giant stars which provided the early chemical complexification of the universe, the violent formation of galaxies (such as our own relatively modest galaxy, the Milky Way, among billions of others), the great antiquity of the Earth, and the expanding universe.

What about biological evolution? Applying the lessons of the Galileo affair would suggest not only that there is no conflict between Christianity and biology but also that the biological facts, once again, must somehow reflect God's purposes in creation. This general view—falling under the rubric of *theistic evolution*—has long been accepted by many scientists in the believing community. For example, this view was expressed by Asa Gray and Charles Babbage, who were contemporaries of Darwin. Reflecting a full century of further scientific progress, in 1973, Theodosius Dobzhansky, a Russian Orthodox believer and acclaimed geneticist, published a famous article entitled "Nothing in Biology Makes Sense Except in the Light of Evolution."[1] Theistic evolution is also endorsed by the American Scientific Affiliation, an avowedly Christian organization. It is not difficult to find practicing scientists who are Christian and who embrace theistic evolution (e.g., Kenneth Miller, Simon Conway Morris, and Joan Roughgarden). Another high-profile scientist, Francis Collins, former director of the Human Genome Project and now director of the National Institutes of Health, founded the BioLogos Foundation (and website) to promote understanding of theistic evolution. Faithfully participating in the cultural discussion, Collins debated Dawkins in a *Time* magazine joint interview, arguing that "God's creative power ... brought it all into being in the first place."[2] Various versions of this view are also supported by Christian philosophers and theologians (e.g., George Coyne of the Vatican Observatory, Ted Peters, Keith Ward, and Pope John Paul II). No doubt, theistic evolution will never satisfy Creation Science advocates or even proponents of ID who subject it to excessive qualification and selective rebuttal. But both of these camps are in their own ways intellectual descendants of Protestant fundamentalism, a movement whose defects have been thoroughly catalogued in many other venues.[3]

In reflecting on evolution from within the Wesleyan tradition, I will not do battle here with the New Atheism, Creation Science, or Intelligent Design—all of which systematically misinterpret the evolutionary story emerging from the sciences as the embodiment of philosophical naturalism and atheism. In fact, I am pleased that some of the Wesleyan and Methodist denominations—such as the United Methodist Church and the Church of the Nazarene—have official statements either endorsing or expressing openness to some version of theistic evolution, as do the Catholic, Anglican, and Episcopal Churches. My present aim is to accept the premise of theistic evolution (the simple conjunction of theism and evolution) and then explore how it may be developed into a much richer perspective that advances contemporary theological insight and articulation. In every age and for every generation, theology must maintain relevance and credibility by interacting with all that we come to know and experience in nature and history. What

---

1. Theodosius Dobzhansky, *American Biology Teacher* 35 (1973) 125–29.

2. David Biem et al., "God vs. Science," *Time* (November 13, 2006) 48–55. Online: http://www.time.com/time/magazine/article/0,9171,1555132-3,00.html.

3. See Ronald Numbers, *The Creationists: From Scientific Creationism to Intelligent Design* (Cambridge: Harvard University Press, 2006). See also "Religion and Science" in Michael Peterson et al., *Philosophy of Religion: Selected Readings*, 4th ed. (New York: Oxford University Press, 2010) 507–70.

is more, theology seeks pure understanding, the ever deepening penetration into the enduring truths of the faith. Critical aspects of that understanding necessarily depend on sympathetically embracing the scientific position on evolution. Taking the integrative and interdisciplinary role of philosophy seriously, I identify here some of the intimate and important ties between theological truth and the scientific facts.

It is commonplace for discussions of philosophical problems in religion—the problem of evil, problems over the divine attributes, the problem of divine action, etc.—to revolve around the implications of standard theism without direct reliance upon Christian doctrines and beliefs. Likewise, in discussing the problem of relating science and Christian belief, theistic evolution per se carries no more theological content than that of standard theism (the claim that an omnipotent, omniscient, perfectly good deity underwrites the physical existence and lawful processes of the universe) and is therefore compatible with Judaism and Islam. Often, basic theistic evolution is supplemented by an appropriate nonliteral reading of disputed passages of scripture in order to construct an approach that Christians find intellectually helpful. In this regard, St. Augustine now seems almost prescient in his commentary on Genesis when he urges Christians to make biblical interpretation, not biblical authority, the proper focus in the encounter with extra-theological knowledge. He even counsels that believers must be ready to seek a different interpretation of a biblical text "if reason should prove that [some factual] opinion [which appears to conflict with the text] is unquestionably true." It is worth quoting at length Augustine's passionate argument regarding how scientific incompetence in believers can negatively affect the perception of the gospel:

> Now, it is a disgraceful and dangerous thing for a [nonbeliever] to hear a Christian, presumably giving the meaning of Holy Scripture, talking nonsense on these [scientific] topics; and we should take all means to prevent such an embarrassing situation, in which people show up vast ignorance in a Christian and laugh it to scorn. The shame is not so much that an ignorant individual is derided, but that people outside the household of faith think our sacred writers held such opinions, and, to the great loss of those for whose salvation we toil, the writers of our Scripture are criticized and rejected as unlearned men. If they find a Christian mistaken in a field which they themselves know well and hear him maintaining his foolish opinions about our books, how are they going to believe those books in matters concerning the resurrection of the dead, the hope of eternal life, and the kingdom of heaven, when they think their pages are full of falsehoods on facts which they themselves have learnt from experience and the light of reason?[4]

Logically, the union of appropriate nonliteral readings of certain biblical passages with theistic evolution is one way of securing the compatibility (i.e., lack of incompatibility) of Christianity and the science of evolution, but it does not provide a coherent and comprehensive account of why reality is the way it is. To develop such an account, we must take the advice of Marilyn Adams, who says that the full intellectual resources of distinctively *Christian* theism must be employed to address the most difficult philo-

---

4. Augustine, *The Literal Meaning of Genesis*, Ancient Christian Writers 41, trans. and annotation J. Taylor (New York: Newman, 1982) 42–43.

sophical challenges facing Christian belief. In the present context, this means that basic theism, even coupled with enlightened biblical interpretation, cannot speak for the total Christian theological vision.[5] Instead we must identify and explore some of the deepest aspects of Christian theology in order to engage evolutionary science. But how, exactly, should this project proceed?

HOW CAN CHRISTIAN FAITH ENGAGE EVOLUTIONARY SCIENCE?

Michael Ruse, philosophical naturalist and preeminent Darwinian philosopher of science, in a talk about difficulties that Christianity faces in engaging evolutionary science, offered what he calls the "five bottom line demands" of the Christian: God created the universe; humans bear God's image; humans are fallen; Christ as Redeemer died for our sins; and hence we have the possibility of eternal life.[6] This poor man's kerygma, an incomplete summary at best, represents an honest attempt to portray expressly Christian ideas that go beyond standard theism. But in the end Ruse still believes that evolution, grounded in science, is the basis for a world system which excludes a Christian (or any) religious perspective. The utter nondirectedness of evolution, as Ruse sees it, has strong anti-theistic implications. In his own words, "naturalism, atheism, and skepticism are more reasonable."

I responded publicly to Ruse at the time, stating that this five-point description of Christian belief is fine as far as it goes but that it is not conceptually rich enough to generate many interesting and powerful implications regarding the facts of evolution. Feeling strangely inspired by Richard Dawkins' litany of a dozen and a half adjectives for the God of the Old Testament (a litany which includes vindictive, bloodthirsty, infanticidal, homophobic, megalomaniacal, and other less than flattering terms), I recited my own list of more than a dozen adjectives to characterize the understanding of Christian theism which I am quite confident is capable of a fruitful encounter with evolutionary science:

> *Classical, ecumenical, historically orthodox, Nicene, Constantinopolitan, Chalcedonian, Trinitarian, creational, incarnational, sacramental, kenotic, perichoretic, ontologically and epistemologically realist, natural law* Christian theism.

Some of these qualifiers may seem overlapping or redundant, but I use them to refer to quite specific and related themes in the Christian picture of reality. Additional qualifiers might be proposed, but this list will serve as shorthand for an amazing vision of God, the universe, and human destiny that accounts for the most profound insights of the sciences.

---

5. Marilyn McCord Adams, *Horrendous Evils and the Goodness of God* (Ithaca and London: Cornell University Press, 1999) e.g., 4.

6. Michael Ruse, "Can a Darwinian Be a Christian?—The Human Problem," paper presented at The Venice Summer School of Science and Religion on the topic Evolution and Human Uniqueness, Venice, Italy (May 29, 2009). For a more thorough discussion of this matter, see Ruse's book *Can a Darwinian Be a Christian? The Relationship between Science and Religion* (Cambridge: Cambridge University Press, 2001).

Referring to Ian Barbour's taxonomy of different models of the science-religion relationship, we must say that a historically orthodox Christian position simply cannot settle for a *conflict model* (a la Dawkins) or even an *independence model* (a la Gould). In fact, even a *dialogue model*, which correctly recommends interaction as a necessary process of reciprocal appreciation and comprehension, does not assume that there can be a unified understanding of reality which integrates all truths in the various disciplines with the truths of theology. Yet the classical conception of created reality as a "uni-verse" (one-truth) suggests that truth in science and truth in theology are intimately tied together in a coherent whole. All of the sciences, then, with their pervasively evolutionary findings, must be taken very seriously by an intellectually robust Christian faith, since they are integral to the "one-truth" we seek to know ever more clearly.

A basic picture of reality is also projected by the sciences—a picture that may be thematically characterized to give us a sense of the kind of world revealed by disciplined empirical inquiry. In my opinion, then, progress toward a unified understanding is achieved as we operate on the basis of an *integration model* in which science contributes to theological reflection and theology provides context for science. Such an approach carefully examines the respective pictures of reality from contemporary science and Christian theology in order to detect important correlations—indeed, profound resonances—between them.

A SKETCH OF THE THEOLOGICAL PICTURE OF REALITY

Let us begin by sketching some of the large themes of classical Christian orthodoxy, followed by those of science, exploring the significance of each theme as we proceed.

Classical, Ecumenical, Historically Orthodox. Classical Christianity is the definition of Christian belief hammered out by councils, synods, and consensual bodies convened during the early life of the church. These conclaves met on a worldwide basis to enunciate a precise understanding of Jesus Christ, the Holy Spirit, the Trinity, and other doctrines and, in so doing, to distinguish authentic Christian belief from heresy and error. The official declarations of the Seven Great Councils—Nicaea I, Constantinople I, Ephesus, Chalcedon, Constantinople II, Constantinople III, and Nicaea II—bound all Christians East and West. Universal Christianity—that is, catholic Christianity—supplies the intellectual content necessary to engage science. To begin, universal Christianity points singularly to the overarching goal of our existence as human creatures. The *Catechism of the Catholic Church* poignantly declares:

> God, infinitely perfect and blessed in himself, in a plan of sheer goodness freely created man to make him share in his own blessed life.... The desire for God is written in the human heart, because man is created by God and for God; and God never ceases to draw man to himself.[7]

We were made for God; we find the meaning of our existence in relation to him. And we are meant to experience God's life taking root and growing in our lives within a worship-

---

7. *Catechism of the Catholic Church* (Liguori, MO: United States Catholic Conference, 1994) 7, 15.

ing community. This great mystery occurs, therefore, in the midst of the people who are called Christ's body. The *Westminster Confession* states: "All saints that are united to Jesus Christ their head, by his Spirit and by faith, have fellowship with him in his graces, sufferings, death, resurrection, and glory, and being united to one another in love, they have communion in each other's gifts and graces...."[8] Indeed, the Apostles' Creed makes "communion of the saints" a necessary item of belief.

Nicene, Constantinopolitan, Chalcedonian. The findings of all of the Seven Great Councils clarify and solidify important elements of Christian faith; but the first councils of Nicaea (325) and Constantinople (381) as well as the council of Chalcedon (451) shall serve as symbolic for our purposes. At Nicaea, of course, the nature of Christ the Son of God was formulated: that he is not simply the most perfect of all creatures but is consubstantial and co-eternal with the Father ("eternally begotten of the Father, God from God, Light from Light, true God from true God"). At Constantinople, the belief that the Holy Spirit is a Person and proceeds from (and therefore must be of the same substance with) the Father was affirmed, thus giving endorsement to the concept of the Trinity ("with the Father and the Son he is worshiped and glorified"). At Chalcedon, the meaning of the Incarnation was further refined: that Jesus Christ our Lord perfectly and forever unites in one Person two distinct natures, human and divine, without confusion of the human with the divine or the diminution of either the human or the divine ("truly God and truly man"). Such theological statements, resulting from the councils, form an important basis for a Christian vision of reality capable of productive engagement with contemporary science.

Trinitarian. Significant theological explanation is often generated by the power of a single crucial insight. Only Trinitarian belief is complex enough to match the depth of experience recorded in the Bible and continued in the ongoing life of the Church. Yet the concept of the Trinity is not merely a summary of experience (the economic Trinity known through creation and salvation); rather it is—following Rahner's Rule—to be identified with the Immanent Trinity (God in Himself in His own eternity, infinity and glory).[9] God's nature is truly, but not exhaustively, made known through his revelatory acts. This means that the proclamation of the "One in Three and Three in One" is not a just another mystical formula. It is a privileged metaphysical insight, vouchsafed to the body of believers: that the Godhead is intrinsically a dynamic personal, interpersonal, social, and relational Being, with the Persons interacting in mutual relations of self-giving love. Reflecting the renaissance of Trinitarian theology in our day, this essay assumes that Trinitarian themes are not simply one area of theology but provide the very framework for theology, including the other theological themes explored below.

Creational, Incarnational, Sacramental. The concept of "creation out of nothing" (*creatio ex nihilo*) reflects the truth that reality is fundamentally divided into two broad domains:

---

8. *The Westminster Confession*, art. 26. See the complete *Confession* in the Appendix in Paul Smith, *The Westminster Confession: Enjoying God Forever* (Chicago: Moody, 1998).

9. Karl Rahner, *The Trinity* (London: Burns & Oates, 1970) 22.

the Creator and the creation. The classical doctrine of creation entails that God freely—without necessity or cosmic conflict—brought everything else into being. Knowledge of the nature of God as Creator entails that the creaturely realm is real, rational, and good.[10] For purposes of this discussion, to be real is to posses the gift of material existence, to be rational is to possess order amenable to mind, and to be good is to have divinely-bestowed worth. To be creaturely, however, also means to be dependent, not self-sufficient—and this contingency means that the Creator is continually keeping the creation from ontological collapse. Humanity, as the crowning aspect of creation, is said to bear the image of God (*imago Dei*), to be made essentially to be like God in certain finite respects and to be destined for communion with God. The doctrine of the Incarnation is both evidence of God's desire to identify intimately with humanity and the first fruit of humanity actually being taken into the divine life. With divinely-given authority, the Church leads us into this mystery of grace by administering the sacrament of the Eucharist. But we may appropriately enlarge the definition of sacrament in the Anglican *Thirty-Nine Articles*—as "a visible sign of an invisible grace"—so that all things in ordinary life and in the larger reality we inhabit potentially become sacramental, avenues of God's grace. We can briefly sum up implications of the creational-incarnational-sacramental nature of Christian faith that relate to present concerns: that God loves matter; that humanity is intimately connected to the material realm; and that the whole of nature (human and subhuman), though finite and contingent, has an ultimate destiny in the purposes of God.

Kenotic. It should be no surprise that one of the most striking descriptions of the humility and condescension of Christ—that "he emptied himself" (Phil 2:7 NRSV)—is one of the richest and most central theological concepts. The Son of God thought it no shame to become one with humanity and share our lot, with the purpose of inviting us into fellowship with himself. Theologian Donald Dawe laments our lack of attention to the full meaning of "self-emptying" (*kenosis*):

> The audacity of this belief in the divine kenosis has often been lost by long familiarity with it.... The familiar phrases "he emptied himself [*heauton ekenosen*], taking the form of a servant," "though he was rich, yet for your sake he became poor," have come to seem commonplace. Yet this belief in the divine self-emptying epitomizes the radically new message of Christian faith about God and his relation to man.[11]

Since love is the essential nature of God, it follows logically that the object of love must be given an appropriate degree of independence for genuinely free response. Divine self-limitation, then, makes possible human freedom, which is a necessary condition for being truly able to love God and to develop all of the relational values that make for human fulfillment. On broader theological grounds, we must conclude that the whole of divinely-created reality, and not just our own species' brief history here, is kenotic in character, as God limits his full power and glory, because this might well be the only way to make a creation at all.

---

10. See Daniel O'Connor and Francis Oakley, eds., *Creation: The Impact of an Idea* (New York: Scribners, 1969) Part I on "Nature."

11. Donald Dawe, *The Form of a Servant* (Philadelphia: Westminster, 1963) 13–15.

Perichoretic. Beginning with the Cappadocian Fathers, Christian theology has used the term *perichoresis* to refer to the mutual inter-penetration and mutual indwelling of the Father, Son, and Holy Spirit within the Trinity. Biblical passages such as "The Father is in the Son, and the Son in the Father" ground this theme, which has been revitalized in our day by John Zizioulas, Jürgen Moltmann, and others.[12] The Father and the Son do not simply embrace each other, but so intimate and harmonious is their communion that they also permeate each other, and dwell in each other eternally, in one Being. All of this suggests that the inner life of God is dynamic, not static, and characterized by self-giving, self-sacrificing love. It is not difficult to imagine why St. Gregory of Nazianzus characterized God's inner life as "the Great Dance."[13] Jesus himself extended the idea of mutual indwelling in an ecclesiastical direction in his prayer, "That they all may be one; as thou, Father, art in me, and I in thee, that they also may be one in us" (John 17:21 NRSV). So, the amazing invitation is for humanity to be drawn into the life of God—to become a partner in the great dance of mutual love relations. According to Jesus, our participation in that Life which is the True Life should be manifest in our unity with each other: "That they may be one." Whatever else *perichoresis* means for the Church, it surely means that we must "dwell within" one another, giving ourselves to one another, or the world will not believe that the Son "dwells within" and "came forth from" the Father. The anthropological implication here is that the image of God which we bear includes the perichoretic relations with other finite persons as essential: that each created person is a distinct center of consciousness and will, and yet whose personhood is partly constituted by relations to other persons. The persons are real, the relations between them are real, and the intrinsic need for relationship is real. Extending the classical Thomistic idea of *analogia entis* (analogy to the being of God), we recognize *analogia relationis* (analogy to the relationality of God) as well.

Ontologically and Epistemologically Realist. Historic orthodoxy assumes a general metaphysical realism: the view that the common reality we inhabit is constituted by real entities with determinate natures which act and react to produce the manifold phenomenon we experience. One could not embrace the Nicene Creed, for example, without presupposing the existence of the self who affirms it (*credo*), the historical reality of other persons, such as Mary and Pontius Pilate, and the real existence of natural objects, such as light and burial places. But the Creed, as well as other formulations of the faith, also assumes the reality of God, the Trinitarian Persons, the resurrected Jesus, the mystical union of the Church, and other theological realities. Thus, ontological realism about theological entities provides the assumptions which form the truth conditions of orthodox belief. Also inherent in orthodoxy is a necessary and broad epistemological realism: the conviction

---

12. See, for example, John Zizioulas, *Being as Communion* (Yonkers, NY: St Vladimir's Seminary Press, 1997) and Jürgen Moltmann, *The Trinity and the Kingdom: The Doctrine of God* (Harper & Row, New York, 1981).

13. St. Gregory of Nazianzus, *Oration* 18.16. See also the quite colorful website entitled "Seeking God in Einstein's Universe: Into the Weirdness" which uses the theme of the dance of the universe to paint a colorful scientific view of reality in relation to the perichoretic understanding of the Trinitarian Persons: http://myslu.stlawu.edu/~aodo/SLU/SOAR/GodEinstein06/Into%20the%20Weirdness.pdf.

that the human mind is suited to know the common realities in our experience as well as the theological realities which are the referents of our creeds, systems, and ordinary religious beliefs. To be precise, the term "critical realism" is preferred these days to denote a version of realism which is sophisticated about the complex conditions of knowledge but which is nevertheless committed to the basic ability of the mind to know objective reality. When fully explicated, the twin realisms here—ontological and epistemological—expose the many anti-realist interpretations of the faith to be both seriously inadequate on their own terms and distortive of the nature of theological belief as it relates to the science-religion discussion. Neo-Wittgensteinian "language-game" interpretations, Kuhnian "socially supported paradigm" interpretations, and Kierkegaardian "existential necessity" interpretations have all been fashionable in assigning some non-correspondence type of "truth" to theology in order to allow religion and science to coexist in different spheres. But today the onslaught of scientific atheism, led by Dawkins and Dennett, is militantly anti-realist about any form of "truth" in religion and even labors for the demise of religion as part of society's progressive enlightenment.[14] Only a robustly realist Christian orthodoxy has the philosophical compass for navigating this intense debate.

Realism about Science, Too. Of course, anti-realist approaches distort not only the proper nature of theology but also the nature of science. While virtually all philosophies of science admit the enormous success of science in predicting and manipulating empirical phenomena, the history of the philosophy of science includes many influential anti-realist interpretations—the Vienna Circle's logical positivism, Popper's falsificationism, Quine's instrumentalism, Kuhn's social constructivism, postmodernism's deconstructionism, etc. At stake here, primarily, is the existence and knowability of unobservable entities; but other areas of anti-realist attention include the scientific method in relation to the justification of scientific beliefs, causal laws, and the notion of scientific progress.[15] Once again, a healthy epistemological and ontological realism—this time in the philosophy of science—affords crucial insight into the nature and intellectual integrity of science, and supports an understanding of science that can credibly interact with realist theology. Only a realist approach to science, therefore, is able to contribute its fair share to an integrated view of reality.[16]

Natural Law. Natural law moral theory extends the above endorsement of a healthy realism to the moral realm as well. No confusion need exist between this classical mean-

---

14. Richard Dawkins, *The God Delusion* (Boston: Houghton Mifflin, 2006); Daniel C. Dennett, *Breaking the Spell: Religion as a Natural Phenomenon* (New York: Viking Penguin, 2006).

15. For surveys of approaches, consult the following: David Papineau, ed., *The Philosophy of Science* (Oxford: Oxford University Press, 1996); James Ladyman, *Understanding Philosophy of Science* (London: Routledge, 2001); Stewart Brock and Edwin Mares, *Realism and Anti-Realism* (Durham: Acumen, 2007).

16. See the following: Ernan McMullin, "A Case for Scientific Realism" in *Scientific Realism*, edited by Jarett Leplin (Berkeley: University of California Press, 1984); Rom Harré, *Varieties of Realism* (Oxford: Basil Blackwell, 1986); Edward Madden and Rom Harré, *Causal Powers* (Oxford: Basil Blackwell, 1976); Stathis Psillos, *Scientific Realism: How Science Tracks Truth* (London: Routledge, 1999); Michael Peterson, "Critical Realism" in *Science and Religion Primer*, edited by Heidi Campbell and Heather Looy (Grand Rapids: Baker Academic, 2009).

ing of natural law as the law of human nature—specifically, our moral nature—and the modern meaning, which pertains to scientific descriptions of regularities in the physical world. Classical natural law thinking, with roots in Aristotle and Aquinas, affirms the objectivity of moral values and principles as well as the human ability to make reliable judgments about them. Moral realism, then, is best treated as part of the larger realist tradition which includes ontological and epistemological realism. In fact, a positive realist ontology of our common human nature supports universal moral insights about how human beings ought to act and be treated. In *The Abolition of Man*, C. S. Lewis observes that the pervasive moral precepts and judgments of humankind are variously called "Natural Law or Traditional Morality or the First Principles of Practical Reason or the First Platitudes."[17] For Christians, the *telos* inherent in human nature is nothing less than our destiny in the life of God, characterized in part by moral and spiritual virtues, thus providing the link between natural law theory and virtue theory.[18] Moral realism bears on the science-religion discussion in a variety of ways—including its affirmation that we can know objective nonempirical realities as well as its inherent ability to overcome the alleged fact-value dichotomy by anchoring morality in metaphysical and moral facts about human nature. I will not go into an excursus here about the superiority of natural law moral theory over divine command ethics, but I note that further analysis would reveal fascinating similarities in how the dualism in divine command approaches is related to various other dualisms that present unnecessary obstacles to desired progress in the science-religion area (e.g., interventionism as the primary mode of divine activity in the world, mind-body substance dualism, etc.).

A SKETCH OF THE SCIENTIFIC PICTURE OF REALITY

We now move to a characterization of some of the major themes that define the shape of contemporary science.

Fragmentary Accounts Converging on a More Complete Picture. The various scientific disciplines in aggregate constitute an extensive account of the way things are in the natural realm. Each scientific discipline investigates various domains peculiar to it: physics, for example, includes subatomic physics, condensed matter physics, continuum mechanics, and so on. Within each domain, we have gained considerable understanding of the processes involved and have made much progress; nevertheless not all connections among domains are yet completely understood. We are still uncertain, for instance, about how to resolve perplexities over how classical physics and quantum physics relate. Moreover, even though we have made significant connections across major fields of science, we are still working at the project of making more connections. In fact, some relatively new sciences position themselves at the intersection of established disciplines in order to make connections not available within any one of them—for instance, neuroscience seeks to relate molecular biology, genetics, chemistry, and psychology in the study of hu-

---

17. C. S. Lewis, *The Abolition of Man* (New York: Macmillan, 1947) 56; see also 84.

18. For a recent exploration of this linkage, see Craig Boyd, *A Shared Morality: A Narrative Defense of Natural Law Ethics* (Grand Rapids: Brazos, 2007).

man cognitive, behavioral, and emotional functions. While all of the sciences have made enormous strides, and the connections we have already made fill in quite a picture of the way things are, much remains to be discovered. So we take the partial and progressive nature of science simply to reflect human finitude and to motivate further progress.

Interplay of Chance and Necessity. As Jacques Monod convincingly argued, both chance and necessity form the warp and woof of the universe; indeed, they are required for continual dynamic development.[19] From a scientific perspective, the origin of life begins in the chance aggregation of simple molecules into complexes capable of self-replication. But they are able to reproduce themselves through the regularity of their chemical interaction with the environment, as they acquire simple molecules as a kind of "food." So, on the one hand, chance brings about novelty and catalyzes change within complex systems. Necessity, on the other hand, reflects the laws inherent in the universe and allows preservation and selection. The role of physical necessity, then, is not the total determination of events but the provision of a stable context in which particularity occurs—i.e., this happens rather than that. The basic polarity of necessity and chance within material reality itself sets up both the predictability and the unpredictability that we encounter in the sciences, an openness within structure. We must remember that, on strictly scientific grounds, there is no need to follow Monod in interpreting chance as "blind" and thus inconsistent with significance and meaning, since this would commit the fallacy of confusing chance *within* a possible world with chance *among* possible worlds. Frankly, total causal determination is just as much a threat to meaning, but in an opposite way.

Process of Evolving and Emerging Complexity. The scientific narrative begins with the initial singularity, when the universe was just a tiny, expanding point of energy, and moves through early cosmic history when the universe became grainy and lumpy with stars and galaxies, and leads to the current cosmos, which is populated by rich and diverse structures, including scientists and theologians who debate what it all means. The processes that brought about this amazingly fruitful transformation are deeply evolutionary in character, at both the cosmic and biological levels—and these processes result from the fertile interplay of chance and necessity. Absolute necessity would characterize a world too rigid to permit anything really new to emerge, whereas pure chance would make the world too haphazard to allow anything really new to persist. In biology, we know that a degree of chance genetic mutation is required for there to be new forms of life. But without a degree of stable genetic transfer between generations, no new species could be established on which natural selection could operate. In general terms, then, the sciences find themselves in a regime where the symbiotic relation of order and contingency produces wholly new forms of complexity: life from inanimate matter; consciousness from life; human self-consciousness from consciousness.[20] These radically new forms

---

19. Jacques Monod, *Chance and Necessity: An Essay on the Natural Philosophy of Modern Biology* (New York: Knopf, 1971).

20. Interestingly, these events are exactly the sort of major junctures in evolutionary history which Antony Flew credits with prodding his intellectual journey away from the position of atheism to a kind of deistic position which accepts an intelligence beyond the universe. He astutely steers between the unac-

were unforeseeable based on initial conditions together with the relevant laws. "The evolutionary picture," writes historian of science Owen Gingerich, "is one of a zigzag, opportunistic process."[21]

Fine-tuned Anthropic Potentiality. Much of the debate over the evolutionary contour of the sciences focuses on the chance part of the equation, but the exact nature of the necessity involved should not be considered any less significant. Science now recognizes that lawful regularity had to take a very specific, precisely quantifiable form if it were to be possible for carbon-based life to evolve anywhere in the universe. Although life only seems to have developed after about ten billion years of cosmic history, the cosmos was pregnant with this possibility from the Big Bang onward. Since the early universe contained only hydrogen and helium, carbon-12, with its capacity to generate long chain molecules, had to be generated. But there is only one place in the whole universe where carbon-12 atoms can be made: the interior nuclear furnaces of the stars. It is not a sentimental metaphor but rather literal truth that we are people of stardust! Astronomer Fred Hoyle arrived at the remarkable insight that a statistically improbable enhancement effect at just the right energy level—enabling the triple-alpha process—allowed stellar carbon production. Only slight differences in the physics of the situation would have made the production of carbon completely impossible.[22] Ironically, Hoyle's discovery of stellar nucleosynthesis made it difficult for him to maintain his life-long commitment to atheism, and so he posited a "super-intellect" behind the laws of nature without giving it the status of deity.[23] But Hoyle's discovery is only one of many that point to the delicate balance of forces in the universe which make life possible.[24]

Anthropic Potentiality Continued. In biology, we find a similar thesis about the anthropic potential of the universe offered to counter a position held by the late Steven Jay Gould of Harvard. In *A Wonderful Life*, Gould claims that if we were to rewind the tape of

---

ceptable extremes of scientific reductionism and materialism, on the one hand, and the position of the Intelligent Design movement, on the other. See Flew, *There is a God: How the World's Most Notorious Atheist Changed His Mind* (New York: HarperOne, 2007).

21. Owen Gingerich, *God's Universe* (Cambridge, MA: Belknap, 2006) 33.

22. Although the process of stellar nuclear reactions is fairly straightforward, involving two atomic nuclei, which are in motion at tremendous speeds, collide, fuse, and form a heavier element. However, the clear exception is carbon because the intermediate phases from helium to carbon involve highly unstable nuclei. The probability of the necessary three helium nuclei coming together at the same instant is so small that it prompted Hoyle to notice a rare energy effect to boost the reaction and thus lead to the great abundance of carbon required for life in the universe.

23. Fred Hoyle, "The Universe: Past and Present Reflections," *Annual Reviews of Astronomy and Astrophysics* 20 (1982) 16. Also see Hoyle's *Intelligent Universe* (London: Michael Joseph Limited, 1983).

24. In light of this anthropic fertility, some thinkers have developed versions of the Anthropic Principle, offered Anthropic Arguments for God, etc.; but these are not to be confused with the quite specific arguments of the Intelligent Design movement which propose design as an alternative to natural selection. For two examples of reasoning about anthropic potentiality, see John Barrow and Frank Tipler, *The Anthropic Cosmological Principle* (Oxford: Clarendon, 1986); Neil Manson, *God and Design: The Teleological Argument and Modern Science* (London: Routledge, 2003). Regardless of the final appraisal of anthropic considerations, they surely show that science contributes at some level to our thinking about God.

evolutionary development on planet Earth and then run it forward again, the outcome would be entirely different, most certainly without humans and maybe without any form of intelligence at all. Myriad contingencies in the development of life, Gould contends, make the probability of human intelligence vanishingly small.[25] To the contrary, Simon Conway Morris, noted Cambridge paleobiologist, argues that, while the particularities (of five fingers on each hand, thirty-two teeth, etc.) are unlikely on a re-play of evolutionary history, the emergence of more general biological properties is highly likely indeed because there are only a limited number of ways in which eyes can work, brains can work, etc. Across different species, the recurrent tendency of biological organization to arrive at the same "solution" to a particular "need" gives rise to the concepts of "evolutionary convergence" and "evolutionary trajectory," which make human intelligence a "virtual inevitability." Morris writes:

> [I]f contingent happenstance dogs every step of evolution then assuredly the emergence of humans is a cosmic accident.... Yet convergence tells us two things: that evolutionary trends are real, and that adaptation is not some occasional cog in the organic machine, but is central to the explanation of how we came to be here.[26]

Morris further argues that the Earth, our local solar system, and the Milky Way Galaxy which we inhabit are uniquely constituted to be abodes for organic evolution, greatly unlike other systems in the universe—making our situation an odd collaboration of innumerable conditions that are remarkably well arranged for life. But what about intelligent or at least sentient life elsewhere in the universe? Overly ambitious values plugged into the Drake Equation[27]—such as those offered by Carl Sagan a few decades ago—have yielded a probability far above 1 for intelligent life elsewhere in the universe!? But honest recognition of the complex conditions required for life suggests both that Sagan's 1985 book *Contact* (made into the 1997 Jodie Foster film by that title) as well as researchers at the SETI Institute (Search for Extraterrestrial Intelligence Institute) are overly optimistic about the chances being high for extraterrestrial life, let alone intelligent life, and that we humans occupy a peculiarly favorable context in the whole of physical reality.

Relationality. At a variety of levels, a deep-seated interconnectivity inherent in the fabric of the physical world—as opposed to localized, atomistic individuality—is revealed to us by contemporary science. Impressive examples of this relationality are not difficult to find. Classical Newtonian physics conceived of physical processes in terms of the colli-

---

25. Steven Jay Gould, *A Wonderful Life: The Burgess Shale and the Nature of History* (New York: Norton, 1989) 50.

26. Simon Conway Morris, *Life's Solution: Inevitable Humans in a Lonely Universe* (Cambridge: Cambridge University Press, 2003) xv; see also xi–xii.

27. The Drake equation states that: $N = R^* \times fp \times ne \times fl \times fi \times fc \times L$. Where N is the number of civilizations in our galaxy in which communication might be possible; and R^* is the average rate of star formation per year in our galaxy, fp is the fraction of those stars that have planets, ne is the average number of planets that can potentially support life per star that has planets, fl is the fraction of the above that actually go on to develop life at some point, fi is the fraction of the above that actually go on to develop intelligent life, fc is the fraction of civilizations that develop a technology that releases detectable signs of their existence into space, and L is the length of time such civilizations release detectable signals into space.

sions of individual atoms moving in the container of absolute space in the course of unfolding absolute time. However, twentieth century physics is shaped by Albert Einstein's theory of special relativity, which maintains that judgments of simultaneity and of time duration are not absolute but instead are relative to the state of motion of the observer. In Einstein's general theory of relativity, space is likewise not absolute but is closely related to matter and time in a kind of interconnected package: matter curves spacetime, and spacetime curves the paths of matter. Another example is the work by Einstein, Boris Podolsky, and Nathan Rosen showing that quantum theory implies that two particles, once they have interacted, remain mutually entangled, regardless of how far they are separated, in effect, becoming a single system—the famous EPR effect. Still another case of amazing relationality within the universe is provided by chaos theory in which an infinitesimally small uncertainty concerning initial conditions can lead to enormous uncertainties in predicting subsequent behavior. Literally, the effect of moving an electron on a distant galaxy might be amplified over a long period of time to alter events on Earth. Generalizing this point, James Gliek states:

> There are fundamental laws about complex systems, but they are new kinds of laws. They are laws of structure and organization and scale, and they simply vanish when you focus on the individual constituents of a complex system—just as the psychology of a lynch mob vanishes when you interview individual participants.[28]

Atomism, reductionism, and determinism in science have long been superseded by relational concepts of a higher order subsuming the laws of particular levels, of the interaction of parts and wholes, and of continuity and emergence.

Relationality in the Life Sciences. The sciences in aggregate are moving in a decidedly holistic direction, with more and more relationships coming to light and regularly reinforced by new breakthroughs. Who among us can forget the astonishing announcement in 1987 in the journal *Nature* that three geneticists had identified humanity's most recent common ancestor, a woman who lived in Africa 200,000 years ago? This claim was subsequently discussed in *Time* and *Newsweek* cover stories. Given the name "Mitochondrial Eve," this woman is the one to whom all people living today can trace some of their genetic heritage through their mothers.[29] Since the successful mapping of the human genome in the 1990s, we see even more clearly the connectedness of biological life. Although paleontology, biogeology, comparative anatomy, and embryology gave early support to the universal Tree of Life evolutionary concept, now molecular biology,

---

28. James Gliek in the closing address at the 1990 Nobel Conference at Gustavus Adolphus College; quoted by Steven Weinberg in *Dreams of a Final Theory* (New York: Random, 1992) 61.

29. Rebecca Cann, Mark Stoneking, and Allan C. Wilson, (1987), "Mitochondrial DNA and Human Evolution," *Nature,* 325 (January 1, 1987) 31–36. Also see Michael Lemonick and Christina Garcia, "Everyone's Genealogical Mother," *Time* (January 26, 1987) 26; and John Tierney, Lynda Wright, and Karen Springen, "The Search for Adam and Eve," *Newsweek* (January 11, 1988) 46–52. Scholarly discussions continued in such venues as *Science, Proceedings of the National Academy of Sciences,* and *The New England Journal of Medicine.* Also see http://www.pbs.org/wgbh/nova/neanderthals/mtdna.html. There is, of course, appropriate debate over rate of mutation and other scientific aspects of the inference to a common mother from mtDNA.

utilizing advanced computer technology, completely sequences the DNA of living organisms for comparison in precise quantifiable terms. The astounding similarities at the molecular level confirm the philogenetic design of the Tree of Life; indeed a computer—without the fossil record or anatomical observations of various life forms—can now construct the Tree based solely upon the similarities of the DNA sequences of multiple organisms. Francisco Ayala states:

> Molecular biology proves evolution in two ways: first by showing the unity of life in the nature of DNA and the workings of organisms at the level of enzymes and other protein molecules; second, . . . by making it possible to reconstruct evolutionary relationships that were previously unknown, and to confirm, refine, and time all evolutionary relationships from the universal common ancestor up to all living organisms.[30]

Evolution is the only rational way to account for the molecular uniformity of all organisms, given that numerous alternative structures and fundamental processes are in principle equally likely. Moreover, the fact that damaged or "junk" DNA (mutations that do not affect function and thus are not subject to negative selection), once it appears and accumulates and is passed on over time, such that species further down that branch of the Tree carry the same form of damage, makes the probability that evolution did not occur infinitesimally small. All of this means that the evolution of all living things through common descent possesses an extraordinarily high degree of probability conferred by thousands of (published) empirical tests, as high a probability as science can generate.[31] The evidence is compelling that the various species, each of which is grouped around a branching node of the Tree of Life, did indeed have a common genetic ancestor. Humans as well have been shown to share common descent with chimpanzees, and in fact to display a smaller degree of genetic difference from the other primates than the genetic differences between many other related animal species, meaning that the elapsed time since this common bifurcation point is relatively short.[32]

TOWARD A UNIFIED VISION

As Edwin Burtt has taught us, the enterprise of science requires metaphysical interpretation—not because of its inherent incompleteness and continual need for further progress, but because it rests on assumptions not provable by its own methods and because its findings raise philosophical questions not answerable on its own terms.[33]

---

30. Francisco Ayala, *Darwin's Gift to Science and Religion* (Washington, DC: Joseph Henry, 2007) 118.

31. It is actually quite fair to say that evolution shares equal status with such established concepts as the roundness of the Earth, its revolution around the sun, and the molecular composition of matter. See Ayala, *Darwin's Gift*, 130–32.

32. See, for example, Nick Patterson, Daniel J. Richter, Sante Gnerre, Eric S. Lander, and David Reich, "Genetic Evidence for Complex Speciation of Humans and Chimpanzees" *Nature* 441 (29 June 2006) 1103–108. Or, see http://www.nature.com/nature/journal/v441/n7097/full/nature04789.html. See also Francis Collins, *The Language of God : A Scientist Presents Evidence for Belief* (New York: Free Press, 2006) 137–41.

33. Edwin A. Burtt, *The Metaphysical Foundations of Modern Science* (New York: Routledge and Kegan Paul, 1924).

PART TWO: CONTRIBUTION TO CURRENT THEOLOGICAL PROBLEMS

It was Wittgenstein who remarked that, when the totality of scientific facts has been catalogued, all that is really important remains unsayable.[34] But we cannot acquiesce in Wittgensteinian silence about a larger metaphysical framework for science since the human drive to make total sense of reality cannot be suppressed. Furthermore, it is not just the enterprise of science per se that requires metaphysical interpretation, or meta-interpretation, as John Polkinghorne calls it: *the overall evolutionary shape of science must also be thoroughly addressed within any comprehensive worldview.* The atheistic community, of course, co-opts the scientific facts of evolution to serve as the basis of a reductionistic and materialistic worldview—a view which asserts the sufficiency of empirical inquiry, the self-existence of the physical, the survival basis of values, the complete continuity of humanity with the animals, and the lack of ultimate meaning in the universe. No wonder so many people, both laity and academics, cannot distinguish the science from the philosophy! Yet we must not surrender the truths of evolutionary science to philosophical naturalism. Classical Christianity's picture of reality involves themes which, properly understood, are profoundly evolutionary and thus constitute part of a welcoming metaphysical interpretation of the scientific facts. Evolution, then, is an absolutely essential concept—not only scientifically, but also theologically. For this reason, John Haught speaks of "*evolutionary* theology," explicitly adding that qualifier which was always implicit in my earlier list.[35]

There is indeed a strangeness to what we know scientifically about ourselves and our place in the universe. As told by astrophysics and astrochemistry, the process of cosmic evolution began with the Big Bang, the high energy point from which all else sprang, until cooling allowed hydrogen and helium to form, and then continued expansion and cooling allowed gravity to take over and condense matter into galaxies and their stars, when the stars could become nuclear cookeries to form the other elements and then explode in death to scatter the new elements into the environment, eventually resulting in the condensation of second generation stars that could attract planets made of materials that would permit next big development. On at least one planet, Earth, conditions of temperature, radiation, and chemical environment permitted the coming into being of quite elaborate molecules with the power of replicating themselves. From this point, the evolutionary story, as continued by genetics, anthropology, paleontology, and molecular biology, provides much finer granularity to the picture of how evolution has played out on Earth. This all may seem strange, but truth is sometimes like that. Accepting the scientific story at its own level, a classically Christian meta-interpretation—in contrast to one that is obsessed with beginnings—is guided by the conviction that creation is not only past (*creatio originalis*) but ongoing (*creatio continua*). Creation therefore necessarily

---

34. Ludwig Wittgenstein, *Tractatus Logico-Philosophicus* (London: Routledge, 2001) Propositions 6.52 through 6.53.

35. John Haught, *God after Darwin* (Boulder, CO: Westview, 2000) 36 [emphasis mine]. Regarding biological evolution, Robert John Russell further explains: "It is . . . reductionistic and materialistic philosophy as an interpretation of evolution that Christians must oppose. In its place Christians must offer an alternative interpretation of neo-Darwinian evolution that recognizes it as ultimately the work of God." Robert John Russell, "Evolution and Christian Faith," *America: National Catholic Weekly* 194.6 (February 20, 2006): http://www.americamagazine.org/content/article.cfm?article_id=4627.

involves God's progressive ordering, blessing, and empowering. Psalm 104, for example, certainly suggests a Creator who is continuously and creatively active.

Classical orthodoxy teaches that the self-existent, self-sufficient, self-giving Triune God created in order invite the creature into his own divine life. This intimate communion is the goal which can only be achieved by kenosis broadly understood: that God allows the created other truly to be itself, indeed, to "make" itself, thus developing a self-identity distinct from the Creator that can return freely in love to the Creator. A genuinely kenotic creation, then, makes possible a greater good than a ready-made creation ever could, since it allows real contingency, which is nothing less than openness to alternative possibilities within lawful structure so that divinely given potentiality can be brought to specifically realized actuality in the historical process of the world. Wolfhart Pannenberg observes that taking contingency seriously as a direct implication of the doctrine of creation is crucial to detaching religious thinking from mechanistic, and therefore static, ideas of design—and thus ultimately to seeing design as a comparatively secondary issue. Pannenberg explains:

> Much more important in the dialogue between theology and science is the issue of contingency—both in the broad sense of the contingent emergence and existence of everything created and in the more special function of contingency as a source of novelty.[36]

Contingency as a source of novelty means that there can be an actual history—of both nature and human affairs—and a meaningful future. Contingency is integral to a comprehensive concept of kenosis that avoids the determinism which the denial of contingency implies. Of course, the kenotic openness of reality means that there will be cost as contingencies within the subhuman creation sometimes lead to blind genetic alleys and even to harmful genetic mutations such as cancer, as the evolving creation seeks ever new kinds of fruitfulness—a point that must be addressed in any comprehensive theodicy.[37] Contingencies at the human level include the goods of creative invention, noble actions, and selfless service as well as the evils of betrayal and murder. So, the good and the bad occur in the realm of freedom made possible by that great creative act.

In *The Trinity and the Kingdom*, Moltmann anchors the original act of creation and its continuance in the inner-trinitarian love of the Father for the Son. The Father's engendering love for the Son calls creation into life through the power of the Holy Spirit. The indwelling Spirit, then, permeates the entire cosmos—every atom, super nova, and biological form—with life-giving energy. In *God in Creation*, Moltmann writes: "Through the powers and potentialities of the Spirit, the Creator indwells the creatures he has made, animates them, holds them in life, and leads them into the future of his kingdom."[38] This

---

36. Wolfhart Pannenberg, "Contributions from Systematic Theology" in *The Oxford Handbook of Religion and Science*, ed. Philip Clayton (New York: Oxford University Press, 2006) 363.

37. See my paper "The Strong Darwinian Problem of Human Pain," which was a product of the Venice Summer School of Science and Religion on the topic of Evolution and Human Uniqueness, Venice, Italy (May 26–30, 2009), funded by the John Templeton Foundation.

38. Moltmann, *God in Creation: A New Theology of Creation and the Spirit of God*, trans. by Margaret Kohl (Minneapolis: Fortress, 1993) 14.

pneumatological approach to creation is thoroughly perichoretic, displaying the Spirit's transcendence (containing creation) and immanence (contained within creation). This is not a dominance-submission model of God and creation but rather a deeply relational one in which God not only brings creation into existence but also enters into it. And the free loving response he seeks is cooperation with the Spirit. Indeed, the Spirit forms a pattern of relationships with creation analogous to the perichoretic relations within the life of the Trinity. Thus, the unfolding future of the world is not a pre-determined script but more like an improvisation between God and creatures.

John Polkinghorne affirms the Spirit's providential guidance in the workings of the world studied by science:

> The actual balance between chance and necessity, contingency and potentiality, which we perceive seems to me to be consistent with the will of a patient and subtle Creator, content to achieve his purposes through the unfolding of process and accepting thereby a measure of the vulnerability and precariousness which always characterize the gift of freedom by love.[39]

Providential guidance is also seen in the astonishing drive within creation towards increasingly elaborate forms of life, which eventually results in a rational, self-aware creature that can be said to bear the divine image. Fundamental anthropic fertility was built into the fabric of the universe from the start, but its actual form of realization was explored and fulfilled by the contingency of evolving history. So, Gould's conviction that the chanciness of evolution would never again produce soulish animals lacks the theological insight that God has willed that there be rational-moral-physical creatures capable of intimate fellowship with himself. Intriguing echoes of this theme can be found in the words of eminent scientists, words consistent with the convergence theory of Simon Conway Morris. Princeton physicist Freeman Dyson has suggested that the universe, in some sense, "knew we were coming."[40] In *The Goldilocks Enigma*, Paul Davis, cosmologist and recipient of the Faraday Prize, argues for a grand cosmic plan that makes the universe "just right" for life.[41] Of course, the fact that that biological life should emerge and that rational and moral capacities should come to be present in animal form is, again, part of the oddity of it all.[42] What this must mean is that the theme of relatedness in God's economy is played out both in our intimate connection to matter and in our destiny in the higher life of God. Relatedness is, moreover, exemplified in the most astounding way in the Theandric One, God uniting with humanity forever. So, both creation and incarnation symbolize that the special dignity of humankind depends neither on its inhabiting

---

39. John Polkinghorne, *One World: The Interaction of Science and Theology* (West Conshohocken, PA: Templeton, 2007) 82.

40. Freeman Dyson, *Disturbing the Universe* (New York: Harper & Row, 1979) 250.

41. Paul Davies, *The Goldilocks Enigma: Why Is the Universe Just Right for Life?* (New York: Houghton Mifflin, 2007); previously titled *Cosmic Jackpot*.

42. Of course, we Thomists have always affirmed the connectedness of humanity with the rest of physical nature: the soul is the form, or immensely complex information-bearing pattern, of the body. And this is entirely consistent with bearing the divine image.

the center of the universe nor on *Homo sapiens* being a separately and instantaneously created species.

The doctrine of creation assigns value and meaningfulness to the universe and its history. And the creaturely status of humans and the rest of nature entails that nothing that allows itself to be taken into the life of God will be irretrievably lost. Scientists tell us that the universe will come to an end—either in a "big crunch" as gravity overcomes the expansive effect of the Big Bang or by continued expansion as galaxies fly farther apart until they become gigantic black holes and collapse in upon themselves. Things will end in either a bang or a whimper, but end they will. And each human being—as a psychosomatic unity—ends in death. Science can tell us in great detail about death but cannot envision a destiny beyond death. Yet science is not the last word. If all is not to be futility, the doctrine of creation must be inseparably linked to eschatology, which projects the hope that there is a destiny beyond death, a hope anchored in the faithfulness of the Creator who is also Redeemer. The damage suffered by all of creation, then, is being overcome by the Spirit's activity which uplifts, restores, and transforms—making redemption not only personal but corporate and cosmic as well. Christians believe that the new creation, arising from the old, has already begun with the resurrection of our Lord Jesus Christ, who has become the bridge between the divine life and creaturely existence. So, the ground for eschatological hope is the faithful love of God testified to by the Resurrection.

The intimate relatedness of reality makes this one world, a cosmos, not reducible just to the universe described in theological terms (since science illuminates natural phenomena in a way theology cannot) or to the universe as studied by science (since theology supplies revelatory content not available to science). All things are connected in the God who is the very source of their connection—such that perspectives not only from science and theology, but from ethics and aesthetics as well, tell us one-truth:

> In the beginning was the Word, and the Word was with God, and the Word was God. He was in the beginning with God; all things were made through him, and without him was not anything made that was made. (John 1:1–3 RSV)

Although the concept of Christ as the Word (*logos*) implies order, unity, and intelligibility in creation, a Trinitarian-kenotic-perichoretic Christian understanding goes even further in affirming creation's decidedly evolutionary character in God's economy, establishing mutual and deep confirmation between the evolutionary themes of theology and science. Christian faith, then, must see science as revealing a world which is a reflection of God's ways—making science itself sacramental, a visible sign of an invisible grace. And science, like all sacramental realities in the created world, is but a shadow of the greatest sacrament, the Incarnation in which "the Word became flesh and dwelt among us, full of grace and truth; we have beheld his glory, glory as of the only Son from the Father" (John 1:14 RSV).

Evolutionary thinking is integral to a complete vision of reality—a vision which both subsumes and transcends the results of natural theology, biblical theology, and a theology of nature as it seeks to incorporate all we know into the synthetic activity of systematic theology. The Wesleyan theological tradition—as our historical expression of classical orthodoxy—will find this holistic vision fruitful as it seeks to be an ever relevant witness to the Creator and Redeemer who bestows the gift of finite existence, works more by process than by episodic interruption, and ultimately offers liberation from transience and decay as the hope of all creation and fulfillment of all human longing.

11

Kenosis and Emergence

A Wesleyan Perspective

Bradford McCall

INTRODUCTION

MY FIRST INTERACTION WITH Larry Wood was during the Summer semester of 2004, in a course entitled "Method and Praxis in Theology." Dr. Wood's course rekindled in me a desire to relate my former education in biology with the faith that I then professed. Indeed, his course sought to critically analyze contemporary theological methods and identify the influence of postmodern science upon contemporary doctrine. I remember Dr. Wood telling us that Wesley once said to a preacher that the study of logic was the single most important thing to study next to the Bible if they were going to understand the Bible properly and thereafter preach it effectively. The foundation that Dr. Wood gave me through that course in connecting theological method with Christian doctrine, especially the doctrine of divine revelation, has served me well in the subsequent years. This essay is an attempt to demonstrate that methodology concerning a hot topic in recent philosophical reflections: emergence. It is my hope that it will serve as appropriate example of a Wesleyan-influenced, Evangelical theology of creation in the postmodern world.[1]

Emergence is, in brief, the view that novel and unpredictable occurrences are naturally produced in nature, and that said novel structures, organs and organisms are not reducible to their component parts.[2] Philip Clayton proffers that emergence is a fruitful paradigm in explaining evolutionary progress in the physical world, which represents

---

1. Note that I herein intend to contribute, at least minimally, to the development of a systematic theology of creation. I agree wholeheartedly with Joel Green who notes that a proposed synthesis of theology and the bible should proceed by clearly identifying where and how to locate the disciplinary interface, where and how to locate the structures of accountability to ensure respect given to both fields, and where and how to locate the means for validating constructive work (Joel B. Green, "Scripture and Theology: Uniting the Two So Long Divided," in Joel B. Green and Max Turner, eds., *Between Two Horizons: Spanning New Testament Studies & Systematic Theology* [Grand Rapids: Eerdmans, 2000] 42).

2. Jaewong Kim, "Making Sense of Emergence," *Philosophical Studies* 95 (1999) 3–36.

explanatory power beyond that of physics alone.³ Whereas Clayton has offered an explanative and informative survey of emergence theory, I want to supplement his account in this essay by unpacking the metaphysical realities that give rise to emergence. I will use Clayton's text as the source of my extrapolations, contending that a richer metaphysical account *ironically* results in greater autonomy for the biological sciences.

In *Creation and Reality*, Michael Welker offers "initial steps toward correcting both the classic theistic caricature of God the Creator and a corresponding religious understanding of reality."⁴ New approaches to creation are a "burning theological interest," for modern religious depictions are "boring, vapid, and banal."⁵ Even when and where the bible is granted authority in faith and practice, patrons seem to no longer read it attentively and imaginatively.⁶ In this essay, I seek to offer a new approach to creation, building upon the notions of emergence and kenosis. I argue that the existence and viability of emergence theory depends upon the primal kenotic act of God the Spirit *pouring* himself *into* creation.

In what follows, one will find three distinct parts. In the first part of this paper, I shall review and interact with Clayton's seminal work, *Mind & Emergence*. In the second, I present the biblical basis of kenosis of the Spirit *into* creation, as well as discuss former conceptions of the kenosis and science connection. In the third and final part of this paper, I make my own constructive theological proposals regarding the connections between kenosis of the Spirit into creation and emergence theory.

A REVIEW OF CLAYTON'S UNDERSTANDING OF EMERGENCE

Philip Clayton's, *Mind and Emergence*, explicitly covers the revolution brought about by the study of evolution that undercuts both *physicalism* and *dualism*.⁷ In it, Clayton argues that emergence is the philosophical position that best accounts for the data derived from the study of evolution.⁸ Emergentists argue that the reductionary tendencies within

---

3. Emergence provides a way for theists to speak of the response of agents to the divine while remaining consistent with the scientific study of natural history (Philip Clayton, "Emergence From Physics to Theology: Toward a Panoramic View," *Zygon* 41.3 [September 2006] 682).

4. Michael Welker, *Creation and Reality* (Minneapolis: Augsburg Fortress, 1999) 2.

5. Ibid., 4. Part of the reason why theology today is often boring, vapid, and banal is that it has "misconstrued the role of texts and the role of interpreters" (Green, "Scripture and Theology," 30).

6. Ellen F. Davis and Richard B. Hays, *The Art of Reading Scripture* (Grand Rapids: Eerdmans, 2003) xv.

7. Clayton, *Mind & Emergence*, 1. Note that both *physicalism* and *dualism*, to varying degrees, are based on an Enlightenment model of science. Emergence, however, moves beyond the Enlightenment model of science. No longer can one seek to explain all things as being merely reducible to their physical entities or microphysical causes (i.e., *physicalism*), as *physicalism* is inconsistent with standard research theories and practices within biology (Clayton, *Mind & Emergence*, 66). *Physicalism* is also incompatible with emergence because it "rules out forms of natural causality that are more than merely a sum of physical forces" (ibid., 174).

8. Deacon notes that emergence is the "term that that is most often used by scientists to describe the spontaneous appearance of unprecedented orderliness in nature" (Terrence W. Deacon, "Emergence: The Hole at the Wheel's Hub," in Phillip Clayton and Paul C. Davies, eds., *The Re-Emergence of Emergence: The Emergentist Hypothesis from Science to Religion* [Oxford: Oxford University, 2006] 121). He further notes that the term connotes an image of something coming out of hiding, something without precedent, and a bit surprising (ibid.).

the natural sciences are not tenable.[9] In fact, "actualizing the dream of a final reduction 'downwards', it now appears, has proven fundamentally impossible."[10] The pompous nature of the physics of former years has been humbled—epistemically and practically—by a series of revelations within nature that place inherent limitations upon what physics can explain, predict, or know.[11]

Before offering his own definition of emergence, Clayton first depicts the two main classifications of emergence theories within the twentieth century: strong and weak. The strong emergentist position can be labeled ontological emergence, whereas the weak emergentist position could be aptly identified as epistemological emergence. Strong emergentists postulate that evolution produces ontologically distinct levels of organs/isms that are characterized by their own distinct regularities and causal forces.

In opposition, weak emergentists maintain that as new patterns emerge the causal processes remain those that are fundamental to known physics. A property of an organ/ism is weakly emergent if it is reducible to its intrinsic qualities, insomuch as weakly emergent properties are 'novel' only at the level of description (epistemologically). This contrasts with strongly emergent organs/isms in which the cause is neither reducible to any intrinsic causal capacity of the parts nor to any relation between the component parts.[12] Clayton asserts that weak emergence in effect leaves us with the same old dichotomy of physicalism and dualism.[13]

After reviewing and critiquing twentieth century views of emergence, Clayton offers his own view regarding emergence theory. In so doing, radicalizes the *immanence*

---

9. Modern advances in the natural sciences reveal a vastly more complicated world than the reductionist program of the late nineteenth and twentieth century's ever envisioned. As Clayton writes, "[i]t is unfortunate that in recent years the explosion of knowledge in molecular biology has caused all of biology to be painted with a reductionist stroke" (Clayton, *Mind & Emergence*, 94).

10. Ibid., 70.

11. For example, *Heisenberg's Uncertainty Principle* delimits our ability to predict with accuracy the exact location and momentum of subatomic particles, and makes one realize that there exists an inherent indeterminacy within the physical world itself. Moreover, *Chaos Theory* has shown that the future states of complex systems are unpredictable, due to finite knowledge of initial conditions.

12. Clayton, *Mind & Emergence*, 10. That is to say, a strongly emergent phenomenon is "explanatorily, causally, and hence ontologically irreducible to the systems out of which it has evolved" (Phillip Clayton, "Emergence from Quantum Physics to Religion," 310). However, though they are not *reducible*, they are *dependent* upon the systems out of which they have evolved.

13. Emergentists should be monists, but not physicalists, note, which means that all objects and phenomena within the world matrix arise from one basic type of matter-energy "stuff" (Phillip Clayton, "Emergence from Quantum Physics to Religion: A Critical Appraisal," 313). Emergence suggests that significant things can emerge from insignificant starts, and in the end the whole is so much more than the initial components. Emergence allows us to gain victory over reductionism and to tread the treacherous path between physicalism and dualism which may be the perfect solution to the debates that have troubled philosophers, scientists, and theologians for centuries (Antje Jackelén, "Emergence Everywhere?! Reflections on Philip Clayton's Mind and Emergence," *Zygon* 41.3 [September 2006] 625). Clayton himself is an advocate of *strong* emergence. In fact, Peterson classifies Clayton as a *radical* emergentist (Gregory R. Peterson, "Species of Emergence," *Zygon* 41.3 [2006] 705). Radical emergentists emphasize both epistemological and ontological openness. Radical emergence is good for both theology and science; nevertheless, radical emergence also has its dangers, possibly leading to what might be referred to as an emergence of the gaps (ibid., 709).

of God.[14] Clayton defines emergence as "the theory that cosmic evolution repeatedly includes unpredictable, irreducible, and novel appearances."[15] He notes that emergence is "that which is produced by a combination of causes, but cannot be regarded as the sum of their individual effects."[16] Moreover, "emergence is the theory that cosmic evolution repeatedly includes unpredictable, irreducible, and novel appearances."[17]

Clayton seeks to develop the role of emergence in the natural sciences and in evolution, which may be Clayton's most important contribution to the dialogue between theology and science found within *Mind and Emergence*. He notes that particularly within biology, one can see multiple instances of where that which emerges becomes a causal agent in its own right. He states that the biggest question facing scientists today is "how nature obtains order 'out of nothing,' that is, how order is produced in the course of a system's evolution when it is not present in the initial conditions."[18] Clayton argues that whereas "biological processes in general are the result of systems that create and maintain order (stasis) through massive energy input from their environment," there comes a point of sufficient complexity after which a phase transition suddenly becomes almost inevitable.[19] Emergence in evolution therefore "consists of a collection of highly convoluted processes that produce a remarkably complex kind of combinatorial novelty."[20]

Clayton implies that the resurgence of emergence in the twentieth century has done much to deflate the bottom-up "new synthesis" that resulted from Watson and Crick's discovery of the DNA molecule in 1956, which was linked to Neo-Darwinian evolutionary thought.[21] The "new synthesis" is *in process* of being replaced by an "interactionist consensus" in which neither genes nor environments, neither nature nor nurture, suffice wholly for the production of phenotypes.[22] Within this interactionist paradigm, "fully adequate explanations of biological phenomena require the constant interplay of both

---

14. One could perceive this creative activity of the Spirit as being either inside the chaos, picturing God as immanent, or as the Spirit reaching down to create order according to the laws of nature, which pictures God as transcendent (Steven D. Crain, "God Embodied In, God Bodying Forth the World: Emergence and Christian Theology," Zygon vol. 41.3 [2006] 666). Much recent theology, however, like that of Jürgen Moltmann (*God in Creation* [Minneapolis: Augsburg Fortress, 1993]), John Haught (*Deeper than Darwin: The Prospect for Religion in the Age of Evolution* [Cambridge: Westview, 2003]), and Denis Edwards (*Breath of Life: A Theology of the Creator Spirit* [Maryknoll: Orbis, 2004]), speaks eloquently of God's immanence in nature. It should be noted that the term *ruach* denotes God's active and creative presence throughout creation.

15. Clayton, *Mind & Emergence*, 39.

16. Ibid., 38.

17. Ibid., 39.

18. Ibid., 73.

19. Ibid., 78. Note Clayton's general agreement with Stuart Kauffman, *Investigations* (Oxford: Oxford University, 2000) 35.

20. Clayton, *Mind & Emergence*, 85. Cf. Terrence Deacon, "The Hierarchic Logic of Emergence," in Bruce H. Weber and David J. Depew, *Evolution and Learning* (Cambridge: MIT, 2003) 273–308.

21. Note this implication is inferred by his placement of the section describing the "new synthesis" in biology into this chapter. Said "new synthesis" posits that the behavior of organisms—and even *ecosystems*—can be explained solely by referencing the gene reproduction and mutation that underlies them.

22. Cf. Jason S. Robert, *Embryology, Epigenesis and Evolution: Taking Development Seriously* (Cambridge: Cambridge University, 2004) 2.

bottom-up and top-down accounts."²³ Genotypes produce phenotypes that interact with specific environments, which then reproduce genotypes (*ad infinitum*). Clayton agrees, and states that there "is increasing evidence that emergence represents a fruitful ... meta-scientific ... framework for comparing the relations between the diverse realms of the natural world."²⁴

So, having covered Clayton in this past section, what does he contribute to our understanding of emergence, particularly from a Wesleyan perspective? I'd like to suggest at least four things: emergence, according to Clayton, is in direct opposition to reductionism; after all, if reductionism is possible, then emergentism turns into to either mechanism or vitalism. Moreover, Clayton takes very seriously both evolutionary continuity and the increase in complexity of organization. Further, Clayton's strong emergentism focuses more-so upon the whole than upon the parts, yet is inherently monistic. And finally, according to Clayton, emergence theory represents an explanatory ladder of nature that eventually leads outside the natural sciences, to which we now turn. Indeed, in the next section, I seek to contribute to Clayton's view of emergence, adding relevant Biblical data that supports the notion of the Spirit's kenosis into creation.

FORMER CONCEPTIONS OF THE KENOSIS AND SCIENCE CONNECTION AND THE BIBLICAL BASIS OF KENOSIS OF THE SPIRIT INTO CREATION

The Bible gives good grounds for illustrating the Holy Spirit as being the active agent of God in the world, particularly regarding the Spirit as life-giver and animator of all creation.²⁵ It is the position of this paper that just as the Spirit kenotically entered into the chaotic seas through which the Jews passed in their Exodus (Exod 14:21), so too was the Spirit of God parting the chaos of the primordial waters,²⁶ thereby preparing and causing creation to leap forth.²⁷ The Spirit of life hovered over the primordial waters and transformed the chaos into the cosmos. As the Spirit blows, God speaks forth his creative Word, imparts information,²⁸ and something that is separate from God is formed from

---

23. Clayton, *Mind & Emergence*, 95.

24. Ibid., 93.

25. Cf. Paul's assertion that the Spirit of God "gives life" in 2 Corinthians 3:6.

26. Goergen asserts that without and apart from the Spirit, there would be absolute chaos in the material world (Donald J. Goergen, *Fire of Love: Encountering the Holy Spirit* [Mahwah, NJ: Paulist, 2006] 108).

27. Cf. Michael Lodhal, *Shekhinah/Spirit: Divine Presence in Jewish and Christian Religion* (New York: A Stimulus, 1992) 43.

28. Peterson notes that "[n]onreductive physicalists, as well as other emergentists, sometimes identify emergent entities with information" (Gregory R. Peterson, "Species of Emergence," 702). Bonting attempts to bring the various activities ascribed to the Spirit (Hebrew *ruach*, Greek *pneuma*) under one heading, which he identifies as the *communicator* of information (Sjoerd L. Bonting, "Spirit and Creation," *Zygon* 41.3 [2006] 713). The Spirit, then, functions as a transmitter of information – from God to us and from us to God. Interestingly, Clayton elsewhere notes that "God could guide the process of emergence by introducing new information (formal causality) and by holding out an ideal or image that could influence development without altering the mechanical mechanisms of evolution or adding energy from the outside (final causality)" (Phillip Clayton, "Divine Causes in the World of Nature," in Ted Peters, Muzzafar Iqbal, and Syed Nomanul Haq, eds., *God, Life, and the Cosmos: Christian and Islamic Perspectives* [Aldershot: Ashgate, 2002] 273).

chaos. Creation begins not with the Word, as per se, but rather with the Spirit, as the Spirit's presence precedes and is presupposed by the speaking of the Word.[29]

In Gen 1:2, the Spirit moved upon the face of the waters, which constitutes a creative act. The Hebrew word used in Gen 1:2 for "moved" is *rahap*, which means literally to "vibrate" (vibration is energy). Thus, it was the Spirit that introduced energy (or pure information)[30] into the formless void. The verb used in Gen 1:2 depicts the presence of the Spirit hovering mysteriously over the waters, preparing for the acts of creation to follow. It is interesting to note that the Hebrew verb, *ârâh*, has been translated "hovering" (as a bird over her young, see Deut 32:11), whereas the Syriac cognate term means "to brood over; to incubate." That the Spirit was hovering like a mother stork might hover over her nest is a portent of life to come from the dark, murky depths of the chaos below.[31] Additionally, the original terms *to'·hü* and *bo'·hü*, of Gen 1:2, which are often translated as *without form* and *void*, are of uncertain etymology; but wherever they are used, they convey the idea of confusion and disorder. One may postulate, then, that the Spirit is ultimately responsible for both the conditions for life, as well as life itself. The Spirit is the "executive arm" (i.e., the enacting or effectual arm) of the Trinity in that the Spirit was active as the Son spoke each word in the primal creating moments recorded in Gen 1.[32]

Thus, the light that first illuminated the earth was caused by the impartation of information and order by the inspiriting of the Spirit of God. When God inspirits formless and chaotic matter, nothing becomes something, and the disorderly becomes orderly. Since the level of order required for the origination of complex life was extremely high,[33] it is especially important to acknowledge that the Old Testament begins by presenting the function of the Spirit as being the giver and communicator of orderly information and, consequently, of complex biological life.

A pneumatological rereading of Genesis 1 and 2 shows the predominant conceptions of creation as *creatio ex nihilo* to be false abstractions. The summarizing conceptions of creation, according to Welker, are "very vague, mostly even obscure."[34] I contend that creation in Genesis is not a creation out of nothing, as a onetime event, but is instead a continuous creation, a transformative process of producing higher aggregate conditions out of an absence of structure and order. *Creatio continua* (continuing creative activity) operates as an enabling condition for all that occurs thereafter. Indeed, on the third day[35]

---

29. D. Lyle Dabney, "The Nature of the Spirit," in Michael Welker, ed., *The Work of the Spirit* (Grand Rapids: Eerdmans, 2006) 73.

30. The Spirit as God's *energeia*, through which God the Father calls all aspects of creation into being, fits very well with modern cosmological theory (Sjoerd L. Bonting, *Spirit and Creation*, 721). In reference to the Big Bang, the Spirit brings in the information needed to transform the explosion into an orderly process of cosmic evolution (ibid., 723).

31. Note that the Spirit is described as a *dove* in Matt 3:16.

32. After the introduction of energy (or pure information) by the Spirit into the formless, chaotic matter, there was light (Gen 1:3).

33. As per Stuart Kaufman, cited in Radu Popa, *Between Necessity and Probability: Searching for the Definition and Origin of Life* (New York: Springer, 2004) 73.

34. Welker, *Creation and Reality*, 6–7.

35. This is neither time nor space to speculate upon what the term 'day' might mean or connote.

of the Genesis account, in the midst of God's creativity, God's creating interacts with that which was created in order to produce further acts of creation, insomuch as the process of *creatio continua* becomes one with the process of *creatio ex creation* (creation out of creation). We read on day three: Then God said, "Let the *earth put forth* vegetation: plants yielding seed, and fruit trees of every kind on earth that bear fruit with the seed in it" (1:11). On day five of the Genesis account, God commands, "Let the *waters bring forth* swarms of living creatures . . ." (1:20), and again, "Let the *earth bring forth* living creatures of every kind . . ." (1:24).

According to Welker, neither Genesis 1 or 2 "describes God as a highest being who in pure self-sufficiency does nothing other than produce and cause creaturely being."[36] Moreover, he stipulates that in Genesis 1 and 2 God's action corresponds to only a few ways in which we normally construe causation and production.[37] Seven times God is listed as evaluating.[38] Three times God is listed as naming.[39] Three times God is listed as acting upon what is already created in order to separate it and give it order.[40] The latter three instances of God's action give credence to the notion of God acting upon formless matter, and thereby giving it order, structure, and complexity. Thus, the creating God is not merely an actor within creation, but also a reactor to creation. Indeed, God's action is an action that reacts, and is an action that lets itself be determined. Genesis 1 and 2 depict a creation that has its own activity, is itself productive, and is itself causative.

In the Genesis narrative, then, one is not able to derive a clear demarcation between God's creativity and the creature's activity. On the one hand, God's activity is clearly active in production and causation. On the other hand, God is equally reactive to that which is created. From this data, an abstract, minimal definition of creation as related within the Genesis narrative follows: "creation is the construction and maintenance of associations of different, interdependent creaturely realms."[41] The study of creation must, therefore, focus upon the interdependencies of natural and providential processes, because creation as a whole, both the reality and nature of it, continually flow into each other.

Not only did God the Spirit create the world at one point in the past, but he now continually upholds it.[42] Indeed, Paul the Apostle expresses God the Son's creative work as that by which "all things were created" (Col 1:16), which is an act of definitive causation (a "coming to be"). The speaking forth of the Word of God, which Paul here has in mind, however, necessarily presupposes the *Breath* of God (i.e., *pneuma/ruach*—God the Spirit). Moreover, the very next verse explains that "in Him all things hold together" (Col 1:17), which connotes the continual creative act of the Spirit.[43] It is important, therefore,

---

36. Welker, *Creation and Reality*, 9.

37. Ibid.

38. Gen 1:4, 1:10, 1:12, 1:18, 1:21, 1:25, and 1:31.

39. Gen 1:5, 1:8, 1:10.

40. Gen 1:11, 120, 1:24.

41. Welker, *Creation and Reality*, 13.

42. This statement is adapted from Newton, as cited in Christopher Southgate, *God, Humanity, and the Cosmos* (New York: T. & T. Clark, 2005) 281. For further support, see Goergen, *Fire of Love*, 114.

43. For support of this notion, see: Keith Ward, *God, Chance, and Necessity* (New York: Oneworld, 1996) 78.

to view the Spirit not only as originator of creation, but also as sustainer of creation, upholding its order, and giving it life.[44] As Polkinghorne writes, "Part of a notion of *creatio continua* must surely be that an evolving universe is one which is theologically understood as being allowed, within divine providence, 'to make itself.'"[45] Rather than bringing into being a ready-made world of unalterable character, the Godhead allows the creation, kenotically empowered by the Spirit, to develop according to its own pace. As Vanstone notes, the activity of the Spirit within creation proceeds by no assured program, but is precarious instead.[46] This evolving fertility is not a linear progression, but is staggered, as the Spirit is not the manipulator of creation, but its director instead. The Spirit makes things able to make themselves. Theologians today are correct, then, to perceive this long process of evolutionary emergence as God's continued creation, mediated by the interplay of laws and chance.[47] No picture of creation is complete that neglects either the definitive or the continual creative work of the Spirit. Thus, the reality of creation deals with both origins and continual operation.

The Spirit is seen at various junctures within the Bible to operate via proximate causation. For example, Ps 104:30 (NKJV) states, "When you send your Spirit, they are created, and you renew the face of the earth." Here the term create (*bara*) is used, not of the initial *generation* of life, but of its continual *regeneration*, as the context speaks of the Spirit causing "the grass [to] grow for the cattle, and plants for man to cultivate" (vs. 14). It is "He [the Spirit, i.e., who] makes springs pour water into the ravines; [and flow] between the mountains" (vs. 10) and who "bring[s] darkness, [and] it becomes night" (vs. 20). It is the Spirit that continually provides food for all living things (vs. 28). The repeated emphasis within Ps 104 is the notion that God preserves of the world, which presupposes that God creates through the power of the Spirit, as well as that the presence of the Spirit is the condition for both potentialities and realities of creation.[48] The psalmist knows nothing of outright spontaneous generation, for God sends forth his Spirit, and all things are created.[49] The Spirit is repeatedly depicted in this psalm as the presence of God, as well as the means by which God acts within his creation.[50]

---

44. Sjoerd Bonting, "Spirit and Creation," *Zygon* 41.3 (2006) 724.

45. John Polkinghorne, *Serious Talk* (Philadelphia: Trinity, 1995) 84.

46. W. H. Vanstone, *Love's Endeavor, Love's Expense* (London: Darton Longman & Todd, 1977) 62.

47. Manuel G. Doncel, "The Kenosis of the Creator and of the Created Co-creator," *Zygon* 39.4 (2004) 798. Note that as a consequence of positing *creatio continua*, one must insist that the Spirit of God's providential power is manifest in the unfolding of creation in evolutionary history (John Polkinghorne, "Kenotic Creation and Divine Action," in John Polkinghorne, ed. *The Work of Love* [Grand Rapids: Eerdmans, 2001] 96). In affirmation of this understanding of the ongoing evolution of the creation as being God's manner of creation from the viewpoint of a theologian, see Goergen, *Fire of Love*, 89–105.

48. Jürgen Moltmann, *God in Creation*, 10.

49. Interestingly, Jürgen Moltmann gives the Spirit a near monopoly in creation. He speaks of the life-giving action of the Spirit, since he bases his claim on Ps 104:30, "When you send forth your spirit [*ruach*], they [the animals] are created" (NRSV). From this text Moltmann concludes: "This presupposes that God always creates through and in the power of his Spirit" (Moltmann, *God in Creation*, 9).

50. Bonting, "Spirit and Creation," 715.

The Greek verb *kenóō*, from which the term kenosis is derived, can mean either "to empty," or "to pour out." Its Hebrew equivalent is used, for example, in Isa 32:15: "Until the spirit be poured upon us from on high. . . ." The various cognates of the verb translated in the Septuagint (LXX) by kenosis appear fourteen times in biblical Hebrew. In its original sense, the verb *ârâh* refers to a cause of movement leading to a mass out being poured out of a container. Thus, the word means "to pour out" in reference to Rebekah's pouring out water from her pitcher into the trough (Gen 24:20, the verb in the LXX is *ekkenów*).[51] In the original Hebrew of Gen 24:20, the term is וַתְּעַר, a primitive root, meaning to be (i.e., causatively to make). Hence, it is appropriate to translate said term as either to empty, or to pour out. Whereas the pitcher was emptied, the trough was made full (which is addition) by the emptying of the pitcher. It is therefore concluded by me that a fruitful approach to understanding the verb *kenóō* is to realize it also means "to pour out."[52] I posit that the kenosis of the Spirit into creation had a similar effect as the Rebekah's pouring out water into the trough.

Christ poured himself into humanity so that it could be reconciled to the Father and that it might become acceptable to the Father (Phil 2:5–11). God the Son enters into the limited, finite situation of humankind, descending into it, thereby embracing the whole of human existence in his being. It needs to be noted that the kenosis of the Son referred to in Phil 2:5–11 cannot be understood as a subtraction of deity, but the addition of humanity instead. In the Philippians passage, the verb often translated as "emptied" is explained, expanded, and extrapolated by three participles that directly follow it: 1) taking the form of a servant, 2) becoming in the likeness of men, and 3) being found in fashion as a man.[53] This reference to Christological kenosis, then, also has the net effect of addition.

Furthermore, the Philippians usage of the term kenosis eerily resembles that which is found in Isa 53:12, which reads that "[h]e *poured out* his soul to death." What God does

---

51. Palmer indicates that meaning is a matter of context, and that the explanatory procedure provides the arena for understanding (Palmer, *Hermeneutics*, 25).

52. It is crucial to recognize that the texts of Scripture do not possess a single meaning, limited to the intent of the original author. Rather, Scripture has multiple complex senses (Davis and Hays, *The Art of Reading Scripture*, 2–3). Nevertheless, "Scriptures are our guide, and we, their apprentices" (W. S. Johnson, "Reading the Scriptures Faithfully in a Postmodern Age," in Davis and Hays, *The Art of Reading Scripture*, 109). Dostal agrees, and notes that a "philosophical or literary work always surpasses what the author understands (Robert J. Dostal, "Gadamer: The Man and His Work," in *The Cambridge Companion to Gadamer*, ed. Robert J. Dostal [Cambridge: Cambridge University, 2002] 13).

53. One can discern, then, that I do not hold to the notion that Christ 'emptied' himself of his divinity on the cross, as popularly understood. Rather, I perceive him to have 'poured it out'. This position of my own somewhat challenges the prevailing interpretation of the Christological kenosis. However, I believe it to be in keeping with what Davis writes of critical traditioning. She states such traditioning "denotes the willingness to engage in radical rethinking of a formerly accepted theological position" so that we may "learn something previously unimaginable about the fundaments of life with God" (Ellen F. Davis, "Critical Traditioning," in Davis and Hays, *The Art of Reading Scripture*, 170, 177). In positing my conception of kenosis in terms of the primal act of the Spirit into creation, I am inculcating Gadamer's insistence that to understand anything is, in essence, to apply it (cf. Jean Grondin, "Gadamer's Basic Understanding of Understanding," in *The Cambridge Companion to Gadamer*, ed. Robert J. Dostal [Cambridge: Cambridge University, 2002] 38–39).

particularly and punctiliously by the kenosis of the Son into human form, I posit, God does generally and continually by the kenosis of the Spirit into creation. The Spirit is the *Breath* of life, the very giver of life, and is thus the creative power of the Father. The Spirit, then, is the vital energy that enlivens, as well as the potent force that enervates innovation. The kenosis of the Spirit into creation, the pouring out of life, makes possible not only otherness as properly conceived, but also its actualization. I draw this principle from the usage of kenosis in reference to God the Son, believing it illustrative of the kenosis in reference to God the Spirit.[54] There is an inherent others'-centeredness in kenosis, as one can see in Rebekah's case, as well as in Christ's kenosis. It may be extrapolated, further, that the same others'-centeredness is present with the Spirit's kenosis into creation.

I would like to make the argument that the biblical connotations of the term kenosis, just reviewed and elaborated upon, have potent application to theological constructs regarding God's action within the world. In fact, the science and religion dialog has long wrestled with the topic of God's action in the world, and models for conceiving divine action heretofore have been unsatisfactory.[55] Classical Interventionism should be dismissed as illogical because God's action in the world would be inconsistently intermittent if actualized as pure intervention; God acting only as the Creator of the world is deistic, and thereby delimits divine action in perpetuity; Thomistic understandings of God as the primary Cause and creatures as secondary causes results in unnecessary bifurcations; and a full-blown Process theology is unable to sustain the eschatological guarantees of God as revealed in Scripture.[56] The resurgence of kenotic theology has thus been helpful in reformulating divine action in an evolutionary world.

CONNECTION BETWEEN KENOSIS OF THE SPIRIT INTO CREATION AND EMERGENCE THEORY

Several years ago, a collection of essays by theologians and scientists explored creation as *The Work of Love,* pointing to divine action as kenosis.[57] In said book, John Polkinghorne adopts the understanding of kenosis that is an affirmation of God's voluntary self-limitation,[58] one that allows creatures to enjoy power and freedom. Classical theology, according to Polkinghorne, envisions God in total control and invulnerable to the point that there is no reciprocal effect of creatures upon the divine nature. According to Polkinghorne's view of kenosis, however, the kenotic Creator interacts with creatures; the word "interact" is preferable to "intervene," in this volume, apparently because in-

---

54. This kenosis of the Spirit can also be seen, for example, in his descent upon Jesus at baptism. Indeed, the Spirit was poured into Jesus so as to empower Jesus for his crucial ministry of imparting life to the masses, which resulted in Jesus' own temporal and bodily death.

55. See Southgate, *God, Humanity, and the Cosmos.*

56. Amos Yong, "From Quantum Mechanics to the Eucharistic Meal: John Polkinghorne's Vision of Science and Theology," in *The Global Spiral: A Publication of Metanexus Institute* 5:5 (2005). Online: http://www.metanexus.net/Magazine/ArticleDetail/tabid/68/id/9285/Default.aspx.

57. John Polkinghorne, ed., *The Work of Love* (Grand Rapids: Eerdmans, 2001).

58. Note that although I do not exactly agree with the understanding of kenosis as self-limitation, I nonetheless find much value in the essays contained within the Polkinghorne volume.

tervene carries connotations of an interruption of natural processes. For Polkinghorne, kenosis connotes the risk of the creating Spirit in submitting to the quasi-free process of evolutionary creation, which qualifies, in a kenotic way, the operation of the Spirit. Polkinghorne notes that the kenotic Spirit is the exemplar of humility, for he kenotically interacted with the created world, and as such, at least in some qualified sense, limits his eternality and omnipotence.[59] The volume conceives kenosis as God's entirely voluntary self-limitation. Thus, the Spirit was, as it were, "taking a risk" in creating a world kenotically, for it necessarily involves both chance and randomness through the processes of evolution.[60]

Polkinghorne's view of kenosis is similar to Moltmann's, who notes that kenotic self-surrender is "God's Trinitarian nature, and is therefore the mark of all his works 'outward.'"[61] The kenotic creating Spirit does not overrule creation or its creatures, but continuously *interacts* with them instead. A summarization of *The Works of Love*'s view on kenosis is that God allows the created other to be and to act, insomuch as while all that happens is permitted by God's general providence, not all happenings are in accordance with God's will. Such an understanding is basic to the interpretation of evolutionary history as creation making itself.

I find Polkinghorne's theory of kenosis, here, helpful, but incomplete. I argue that kenotic theology must maintain that the Spirit completely shares and imparts himself *into* creation. The Spirit "poured himself out" into creation, thereby causing it to leap forth from chaos and become a structured and orderly system of life-bearing entities. As a result of this *Breath* of God imparted, nature gives birth to life, and life-bearing entities burst upon the environment.[62] The Spirit is the life-giving force that enables creation to strive toward becoming its fullness via the process of evolution. The creation of ordered matter has its ontological origin in and through the agency of the Spirit of God. Creation is thus a kenotic act of self-offering. One may accurately posit that creation in a qualified sense, possesses the Spirit of God from its very origin. Instead of reducing the created world into a pantheistic entity, however, God is an 'all embracing unity' and the world exists 'in' (panentheism) God in the sense that God is the ground of being for the created world; being panentheistic in relation, there is both distinction and relatedness between the Spirit and creation.

According to Kathryn Tanner, the Spirit has historically been seen to either work immediately (proximately, i.e.) or gradually.[63] In this view, the Spirit could be seen just

---

59. John Polkinghorne, "Kenotic Creation and Divine," in *The Work of Love*, 106.

60. Arthur Peacocke, "The Cost of New Life," in *The Work of Love*, 27.

61. Jurgen Moltmann, "Kenosis in the Creation and the Consummation of the World," in *The Work of Love*, 141.

62. Holmes Ralston III, "Kenosis and Nature," in *The Work of Love*, 58.

63. Kathryn Tanner, "Workings of the Spirit: Simplicity or Complexity?," in *The Work of the Spirit*, Michael Welker, ed. (Grand Rapids: Eerdmans, 2006) 87. The gradual model of the working of the Spirit requires methods of inquiry typical of modern science, and holds great promise for the science and religion dialog (ibid., 105). Moreover, Goergen contends, which I also affirm, that as the source of creative evolution, the Spirit works from *within* creation to generate ever increasing complexity, as opposed to externally compelling and manipulating creation (Goergen, *Fire of Love*, 106).

as much at work in the ordinary events of history as in its unusual happenings. Just as God usually works within, rather than overriding, the normal course of human affairs, so too does God work within the natural processes of nature, for "the same Spirit doth not breathe contrary notions."[64] The Spirit works modestly, in a continuous fashion *in* and *through* natural processes.[65] The notion of emergence is compatible with the impersonal kenotic working of the Spirit in empowering creation from within in an almost hidden manner.[66] This hiddenness of the Spirit comports well with the Orthodox theologian Vladimir Lossky's statements to the effect that the Spirit remains "unmanifested, concealing himself even in his appearing."[67] By the Spirit's kenosis into creation, creation itself is then enabled, using Clayton's language, to participate in the processes of production and reproduction. In the following two sections, I will explore further the notion of the Spirit's kenosis into unordered matter in discussing primordial chaos, as well as the potentialities that are inherent within matter.

Kenosis and Primordial Chaos

In an interesting contribution to the volume entitled *The Work of the Spirit*, Amos Yong discusses the contributions of pneumatology to the broad notion of divine action.[68] Yong invokes the Spirit as acting upon primordial chaos. It is my contention that primordial chaos is the great confusion of matter out of which the Spirit, by kenosis, generated order, structure, and ultimately all of life. Primordial chaos, in and of itself, is incapable to produce the formation of an ordered, structured, and functional collocation of atoms, because it is by definition random processes. Indeed, primordial chaos lacks the favorable environment that is requisite for enduring and functional patterns of matter to emerge. In fact, in primordial chaos, matter did not exist as such; rather there was indeterminate and unconditioned disorder.

According to Yong, the Spirit causes the emergence of order and presides over it from within through the processes of division, distinction, differentiation, and particularization.[69] The Spirit creates by infusing the primordial chaos with pure and directed information, which resulted in an evolutionary process that was imbibed with fertility. Yong's assertion gains support by Morowitz, who argues that the Spirit powers—even

---

64. Richard Sibbes, *Works*, ed. A. B. Grosart, 7 vols. (Edinburgh: James Nichol, 1862) 5:427.

65. Michael Welker, "Spirit in Philosophical, Theological, and Interdisciplinary Perspectives," in *The Work of the Spirit*, 227.

66. Hiddenness is at the heart of kenosis, notes Ernest Simmons. Further, the Hebrew *ruach*, as well as the Greek *pneuma*, both carry with them a sense of hidden and unseen forces ("Towards Kenotic Pneumatology: Quantum Field Theory and the Theology of the Cross," [*CTNS Bulletin* 19.2 (1999)] 11–16).

67. Vladimir Lossky, *The Mystical Theology of the Eastern Church* (Cambridge: Clarke, 1957) 169. Interestingly, Creegan argues that God's trinitarian nature, God's hiddenness, and God's incarnation give us reason to believe that we should be able to discern divine presence in the natural world, but only within the natural processes and thereby only in a somewhat obscured fashion (Nicola H. Creegan, "A Christian Theology of Evolution and Participation," *Zygon* 42.2 [2007] 500).

68. Amos Yong, "*Ruach*, the Primordial Chaos, and the Breath of Life: Emergence Theory and the Creation Narratives in Pneumatological Perspective," in *The Work of the Spirit*, 183–204.

69. Ibid., 194–95, 202.

empowers—emergence by being the selection rules between God's immanence and the development of the earth. He writes, "Emergence selects the restricted world of the real from the super-immense world of the possible."[70] The Spirit is the intermediate between physical laws and chaotic matter. In this sense the Spirit acted as a liaison between the primordial chaos, which was the source of variation and novelty, and the resultant ordered and structured creation of the Genesis account. Thus, the movement from chaos to cosmos was directed by the Spirit.[71]

Kenosis and Creation Understood as Potentiality

Primordial chaos, due to its intrinsic unpredictabilities, allows the *Possibility of God* (i.e., the Spirit[72]) much leeway in action. This primordial chaos was essential to God's subsequent creation because it was the source of innumerable potentialities,[73] without which the immense variety of nature would not be possible.[74] The Spirit's kenosis into creation leads to the realization of manifold potentialities. This divine *Possibility* swept over the primordial chaotic abyss and by kenosis into this primal creation, the complex activity of ordering within the chaotic primordial waters was onset. Because of the Spirit hovering over the waters, "the chaos becomes promise."[75]

In creation, the Spirit kenotically bestows both *potentiality* and "being" ("Let there be..."). In this view, "instead of being daunted by the role of chance in genetic mutations as being the manifestation of irrationality in the Universe, it would be more consistent with the observations to assert that the full gamut of potentialities of living matter could be explored only through the agency of the rapid and frequent randomization which is

---

70. Harold J. Morowitz, *The Emergence of Everything* (Oxford: Oxford University, 2002) 197.

71. This primordial chaos did not contain its own information (only non-directed energy instead), and therefore had to be infused with such by the Spirit. Thus, one may accurately note that the Spirit is the agent of causation by the interjection of both concretion and specification through information (John Polkinghorne, "The Hidden Spirit and the Cosmos," in *The Work of the Spirit*, 169). Primordial chaos without an input of active information by the Spirit of God would remain forever indeterminate and unstructured (cf. James E. Huchingson, "Chaos, Communications Theory, and God's Abundance," *Zygon* 37 [2002] 395–414). For Bulgakov, ordered matter is the direct result of the kenotic action of the Spirit of God into creation (Sergius Bulgakov, *The Comforter* [Grand Rapids: Eerdmans, 2004] 345). Matter's receptivity to spirit, which has form as a requisite, also has as its precondition the creaturely descent of the Spirit, His kenosis into creation (ibid., 221). Thus, the Spirit of God seems at first to have created the elementary principles of all things, creating formless masses of matter, which was without arrangement or distinction of parts.

72. For justification of this terminology, see D. Lyle Dabney, "Naming the Spirit: Towards a Pneumatology of the Cross," in *Starting with the Spirit*, eds. Gordon Preece and Stephen Pickard (Adelaide: Openbook, 2001) 58. Also, creation from a pneumatological standpoint begins with the Spirit, and thus one should interpret the world as not defined by necessity, but by possibility instead, for the Spirit is the possibility of God (Dabney, 78). Michael Lodahl also notes that the "Spirit of God is identified as the possibility of God" ("From God to Creation: Pursuing the Trinitarian Reflections of Gregory of Nyssa as a Critique of Creation ex Nihilo," Paper presented to the American Academy of Religion, 2004 Annual Meeting, 4).

73. Note that within this section the terms potentialities and possibilities are used synonymously.

74. James E. Huchingson, "Chaos, Communications Theory, and God's Abundance," *Zygon* 37 (2002) 398.

75. G. T. Montague, *The Holy Spirit: Growth of a Biblical Tradition* (New York: Paulist, 1976) 67.

possible at the molecular level of DNA."⁷⁶ The way in which "chance" operates within the world to produce new structures, new entities, and even new species, can only be understood as an actualization of the potentialities that the creating Spirit imbibed within creation. Thus, the creating Spirit's intention and purpose is actualized through the operation of "chance" and "random" events. One can perceive God within evolution—and even within chaotic systems—then, as the processes themselves. In fact, these processes, unveiled by the biological sciences, are God-acting-as-Creator. Chaotic systems, perhaps wrongfully labeled, interlace both order and disorder. If the system is too far on the orderly side, the possibility for novelty is greatly reduced, as the system itself is too rigid for anything except a rearrangement of what already exists. Conversely, if the system strays too far on the side of disorder, a random world of proverbial anarchy results.⁷⁷ The potential for novelty and relative stability lies between the two poles of order and disorder within chaotic systems.

In dialog with Polkinghorne, I posit that the endowment of potentiality and regularity was instituted by, and relies upon, the kenosis of the Spirit into creation. The Spirit, in this kenotic model, is seen as working within the seeming openness of nature, in conjunction with the unfolding of potentiality, and hence is not what might be called a "Spirit-of-the-gaps" (akin to the God-of-the-gaps). Moreover, the Spirit enables emergence by endowing creation and creatures with the ability to unfold by apparent natural processes according to their own inherent potentialities and possibilities. Simpson writes that "within the framework of the evolutionary history of life, there have been not one but many different kinds of progress," which is a correlate to the notion of the actualization of possibilities.⁷⁸ Moreover, Popper points out that the realization of possibilities, which may be random, depends upon the total situation within which the possibilities are being actualized so that there "exist weighted possibilities which are more than mere possibilities, but [at the same time are] . . . tendencies or propensities to become real."⁷⁹ I posit that there is a definitive lure of the Spirit within the propensities of nature, which seamlessly coalesces with the notion of the Spirit's kenosis into creation, for this potential, as it were, is directed by the ordering activity of the Spirit.

By creating in a kenotic manner, the Spirit both allows and invites the input of creatures in the activity of creation, and reacts according to that input, which invites creation into a cooperative relationship. Indeed, the Spirit did not create in a manipulative, single act, but instead acts in a process in which creation is allowed to develop. This notion of creation through development also leads to an understanding of biological evolution in

---

76. Arthur Peacocke, *Creation and the World of Science* (Oxford: Clarendon, 1979) 94.

77. Polkinghorne, "The Hidden Spirit and the Cosmos," 174.

78. Of which, these are examples: the increasing specialization with its corollary of improvement and adaptability; increase in the general energy or maintained level of processes; increasing complexity, and so forth (G. G. Simpson, *The Meaning of Evolution* [New Haven: Yale University, 1971] 236).

79. Karl Popper, *A World of Propensities* (Bristol: Thoemmes, 1990) 12. Peacocke suggests that there are propensities in evolution, of the Popperian sense noted above, towards the possession of certain features and characteristics, propensities which are built into the evolutionary process. Among these propensities of evolution, Peacocke notes, are "complexity" and "information-processing and storage-ability" (Peacocke, "The Cost of New Life," 30).

which the Spirit is seen as using the development of creatures via a type of continuing creation. There exists overwhelming evidence of a universe marked by development, which points to creation by kenosis. And it should be noted that the Spirit is present "in, with, and under" the processes of biological evolution within the created world.[80] The kenotic creating Spirit is present within the historical contingency of evolution, as well as its lawful regularity.[81] Seen in this manner, the Spirit acts within the causal nexus of creation continually (i.e., natural law, providence, and later human action). Thus, the Spirit did not bring about creation through a definitive action, but instead used a process of evolution guided by natural laws.

CONCLUSION

The earth is an active, empowering environment—even an empowering agent—that brings forth life by various independent processes of self-reproduction. Evolution is the overall process, but emergence punctuates the steps of the evolutionary epic. At the same time, the earth must be seen as an environment of various heterogeneous life-processes. The earth brings forth, but it does not bring forth itself. By releasing the power of the self-directed earth, the Spirit enables—potentially—the continual production, variation, and sustenance of vegetable and animal life.[82] Moreover, in order to be consistent within the causal nexus, the Spirit of God kenotically bestows causal power unto the created order, and in effect thereafter becomes the chief Cause amongst causes.[83] However, the created world is docile before the Spirit, and therefore ever open to the Spirit's causal influence.

The entire mission of the Spirit could be succinctly envisioned as one of kenosis.[84] By extrapolation, one may infer that the Spirit was poured into creation so that it might develop fully in complexity into what the Father had intentioned from the beginning. By focusing on the Spirit, via kenosis into creation, I argue that the Spirit is both directly and indirectly involved in the world from beginning to end. Thus, whereas the Spirit is the primary cause of all things, the Spirit also works through secondary causes. This implies, therefore, that what may commonly be referred to as the natural processes, or even what may be termed random processes, are in reality the indirect acts of the Spirit through secondary causes. I postulate that distinctive, seemingly nondependent, actions are in fact Spirit-caused, though they may appear to be secondarily caused.[85] The apparent secondary causation is due in large part to the fact that the Spirit is the agent of discovery within the various possibilities of God.[86] In this secondary capacity, the Spirit is the remote cause, while natural forces are proximate causes of events. Whereas the Godhead

---

80. Cf. Peacocke, "The Cost of New Life," 32, 86.
81. Polkinghorne, "Kenotic Creation and Divine," 96.
82. Welker, *Creation and Reality*, 42.
83. Reference Polkinghorne, "Kenotic Creation and Divine," 104.
84. Richard Lucien, *Kenosis and Creation* (New York: Paulist, 1997) 116.
85. Compare this postulation with a Neo-Thomist conception of Divine "double agency," as mentioned by Southgate in *God, Humanity, and the Cosmos*, 281.
86. D. Lyle Dabney, "Naming the Spirit: Towards a Pneumatology of the Cross," in *Starting with the Spirit*, eds. Gordon Preece and Stephen Pickard (Adelaide: Open Book, 2001) 58.

created all of the natural processes and laws, the Spirit is God's agent of creation within all of the forces of nature via kenosis.

The Spirit, I affirm, ennobles creation to possess emergent capabilities, as the Spirit imparted propensities into creation that eventuate the rise of higher forms of life. Thus, the *Breath* of life enables and empowers the emergence of creation and creatures. Moreover, this immanent Spirit of emergence endows creation with the ability to unfold by "natural" processes according to their inherent potentialities. This radicalization of immanence comports well with my advocacy of kenosis of the Spirit *into* creation, for in said notion, the Spirit is *intimately interior* to nature, as its source, sustenance and end. Recognize that if theism is to be more than mere deism, it must allow for some sort of divine involvement in the natural world, which leads to the plausibility of some degree of immanence.

In this essay, I have reviewed and interacted with Clayton's seminal work, *Mind & Emergence*. In that book, Clayton contends that emergence is a viable option in contrast to the waning explanatory power of both physicalism and dualism. Moreover, I have presented the Biblical basis of kenosis of the Spirit *into* creation, arguing that the Bible presents the Spirit as being the active agent of God in the world, particularly regarding the Spirit as life-giver and animator of all creation. I also have made my own contribution of the connections between kenosis of the Spirit into creation and emergence theory, which complements Clayton's explanatory survey of emergence theory, and which hopefully will make a positive contribution toward a systematic theology of creation. In using Clayton's text as the source of my extrapolations, I have contended in sum that a richer metaphysical account *ironically* results in greater autonomy for the biological sciences.

12

Revisiting the Day of Atonement

GRAHAM MCFARLANE

One of the really surprising things about the present bewilderment of humanity is that the Christian Church now finds herself called upon to proclaim the old and hated doctrine of sin as a gospel of cheer and encouragement. The final tendency of the modern philosophies—hailed in their day as a release from the burden of sinfulness—has been to bind man hard and fast in the chains of an iron determinism. The influences of heredity and environment, of glandular make-up and the control exercised by the unconscious, of economic necessity and the mechanics of biological development, have all been invoked to assure man that he is not responsible for his misfortunes and therefore not to be held guilty. Evil has been represented as something imposed upon him from without, not made by him from within. The dreadful conclusion follows inevitably, that as he is not responsible for evil, he cannot alter it; even though evolution and progress may offer some alleviation in the future, *there is not hope for you and me, here and now.*[1]

THE PRECOCIOUS NATURE OF Dorothy Sayers's words, written over six decades ago, have remarkable clarity today. Perhaps now, more than ever, the modern sense of progress has been dealt a terminal blow even though it may take several decades before the consequences take shape and develop into whatever comes after the Enlightenment project. Despite all our self-knowledge the sense of impotence remains concerning the human ability to change. And yet, too, our growing knowledge regarding the human condition sets the stage for an even more ancient way of not only understanding the human condition but also its solution. In our highly therapeutised society it is no longer anachronistic to believe the human condition to be one of inner bondage. Nor is it fallacious to claim some form of soteriology as the solution. The time is ripe, therefore, to reconsider the biblical remedy to the problem of human bondage.

---

1. Dorothy L. Sayers, *Creed or Chaos? Essays in Popular Theology* (London: Methuen, 1947) 41; italics added.

PART TWO: CONTRIBUTION TO CURRENT THEOLOGICAL PROBLEMS

How?

The answer involves articulating what might be described as a "worldview." Put simply, this socio-metaphysical construct empowers us to answer several existential questions:

1. What is prime reality?
2. What is the nature of the world around us?
3. What is human being?
4. What happens to a person at death?
5. Why is it possible to know anything at all?
6. How do we know what is right and wrong?
7. What is the meaning of human history?[2]

Our worldview is, thus, "the shared framework of ideas held by a particular society concerning how they perceive the world ... The worldview gives shape and order to the multitude of outward manifestations of a culture."[3] Without a worldview it is less likely that we can both analyze and diagnose our social and political contexts, and provide solutions. Tom Wright identifies four criteria for this task:

- Worldviews provide the stories with which we understand reality
- The worldview-stories enable us to answer the basic question of human existence
- We express our answers to such questions through cultural symbols
- Our worldview provides ways of living in the world.[4]

This is important as we ask questions concerning the human condition—our humanity is constructed by our wider social engineering. The question then becomes how successful is our worldview in "explaining" or "describing" our inability to achieve the sense of freedom for which we appear to be wired?

I want to argue that only a specifically *relational* understanding of the Christian story—or worldview—affords us sufficiently robust answers to questions posed above by Wright concerning the human condition:

- that its genesis is located in the original creation stories: that Adam was not an individual but a person who needed a neighbor to love and be loved by; that to be a person is to live a life of faithful obedience that revealed one's complete love of God:[5]

---

2. James W. Sire, *Naming the Elephant: Worldview as a Concept* (Downers Grove, IL: InterVarsity, 2004) 134–35. The term comes from *Weltanschauung*, a way of looking at the world, of viewing the world, first used by Kant (1724–1804).

3. David Burnett, *Clash of Worlds* (Nashville: Thomas Nelson, 1993) 13–14.

4. Nicholas T. Wright, *The New Testament and the People of God* (London: SPCK, 1993) 123–24.

5. See Gerhard Van Groningen, "Covenant" in *Evangelical Dictionary of Biblical Theology*, ed. Walter A.

- that the call into existence as the people of God[6] was this; that they might love the LORD with all their heart, soul, mind and strength and be a witness to the gentiles nations around of their God[7], and in this sense, loving them as themselves. In so doing, they fulfilled the Law of God;[8]

- that this Law became the standard by the people of God were assessed and would be the hallmark of the Lord God's Messiah;[9]

- that Jesus' teaching about the Kingdom of God and his own mission is the fulfilling of this same Law:[10] he loved the Father with all his heart, soul, mind and strength;[11] he loved his neighbour as himself;[12]

- that Paul understands this to be the fulfillment of the Law:[13] hence his passion for the Gentiles; hence his concern for the poor in Jerusalem;

Why is it so important to go back to such basics and re-articulate what is normative for the Old Testament and New Testament people of God? It is necessary not only because we have become somewhat illiterate today to this most fundamental heuristic construct but much more presciently because without it we can neither diagnose our true condition or offer a viable and dynamic solution. The moot point here is that this worldview provides us with is a fundamentally *relational* understanding of reality in general and of human existence in particular and explains our inability to be free. It will be against this backdrop that we can offer a *gospel* that is indeed "good news" for our contemporaries. Seen within this worldview we discover that human beings are not the sum total of their biological existence. As Patrick Miller states, "[T]he language of the soul is a reminder that here is something in the human reality that transcends the most complete analysis of the physiology and neurology of the human brain."[14] It is a *relational* understanding of human identity—both in relation to God, self and neighbour. *Consequently, whilst human personal identity may well be contoured by the physical body*

Elwell (Cumbria: Baker, 1996) 124–32, esp. 125–26 for the belief that whilst the term "covenant" is not used in Genesis 1–5 "the basic elements of covenant are imbedded" in the creation account, p. 125.

6. Gen 12:1–3. See James Hamilton, "The Seed of the Woman and the Blessing of Abraham," *Tyndale Bulletin* 58.2 (2007) 253–73 where Hamilton argues correctly that hints of God's primal intentions with Adam and the promise of Eden continue with the divine promise to Abraham and a land of blessing.

7. Terence Fretheim, *God and World in the OT: A Relational Theology of Creation* (Nashville: Abingdon, 2005) 7.

8. Deut 6:1–15; 11:8–32. The possession of God's covenant blessing and promise is directly linked to the degree that the people of God fulfil their side of the relational expectations of the Covenant.

9. Jer 31:31–37.

10. Matt 5:17–18.

11. John 14:31.

12. John 15:13. Love of God was understood to be a summary of the entire Law (Deut 5:29).

13. Rom 13:10; Gal 5:14.

14. Patrick D. Miller, "What is a Human Being? The Anthropology of Scripture" in *What About the Soul? Neuroscience and Christian Anthropology* (Nashville: Abingdon) 64.

it is also constituted by the relationships that enable us to identify the different aspects of our personal identity.[15]

THE PROBLEM WE FACE AND HAVE TO OVERCOME

The Judaeo-Christian faiths articulate the problem we face as *sin*. We can identify two aspects of sin at this point. The first is this: *sin not an anthropological, or sociological or psychological term*: its primary meaning is *theological*. It is only known in relation to God. The second is this: *sin is so much a part of us that it is best understood as a dysfunction of my person first, my actions second.*

Sin, as a relational dysfunction, causes "irreparable dislocation" according to Colin Gunton and Christoph Schwöbel, not because it creates something new. Rather, its malignancy is demonstrated in the fact that "it forces human beings to relate to creation in a way that contradicts its proper order."[16] What we see, then, in the phenomenon of sin is the outworking of a personal relational dysfunction, be it individual or corporate, personal or social, national or global. In essence, the act of sin is but the external manifestation of an interior personal reality—*refusal to live in faithful creaturely obedience and dependence upon God and in relation to one's neighbour*. Its consequences are simple—death. And it is a death that is "not merely the end of a biological organism, but the awful outworking of our human destruction of God's intention."[17]

In response to this dysfunctional sociality we are called into covenant relationship that expresses itself three-dimensionally: with God, with self and with neighbour.[18] Life within *this* particular matrix of relationships leads to relational fecundity that can only be described in terms of a super-abundance that is both material (you will get the land—Gen 12:1–3; 13:14–17; 15:7, 18; 17:8) and personal (your descendents will outnumber the stars—Gen 12:3; 18:18; 22:18; 26:4; 28:14; Ps 72:17; Jer 4:2; Zech 8:13). These are the relational expectations that constitute the Lord God's relationship with Israel and creation. It is only set against this backdrop that our sin is understood correctly: as a relational pathology.

Sin is the breakdown of the relational expectations that constitute our very selves. When these expectations are broken, an "anti-force" is released. The Bible names this power as "sin." As a result, the relational expectations that constitute creaturely *and* covenantal relationship become distorted and broken to various degrees. Since human sociality operates at several levels and in various ways we should not be too surprised to discover that

---

15. R. Larry Shelton, *Cross & Covenant* (Milton Keynes: Paternoster/Authentic Media) 2006 is an extended argument for a narrative understanding of what the God-human expectations look like within the context of covenant.

16. Colin E. Gunton and Christoph Schwöbel, *Persons, Divine and Human* (Edinburgh: T. & T. Clark, 1991) 149.

17. Stanley J. Grenz, *Theology for the Community of God* (Grand Rapids: Eerdmans, 2000) 581.

18. "Covenant loyalty, not sinless perfection, is the primary and fundamental issue in Deuteronomy ... Failure to do the whole law functions in Deuteronomy as idiomatic expression which means to abandon the covenant with Yahweh and to serve other gods," Jeffrey R. Wisdom, *Blessing for the Nations and the Curse of the Law* (Tübingen: Mohr/Stiebeck, 2001) 61–62.

the problem, too, operates at various levels of human intercourse: the divine, the personal and the social. And it is on these grounds that there are also degrees of severity regarding the problem being addressed. Certain sins have a more *common* identity: they constitute the inevitable breakdowns of relationship that are easily resolvable through payment or cleansing. Such relational dysfunctions, described in the OT as khet[19] or avon[20] sins, leave one socially (and financially) impoverished, but not cut off from the community of faith or the wider created order. These less volitional and thus less personal sins are resolvable in that whilst they are rooted in our actions they are resolvable with a bit of good Jewish common sense and some cognitive behavioural programming. As such, then, these are not the kind of relational breakdowns and dysfunctions that cut us off from fellowship with God, neighbour or self permanently.

What *is* problematic are those external actions that demonstrate an internal reality which evidences volitional and personal actions, intentional rebellion against the other, whether divine or human. Such unresolvable differences lead, ultimately, to the death of the relationship, whether with God, self or neighbour. It is wilful rebelliousness and constitutes a fundamental breach in covenant.[21] It stems from the inner intentions of the person and is an act of her will. Such sins are sins committed, literally, "with a high hand" (Num 15:30–31). Here, there is no form of restitution since it is a consequence of a much deeper state of relational dysfunction—and is indicative of one's "heart," one's inner existence. The sin becomes a permanent state of affairs. Unless this is addressed things can only go from bad to worse since it cannot be atoned for: it can neither be washed off nor bought off. As such, these *pesha* sins constitute a form of bondage and demonstrate a degree of powerlessness articulated by Dorothy Sayers in our opening quotation. They are external demonstrations of an internal reality, namely, an attitude of heart and thus constitutive of the person him or herself. There is no means of personal atonement without removing the root of the problem, the agent of sin him or herself. The remedy involves total self-destruction. Why? Unlike *khet* or *avon* misdemeanours, *pesha* sins cannot be washed out or bought off. The sin and the sinner are one and the same, the sin being the externalisation of an internal, personal reality. The human pathology is so deep, it grip so radical that it renders us powerless to resolve the issue ourselves. The irresolvability has to do not to do so much with the action, but with the agent: *pesha* sins, sins of the heart, are sins of the personality, of the will and intention.[22] As such, their nature is such that only by virtue of the death of the agent can the actions be stemmed.

---

19. Unintentional sin, a missing of the mark (taken from archery) that carries with it negative consequences: see, Lev 19:17; 20:20; 22:9; 24:15; Num 9:13; 18:22, 32; Isa 53:12; Ezek 23:49.

20. This is a sin knowingly committed but not in a manner that defies God. It is sin carried out as lust or uncontrolled emotion, or to be understood as a "wandering out of the way," John Goldingay, *Atonement Today*, ed. John Goldingay (London: SPCK, 1995) 42; see, Gen 4:13; 19:15; Exod 28:38, 43; Lev 5:1, 17; 7:18; 10:17; 16:22; 17:16; 19:8; 20:17, 19; 22:16; 26:39, 41, 43; Num 5:31; 14:34; 18:1, 23; 30:15; 1 Sam 25:24; 28:10; 2 Sam 14:9; 2 Kgs 7:9; Job 10:14; Ps 31:11; 69:28; 106:43; Prov 5:22; Isa 5:18; 30:13; 40:2; 53:6, 11; 64:5, 6; Jer 51:6; Lam 4:22; 5:7; Ezek 4:4–6, 17; 7:16; 14:10; 18:19-20; 21:30, 34; 24:23; 32:27; 35:5; 39:23; 44:10, 12.

21. Mark E. Biddle, *Missing the Mark: Sin and Its Consequences in Biblical Theology* (Nashville: Abingdon, 2005) 20.

22. For example, Ps 5:10; 19:13; 25:7; 32:1; 32:5; 36:1; 39:8; 51:1; 51:3; 59:3; 65:3; 89:32; 103:12; 107:17,

We can summarize the implications thus:

At the relational level chaos erupts at the very apex of creation whereby human beings experience three-dimensional alienation:

- alienation in relation to one's self—since our own sense of self is dependent upon a more primary relationship with God who calls us into being and from whom we derive our true identity;

- alienation in relation to the "other"—since to be an embodied "self" requires the presence of other embodied beings with whom we can experience immediate relationship;

- alienation in relation to the Creator—since all ongoing acts of self-determination are directed against God.

TOWARDS A SOLUTION

A specifically Christian worldview affords us an explanation and diagnosis concerning our personal impotence to change. There is no hope if we are left to our own devices because our basic human condition is one in which we find ourselves constantly oriented away from at least one aspect of our relational identity in relation to God, neighbor or self. However, as Wright points out above, for a worldview to be of any use it must also proffer an adequate solution.

It is here that the specifically Christian kicks in, as it were, on its own distinctions. It presupposes a worldview of solidarity, identification and interchange.[23] We catch various glimpses of this worldview throughout Scripture: in the interchange of lamb and firstborn in Exod 12; in the more primitive bronze serpent in Num 21:9; in the Day of Atonement in Lev 16; in the liberation of the demon-possessed man at Gerasenes; in Jesus' own interpretation of the Passover, Matt 27:26–29/Lk 22:14–21. Contrary to contemporary, modern thinking Paul, too, can speak of human solidarity, of interchange between humans and the consequences of their actions with significant import to our understanding of Christ's death. Such a view of creation, Morna Hooker reminds us, is "a vitally important factor in the substructure of his thought."[24] Indeed, without it, the benefits of sacrifice are limited, the significance of Jesus' death and his resurrection are of little transferable significance for us, (Rom 8:3). We inhabit, then, a world in which interchange is possible. Without this pre-requisite the resolution of the irredeemable would remain an impossibility.

Isa 24:20; 43:25; 44:22; 50:1; 53:5, 8; 57:4; 58:1; 59:12,20, Ezek 14:11, 18;22, 28, 30, 31; 21:24; 33:10, 12; 37:23; 39:24.

23. Morna D. Hooker, *From Adam to Christ* (Cambridge: Cambridge University Press, 1990) esp. ch. 1; Clinton E. Arnold, *Ephesians: Power and Magic* (Grand Rapids: Baker, 1992) 136–37.

24. Hooker, *From Adam to Christ*, 41.

GOING BACK TO BASICS

The dynamics of sacrifice—how it actually "works"—turn on the biblical notion that not all sins are the same. We have already identified three types of sin: *khet, avon* and *pesha*. With these 3 types of sin is the notion of clean and unclean: the unclean infiltrates a "place"—community, land, people—and takes on a life of its own. This is no ancient worldview operating here. We can describe sin, in this sense, in *medical* terms, as a virulent agent in a manner not too dissimilar to contemporary viruses such as AIDS. In the normal state of human affairs when sin is allowed to carry on as normal the effects of such sin simply spread. Alternatively, we can describe sin in *social, interpersonal* terms, where sin spreads like gossip: a word, here and there, until the "word" takes on a whole world of its own wreaking its havoc and destruction. Or, we can describe it in *psycho-behavioural* terms, where the compulsive behaviour of an individual, be it sexual, chemical, calorific or adrenal, compounds and expands until the behaviour ends in self-destruction. In the light of such examples we are not at all "off-track" in describing the problem the cross overcomes, then, within the ancient worldview of Israel. It resonates too distinctly with today's world to assume, as C. S. Lewis puts it, such cultural and epistemic imperialism.[25]

Once we see the problem in this light of course we recognize this to be the corporate status of humanity. When we are confronted by the Creator's relational standards we discover our true condition to be one that is very much far from the mark. We find ourselves, then, in a somewhat precarious state of affairs, well put by Miroslav Volf when he concludes: "The world is sinful. That's why God doesn't affirm it indiscriminately. God loves the world. That's why God doesn't punish it in justice.

What does God do with this double bind? God forgives."[26]

The question this begs is simple: "How?"

SACRIFICE IN ACTION: YOM KIPPUR—THE DAY OF ATONEMENT.

In order that forgiveness may occur, an additional means of reconciliation is needed for deliberate, rebellious sin. For this, we need to turn to the ancient Israelite festival mentioned in the Holiness Code[27] and outlined in Leviticus 16, the Day of Atonement, where, interestingly, we discover the only two uses of *pesha* in verses 16 & 21. The means by which atonement is procured on Yom Kippur is presented as a series of successive actions whereby the priest and people, as well as the Holy of Holies, are cleansed of contamination. It can be summarized as follows:

- the bull for the sin-offering of the high priest is ritually slaughtered;
- identical male goats are brought to the priest;
- lots are cast & one is dedicated to the Lord and the other to Azazel;[28]

---

25. Clives S. Lewis, *Surprised by Joy* (London: Fount, 1998) 161.

26. Miraslov Volf, *Free of Charge: Giving and Forgiving in a Culture Stripped of Grace* (Grand Rapids: Zondervan, 2005) 140.

27. Lev 23:26–32.

28. "Azazel enjoys the distinction of being the most mysterious extra human character in sacred literature," in Isidore Singer, ed., *The Jewish Encyclopaedia* (KTAV) 286.

- the goat to the Lord is killed and its blood mixed with that of the other bull;
- the mixed blood is carried to the Holy of holies and is spread on and in front of the cover of the ark;
- the other parts of the Temple are cleansed with the mixed blood;
- the goat for Azazel is presented to the high priest who lays hands upon it, confessing over it the sins of Israel, including their pesha;
- the goat is driven alive into the wilderness;
- the remains of the bull of the sin offering and the goat to the Lord are ritually disposed.

Two distinct modes of action operate here within the one ceremony.

On the one hand, there is a recognition that some sins are so catastrophic in their consequences that they deem the physical place where they occur so odious that the possibility of engagement is lost—the offended party, the one sinned against, cannot go back there until something happens to rectify the situation. We see this same dynamic taking place in the Day of Atonement: one goat purifies the temple of any uncleanness thus making it possible for the Lord God to be with his people once again (Lev 16:16).

On the other hand, when we are sinned against—deliberately, intentionally, purposefully—this act results in the breakdown of the relationship, in a barrier between the parties. Until the breakdown is dealt with, the barrier is removed, it is impossible for the relationship to be restored. Again, we see this dynamic in operation: another goat takes the offences away so that the people of God can come back to God and be in relation with him as he comes back to the cleaned-up temple (Lev 16:21). Of interest is the fact that it is not the blood sacrifice, therefore, that takes away the sin and establishes forgiveness, as in Lev 29:22. The blood cleanses the meeting place between God and people. The physical body removes the offending sins from the people so that they are free to relate once again.

It is quite clear that the Day of Atonement defied normal convention. It appears to step across prescribed boundaries seeking, in turn, a solution *outside* the normal legal boundaries of Israelite religion. It represents, rather, an *excessive* act that exceeds the law's normal conditions, what Frances Young describes as an "annual super-sin offering."[29] This is not the offering of penance by the sinner. On the contrary, it is an act performed by the *offended* One in order to restore relationship with the offending party so that the fabric of *creaturely* existence may be restored and *relationship* may proceed. It is a *proactive* response on the part of the One who, though having been alienated by human response and action moves towards his creation in an action of supreme love. The scapegoat, in Finlan's words, is "*sent beyond the pale*" having become "a loathsome" thing.[30]

---

29. Francis M. Young, *Sacrifice and the Death of Christ* (London: SPCK, 1975) 29.
30. Stephen Finlan, *The Background and Contents of Paul's Cultic Atonement Metaphors* (Atlanta: Society of Biblical Literature, 2004) 81.

It has become a cursed object in order that the curse of sin may be removed from the people and fellowship with God may be restored.

Once again, we are back to the centrality of sacrificial language. McIntyre sums it up perfectly when he comments that, "Whenever God offers to men and women his forgiveness . . . that forgiveness springs from love which is intrinsically sacrificial and costly."[31] The point must be stressed: at the level of *what is happening* it appears that a life is being forfeited and that mercantile or legal language could convey the act. However, at the level of *how this is happening* the sacrifice does not act as a replacement object to be punished but rather as the 'space' wherein the offended party extends the *gift* of reconciliation and the offending party exercises *trust* in the one seeking reconciliation. It is by *grace* through *faith*—not a work, (Eph 2:8; Gal 3:11; Heb 10:38) It is *gift*—without it we would simply be given up to the consequences of our dysfunctional relationships and the laws of creation and covenant would be fulfilled. Justice would be met. We would bring upon ourselves the inverse of blessing: a curse that leads to death as the *wrath* of the Creator, the inbuilt consequences of sin.

Consequently, in the Day of Atonement to make sacrifice is "to make a confession."[32] It transcends the code and conditions of the law and is the very reversal of the *lex talionis*.[33] It is an act of grace from start to finish where the Lord God is the subject of atonement. The entire ceremony presupposes that the God of Israel has already decided to make himself present to the people. Consequently, the ceremonial actions do not *cause* God to forgive as though there were some mechanical or automatic response. Rather, the entire ceremony "proclaims the freedom of God's grace."[34]

Sacrificial atonement is, thus, an act of supreme personal renunciation. Jensen's understanding of forgiveness describes how reconciliation—the kind required when confronted by the unforgivable—is possible. "To forgive means to exhaust in one's own being the consequences one has suffered so that those consequences will not cause further damage (psychological, social, financial, etc.) to the victimizer; or, to determine that even if given the opportunity to cause retaliative damage to the victimizer, one would not do so."[35]

This is what God in Christ has done for us. We can identify key aspects of what it means to describe Jesus' death as a "sacrifice." In light of the dynamic of hyper-sacrifice as demonstrated in the Day of Atonement we can say, on the one hand, that:

---

31. John McIntyre, *The Shape of Soteriology: Studies in the Doctrine of the Death of Christ* (Edinburgh: T. & T. Clark, 1992) 115.

32. Eberhard Jüngel, *Theological Essays II* (Edinburgh: T. & T. Clark, 1995) 172.

33. Richard Holloway, *On Forgiveness: How Can We Forgive the Unforgiveable?* (Edinburgh: Canongate, 2002) 82.

34. Markus Barth, *Was Christ's Death A Sacrifice?* (Edinburgh: Oliver & Boyd, 1961) 23.

35. Paul Jensen, "Forgiveness and Atonement," *Scottish Journal of Theology* 46 (1993) 154.

- Jesus Christ becomes "the absolute victim."[36] In him the full weight of the consequences for our relational dysfunction comes to bear and is absolutized. He is shamed, spat upon, ridiculed, mocked, humiliated, flogged, beaten, abused, insulted, abandoned, tortured and sent outside the symbolic boundaries of civilised society. The symbolic identification with the "cursed" and the scapegoat are not missed.[37]

- Jesus becomes the one who is cursed: he is the one on whom the irredeemable sins are placed and by whom they are removed. He takes our sins out of the "relational zone"[38] and redeems us from the curse of the Law by becoming what we are—cursed (Gal 3:13).

- The one *with* life becomes the very *anti-life* that our sin generates. Only in this act of sacrificial exchange can relationship be restored. The one who fulfilled the Law, who loved God with his entire heart, soul, and mind and was obedient even to the point of death, and loved his neighbour as himself he, the sinless one, removes our sin once and for all (Heb 10:14) as the scapegoat did annually on the great "reversal ritual" of the Day of Atonement.[39]

- His physical life is substituted for ours (Rom 5:6–10).[40] He becomes what we should become so that we might become who he is. In this manner, Jesus Christ acts as our "head," breaking the virulent power of sin in his body in order that *his* life may be restored in ours.

On the other hand, this act of self-sacrificial love becomes the prototype of a new way of relating;

- Through the sacrificial act of Jesus—bloodshed on an even bloodier and cursed cross—the place of contact, the locus of habitation is once again cleansed so that God can relate to his people, inhabit their space, dwell in their hearts.

- Christ deals with sin for us and condemns it (Rom 8:3). As such human beings are no longer "covenantally dysfunctional."[41] If sin's power has been destroyed by our sin and curse-bearer, then the relational expectations can begin to be fulfilled. A new covenant is established (Heb 9:19–21) and the blessings of the new covenant can be enjoyed.[42] Thus, the imperative of Gal 3:10–14 is that these

---

36. Rowan Williams, *Resurrection* (New York: Pilgrim, 1982) 16.

37. *Frederick* A. Niedner argues that the imagery of Yom Kippur is being used in the Barabbas and Jesus narrative in Matt 27:15ff. See "'His blood be on us, and on our children!': A Biblical Economy of Forgiveness," *The Cresset* 62/6 (1999) 14–16.

38. Jensen, "Forgiveness and Atonement," 154.

39. Finlan, *Background*, 99.

40. Ibid., "The scapegoat is a particularly *physical* kind of rite, in that sin or disease is loaded onto the body of a living creature, which is then abused and driven out."

41. Michael J. Gorman, *Cruciformity: Paul's Narrative Spirituality of the Cross* (Grand Rapids: Eerdmans, 2001) 106.

42. Scot McKnight, *Jesus and His Death* (Waco: Baylor University Press, 2005) 298.

blessings are not the sole prerogative of Jews. By being placed outside the covenant and breaking the curse upon those excluded from the blessings, Jesus has now made it possible for them to join the covenant and enjoy its blessings.

- Christ inaugurates the eschatological blessings. We make sacrifices to the degree we believe in the future: we sacrifice *for* something.[43] Thus, not only is there a negative exchange—our sin for his wholeness—there is also a positive exchange—the gifting of the Spirit. Here the benefits of the sin-exchange become loaded with overtones concerning the Spirit (Rom 8:1–11). Instead of *anti-life* we are now recipients of the *Giver of life*, the Holy Spirit. What was oriented towards death is now enlivened by the very life-force of creation itself, the Spirit of God.

---

43. See John Milbank, "The Midwinter Sacrifice," in *The Blackwell Companion to Postmodern Theology*, ed. G. Ward (Oxford: Blackwell, 2001) ch. 6.

13

Bind Us Together?

A Sketch of Shame and Violence in the Day of Atonement and Communion

AARON PERRY

THE WESLEYAN TRADITION HAS shaped its pastors to think in terms of community. Books, conferences, and lectures on small groups have all been developed to help pastors discover and reflect on what keeps communities together and what breaks them apart. One crucial topic with respect to the health of a community is shame. It plays a significant role in shaping how people relate socially and interpersonally. In this essay, I offer a sketch for an interpretation of the ritual violence of the Day of Atonement as a response to a community suffering shame which then draws out potential implications for the death of Christ and communion. First, I will consider recent sociological and psychological studies with regard to the relationship between shame and violence. Second, I will examine the ability of ritual and non-ritual violence both to create and sustain community relations. Third, I will offer one interpretation of the Day of Atonement in light of this discussion. This sketch will suggest that the Day of Atonement may provide a curtailed outlet for violence, while utilizing this same ritualized violence to unite the community, thereby removing one cause of shame. From here, I will consider avenues for further discussion, specifically how the Christian practice of communion may serve as a reminder and completion of the ritual violence which created the covenanted community of the church. I will conclude with areas this sketch establishes as important for further research.

WHAT IS SHAME?

Not only is shame a category that provides insight to community, it is also a potential resource for hamartiology.[1] Chronic shame can heighten the crippling nature of negative shame—a desire to hide that is rooted in worthlessness rather than value—and destroy the opportunity for community. One of the most troubling aspects of shame is that it is

---

1. See, for example, Alan Mann, *Atonement for a Sinless Society: Engaging with an Emerging Culture* (Milton Keynes: Paternoster, 2005).

difficult to describe. While there is no stable core to all of shame's variety of experiences, some elements are more prevalent.[2] For example, the shamed often desire to hide or cover. Second, there is often a "split" of the shamed individual: they believe an incongruity exists between the self they present to others and the self they experience.[3] Both of these experiences reveal that one's relationships are central to shame: shame hides the self from others, while an incongruity between selves is intelligible only when others are involved.[4]

Shame need not always be considered in a negative fashion. Shame can lead us to greater forms of discretion about what we will not do or should not do.[5] This positive, "discretionary" shame has a "positive function of insuring a modicum of modesty, privacy, propriety, and prudence."[6] Discretionary shame keeps a person's world intact when her personal or communal boundaries are broken, thereby serving their wellbeing.[7] As such, positive shame is "part of the social 'glue' that binds solidaristic relations."[8] Discretionary shame keeps up needed boundaries—both to maintain healthy distances from many and to establish closer proximities to a select few.

Disgrace shame, however, goes in the opposite direction. Rather than protecting, disgrace shame harms the individual.

> [D]isgrace shame is a painful experience of the disintegration of one's world. A break occurs in the self's relationship with itself and/or others. An awkward, uncomfortable space opens up in the world. The self is no longer whole, but divided. It feels less than it wants to be, less than at its best it knows itself to be.[9]

This type of shame becomes intensely personal, limiting proper relationships with the self and others. Robert Albers notes that the "experience of disgrace shame shakes the essential foundation of the divine-human relationship and the individual-group relationship."[10] The important distinction to make is that while discretionary shame be-

---

2. Stephen Pattison (*Shame: Theory, Therapy, Theology* [Cambridge: CUP, 2000]) uses the illustration of an onion. At the center of the layers of shame, there is no "real onion" (39).

3. Ibid., 73. This is not a split in the sense of dissociative identity disorder, but the experience of *being* one person but being seen for another.

4. This, of course, is an ancient idea going back to Aristotle [*Nicomachean* Ethics, Book IV chapter 9 (February, 2009). Online: http://classics.mit.edu/Aristotle/nicomachaen.4.iv.html] for whom shame is a feeling of dishonor one experiences, which presupposes relations.

5. Robert H. Albers, "Shame: A Dynamic in the Etiology of Violence," *Dialog* 36.4 (1997) 254–65; Carl D. Schneider, *Shame, Exposure and Privacy* (New York: Norton, 1977). Aristotle [*Rhetoric*, Book II chapter 6 (August, 2008). Online: http://www.public.iastate.edu/~honeyl/Rhetoric/rhet2-6.html] also mentioned shamelessness "as contempt or indifference in regard to these same bad things (that cause us shame)." Though, it should be mentioned, shame is not a virtue for Aristotle.

6. Ibid., 255.

7. Ibid., 256.

8. Larry Ray, David Smith, and Liz Wastell, "Shame, Rage, and Racist Violence," *British Journal of Criminology* 44 (2004) 353.

9. Schneider, *Shame, Exposure and Privacy*, 22, as cited by Albers, "Shame," 256.

10. Albers, "Shame," 257.

lieves in the individual's value, disgrace shame believes the self lacks value. It is this type of negative shame which is most pertinent for this paper.[11]

The personal nature of negative shame is best seen in terms of identity. "[S]hame is about something [one is]."[12] This forces us to distinguish shame from guilt. Stephen Pattison shows the difference this can make in terms of the use of metaphors:

> While guilt pertains to a world characterised by metaphors in which persons offend against rules, incur debts, are punished and have to make active reparation, shame pertains more to a metaphorical world in which persons are excluded, found to be 'dirty' or polluted, and stand in need of cleansing and acceptance in order to be reintegrated into society.[13]

The lack of consideration of one's value forces one's alienation from the community. Here we see why Aristotle notes that community is a precondition of shame.[14] If shame is an exclusion, there must be a community to which inclusion is necessary or one desires. This sense of alienation is not fully described via the metaphor of defilement, however.

Shame can also result in a lack of ability to give adequate gifts to assure and earn social acceptance. Frederick Turner writes,

> Shame ... comes from the consciousness of a lack of ability to give.... The shame one feels at being excluded from the communion of the "right" people ... derives basically from a suspicion that our own gift to society was not acceptable and thus that our exclusion from the human exchange system may, shamefully, be justified.[15]

Note Turner's language of *right people*. Again, community, a group of people, is the precondition for shame in that there *are* right people. The shamed person, as a result, becomes distrusting of relationships[16] and, operating from outside of relationships, believes the excluding judgment they perceive put on them by the community.[17] Putting this in

---

11. See also John Braithwaite, *Crime, Shame, and Reintegration* (Cambridge: Cambridge University Press, 1989). Braithwaite studies the use of shame in reintegrating people into societies, from a penal/reform perspective, distinguishing between reintegrative and stigmatizing shame. Thomas Scheff and Suzanne Retzinger describe stigmatizing shame as "involving assigning a master status to a person based on their lawbreaking" [Thomas J. Scheff and Suzanne M. Retzinger, *Emotions and Violence: Shame and Rage in Destructive Conflicts* (Lexington, MA: Lexington, 1991) 72].

12. James W. Fowler, "Shame: Toward a Practical Theological Understanding," *The Christian Century* 110:24 (August 25–September 1, 1993) 816.

13. Pattison, *Shame*, 88.

14. Aristotle notes that shame is felt whenever those whose opinion matters to us are involved. *Rhetoric*, Book II, Chapter 6. Online: http://www.public.iastate.edu/~honeyl/Rhetoric/rhet2-6.html.

15. Frederick Turner, "Shame, Beauty, and the Tragic View of History," *American Behavioral Scientist* 38:8 (August 1995) 1066–67. Turner's argument, of course, rests on the premise that community and proper standing within community is founded on reciprocal exchange. Such a consideration is not foreign to Christian thought. Augustine roots community in the mutual sharing of objects of love [*City of God*, book XIX, article 24, from *From Irenaeus to Grotius*, eds. Oliver O'Donovan & Joan Lockwood O'Donovan (Grand Rapids: Eerdmans, 1999) 162]. This notion of lacking valuable gift could, perhaps, be rephrased as lack of *acceptable sacrifice*, the implications of which will be clear later in this paper.

16. Pattison, *Shame*, 167.

17. Pattison (*Shame*) captures the acceptance of excluding judgment when he writes, "I believe myself to

an Augustinian framework, we could say that just as the shamed person has no loveworthy gift for the community in which they may share, so does the person consider themselves of little value and, as a result, lacks in self-love.[18] The shamed person is defiled and requires cleansing, but lacking this cleansing, seeks to hide and cover themselves. "To see chronically shamed people as people who essentially experience a sense of themselves as excluded, inferior, defiled, polluted and polluting, indeed as toxic dirt, is not far-fetched."[19]

This break in social relationships both causes and is caused by shame. The lack of things binding individuals together in community, whether because the individual considers their gift to the community of little value, or because the shamed perceives a judgment from the community, leads to isolated individuals. However, since individuals still reside in some forms of community, communities themselves experience this same lack of coherence because they have nothing to share: they lack bonds; there are no common objects of love.[20] Consider manufacturing as an example:

> Communities once defined by the shared experience of the manufacturing industry lose coherence and stability along with affluence; long-cherished cultural expectations or working-class masculinity become unrealizable with the erosion of their material basis; and the inherited meanings of territory and neighbourhood become fractured and uncertain.[21]

As a result, shame may also infiltrate and work through "the collective consciousness of communities or even nations."[22] This sense of national shame can be highlighted in a generational sense: parents that suffer shame produce shame in their children; when shame is nation-wide, brought on, say, by a[n inter]national war, an entire generation may be raised in this shame and, in turn, raise the next generation in a similar way,[23]

---

have been a shame-bound person for most of my life, regarding myself as unworthy, valueless and defiled, with a deep desire to hide myself away from the 'legitimate' negative judgment of others" (7).

18. James Gilligan ("Shame, Guilt, and Violence," *Social Research* 70:4 [Winter 2003]) writes, "Just as pride means self-love (and its various synonyms, such as self-esteem, self-respect, or feelings of self-worth), shame means lack or deficiency of self-love" (1153).

19. Pattison, *Shame*, 90.

20. For an Augustinian examination of community, see Oliver O'Donovan, *Common Objects of Love* (Grand Rapids: Eerdmans, 2002).

21. Ray, Smith, and Wastell, "Shame, Rage and Racist Violence," 364.

22. Albers, "Shame," 257.

23. For an example of this, see Mary Katherine Armstrong, "Child Abuse, Shame, Rage and Violence," *The Journal of Psychohistory* 31 (Summer 2003). Armstrong uses the example of a 17 year-old German boy whose parents were born in the rebuilding of Germany after World War II, whose own parents, in turn, had lived through World War II, whose parents, in turn, had seen the rise of national socialism.

The reason that such shame is passed on could be, in part, neurological. Martin H. Teicher ["Scars that Won't Heal: The Neurobiology of Child Abuse," *Scientific American* 286:3 (March 2002)] writes, "Because childhood abuse occurs during the critical formative time when the brain is being physically sculpted by experience, the impact of severe stress can leave an indelible imprint on its structure and function. Such abuse, it seems, induces a cascade of molecular and neurobiological effects that irreversibly alter neural development" (May 2007, http://www.theannainstitute.org/stwh.html). Persons suffering particular effects of such abuse may suffer borderline personality disorder. Amazingly, though the language of shame is not

transmitting "forms of racial, religious and national prejudice"[24] stretching even into "[p]atterns of character, perduring types of perception, emotion, and motivation ... in ... international relationships."[25]

VIOLENCE AS A RESPONSE TO SHAME

We have now briefly examined the experience of shame, its causes, and its lasting effects. We have also seen how some chronically shamed simply accept the judgment of a community that has excluded him or her. This is not the only response shamed people take, however.

Shame alerts people to a disruption in relationships. It signals an interruption in reciprocal trust in a relationship[26] and the resulting necessity to alter behavior to rescue the relationship.[27] In this sense, shame may actually *prevent* "negative reactions such as violence and anger," facilitate restoration of relationship.[28] If shame *moves outside of restoration*, however, becoming what Pattison calls "chronic shame," the responses are negative.[29] Because people are communal beings, a simple acceptance of exclusion cannot last indefinitely. As a result, a chronically shamed individual will often respond to shame by attacking the self, avoiding the other, or attacking the other.[30] Attacking the other works to confirm the worth of the shamed and to restore honor. Without retaliatory violence, the shamed is often considered worth nothing. For example, when a woman's honor is not (violently) avenged, her shame is confirmed.[31] As a result, violence is a response to

---

present in Teicher's article, he notes that persons suffering borderline personality disorder may exalt and then vilify individuals, which is a trait of scapegoating, and be prone to eruptions of anger. Both of these, as will be seen, are symptoms of shame. Individuals may also see in "black and white" terms. This may be connected with a similar phenomenon in war that the world is construed in black and white [Chris Hedges, *War is a Force that Gives us Meaning* (New York: Public Affairs, 2002), as referenced by Stanley Hauerwas, "Sacrificing the Sacrifices of War," *Criswell Theological Review* 4:2 (Spring 2007), 81]. This connection is possible, especially considering Teicher's ("Scars that Won't Heal") belief that "molecular and neurobiological effects ... alter neural development in an adaptive way that prepares the adult brain to survive and reproduce in a dangerous world" (Online: http://www.theannainstitute.org/stwh.html).

24. Scheff and Retzinger, *Emotions and Violence*, 105.

25. Ibid., 37. It should be noted that Scheff and Retzinger prefer to work with "national character" as an *hypothesis*, more tentative than uses earlier they previously saw as assumptions (37). See also Albers, "Shame," 257.

26. Gershen Kaufman, *The Psychology of Shame* (London: Routledge, 1993) 29–31 cited in Pattison, *Shame*, 79.

27. Scheff and Retzinger, *Emotions and Violence*, 64. Pattison does not refer to shame as a feeling, however certain feelings are associated with the experience of shame.

28. Ibid., 79.

29. Scheff and Retzinger (*Emotions and Violence*) talk about this kind of shame as "unacknowledged shame" (69).

30. Pattison, *Shame*, 110–14. For an example of violence against the self as a response to shame, see Gilligan, "Shame, Guilt, and Violence," 1151. Here he mentions suicide as a way of gaining respect.

31. Gilligan, "Shame, Guilt, and Violence," 1156–57.

ward off shame and restore value, even achieving equilibrium, if not reconciliation, in a relationship.[32]

Just as shame had consequences for the individual, so can its response be accomplished in a group and society.[33] One example that Pattison gives of the violence and rage in communities suffering shame is that of scapegoating, where the shamed group finds one similar to them in order to project their feelings and experience onto the scapegoat and, by excluding them, force these feelings and experiences away from the community. The scapegoat may then attempt a similar maneuver.[34] If we return to the cause of shame resulting from lack of community by lack of love-worthy gift, itself the precondition of shame, then violence may only partially deal with shame:[35]

> Anger and rage ... have frequently been seen as reactions that are often intrinsic to shame. These aggressive reactions associated with scripts of attacking the other, while they can have constructive aspects to them, are often deeply corrosive of the respectful, trusting relationships between people and in society as a whole.[36]

Since violence serves to diminish trusting relationships, there is a cyclical nature to violence as response to shame: shame may lead to violence which undercuts the long-term possibility for relationship or community, the loss of which contributes to shame, which may be counteracted with more violence.[37]

VIOLENCE AND COMMUNITY

But now a strange phenomenon comes into play. Violence also has the ability to *create and sustain* communities—achieving equilibrium in relationships, thereby eliminating, albeit temporarily, one of the root causes of shame. In their book, *Blood Sacrifice and the Nation: Totem Rituals and the American Flag*, Carolyn Marvin and David Ingle begin by asking the question, "What binds the nation together?"[38] Here it is essential to note that Scheff and Retzinger ask almost the exact same question, but with a different sociology: "What forces bind members of a society together? What forces tear them apart? What forces cause cooperation and conflict?"[39] Scheff and Retzinger ask what binds individuals together, whereas Marvin and Ingle begin with the community. Scheff and Retzinger's answer, "attunement," by which they mean "mutual understanding and mutual ratification"[40]

---

32. Herbert E. Thomas, "Experiencing a Shame Response as a Precursor to Violence," *Bulletin of the American Academy of Psychiatry Law* 23.4 (1995) 588. See also Gilligan, "Shame, Guilt, and Violence," 1154. See also Scheff and Retzinger, *Emotions and Violence*, 66.

33. Pattison, *Shame*, 115. See also Pattison's preceding discussion of this phenomenon (110–14). Pattison also sees chronic shame impacting individuals, families, and societies (154).

34. Ibid., 115. This idea of transference is also found in Kaufman, *Shame*, 83–84.

35. Thomas, "Experiencing a Shame Response as a Precursor to Violence," 588.

36. Pattison, *Shame*, 127. Pattison (*Shame*) defines rage as "uncontrolled anger" (127).

37. Albers, "Shame," 261.

38. Carolyn Marvin and David W. Ingle, *Blood Sacrifice and the Nation: Totem Rituals and the American Flag* (Cambridge: Cambridge University Press, 1999) 1.

39. Scheff and Retzinger, *Emotions and Violence*, 21.

40. Ibid., 21.

is much different from that of Marvin and Ingle, who argue that "violent blood sacrifice makes enduring groups cohere...."[41] Both, however, have grounded their notion of community in terms of shared *practices*: one suggests communication tactics, while the other proffers shared violence in sacrifice.[42] As a result, it is not necessary for attunement to be *incorrect* in order to consider violent sacrifice as a practice a community may hold in common.

So, how does the practice of sacrifice bind the nation together? Marvin and Ingle believe that the ritual killing of the community's own members at their own hands in honor of their totem binds them together. From this action, they define nation as "the shared memory of blood sacrifice, periodically renewed."[43] Marvin and Ingle distinguish this "felt" nation from the nation-state, which is the "agreement about killing rules that compels citizens to sacrifice themselves for the group," at the impetus of the felt nation.[44] The shared story of sacrifice for a common object in the felt nation encourages the continued and ratified sacrifice by this original shared myth/reality, becoming the formal nation-state. The sentiment created by these willing deaths is strong enough to make a group cohere, at least temporarily, which, they believe, shows the nation's dependence on war. While Marvin and Ingle acknowledge that no nation-state survives forever, they argue that what does survive is this *pattern* of group coherence. As a result, they seek to "illuminate the dynamics of patriotic nationalism," by showing "violence as an essential social resource."[45]

The use of violence, then, requires strict strategy. For Marvin and Ingle, "What is really true in any society is what is worth killing for, and what citizens may be compelled to sacrifice their lives for."[46] Because in the United States religious denominations are not permitted to kill, Marvin and Ingle highlight that nationalism is the sole motivation for sacrificial killing and death, thereby making the nation the only *real* community.[47] The strict and strategic use of violence is limited to one authority, thereby eliminating fragmentation.

---

41. Marvin and Ingle, *Blood Sacrifice and the Nation*, 1.

42. The Latin origin community, *communitas*, is intimately connected to *communis*, common, which has a probable origination of sharing *common practices*.

43. Ibid., 4; note the cyclical nature of violence, mentioned in the last section. John Milbank ("Stories of Sacrifice," *Modern Theology* 12 [January 1996]) notes that Wellhausen sees the "centralization of sacrifice (as having) a beneficent purpose, (seeing) the hand of providence ... most of all at work in the emergence of politically-governed nations" (31). Friedrich Nietzsche ("Second Essay," *Genealogy of Morals* [February 2008] http://www.mala.bc.ca/~johnstoi/Nietzsche/genealogy2.htm) makes a related observation: "When the human being considered it necessary to make a memory for himself, it never happened without blood, martyrs, and sacrifices—the most terrible sacrifices and pledges (among them the sacrifice of the first born), the most repulsive self-mutilations (for example castration), the cruellest [sic] forms of ritual in all the religious cults (and all religions are at bottom systems of cruelty)—all that originates in that instinct which discovered that pain was the most powerful means of helping to develop the memory."

44. Ibid., 4.

45. Ibid., 8.

46. Ibid., 9.

47. Ibid., 9–10.

The violence which brings coherence is powerful and its order is created by the effective fusion of violence with myth—the shared memory of sacrifice.[48] As a result, "[b]lood sacrifice links the citizen to the nation."[49] The myth becomes compelling to those who live in its grasp and are formed by it. However, because this myth of sacrifice to a common object is not consciously recognized, it is not labeled "primitive." What is called "primitive," instead, is that violence "from which we seek to distance ourselves. Defined by violence, classified as primitive, the Other is not us. . . . Calling others primitive, the labelers purify themselves."[50] This scapegoat mechanic is easily connected to shame: The means used for group coherence (violence) are not considered worthy of one group, so they are transferred to others, thereby *hiding* the presence of these means in the original group. Those who transfer the primitiveness to another group are *purified*.

Marvin and Ingle, relying on René Girard's scapegoat theory, emphasize that such forms of violence bring coherence only when they are held in wide agreement. In other words, "[w]ar must be popular."[51] Since the agreement on who may kill and who may be killed is what holds a group together, it must be widespread otherwise there is fragmentation. (Hence the reason for the strategic use of violence). Thus, Marvin and Ingle believe that "[o]rganizing, not eradicating violence is the task of group survival."[52] Whenever the ritual of violence is not widely shared, it is failed, and the greater its failure, the greater the division. All rituals eventually fail to warrant widespread sacrifice, and new rituals must take their place which rally the group to another agreement on the authority to kill and the value of the group for whom their life is given/sacrificed.[53]

When it is uncontained, violence, this focused killing energy directed toward another, spirals out of control:[54] sacrifice given for the sake of the group forms a group from which violence is focused and directed outwards. One need only think of rival gangs who achieve unity in their violence against another gang, but who initiate new members with violent beatings. The violence one is willing to suffer to gain entry to the community is then turned outward. With this in mind, Marvin and Ingle ask a haunting question, "[A]re we forever doomed to suffer violence and inflict it?"[55] Marvin and Ingle have what some would call a pessimistic view, arguing that no, we cannot avoid and eliminate violence. At best, we can learn from social violence, just as we learn from natural violence (tornadoes, tsunamis, etc.). Even some forms of non-violence act as redirections that result in violence elsewhere.[56] "The question is never how to get rid of violence, but which

---

48. Ibid., 63.

49. Ibid.

50. Ibid., 64. The form of transference resembles reactions to shame noted above; indeed, Marvin and Ingle refer to the outsider as a "scapegoat" (79).

51. Ibid., 90.

52. Ibid., 71.

53. Ibid., 93.

54. Ibid., 312–13.

55. Ibid., 313.

56. Ibid., 313–15. Stanley Hauerwas ("Sacrificing the Sacrifices of War") writes, "In an odd way pacifists can be as dependent on the existence of war to make their world intelligible as those who think that war

set of killing rules we will submit to.... Wherever we are, killing rules are in effect."[57] This is no difference for religious people, either; they have merely substituted the power to which they believe has authority to kill. This violence creates community: "Where blood is not at stake, groups are not enduring."[58]

This conclusion ought to give a Christian pause. Is not the church called to be a non-violent community?[59] Wasn't Jesus non-violent? If Marvin and Ingle are correct, then how does a Christian live in radical obedience to a crucified Messiah? Is such obedience possible? More to the point, why should Marvin and Ingle go unchallenged critically? Unfortunately the nature of this paper prevents us from going deeper into the sociological conversation their work requires. Instead, I wish to offer a sketch of how one might proceed with the above in mind, given a devotion to Christian faith. This does not mean that social sciences dictate exegesis of Scripture. (Indeed, inasmuch as Marvin and Ingle acknowledge René Girard as a source,[60] they implicitly acknowledge that Scripture has played a role in opening their eyes to the secret violence we are not "meant to notice,"[61] because, for Girard, the Christian faith and its Scripture have contributed to the unmasking of sacrificial violence.[62]) However, it does provide an exegetical pencil with which we can sketch an interpretation of the Day of Atonement. In this direction we now turn.

SHAME, VIOLENCE, AND SCRIPTURE

In order to complete this sketched interpretation, I will look at early narratives in Scripture and show how they have elements of shame which show one threat Israel faced. I will suggest that sacrificial violence brought group coherence to Israel, thereby partially dealing with this threat of shame.

Earlier we saw that shame had elements of hiding and covering. Both of these elements are found in the Adam and Eve narrative, where they cover themselves (Gen 3:7) and hide from God (Gen 3:8). Blaming the serpent is also a scapegoating action.[63]

---

at the very least must be tragically accepted" (78). The pacifist lifestyle, for Hauerwas, is not a strategy; it is a witness to the gospel. To this extent, the pacifist lifestyle may even increase violence and injustice. The pacifist lifestyle is "not to make the world more just, but to make the world the world" (93).

57. Ibid., 313.

58. Ibid., 315.

59. In his intriguing and insightful essay, "Sacrificing the Sacrifices of War," which forms part of the flow of the argument of this paper, Hauerwas draws a close conclusion. Since his context is war and not simply violence, he asserts that the church is the end of war (93). However, in the essay Hauerwas sees war as compelling because it "sacrifice[s] ... our unwillingness to kill" (80). As a result, the church, which recognizes the end of sacrifice in Christ (80), cannot commit this sacrifice. I am sympathetic to this conclusion, but believe another political theology could possibly give more resources to think differently about war.

60. Marvin and Ingle, *Blood Sacrifice and the Nation*, 10, 73, 78–79. Naturally, there is also critique and reworking of Girard as well.

61. Ibid., 315.

62. René Girard, *The Girard Reader*, ed. James G. Williams (New York: Crossroad, 1996) 275; René Girard, *I See Satan Fall like Lightning*, trans. James G. Williams (Maryknoll, NY: Orbis, 2001) 178–81, as referenced by Hans Boersma, *Violence, Hospitality, and the Cross: Reappropriating the Atonement Tradition* (Grand Rapids: Baker Academic, 2004) 139.

63. Victor Hamilton [*Handbook on the Pentateuch* (Grand Rapids: Baker, 1982)] distinguishes between

Immediately following is the story of Cain and Abel where Cain's anger in response to God's rejection of his sacrifice (Gen 4:5–6) is manifest in conjunction with a *downcast* face, which is a form of hiding.[64] Cain's response also involves violence in the murder of Abel and an attempted cover-up, hiding, in Abel's burial (4:10). The shame of the Cain and Abel story is noted by James Gilligan who sees in Cain a reflection of some of the murderers with whom he has worked in penitentiaries: God disrespected Cain in favor of Abel and so Cain reacted violently to this insult, thereby re-obtaining self respect.[65] Frederick Turner makes explicit reference to the shame of Adam and Eve and Cain and Abel.[66] If these stories reflect the foundation of Israel *and* humanity at all, and their narrative location in Scripture suggests that they do so theologically, then they hold implications for the problems of sin besetting the Israelite community[67] *and* the role shame plays in the systemic sin that humanity suffers.

The Day of Atonement then, because it deals with the national and systemic sin of Israel, can be considered as a response to shame. The Day of Atonement has connection with the ritual sin-offering. Frances Young describes it as "sort of 'super-sin-offering,'"[68] by which she means that it extends and intensifies the function of the sin-offerings which "were a means given by God himself for *wiping away* the sins which prevented his chosen people from fulfilling the obligations of the covenant-relationship. . . ."[69] As we noted above, shame is both caused by and results in fractured relationship, and Young's consideration of its solution—being wiped away—fits with the language of defilement which the shamed experiences. John Goldingay agrees with this metaphor, arguing that sin offerings are better understood as "purification offerings."[70] As such, "Levitical offerings draw attention to another aspect of the problems caused by our failure and wrongdoing: the *stain* it leaves."[71] Again, here we see the language of shame applied to the defiling effects of systemic sin in the Israelite community, ritually counteracted by the sin-offering, which is intensified by the Day of Atonement.[72]

---

the shame and guilt that Adam and Eve suffer in this story, and notes a *scapegoating* attempt in the story (48), where Adam and Eve blame the serpent, as we might expect from the notes above.

64. For a theological and psychological examination of the importance of the face in relationships, specifically with regard to forgiveness, see F. LeRon Shults and Steven J. Sandage, *The Faces of Forgiveness* (Grand Rapids: Baker Academic, 2003).

65. Gilligan, "Shame, Guilt, Violence," 1156. Forrest Wood Jr., ("Averting Violence: Social and Personal," *Perspectives in Religious Studies* 14 [Spring 1987] 29) sees this story as one of "unacceptance," which is an element of shame seen above.

66. Turner, "Shame, Beauty, and the Tragic View of History," 1061.

67. For a consideration of shame in the Psalms, see Walter Brueggemann, "Voice as Counter to Violence," *Calvin Theological Journal* 36 (April 2001) 22–33. Brueggemann writes, "Israel is 'a shame society.' Israel understands the social power that makes one crawl into a hole and become invisible. Israel seeks protection from God against the negating power of humiliation" (28).

68. Frances M. Young, *Sacrifice and the Death of Christ* (London: SPCK, 1975) 29.

69. Ibid., 28. Emphasis mine.

70. John Goldingay, "Old Testament Sacrifice and the Death of Christ," from *Atonement Today*, ed. John Goldingay (London: SPCK, 1995) 8.

71. Ibid., 8. Emphasis mine.

72. John H. Hayes ("Atonement in the Book of Leviticus," *Interpretation* 52 [January 1998] 5–15) agrees with Goldingay that the "sin offering" should be translated "'purification' or 'purgation' sacrifice" (8). He also

PART TWO: CONTRIBUTION TO CURRENT THEOLOGICAL PROBLEMS

Let us examine the Day of Atonement further. On this Day, Aaron would select two goats and draw lots for them. One would be sacrificed as a sin offering (Lev 16:9), while the other would be selected as a scapegoat (Lev 16:10).[73] Aaron would lay his hands on the scapegoat and confess all the sins of the Israelite community after which it was led into the desert, banished from the community, taking with it the sins of the people (Lev 16:21–22).[74] This symbolized that "the people and the land had been *purged* of their guilt"[75] which is clearly shame language.[76]

The community is safeguarded and restored by the Day of Atonement, the intensification of its preceding and subsequent ritual sacrifices by cleansing from one goat and the exile of the other. The individuals are brought together because the defilement of sin is wiped away. Perhaps we could also say that for the individual to be at-one with God, they would have to be at-one with their neighbor since the means of their atonement are the same means of atonement for their neighbor. The transference of stain to the goat leaves the community clean. The people are bonded; their sin is cleansed. But this sacrificial ritual was *only to take place within prescribed boundaries*. Leviticus 17:1–7 forbids the sacrifice of ox, lamb, or goat either inside or outside the camp. Proper sacrificial practice was connected with right location (Tent of Meeting) and authority (Priest). Included in the prescribed violence of the Day of Atonement is a limitation of its practice and an agreement of its execution.

---

makes an important note to distinguish the Day of Atonement from normal sin offerings: "The blood of the purification sacrifice is never applied to humans but only to parts of the sanctuary" (8). This could emphasize the systemic purification happening not simply for individual impurity, but for national impurity, even in the tools used to counteract defilement.

73. John R. W. Stott (*The Cross of Christ* [Downers Grove, IL: InterVarsity, 1986] 144) points out that, according to v. 5, the two goats comprise one sin offering and so cannot be divided too strongly.

74. There is a long tradition of speculation that this goat was killed by Azazel. This exile was still a form of violence.

75. R. K. Harrison, *Leviticus: An Introduction and a Commentary*. Tyndale Old Testament Commentaries (Downer's Grove, Ill: InterVarsity, 1980) 171. See also Gordan J. Wenham, *The Book of Leviticus*. The New International Commentary on the Old Testament (Grand Rapids: Eerdmans, 1979) 26; John E. Hartley, *Leviticus*, Word Biblical Commentary (Dallas, TX: Word, 1992) 238. Hartley (*Leviticus*) goes so far as to say that the goat, once confessed over, becomes a "terrible polluting force" (241).

76. Goldingay ("Old Testament Sacrifice and the Death of Christ") insists on *not* using guilt language. He writes, "The laying on of hands identifies offerers and offerings and indicates that they truly represent them; something of themselves passes over with the gift to the recipient. In the case of the purification offering and the Day of Atonement ritual, the stain is transferred to the offering (cf. Lev 16:21) and is destroyed in it. Here there is indeed a sense in which the offering substitutes for the offerer, though it is not that the offering is vicariously punished.... By laying hands on the offering, the offerers identify with it and *pass on to it not their guilt* but their stain. The offering is then not vicariously punished but vicariously cleansed" (10, emphasis mine). I do not follow Goldingay in his separation of punishment from cleansing, however, and see no reason why cleansing need not include punishment. Indeed, if banishment from community, which the scapegoat suffers, is *not* punishment, then how does one understand exile? There is no need to draw a necessary dichotomy between punishment and cleansing. For a critique of Goldingay, see Henri Blocher, "The Sacrifice of Jesus Christ: The Current Theological Situation," *European Journal of Theology* 8:1, 23–36. Interestingly, Hayes ("Atonement in the Book of Leviticus") sees the scapegoat ritual as "concerned with the removal of pollution ... from the people," but sees no element of impurity in Leviticus 16:21. For him, what is removed from the people are their "iniquities, transgressions, and wrongdoings" (13).

How should we understand how this ritual, sacrificial violence bonds the group together? Marvin and Ingle's narrative may provide an interpretive lens. Recall that for Marvin and Ingle an agreement of ritual killing authority to which the group made sacrifices was what brought group coherence. The sacrificial violence of the Day of Atonement, in both the sin offering and the scapegoat, is participated in by the whole community: The Priest's hands transfer the guilt *of* the whole community for the sake of the *whole* community. Moreover, the injunctions against sacrificial practice outside of these parameters are forbidden, punished by the offender's separation from community, which reinforces the punishment which the scapegoat originally takes.[77] The one who rejects and engages in disobedient practice of this divine provision is rejected and excluded. The authority of the ritual killing is the Priest but only then under the direction of God.

The gruesome story of the stoning of a blasphemer in Leviticus 24 may also reinforce this view. Here, when a man of Israelite and Egyptian descent blasphemes the name of the LORD, the community waits *on the LORD* for their instructions in dealing with him (Lev 24:12). The LORD has the ability to command his death, which he does, and the blasphemer is stoned outside the camp, and the community acts in obedience to the authority of the One who can kill. However, just as Leviticus 17 sanctioned and controlled sacrificial violence, so does Leviticus 24 limit violence with the *lex talionis*, which is for both alien and native Israelite (Lev 24:17–22). God, the killing authority, not only commanded violence, but limited it, as well.[78]

How could this ritual have counteracted shame? This restoration and binding of the community counteracts shame because by "creating a sense of group solidarity and well-being, people [are helped] to de-objectify themselves and to forget their sense of shame."[79] Restored relations, procured by the sacrificial guidelines God gives, eliminate the isolation that Israelites suffered from the narratives of Cain and Abel, Adam and Eve.

Here, then, we can provide just the initial sketch of these elements: The community of Israel suffered from shame, not surprisingly considering some of their foundational narratives had elements of shame. This shame threatened to undo the community. God's provision of ritual sacrifice, however, provided cleansing of sin; sin was transferred to another and, on this other, banished from the community, allowing Israel to live in peace. This violent sacrifice, instituted by God and limited to specific instances, served to bind the Israelite community together in their acknowledgement of his authority. This binding, finally, served to heal certain isolating effects of shame.

---

77. Part of the narrative of limiting violence is found here, if sacrificial practice away from the shrine was previously practiced, and is now replaced. See Herbert Chanan Brichto, "On Slaughter and Sacrifice, Blood and Atonement," *Hebrew Union College Annual* 47 (1976) 24.

78. Brichto ("On Slaughter and Sacrifice, Blood and Atonement") affirms that the taking of animals lives is not a "natural right of man but a right granted to him—on this recognizance—by the Creator of life" (28). This lines up well with the prohibition of sacrificial violence separated from God's prescribed methods: Only God has authority to take life or to direct the manner and opportunity of its taking.

79. Pattison, *Shame*, 160.

PART TWO: CONTRIBUTION TO CURRENT THEOLOGICAL PROBLEMS

POTENTIAL IMPLICATIONS FOR THE PRACTICE OF COMMUNION

Obviously this is simply a sketch. A fully developed argument would engage critically with the first two elements of shame and violence, which I have not done. Still, this sketch provides avenues forward in conversations surrounding atonement, specifically theories of penal substitution and ransom and therefore warrants more research. Specifically biblical and theological examinations of the role of shame in the Old Testament and how this research may critically engage contemporary psychological and sociological studies. While there is not space for such work in this paper, I do wish to offer one area, the Christian practice of communion, in which this sketch may offer opportunity for further reflection. Ephraim Radner's theological commentary of Leviticus provides the reasoning for why this further reflection may be possible.

Radner asserts that "Jesus fulfills the whole of the law in its forms and purposes."[80] This means that the "holocausts and offerings, the very beasts and their blood, find their perfect place in Christ."[81] Moreover, as Jesus is before all things and all things hold together in him, then without "the death of Jesus in his flesh and blood, there would be no sacrifices of animals and grain at all, anywhere. They speak of him; they tend toward him; they exist only because of him (Col 1:15–20)."[82] The reality of the cross both grounds *and* resets the reality of the sacrifices. Hebrews affirms grounding and resetting by recording that the blood of Jesus does what the blood of bulls and goats cannot do; it cleanses our consciences (Heb 9:13–14). The shame language of 'cleanse,' connected to aspects of shame in the sacrificial system, has now been applied to the efficacy of Jesus' sacrifice. As a result, may it be possible to see shame overcome both in the sacrificial system, specifically the Day of Atonement and the sacrifice of Jesus?[83]

Some will immediately answer "No" because of the Old Testament injunctions against sacrifice (e.g., Ps 40:6, 51:16; Is 1:11; Hosea 6:6). Can we understand God's extensive regulation of sacrifice while at the same time his frustration and rejection of the practice? Blaise Pascal comments on this tension: "Those who ordained these sacrifices knew their uselessness; those who have declared their uselessness, have not ceased to practice them."[84] Pascal believes this tension is surpassed by reading the sacrifices in a figurative manner, in which they point to Christ. Such figurative reading,

> by attaching each reality—the positive and negative character of the sacrificial ritual in the eyes of God—to the full historical ministry of Jesus whose own life

---

80. Ephraim Radner, *Leviticus*, Brazos Theological Commentary of the Bible (Grand Rapids: Brazos, 2008) 288.

81. Ibid., 288.

82. Ibid.

83. Radner (*Leviticus*) refers to the Day of Atonement as primarily a "ceremony of the sanctuary," of Creator coming near to creature (170–71). Naturally, this is in line with Hebrews 2 and how we have been brought near, now having access to the Father (2:14–18).

84. Blaise Pascal, *Pensées*, *IntraText Digital Library* (December 2007, http://www.intratext.com/IXT/ENG1277/_P8.HTM) frag. 578. I owe this line of thinking to Ephraim Radner and the Introduction to his commentary on Leviticus.

in the Father's purposes is marked by a deep obscurity... expresses the profound reality of created human nature and redemption.[85]

How does this contradiction of God's pleasure and rejection of sacrifice happen? Radner's synopsis here is excellent and it serves to quote him at length:

> Because Scripture is the living word of God, our engagement with its reading represents God working with us. And the very details of Scripture, as they exercise our understanding and care, are therefore instruments of the primary mission of God in our souls. Leviticus—even before it is examined—must be assumed to be a means by which the truth of God is exposed to us for our eternal destiny. The whole of reality comprises two foundational truths according to Pascal: the redemptive love of God, and the corruption of human life and nature. If, that is, Leviticus stands upon a contradiction regarding the character of its referents and their enduring effect—for example, opposing views of sacrifice—it can only be because these referents themselves must be examined as caught up within and as markers of the contradiction itself. That is, what Leviticus says about the sacrifices must somehow mean something that also comprehends what the Prophets themselves say about sacrifice. The two are not simply alternative readings of sacrifice, to be laid before the reader or church and chosen as discerned for this or that moment of history. Each part of Scripture must also represent and express the reality of the world's [sic] as a whole, as Pascal explains it. It is the holding together and exposing of these two truths of redemption and corruption simultaneously that the Christian faith represents and that Jesus himself embodies in the flesh of space and time and that Scripture's writing and reading enacts.[86]

The sacrifices, including their violence, prefigure Christ, and reveal both the redemption of God *and* the corruption of the world for God's purposes.[87] This means that anthropological and/or sociological interpretations of violence vis-à-vis shame, as offered above, are insufficient, but *may* illumine God's particular purposes in their revelation.

Therefore, I propose that we *may* examine shame and violence in the ritual sacrifice by approaching the cross as an event that may be worked into the "broader range of historical life than ... [as a] ... single transaction for sin."[88] This "broader range" fits with the element that shame may be corrected by *ritual practices*, as noted above. The most significant Christian ritual that notes the cross is Holy Communion: the broken body and spilled blood of Christ given for us. If the cross and sacrificial practices have the same purpose of God drawing near and this is done by his overcoming shame, only now to an extent that the blood of bulls and goats could never do, then the interpretation offered regarding chastened but sanctioned violence above also applies to the death of Christ. Just as Marvin and Ingle suggested that unity around killing energy binds a nation together, communion may have the possibility of recognizing the horrible violence suffered by the Son and recognizing the proactive role played therein by the Triune God,

---

85. Radner, *Leviticus*, 20. This figurative reading of Leviticus is affirmed by Ehsan Ahmed, "Pascal, the Pensées, and the Figure of the Lamb: A Physiognomy," *Neophilologus* 80 (1996) 29–40.

86. Radner, *Leviticus*, 20–21. Emphasis mine.

87. Ibid., 287–99.

88. Ibid., 163.

we are bound together by this *divine* violence, and in this *binding* can find healing for the shame we suffer. This violence is not from the heart of God, however, but bounds from his love which reveals both the depravity of our sin *and* God's great redemption.

A further area of reflection, connected with communion, is the Christian examination of violence. Let's follow the sketch and say that God intends to overcome human shame in the crucifixion. If this is the case, then we see the fractured world and therein our fractured selves because we see the reality of evil most clearly in the death of Jesus. As Karl Barth writes, "From this point alone can we grasp the fact, the extent, and the content of the impeachment of [humanity]."[89] With this in mind, communion's link to the cross uncovers the reality of our sin, our true selves, and allows our true selves to gather in unity around the sacred space of the body of Jesus. We are safe to do so because we focus not on ourselves, but on Christ, and from him receive healing for our shame. This healing comes in our bondedness, not only to each other, but to God. We receive healing *from* Christ because we are *with* Christ. Just as the sacrifices were a practice that breached the gap between Creator and creature, so does communion Spirit-ually restore Christ to our presence and us to his, our unveiled faces seen by the face of the Savior.

Second, we recognize in communion the horror of violence, caused by our sin, but *used* and *manipulated* by God for his purposes and for our benefit. For the Christian community, the violence instituted and limited in the sacrifices which bound Israel together may prefigure the violence which may bind us together in the cross and in this binding restore our fellowship and heal our shame. We see God's creative abilities to use violence to his ends and are humbled by the role we have played. Communion, the broken body and spilled blood of Jesus, reminds us of the community binding power of violence that only God has orchestrated and used for ultimate and eternal ends.

---

89. Karl Barth, *Dogmatics in Outline* (New York: Harper & Row, 1959) 105.

14

Prima Gratia, Prima Fide, and *Prima Scriptura*

Reforming Protestant Principles

Don Thorsen

During the sixteenth century, three theological principles came to identify the Protestant Reformation: *Sola gratia, sola fide,* and *sola scriptura. Sola gratia* (Latin, "grace alone" or "by grace alone") emphasizes that salvation occurs by God's "grace alone" and not by human merit. *Sola fide* (Latin, "faith alone" or "by faith alone") is similar in that it emphasizes that people accept God's gracious offer of salvation by (or through) "faith alone" rather than by human will or good works. *Sola scriptura* (Latin, "scripture alone") emphasizes that "scripture alone," rather than ecclesiastical authority or human opinion, represents religious authority. As such, it is sometimes called the "formal principle" of the Protestant Reformation, or the "scripture principle."

However, there has always been debate with regard to the extent of exclusivity to which the Protestant Reformers, and others who followed in their tradition, held to the *sola* principles. In *theory, sola gratia, sola fide,* and *sola scriptura* became powerful slogans for identifying, defending, and promoting the Protestant Reformation. Protestants continue to tout them. However, in *practice*, there are many reasons to question the Protestant principles both in terms of how the founders used them and especially in terms of how Protestants have used them since the time of the Reformation. In many ways, Protestantism includes more than grace alone, more than faith alone, and more than scripture alone. The Latin word *prima* ("primarily") makes more sense in describing the complex understanding of Protestant Reformers and their nuanced articulation of salvation and religious authority. The concept of *prima* makes even more sense in describing the diversity of beliefs, values, and practices in the subsequent development of Protestant Christianity.

John Wesley is a pivotal example of a Protestant who affirmed the Reformation tradition, yet went beyond it in all three of its principles. Most notable is Wesley's complex understanding of religious authority. Albert Outler says:

PART TWO: Contribution to Current Theological Problems

> The great Protestant watchwords of *sola fide* and *sola Scriptura* were in fact fundamentals in Wesley's formulation of a doctrine of biblical authority. But early and late in his career, Wesley interpreted *solus* to mean "primarily" rather than "solely" or "exclusively."[1]

In Latin, *prima*—rather than *solus*—is the appropriate adjective for modifying nouns such as faith and scripture.

In addition to religious authority, Wesley's complex understanding of salvation affirmed more than grace alone and faith alone. Grace worked in prevenient as well as justifying ways; and people's acceptance of salvation involved more than just faith. Salvation was a lifelong process that required responsible thoughts, words, and actions on the part of believers. Wesley's *prima* understanding of the Reformation principles is as important to the present age as it was to Wesley's age. In fact, his theological contributions become increasingly important to the so-called postmodern trajectory of our age. Wesley's complex, dynamic, and holistic understanding of grace, faith, and scripture are crucial to both our personal Christianity and to the nature and mission of the church.

Although the *sola* principles remain important for understanding the history of Protestant Christianity, they are best understood theologically from a Wesleyan perspective as representing *prima* principles because Protestants—past and present—think that salvation and religious authority include more than grace, faith, and scripture alone. Salvation should be thought of in terms of *prima gratia*—initiated primarily by God's grace—and *prima fide*—accepted primarily through faith. Likewise, religious authority should be thought of in terms of *prima scriptura;* scripture represents the primary religious authority of Protestantism but not its exclusive religious authority. Church tradition, logical reflection, and relevant experience all play important and authoritative roles in the founding and continuation of Protestantism.

In order to better understand, teach, and advance the received tradition of Protestant Christianity, it is helpful to re-examine the *sola* principles in terms of a more realistic and relevant perspective as *prima* principles. The *prima* principles help us to understand the history of Protestantism; we need to understand them in their historical context. They also help us understand our personal Christian vocation and the nature and mission of the church in our present, global, inter-religious context. The *prima* principles, in fact, are crucial to fulfilling God's redemptive mission in the world in the present age.

I will begin by discussing *sola scriptura* in its historical context—its spirit and mythic quality. I will continue by talking about the conceptual progression from *sola scriptura*, to the Anglican *via media*, and finally to the so-called Wesleyan quadrilateral. Because Wesleyan scholars first promoted *prima*, rather than *sola*, principles in relation to religious authority, I will present an extended discussion of the topic. After discussing the quadrilateral, I will proceed by talking about the *sola gratia* and *sola fide*. In addition to looking at them in their historical context, I will talk about their relevance to individuals as well as to the nature and mission of the church. Thinking of these Protestant principles as *prima*, rather than *sola*, principles will help in communicating biblical and historic

---

1. Albert Outler, "Introduction," in *John Wesley*, ed. Albert C. Outler (New York: Oxford University Press 1964), 28.

Christianity in ways that are relevant and persuasive in the progressively postmodern world in which we live.

SOLA SCRIPTURA

Sola scriptura represents the Protestant Reformation emphasis upon scripture as the only reliable religious authority—scripture alone. Anticipated by John Wycliffe in the fourteenth century, the cry of *sola scriptura* became widespread among Protestant reformers during the 16th century. Because of the political and religious authority of the Roman Catholic Church, resistance to the traditions and magisterial authority of the church was a matter of life and death. Thus, Protestant reformers such as Luther, Zwingli, and Calvin needed to be very precise about their rationale for defying centuries of Christendom.

Spirit of Sola Scriptura

Although Luther made a simple appeal to the authority of scripture alone, it was not a simplistic appeal. On the contrary, Luther did not think we could rightly appeal to scripture without reference to either church tradition or reason. The spirit of *sola scriptura* included a more comprehensive and dynamic method of religious reflection, formulation and application. For example, in Luther's famous stand against the Roman Catholic Church at the Diet of Worms, he significantly appealed to more than scripture. Although Luther appealed primarily to scripture, he also appealed to reason and to conscience. Luther said:

> Since then your serene Majesty and Your Lordships seek a simple answer, I will give it in this manner, neither horned nor toothed. Unless I am convinced by the testimony of the Scriptures or by clear reason . . . I am bound by the Scriptures I have quoted and my conscience is captive to the Word of God. I cannot and I will not retract anything, since it is neither safe nor right to go against conscience. . . . May God help me. Amen.[2]

Despite his affirmation of *sola scriptura*, Luther does not speak simplistically of scriptural authority. On the contrary, a more sophisticated, broadly conceived, and relevant approach to theology and ministry occurs.

Luther as well as Melancthon—Luther's colleague at Wittenberg University and collaborator in the Protestant Reformation—used diverse religious authorities, despite their affirmation of *sola scriptura*. The Augsburg Confession provides one of the best examples. Although it reflects Luther's theology, Melancthon was the primary author of the document. In the Augsburg Confession, the following is stated about justification:

> This teaching about faith is plainly and clearly treated by Paul in many passages, especially in Eph 2:8, 9, "For by grace you have saved through faith; and this is not your own doing, it is the gift of God—not because of works, lest any man should boast," etc.

---

2. Martin Luther, "Career of a Reformer: II," in *Luther's Works*, vol. 32, eds. G. Forell and H. Lehmann (Philadelphia: Muhlenberg, 1958) 112–13.

PART TWO: CONTRIBUTION TO CURRENT THEOLOGICAL PROBLEMS

That no new interpretation is here introduced can be demonstrated from Augustine, who discusses this question thoroughly and teaches the same thing, namely, that we obtain grace and are justified before God through faith in Christ and not through works. His whole book, *De spiritu et litera* (*The Spirit and the Letter*), proves this. Melancthon echoes Augustine, saying

> Although this teaching is held in great contempt among untried people, yet it is a matter of experience that weak and terrified consciences find it most comforting and salutary.[3]

In the preceding paragraphs, we see Melancthon's use of 1) scripture, 2) tradition, namely, Augustine, and 3) experience, which is explicitly mentioned in the document. Clearly, more than scripture is present in key Reformation documents.

Like Luther and Melancthon, Calvin affirmed *sola scriptura* with sophistication, breadth and relevance. For example, Calvin spends a great deal of time talking about the relationship between scripture and other religious authorities, especially church tradition, since he clearly distinguished between Roman Catholic traditions and those of the Reformers. In the *Institutes of the Christian Religion,* Calvin states in Book One, chapter VI that "Scripture Is Needed as Guide and Teacher for Anyone Who Would Come to God the Creator."[4] Immediately thereafter, Calvin talks in chapter VII about how scripture must be confirmed by the witness of the Holy Spirit and by how some traditions, for example, as found in Augustine, contribute positively to Christian theology.[5] This chapter talks about the experience of the Holy Spirit as well as the benefit of church tradition, rightly discerned. Chapter VIII is entitled, "So Far as Human Reason Goes, Sufficiently Firm Proofs Are at Hand to Establish the Credibility of Scripture."[6] Thus, Calvin appeals to reason as well as experience and church tradition in how he goes about the task of theology. Although he might explicitly affirm *sola scriptura*, a more complex and dynamic approach occurs.

Alister McGrath speaks of the Reformers as having a matrix of religious authority, which includes multiple factors in reflection upon and in the application of scripture, especially with regard to the church and ministry. McGrath says:

> Although it is often suggested that the reformers had no place for tradition in their theological deliberations, this judgment is clearly incorrect. While the notion of tradition as an extra-scriptural source of revelation is excluded, the classic concept of tradition as a particular way of reading and interpreting scripture is retained. Scripture, tradition and the *kerygma* are regarded as essentially coinherent, and as being transmitted, propagated and safeguarded by the community of faith. There is thus a strongly communal dimension to the magisterial reformers' understanding

---

3. Text from *The Book of Concord*, ed. and trans. Theodore G. Tappert (Philadelphia: Fortress, 1959) Art. IV, "Justification," 30; Art. XX, "Faith and Good Works," 42–46, quoted in *Readings in Christian Thought*, ed. Hugh T. Kerr, 2nd ed. (Nashville: Abingdon, 1990) 156.

4. John Calvin, *Institutes of the Christian Religion*, vol. 20, Library of Christian Classics. Trans. Ford Lewis Battles (Philadelphia: Westminster, 1960) 69–73.

5. Ibid., 74–80.

6. Ibid., 81–92.

of the interpretation of scripture, which is to be interpreted and proclaimed within an ecclesiological matrix.[7]

The Westminster Confession, the primary affirmation of Reformed theology in English, affirms *sola scriptura*. However, it does not present a simplistic understanding of the principle of religious authority. On the contrary, the Westminster Confessions allows for other dynamics that are necessary. Chapter 1: "Of the Holy Scripture" says the following:

> The whole counsel of God concerning all things necessary for His own glory, man's salvation, faith and life, is either expressly set down in Scripture, or by good and necessary consequence may be deduced from Scripture: unto which nothing at any time is to be added, whether by new revelations of the Spirit or traditions of men. Nevertheless, we acknowledge the inward illumination of the Spirit of God to be necessary for the saving understanding of such things as are revealed in the Word: and that there are some circumstances concerning the worship of God, and government of the Church, common to human actions and societies, which are to be ordered by the light of nature, and Christian prudence, according to the general rules of the Word, which are always to be observed.[8]

In explication of *sola scriptura*, reflective of the Westminster Confession, Kenneth Samples says it "implies the authority, clarity, and sufficiency of Scripture, and uniquely gives Scripture alone the role of final arbiter in all matters of faith and morals."[9] However, as the final arbiter, it considers more than scripture alone, literally understood.

Myth of Sola Scriptura

Sometimes people misunderstand the sophistication with which the founding reformers understood and applied *sola scriptura*. Any principle used second hand runs the risk of it being used either honorifically or naively, without the benefit of knowing the context of the lengthy, painstaking work of the originators. Consequently, it takes on "mythic" qualities, that is, *sola scriptura* becomes more than a statement of religious authority. It becomes an archetypal symbol of Protestantism as a whole, distinguishing it from Roman Catholicism and Orthodoxy as well as other religions. As such, its existence becomes sacrosanct, something that is zealously affirmed regardless of critical issues related to is its understanding and application. Having mythic power, *sola scriptura* becomes self-sealing no matter how it is used. *Sola scriptura* becomes a shibboleth or test of fidelity to the principles of the Protestant Reformation. Unfortunately, sometimes it is used in ways incommensurate with its originators. One could argue that this happened and, indeed, continues to happen with *sola scriptura*. For example, it happened contemporaneously to Luther and Calvin.

---

7. Alister McGrath, *The Genesis of Doctrine: A Study in the Foundations of Doctrinal Criticism* (Oxford: Basil Blackwell, 1990) 130.

8. Westminster Confession, "Of the Holy Scripture," Presbyterian Church in America, http://www.pcanet.org/general/cof_chapi-v.htm#chapi (accessed 6 May 2005), II.6.

9. Kenneth R. Samples, "What Think Ye of Rome: An Evangelical Appraisal of Contemporary Catholicism," *Christian Research Journal* (Spring 1993) 32.

PART TWO: CONTRIBUTION TO CURRENT THEOLOGICAL PROBLEMS

The Anabaptist movement affirmed *sola scriptura* more radically than had Luther and Calvin, which is why—in part—the Anabaptist movement is referred to as being part of a "radical Reformation." Reformers such as the Zwickau Prophets and Thomas Müntzer were radical for various reasons, including their belief in the exclusive affirmation of scriptural authority without need for any admixture, other than the Holy Spirit. Literally, this view emphasized how individuals need no input other than their own insights, thoughts, and decisions about understanding and applying scripture.

Keith Mathison notes that the radical reformers of the sixteenth century went beyond Luther and Calvin's rejection of the magisterial authority of the Roman Catholic Church over the interpretation of scripture. The radical reformers rejected non-biblical input "in and by the Church within the hermeneutical context of the *regula fidei*," that is, the "rule of faith," which reflects biblical interpretation through the baptismal formulas of the ancient church, ecumenical creeds, and development of subsequent church tradition.[10] This restorationist approach to scripture and scriptural interpretation ("back to the Bible!") wants only the Bible, arguing that an individual unaided by anything or anyone other than the Holy Spirit was spiritually, theologically and ecclesiastically self-sufficient. Although naïve in its individualism, this type of biblicism has perennially reigned among the more fundamentalist, conservative and evangelical Christians. For example, Mathison says the following about the influence of anabaptistic individualism in the United States:

> In eighteenth-century America, this anabaptistic individualism combined with Enlightenment rationalism and democratic populism to create a radical version [of tradition], which has prevailed to this day. This doctrine has become the standard evangelical position on scriptural authority. Recognizing the many errors inherent in this doctrine, many evangelicals who wrongly believe it to be the Reformation doctrine of sola scriptura have left evangelical Protestantism.[11]

Although the radical reformers thought that they were taking Luther and Calvin's understanding of *sola scriptura* to its logical conclusion, they—in fact—reduced Luther and Calvin's principle to a simplistic and potentially dangerous understanding of religious authority and theological method. Too often in church history, Christians have taken this unsophisticated approach—a myth of the Protestant Reformation—to biblical interpretation, ignoring the complexity for which the Protestant reformers struggled and defied the Roman Catholic Church.

Roman Catholics, of course, resisted the Protestant Reformation for many reasons. Among those reasons, they noted the potential "mythic" problems of narrowly conceived religious authority, influenced by individualism, at the Council of Trent. However, Roman Catholics—like the Anabaptists—did not always recognize the methodological sophistication of a Luther and a Calvin. To this day, both Roman Catholics and Orthodox Christians continue to attack the principle of *sola scriptura*, arguing for the historical, social and cultural impossibility of its individualistic approach to scriptural authority

---

10. Keith A. Mathison, *The Shape of Sola Scriptura* (Moscow, ID: Cannon, 2001) 151.
11. Ibid., 152.

and interpretation.¹² Certainly they consider *sola scriptura* both naïve and dangerous to church unity as well as to how Christianity may be applied in life and ministry.

The Protestant apologia for *sola scriptura* also continues today, mostly among conservatively oriented Christians concerned for upholding scripture exclusively, vis-à-vis, other potential religious authorities. Don Kistler, for example, edited *Sola Scriptura! The Protestant Position on the Bible*. In it are articles by prominent authors such as Michael Horton, John MacArthur, and R. C. Sproul. Of scripture, Kister says:

> The battle for the Bible has been raging since the beginning of time. Satan, the great enemy of souls, began his assault with a question: "Hath God said?"....
>
> The slugfest goes on. Romanists add tradition to what is written in Scripture, and place it on an equal plane with Scripture....
>
> Many Charismatics and evangelicals place their personal experience on a par with Scripture, thereby adding to God"s written revelation....
>
> Scripture is complete. God has said everything necessary for us to live the holy life to which He calls us. Nothing further needs to be added to what God has already revealed in His written Word.¹³

These defenders of *sola scriptura* reject the kind of biblicism (and bibliolatry) that can be accused of being unsophisticated and narrow in its theological understanding. Nevertheless, they come precariously close to it. For example, Horton claims an exclusivist understanding of *sola scriptura*. He says, "Not only must we recover the official commitment to the sufficiency of Scripture, it must be the *only* voice we hear from those who assume the momentous task of being God"s spokesmen [*sic*]."¹⁴

James White provides helpful perspective, historically speaking, on what the Protestant Reformation principle of *sola scriptura* does not affirm and what it does affirm. This comparison and contrast of affirmations cannot, of course, be applied to everyone who affirms *sola scriptura*. There are too many factors that come into play with regard to how the principle is understood and applied. Yet, the comparison helps to distinguish between the more sophisticated understanding of *sola scriptura*, reflective of its originators, and more simplistic ways that result in potentially dangerous as well as naive Christian conclusions. White says:

> What *Sola Scriptura* Is Not
>
> 1. First and foremost, *sola scriptura* is not a claim that the Bible contains all knowledge. The Bible is not a scientific textbook, a manual on governmental procedures,

---

12. For example, See Robert Sungenis, *Not by Scripture Alone: A Catholic Critique of the Protestant Doctrine of Sola Scriptura* (Santa Barbara: Queenship, 1997); Joel Peters, *Alone? 21 Reasons to Reject "Sola Scriptura"* (Rockford, IL: Tan Books, 2001); and John Whiteford, *Sola Scriptura: An Orthodox Analysis of the Cornerstone of Reformation Theology* (Ben Lomond, CA: Conciliar, 1996).

13. Don Kistler, "Postscript," in *Sola Scriptura! The Protestant Position on the Bible*, ed. Don Kistler (Morgan, PA: Soli Deo Gloria, 1993) 277–78.

14. Keith Horton, "Foreword," in *Sola Scriptura! The Protestant Position on the Bible*, ed. Don Kistler (Morgan, PA: Soli Deo Gloria, 1993) xviii.

or a catalog of automobile engine parts. The Bible does not claim to give us every bit of knowledge that we could ever obtain.

2. *Sola scriptura* is not a claim that the Bible is an exhaustive catalog of all religious knowledge. The Bible itself asserts that it is not exhaustive in detail (John 21:25). It is obvious that the Bible does not have to be exhaustive to be sufficient as our source of divine truth.

3. *Sola scriptura* is not a denial of the authority of the Church to teach God's truth.

4. *Sola scriptura* is not a denial that the Word of God has, at times, been spoken. Rather, it refers to the Scriptures as serving the Church as God's final and full revelation.

5. *Sola scriptura* does not entail the rejection of every kind or form of Church "tradition." There are some traditions that are God-honoring and useful in the Church. *Sola scriptura* simply means that a higher authority must test any tradition, no matter how ancient or venerable it might seem to us, and that authority is the Bible.

6. *Sola scriptura* is not a denial of the role of the Holy Spirit in guiding and enlightening the Church.

What *Sola Scriptura* Is

1. The doctrine of *sola scriptura*, simply stated, is that the Scriptures alone are sufficient to function as the *regula fidei*, the infallible rule of faith for the Church.

2. All that one must believe to be a Christian is found in Scripture, and in no other source. This is not to say that the necessary beliefs of the faith could not be summarized in a shorter form. However, there is no necessary belief, doctrine, or dogma absolutely required of a person for entrance into the kingdom of heaven that is not found in the pages of Scripture.

3. That which is not found in the Scripture either directly or by necessary implication is not binding upon the Christian.

4. Scripture reveals those things necessary for salvation (2 Tim 3:14–17).

5. All traditions are subject to the higher authority of Scripture (Matt 15:1–9). There can be no understanding of the sufficiency of Scripture apart from an understanding of the true origin and the resultant nature of Scripture. The Reformers had the highest view of the Bible, and therefore had a solid foundation on which to stand in defending the sufficiency of the Scriptures.[15]

It is not necessary to develop this comparison and contrast. Even so, White suggests a more full-orbed presentation of the principle of *sola scriptura*, reflective of the spirit of the early reformers. Despite sometimes poorly conceived and truncated uses of *sola scriptura*, most Protestant leaders understood that Christianity required an awareness and level of theological reflection that involved more than scripture alone, though scripture needed to remain the primary religious authority.

---

15. James White, *The Roman Catholic Controversy*, quoted by John Samson, "Sola Scriptura-By the Scriptures Alone." Online: http://www.fccphx.homestead.com/SolaScriptura.html.

Sola Scriptura to Via Media

In the spirit of *sola scriptura*, the Anglican Church affirmed the primacy of scriptural authority along with the secondary, albeit genuine, religious authority of church tradition and reason. Reflective of the burgeoning Enlightenment, Anglicans such as Richard Hooker advocated reason as the *via media* ("middle way") between scripture and church tradition. Unlike Continental Protestantism, the Church of England was not convinced that *sola scriptura* worked either in theory or in practice. In theory, Anglicans agreed with the Roman Catholic Church that reformers such as Luther and Calvin had gone to an extreme in reducing Christianity to scripture alone. In practice, the Protestant reformers looked nothing like a "restored" first-century church. On the contrary, church tradition significantly influenced the church in Wittenberg as well as the church in Geneva. Thus, there needed to be a more comprehensive, dynamic way of discerning the truth between scripture and tradition. Reason was considered the divine provision by which these sometimes-competing authorities reached a prudent conclusion. Francis Paget summarizes the spirit of Anglicanism, giving the following description of Richard Hooker"s view of religious authority. He says:

> Thus Hooker's appeal in things spiritual is to a threefold fount of guidance and authority—to reason, Scripture, and tradition all alike of god, alike emanating from Him, the one original Source of all light and power—each in certain matters bearing a special and prerogative sanction from Him, all in certain matters blending and co-operating.[16]

In this context, Wesley began his various ministries and theological writings. He did not inherit a narrow, wooden understanding of scripture and scriptural authority. On the contrary, Wesley—with his Oxford University education—received sophisticated schooling in matters of Christian beliefs, values and practices.

Ironically, in the century after Wesley, John Henry Newman and the Tractarians tried to return the Church of England to its Roman Catholic roots rather than it Continental Protestant roots. In a nineteenth century Anglo-Catholic movement, Newman thought that, in Christian antiquity, theological and ministerial decisions were made by general consent about the "rule of faith" passed on by the patristics rather than a *via media*-like balancing of religious authorities, mediated by reason.[17] In the eighteenth century, Wesley also sensed an inadequacy in the *via media*; however, it did not involve a return to restricted Roman Catholic ways of decision-making based upon the magisterial authority of the church and its traditions. On the contrary, it involved an expansion in recognizing the realistic ways Christians made decisions, reflected in the biblical witness as well as in the practices of Christians throughout church history. That realism led to what today has become known as the Wesleyan quadrilateral.

---

16. Francis Paget, *An Introduction to the Fifth Book of Hooker's Treatise on the Laws of Ecclesiastical Piety* (Oxford: Clarendon, 1907) 284.

17. See, for example, John Henry Newman, *Apologia Pro Vita Sua* (London: Longmans, Green & Co., 1914) 130.

PART TWO: Contribution to Current Theological Problems

THE WESLEYAN QUADRILATERAL

The Wesleyan quadrilateral refers to Wesley's understanding of religious authority. It affirms the primacy of scriptural authority along with the secondary, albeit genuine, religious authority of tradition, reason and experience. Although Wesley was not a systematic theologian, his theological understanding of religious authority and theological method had a dramatic impact upon the formulation of his beliefs, values, and practices in the rise of Methodism as well as in his influence upon subsequent theology.[18] The following discussion represents a summary of the quadrilateral drawn from other writings I have done on the subject.[19]

Rise of the Quadrilateral

Wesley did not coin the phrase "quadrilateral." Instead, Albert Outler coined it during the 1960s in an attempt to summarize Wesley's contribution to the theological and ecclesiastical discussion of contemporary issues facing Christians. Outler had no idea of the life the phrase would have, nor was he entirely pleased that he had coined it, since there arose so many misunderstandings and misuses of it.[20] Nevertheless, the quadrilateral has become increasingly prominent in stating the way Christians articulate religious authority.

Let us look more at the development of the quadrilateral. Outler says the following about his coinage of the phrase:

> It was intended as a metaphor for a four-element syndrome, including the four-fold guidelines of authority in Wesley's theological method. In such a quaternity Holy Scripture is clearly unique. But this in turn is illuminated by the collective Christian wisdom of other ages and cultures between the Apostolic Age and our own. It also allows for the rescue of the Gospel from obscurantism by means of the disciplines of critical reason. But always, Biblical revelation must be received in the heart by faith: this is the requirement of "experience."[21]

Although Outler coined the phrase in the context of his involvements with his denomination, the United Methodist Church, he tried to present the quadrilateral with historical respect for the way Wesley utilized scripture, tradition, reason, and experience. Because Wesley was more of a churchman than a theologian, he approached issues of religious belief and practice with the church in mind more than historic and systematic theol-

---

18. Here my focus is on Wesley's understanding of religious authority rather than on theological method. I discuss his theological method in-depth in Don Thorsen, *The Wesleyan Quadrilateral: Scripture, Tradition, Reason, and Experience as a Model of Evangelical Theology* (Lexington: Emeth, 2006) 96–124.

19. In addition to *The Wesleyan Quadrilateral*, see Don Thorsen, "The Wesleyan Quadrilateral in Contemporary American Theology," in *Holiness as a Root of Morality*, ed. John Park (Lewiston, NY: Edwin Mellen, 2006) 47–48.

20. Outler publicly expressed regret that he had coined the term, since it has been so widely misconstrued. See Albert C. Outler, "The Wesleyan Quadrilateral in John Wesley," *Wesleyan Theological Journal* 20 (1985) 16.

21. Outler, "Wesleyan Quadrilateral in John Wesley," 11.

ogy. Thus, as Randy Maddox says, "the term was coined by Albert Outler to emphasize that Wesley relied more on 'standards of doctrine' in his theological approach than on theological Systems or juridical Confessions of Faith."[22] The standards of doctrine represented the practical guidelines for the Methodist movement Wesley founded.

Outler recognized that Wesley affirmed the classic Protestant principle of *sola scriptura*, scripture alone as the primary religious authority. However, Wesley also recognized that Christians used more than scripture in how they went about making decisions about what they believed and what they practiced. Although Christians may not always be conscious of their understanding of religious authority and theological method, they usually function in ways that are identifiable. Thus, according to Outler, "The great Protestant watchwords of *Sola Fide* and *Sola Scriptura* were also fundamental in Wesley's doctrine of authority. But early and late, he interpreted *Solus* to mean "primarily" rather than "solely" or "exclusively."[23]

Spirit of the Quadrilateral

The spirit of the quadrilateral draws from the rich theological heritage it received from Christian wisdom of the ages. It is not a lone spirit in that it looks upon religious authority so uniquely or in an isolated way that does not draw from other tributaries. On the contrary, Wesley's view of religious authority emerged out of Christian tradition, which started from the Bible and developed through various Western and Eastern, Roman Catholic and Protestant perspectives. As such, Wesley did not think that he was a religious innovator. Instead, Wesley thought he was being faithful to age-old wisdom, translating it in ways meaningful to his contemporary context. In so doing, Wesley actually contributed significantly to Christian beliefs and values as well as to Christian practice as manifested in the Methodist movement.

When talking about the nature of religious authority, including the nature of the quadrilateral, it has to be remembered that, ultimately speaking, all authority comes from God. Wesley affirmed this, yet it is easy to lose sight of this fact while arguing about the particular relationship between scripture, tradition, reason, and experience. However, Wesley knew that all authority comes from God and that religious authorities with whom or with which we function are somehow derivative of God's ultimate authority. Even scripture only represents a derived or secondary religious authority. Thus, while the focus of so much of this study is on scripture, tradition, reason, and experience, we must not forget that Christians ultimately look to God alone as their source of religious authority.

With regard to the quadrilateral, Thomas Oden talks about its etymology, which in his opinion functioned since the early patristic writers of the Christian church. He says, "the term *quadrilateral* comes from the image of the four 'fortress cities' of Lombardy, suggesting that if Christian teaching is constructed within such a fourfold fortress, the

---

22. Randy L. Maddox, *Responsible Grace: John Wesley's Practical Theology* (Nashville: Kingswood, 1994) 36.

23. Outler, *John Wesley*, 28.

church can stand secure."²⁴ Later, according to Oden, "The document most commonly associated with the term is the Lambeth Quadrilateral of 1888, which stated four essentials for a reunited church from the Anglican point of view."²⁵ Outler used these sources as a backdrop for formulating the quadrilateral, rather than an abstract geometrical image. Although Wesley may not have used the phrase, its essence appears prominently throughout his writings.

Wesley often appealed to scripture and one of the following: tradition, reason or experience.²⁶ Occasionally, he referred to scripture, reason and tradition, or to scripture, reason and experience.²⁷ Wesley's reference to all four, therefore, is implied more than explicitly stated. Nevertheless, evidence for a fourfold view of religious authority can be found. He did not intend to be innovative in his approach to theology, yet he laid the foundation for an approach to matters of religious faith and practice that continue to be relevant today. From Wesley's perspective, scripture was the inspired, authoritative, and trustworthy revelation of God. One was to study it inductively and critically, relative to his eighteenth century understanding of biblical hermeneutics. However, he was not afraid to apply insights from reason and experience as well as church tradition in interpreting scripture.

Although Wesley gave hermeneutical significance to these four means of doing theology, he considered them complementary with the Protestant principle of *sola Scriptura*. Laurence Wood says, "Wesley held to the *sola scriptura* principle in the sense that the Bible contained the original revelation.... At the same time, tradition, reason, and experience were resources to help interpret the Scriptures."²⁸ Wesley may not have employed the four means as historically and critically as later biblical scholarship. He was, after all, a person of his times. Wood says, "Wesley's four means of theology saved him from extreme literalism."²⁹ Of course, William Abraham argues that scripture, tradition, reason and experience served more as soteriological norms, than as epistemological criteria. Only mistakenly were they turned into foundationalist, intellectualist criteria of truth, rather than being primarily witnesses to God's saving activity in history.³⁰

With regard to tradition, Wesley thought that Protestants undervalued history—especially church history and tradition. Yet, Wesley endeavored to investigate both his

---

24. Thomas C. Oden, *The Living God: Systematic Theology*, vol. 1 (New York: Harper & Row, 1987), 332–33.

25. The Lambeth Quadrilateral affirmed the following: Scripture contains "all things necessary to salvation," as the "rule and ultimate standard of faith"; the ancient ecumenical creeds (Nicene and Apostles") as the sufficient rule of faith; the two sacraments ordained by Christ himself, as the means of grace; "The Historic Episcopate, locally adapted in the methods of its administration to the varying needs of the nations and peoples called of God into the Unity of His Church"; see Oden, *Living God*, 332.

26. See Maddox, *Responsible Grace*, 36 nn. 72, 73, 74.

27. Ibid., 36 nn. 75, 76.

28. Laurence Wood, *Theology as History and Hermeneutics: A Post-Critical Conversation with Contemporary Theology* (Lexington: Emeth, 2004) 107.

29. Ibid., 227.

30. William J. Abraham, *Canon and Criterion in Christian Theology* (New York: Oxford University Press, 1998) 227ff.

immediate ecclesiastical church history as well as ancient traditions that supplemented his religious understanding and his ministry priorities and activities. With regard to reason, "Wesley appealed to reason more than the other two elements of the trilateral hermeneutic. He was prone often to repeat 'all reasonable people believe.'"[31] Although Wesley thought of reason primarily as a tool with which to think critically about scripture and related matters, he thought that reason, logic, and critical thinking were complementary to right belief and practice. Finally, with regard to experience, Wesley thought it could not be ignored in relationship to Christian belief and especially in relationship to Christian practice, both individually and socially, ministerially and publicly. He certainly recognized the potential abuses of experience and appeals to experience, yet Wesley thought it undeniably influenced Christians. They should recognize the experiential dimension of Christian reflection and appropriate it properly, rather than use it naively. Although Wesley did not have a well-developed understanding of experience—relative to contemporary views of it—he thought it included more than personal experience. It also included experience of scientific, behavioral scientific, and other investigations into humanity.

Myth of the Quadrilateral

Once any phrase becomes common parlance, people set out to demythologize it. For example, Ted Campbell calls the quadrilateral a "modern Methodist myth."[32] Of course, there is a lot to be said for this opinion. After all, Wesley did not coin the term. It was not coined till almost two hundred years after Wesley, undoubtedly with alternative motives driving its coinage—motives unrelated or even unfamiliar to Wesley.

One of the more prominent opponents to the use of the quadrilateral is William Abraham. It is not because Abraham is opposed to Wesley. On the contrary, he is a great advocate of Wesley and the Methodist tradition. However, Abraham regrets the non-Wesley usages of Wesley's understanding of religious authority. In particular, he laments the minimization of scriptural authority. For example, Abraham says, "Efforts have been made to treat these four elements dialectically, granting each of the elements relative autonomy. In response since such a dialectic relationship fosters confusion, a call for scrapping the quadrilateral has been issued, suggesting that the quadrilateral invites antipolarization of these four elements."[33]

In defense of the quadrilateral, Stephen Gunter says, "But the misuse of the quadrilateral should not be an excuse to dismiss it. The relationship of these four elements

---

31. John Wesley, quoted by W. Stephen Gunter, "Conclusion," in *Wesley and the Quadrilateral: Renewing the Conversation* (Nashville: Abingdon, 1997) 134; cf. Maddox, *Responsible Grace*, 36.

32. Ted Campbell, "The 'Wesleyan Quadrilateral': The Story of a Modern Methodist Myth," in *Doctrine and Theology in the United Methodist Church*, ed. Thomas A. Langford (Nashville: Kingswood, 1991) 154–61.

33. William J. Abraham, *Waking from Doctrinal Amnesia: The Healing of Doctrine in the United Methodist Church* (Nashville: Abingdon, 1997) 69. See the summary by Carl Schultz, "Biblical Hermeneutics in the Wesleyan Tradition," Houghton University Home Page (10 February 2003): campus.houghton.edu/personnel/gavery/Wesleyweb/biblical_hermenutics.htm.

needs to be seen dialogically, with scripture as the rule and authority in a way that should not be ascribed to the other components."[34] In fact, it would be wrong to think of the four aspects of the quadrilateral in static relationships or even dialectical relationships between only two of the four aspects of it. Instead, proponents see all four aspects in dynamic interaction. The main point of contention with the quadrilateral has usually been in terms of maintaining Wesley's historic emphasis upon the primacy of scriptural authority, vis-à-vis, one or more of the other aspects.

Some contemporary theologians critique the quadrilateral, while adopting it in a modified form. Gary Strauss, for example, affirms dispensationalist theology, and he critiques the quadrilateral for being too linear, envisioning isolated "conversations" between "scripture and tradition" or "scripture and reason" but not between all four at once. This is a critique Strauss believes he shares with John Stackhouse, a prominent evangelical theologian.[35] Of course, such a critique caricatures the quadrilateral because, if anything, it advocates a dynamic interplay and interdependence between the various religious authorities, which is anything but linear. Be that as it may, Strauss says that Stackhouse "perceived a need, therefore, for a revision of the quadrilateral. In its place (a process in which each element contributes to a kind of composite knowledge), he proposed what he described as a four-way conversation between the four elements of the quadrilateral. He holds that, in our process of thought, none of the four can stand by itself as an inviolable authority over the other three due to the reality of our finite and fallen human understanding and interpretation of each."[36] Stackhouse modifies the quadrilateral in describing the nature of evangelical theology. However, the essence of it remains.

In actuality, one could modify the quadrilateral in a variety of ways, appealing to creation, culture, or the behavioral sciences as a variation of three or, perhaps, four or five religious authorities. For example, Luis De Souza argues for a "pentalateral," which includes creation as a fifth component of Wesley's understanding of religious authority.[37] On the other hand, one could say that Wesley affirmed "a unilateral *rule* of Scripture within a trilateral *hermeneutic* of reason, tradition, and experience."[38] However, these various articulations of Wesley affirm the quadrilateral, broadly conceived, and there is no reason to think that either Wesley or Outler, who coined the term, would want to conceive of religious authority too narrowly. One could even cease calling it the

---

34. Gunter, "Conclusion," 131.

35. According to Gary Strauss, Stackhouse provides four criteria: "reliance upon the primary authority of the Bible in all matters of faith and practice; belief in eternal salvation by personal faith in Christ and his atoning work on the cross; the practice of personal piety in the context of a disciplined life; and concern for the evangelism of all people"—see John Stackhouse, Faculty Seminar, Biola University, La Mirada, California, January 1996; summarized by Gary Strauss, "An Evangelical Looks at Homosexuality: From the Wesleyan Quadrilateral to a Postmodern Tetralectic," *Christian Scholar's Review* 26 (Spring 1996) 517–20. Strauss applies Stackhouse's understanding of religious authority to an evangelical assessment of homosexuality.

36. Ibid., 518.

37. See Luis Wesley De Souza, "The Wisdom of God in Creation: Mission and the Wesleyan Pentalateral," in *Global Good News: Mission in a New Context*, ed. Howard Snyder (Nashville: Abingdon, 2001) 138–52.

38. Maddox, *Responsible Grace*, 46.

"Wesleyan quadrilateral," such as Kevin Lawson at Biola University, who refers to it as the "Protestant quadrilateral."[39] By renaming the quadrilateral, it may well be that more people, including evangelical theologians, would be willing to use it as a model for their theological reflection. Regardless, the quadrilateral steadily seems to make headway in shaping present and future evangelical understandings of religious authority.

SOLA GRATIA

Sola gratia was the preeminent teaching of the Protestant Reformers with regard to salvation. Divine grace alone is the ground of salvation, and Christians are justified by grace alone through faith. Protestants such as Luther thought that Roman Catholicism placed too much emphasis on the role of the church, if not also people, for salvation. Any admixture of human or ecclesiastical responsibility robbed God of sovereignty. There should be no synergistic understanding whatsoever of cooperation between people and God. The very suggestion of synergism tempted people; it led to thinking that they merited salvation, which Protestants pejoratively referred to as legalism. Belief in salvation by grace alone was the only way to safeguard a biblical understanding of God's sovereignty and salvation as a gift, not the result of human will or good works.

Spirit of Sola Gratia

Protestant Reformers such as Luther and Calvin revived the spirit of Augustine (354–430), who emphasized the sovereignty of God. In particular, Augustine championed God's sovereignty in reaction to Pelagius' view of God and salvation. Pelagius (354–420/40) left no writings, so we rely upon Augustine for what he considered to be so threatening. Pelagius thought that God created people with the ability to do all that is necessary for salvation. Although their ability is God-given, people must take the initiative for their salvation. People are free to choose that which is good and evil, without the aid of God. Pelagianism was eventually considered a heresy because it was thought to denigrate God's sovereignty by emphasizing how people can earn or merit salvation.

Augustine was equally opposed to what he called semi-Pelagianism. Semi Pelagianism affirms that God needs to act graciously in the lives of people in order to aid in their salvation. They alone, unaided by God's involvement in their lives, is insufficient for salvation. However, people can initiate their salvation, cooperating with God by applying or attaching their will to grace. Augustine thought that semi-Pelagianism made people's will the effective ground of salvation, and that too was thought to denigrate God"s sovereignty. Because of the pervasive effects of sin, Augustine thought that people are totally dependent upon God. Augustine thought that there was nothing whatsoever that people can do for their salvation. People are totally dependent upon God's grace for salvation and for living the Christian life.

The Protestant Reformers thought that Roman Catholicism had allowed the leaven of Pelagianism—of works righteousness—to permeate the church. Since the Pope and

---

39. Kevin E. Lawson, "Developing a Model of Theological Reflection for Educational Ministry Practice: Exploring the Wesleyan Quadrilateral and Stackhouse's Tetralectic," unpublished paper.

magisterium refused to recant their heretical beliefs and practices, Luther, Calvin, and others felt forced to protest and eventually break away from the Roman Catholic Church. Only then would Christianity be able to return to the original teachings of the Bible about God's sovereignty and salvation by grace alone. In order to overturn centuries of degenerative leadership and doctrine in Roman Catholicism, schism was necessary to purify and revive true Christianity.

Myth of Sola Gratia

The boast of *sola gratia* was, in many respects, a reactionary statement created in order to counteract centuries of Roman Catholic hegemony. In order for Luther and others to succeed in breaking away from Roman Catholicism, dramatic choices and distinct theological positions were necessary in order for schism to succeed. The Protestant Reformers' appeal to the Augustinian view of the sovereignty of God helped them to articulate their opposition to views they considered heretical. The appeal to Augustinian tradition aided the appeal to *sola scriptura*, since Augustinianism was thought to promote the primacy of scriptural authority as well as the primacy of grace and faith for salvation.

Of course, it was not true that the Roman Catholic Church advocated Pelagianism or even semi-Pelagianism. Such abuses may have occurred, especially in Germany and Switzerland, and insufficient steps were taken to correct them. However, Roman Catholicism never affirmed Pelagianism or semi-Pelagianism, much less salvation by earning or meriting it. For example, at the Council of Trent (1545–1563), which spearheaded the Counter-Reformation, Roman Catholics discussed the nature of salvation. According to the Council and subsequent teachings, people are saved by grace through faith: "Our justification comes from the grace of God. Grace is *favor*, the *free and undeserved help* that God gives us to respond to his call to become children of God, adoptive sons, partakers of the divine nature and of eternal life."[40]

In order to underscore the similarity—rather than difference—between Roman Catholic and Protestant views of salvation by grace through faith, a joint document was authorized in Augsburg, Germany in 1999. A "Joint Declaration on the Doctrine of Justification" was signed by the Lutheran World Federation and the Roman Catholic Church. The significance and scope of the consensus reached can be summarized in the following two points of the Joint Declaration:

> 40. The understanding of the doctrine of justification set forth in this Declaration shows that a consensus in basic truths of the doctrine of justification exists between Lutherans and Catholics. In light of this consensus the remaining differences of language, theological elaboration, and emphasis in the understanding of justification described in paras. 18 to 39 are acceptable. Therefore the Lutheran and the Catholic explications of justification are in their difference open to one another and do not destroy the consensus regarding the basic truths.
>
> 41. Thus the doctrinal condemnations of the 16th century, in so far as they relate to the doctrine of justification, appear in a new light: The teaching of the Lutheran

---

40. *Catechism of the Catholic Church,* United States Conference of Catholic Bishops, Article 2, Grace and Justification, § 1996. Online: http://www.usccb.org/catechism/text/pt3sect1chpt3art2.htm.

churches presented in this Declaration does not fall under the condemnations from the Council of Trent. The condemnations in the Lutheran Confessions do not apply to the teaching of the Roman Catholic Church presented in this Declaration.

Protestant Reformers too often caricatured official Roman Catholic doctrine as being Pelagian or semi-Pelagian. Such caricatures persist today. (Of course, both sides of the debate were and continue to be guilty of caricaturing the views of one another.) However, it is more appropriate to refer to Roman Catholic beliefs about salvation by grace as semi-Augustinian. This is not a category with which everyone is familiar. Indeed it may not be a category that people like or want to acknowledge as valid. Yet, it is very important for understanding, perhaps, the majority viewpoint of salvation in church history as well as today. The difference between semi-Augustinianism and previous heretical views is that it places emphasis upon the initiation of God for the salvation of people rather than people initiating it. In a sense, God is thought to initiate, facilitate, and complete salvation, including the response of faith on the part of people. This response or cooperation on the part of people represents synergism, but it does not deserve to be called Pelagian or semi-Pelagian. People's choice or free will is enabled by God's grace, so it is not anything that people earn or merit for salvation. Yet, it represents a needed response on the part of people, which is the condition of their salvation. Salvation is not unconditional, as Calvin asserted and, later, the Synod of Dort (1618/9). God foreknows those who will believe, but God does not foreordain it. Foreknowledge is not causative knowledge, which is a distinction between Augustinian and semi-Augustinian beliefs.

Augustinianism was characteristic of Luther and Calvin, and that influence continues among Protestants. However, semi-Augustinianism was and continues to be characteristic not only of Roman Catholicism and Orthodox Churches. For all the influence Augustine had over the development of Christianity, ancient and medieval churches did not follow his lead with regard to issues of salvation related to divine predestination and human freedom. The Second Council of Orange (529), for example, affirmed that salvation involves both divine gift and human task.[41] Likewise, other Protestant developments followed semi-Augustinian rather than Augustinian views. Most notable were the founders of the Church of England, James Arminius and the Arminians in the Netherlands, and John Wesley and the Methodists in Great Britain. Statistically, the overwhelming majority of Christians in church history and today reflect semi-Augustinian and not Augustinian views, which is counterintuitive to many Christians, inside and outside the Protestant tradition.

Not all the Protestant Reformers affirmed Augustinianism, at least, not in its most pronounced form. Luther, for example, is sometimes interpreted as having a semi-Augustinian view of salvation, divine predestination, and human freedom, though his writing on *The Bondage of the Will* strongly suggests Augustinianism. Melancthon, on the other hand, advocated a kind of synergism, which was debated in sixteenth-century Lutheranism, and his views were excluded by the *Formula of Concord* (1577). Melancthon argued that there occurs a coincidence between the Word (or Bible), Spirit, and the hu-

---

41. See Rebecca Harden Weaver, *Divine Grace and Human Agency: A Study of the Semi-Pelagian Controversy* (Macon, GA: Mercer University Press, 1995).

man will not refusing God's grace. He does not believe that the human will occurs prior to grace as an active power or faculty capable of applying grace to the individual. So, Melancthon was not considered heretical, though he advocated a synergistic relationship between God and people for salvation.

Calvin and the Reformed tradition certainly represent the strongest version of Augustinianism, especially in Calvin's affirmation of double predestination.[42] Double predestination affirms that God foreordains both those will be saved (elect) and those who will be damned (reprobate). There is no conditional election; God does not predestine people for salvation based upon any foreseen faith or merit. On the contrary, election is unconditional, and grace is irresistible. Calvin, like Luther, believed that people are saved by grace through faith. Faith is a result of grace and cannot be considered the result of human effort. Paradoxically, faith is still a task, expected by God, regardless of how one interprets the concept of task. In affirming salvation by grace through faith, neither Luther nor Calvin entirely denied human involvement in salvation. Commenting upon the paradox of salvation as both gift and task in Augustine as well as the Protestant Reformers, Roger Olson says:

> In one of his final treatises, titled *On the Predestination of the Saints*, the bishop of Hippo affirmed unconditional election (absolute predestination) and denied free will that could limit or resist the work of God's sovereign grace in those whom God has chosen to save out of the "mass of perdition." During the Protestant Reformation Luther and Calvin hark back to this later writing of Augustine's. None of them, however, entirely denied the human role of salvation; they simply gave

---

42. John Calvin wrote about double predestination, though his followers sometimes prefer to speak in terms of single predestination, leaving the damnation of people a mystery (similar to Augustine). Calvin says: "We call predestination God's eternal decree, by which he compacted with himself what he willed to become of each man. For all are not created in equal condition; rather, eternal life is foreordained for some, eternal damnation for others. Therefore, as any man has been created to one or the other of these ends, se speak of him as predestined to life or to death"; see *Institutes of the Christian Religion*, 3.21.5, 926. In the introduction to the *Institutes*, McNeill refers explicitly to Calvin's double predestination: "Calvin goes beyond Augustine in his explicit assertion of double predestination, in which the reprobation of those not elected is a specific determination of God's inscrutable will. Apparently, the statement of this became a constituent element in Calvin's theology through his never relaxed conviction, borne out by his reading of Scripture and reflection on his own experience, of the unconditioned sovereignty of God. He feels under obligation to close the door to the notion that anything happens otherwise than under the control of the divine will. Man is wholly unable to contribute to his own salvation; nor is election conditioned by divine foreknowledge of a man's faith or goodness" (lviii–lix).

The Westminster Confession, which represents the main statement of Calvinist teaching in the English language, clearly teaches the doctrine of double predestination. For example, the Westminster Confession states the following with regard to "Of God's Eternal Decree": "God from all eternity, did, by the most wise and holy counsel of His own will, freely, and unchangeably ordain whatsoever comes to pass; yet so, as thereby neither is God the author of sin, nor is violence offered to the will of the creatures; nor is the liberty or contingency of second causes taken away, but rather established. II. Although God knows whatsoever may or can come to pass upon all supposed conditions; yet has He not decreed anything because He foresaw it as future, or as that which would come to pass upon such conditions. III. By the decree of God, for the manifestation of His glory, some men and angels are predestinated unto everlasting life; and others foreordained to everlasting death. IV. These angels and men, thus predestinated, and foreordained, are particularly and unchangeably designed, and their number so certain and definite, that it cannot be either increased or diminished."

priority to divine grace and attributed even human choices and actions—insofar as they are meritorious—to God.[43]

Although *sola gratia* wonderfully uplifts the primacy of God's grace for the salvation of people, it does not exclude the human task as well as divine gift required for salvation, holistically and realistically conceived. A more holistic and realistic way of conceptualizing salvation is with *prima gratia* rather than *sola gratia*. God's grace is primarily, rather than solely, involved with providing the gift of salvation to people. People still have the task of receiving God's gift. *Prima gratia* does not imply Pelagianism or semi-Pelagianism; on the contrary, it is better described as Augustinianism or semi-Augustinianism. Both of the latter views allow for some degree of both divine gift and human task, despite lingering differences between the two dimensions of salvation.

Both Grace and Faith

Nowhere do I want to say that people can be saved by any means other than God's grace. I often find it the case, however, that critics of my views immediately accuse me of works-righteousness, Pelagianism, or some other form of historically heretical viewpoint. I do not want to say anything heretical, unbiblical, or—for that matter—contrary to the spirit of historic Christian beliefs, values, and practices. On the contrary, I argue that my emphasis upon *prima gratia*, *sola fide*, and *sola scriptura* better summarize the essence of Christianity. People may disagree, but do not overreact by castigating my views without critically reflecting on the practice of Christians as well as what they tend to say theoretically about their beliefs, values, and practices.

Too often people, including Christians, have difficulty thinking in anything other than either/or categories. Perhaps out of a desire for clear-cut convictions, they want to force God and life into categories they can understand and discuss more easily. Yet, neither God nor life are always clear-cut, easily categorized, or discussed. Frankly, I do not think that scripture is any more clear-cut, easily categorized, or discussed. We need to think critically and, like the Christians who formulated the first creeds, not fear mystery and paradox in the affirmations we make about grace, faith, and scriptural authority.

To me there is not problem in saying that people are saved by God's grace through faith, and that this assertion affirms both divine initiation and people's genuine, albeit of secondary importance, response to God. Such both/and thinking is more representative of scripture and life than either/or thinking that cannot as easily conceptualize or communicate the ways in which God works in the lives of people.

Certainly the Protestant principles emphasize appropriately the priority of emphasizing grace, faith, and scripture, especially in light of the urgency of their affirmations in challenging Roman Catholicism. However, their emphasis should be one of primacy rather than exclusivity. Erring on the side of either/or thinking risks the gospel message of the Bible as well as the dynamic and sometimes inscrutable workings of God through the Holy Spirit today.

---

43. Roger E. Olson, *The Mosaic of Christian Belief: Twenty Centuries of Unity and Diversity* (Downers Grove, IL: InterVarsity, 2002), 271.

PART TWO: CONTRIBUTION TO CURRENT THEOLOGICAL PROBLEMS

SOLA FIDE

Sola fide is usually identified with the Protestant emphasis upon the doctrine of justification as the primary way for talking about salvation. Using forensic language, the Protestant Reformers talked about a legal declaration made, figuratively speaking, of righteousness imputed to people. God forgives people and counts them as righteous on the basis of their faith in Jesus Christ. God accepts people, apart from all human merit, based solely upon the superabundant merit of Christ's work of satisfaction.

Spirit of Sola Fide

Sola fide makes sense most in the company of *sola gratia*, which emphasizes the primacy of God's grace, God's initiative, and God's sovereignty in the salvation process. It does not mean, however, that people do not have a task associated with reconciliation with God. Certainly salvation is made possible by the atonement of Jesus Christ and the empowerment of the Holy Spirit. People are counted as righteous because of the "alien righteousness" of Christ; the impelling cause of it is God alone, through the work of the Holy Spirit.[44]

Faith is not the active cause of justification. Instead it is the means or medium that receives the grace of God in justification. The Word—the Bible—also functions as an instrument bestowed by God and properly received by faith. The same could be said of the sacraments: baptism and the Eucharist. God provides them as the means or medium, and not the cause of salvation.

Justification refers to what God does for the salvation of people, that is, the objective work of Jesus Christ and its effects. Faith refers to the inward, subjective recognition on the part of believers that they are counted as righteous and free from the condemnation of the law. Saving faith accepts the promises of God and the truths of God to the salvation of the believer. It consists of, at least, three components: *notitia*, knowledge; *assensus*, assent; and *fiducia*, trust. Thus, saving faith is not merely intellectual; it is also volitional—a task.

Luther characterizes the believer justified by grace through faith as *simul iustus et peccator*, "both righteous and a sinner."[45] Justification results from imputed rather than imparted righteousness, and people are justified through faith rather than by works. So, it is not because of righteousness as measured by people's merits. Instead people are righteous in God's sight because of the person and work of Jesus Christ. Thus, paradoxically, believers are both righteous and sinner.

---

44. Martin Luther, "Two Kinds of Righteousness," in *Martin Luther: Selections from His Writings*, ed. John Dillenberger (New York: Anchor, 1958) 88.

45. Martin Luther, *Commentary on Romans*, trans. J. Theodore Mueller (Grand Rapids, MI: Kregel, 1954) 130.

Myth of Sola Fide

Christians do not believe that people earn or merit their salvation, even by their faith in Jesus Christ. However, there lingers the idea—the paradox—that, for Christians, salvation is both divine gift and human task. Olson describes it this way:

> In any case, there should be no real doubt that all major Protestant Reformers and their post-Reformation disciples as well as modern Christian theologians affirmed and proclaimed both divine grace and human agency in salvation. Of course they have described that paradox in different ways, and sometimes those differences have caused controversy and division between Protestants—just as they caused the division within Christendom itself during the Protestant Reformation of the sixteenth century.... Suffice it to say here that Christians all together believe that salvation as reconciliation with God and inward renewal from the corruption of inherited depravity and toward the restoration of the image of God is wholly and completely a work of God's grace while at the same time also an event and process involving human agency.[46]

In *theory*, Protestants sometimes say that, with regard to salvation, "God does everything, and I do nothing." Similarly, they say, "I owe everything to God." In a sense, these statements are true. Salvation occurs solely through the divine initiation of God. However, in *practice*, they do something; they believe. From some Protestant perspectives, faith is almost entirely a passive experience. More often, faith is thought to be active; it is understood paradoxically as being attributable to God as well as to people. The customary inclusion of the Protestant principle of *sola fide* along with *sola gratia* reveals—in practice—how the task of faith is inextricably bound up with the gift of grace.

In practice, people—including Protestants—live as if their faith makes a difference. They do not think that they are earning or meriting salvation through their faith. On the contrary, they have faith in that they do not have to earn and merit salvation. That is their hope, their assurance of eternal life. But practically speaking, they take care to believe in the atonement, provided by Jesus Christ and empowered by the Holy Spirit. Indeed they also take care to live obedient lives, though not to earn or merit salvation.

Even if faith is not considered a human admixture to the formula of salvation by grace, then what of obedience? There has been ongoing debate among Christians, from the time of the first century, about the relationship between faith and works. The apostle Paul, of course, argued for salvation by grace through faith:

> For by grace you have been saved through faith, and this is not your own doing; it is the gift of God—not the result of works, so that no one may boast. For we are what he has made us, created in Christ Jesus for good works, which God prepared beforehand to be our way of life. (Eph 2:8–10, NRSV)

On the other hand, James wrote with a different understanding of the relationship between faith and works. He says:

> What good is it, my brothers and sisters, if you say you have faith but do not have works? Can faith save you? If a brother or sister is naked and lacks daily food, and

---

46. Olson, *Mosaic of Christian Belief*, 272–73.

one of you says to them, "Go in peace; keep warm and eat your fill," and yet you do not supply their bodily needs, what is the good of that? So faith by itself, if it has no works, is dead. (James 2:14–17, NRSV)

James concludes his discussion of how faith without works is counterfeit by saying that such faith cannot save (see also Matt 25:31–46; Gal 5:6). Demons know the truth about God, but are not saved (Deut 6:4). Thus, James says, "You see that a person is justified by works and not by faith alone" (James 2:24). In fact, nowhere does the Bible say that people are saved by faith alone. It says the opposite; people are saved "by works and not by faith alone."

This debate continued in the Protestant Reformation, most notably by Luther who considered the book of James as an "epistle full of straw."[47] Luther rejected James' statements that works are a necessary evidence of faith. There are, of course, different ways to interpret the words of Paul as well as James. For example, Christians often say that Paul was making universal statements about salvation for all people, especially unbelievers, while James was talking primarily to a believing audience, who were given exhortations to manifest their faith through love. Thomas Oden says:

> The absence of works indicates that faith is not working actively; hence itself is lacking. In distinguishing between active (true) and inactive (false) faith, James was not contradicting Paul, who viewed saving faith as the condition of the sinner's being made whole.... It is difficult to establish that there is a genuine conflict between Paul and James, for Paul is dealing primarily with the justification that God declares with respect to human sin as viewed in Christ, whereas James is dealing primarily with the way the justified life is made recognizable through acts of love.[48]

Certainly faith and works are inextricably bound up with one another, and we cannot talk about faith for long without also talking about faith working by love, that is, faith that is animated and instructed by love and active in producing good works. In practice, it seems difficult to talk about faith in isolation, as something discussed without reference to faith, on the one hand, and knowledge, assent, trust, volition, and works of love, on the other hand. All dimensions are indicative of faith as gift and task, due to divine and human agency.

Sola fide is a persuasive slogan, emphasizing an essential principle of the Protestant Reformation. However, in practice, a full orbed understanding of faith reflects *prima fide*—primarily faith, rather than faith exclusively, in a reductionistic way. It seems that the Protestant references to the *solas*—scriptura, gratia, and fide—were necessary reactions (or over-reactions) for strengthening the Protestant Reformation from the religious, social, political, economic, and military hegemony of Roman Catholicism and the Holy Roman Empire. Due to necessity, the *sola* principles were understandably reductionistic in order to identify, promote, and defend Protestantism. It was a life or death situation, and desperate times require extreme measures.

---

47. Martin Luther, "Preface to the Epistle of St. James," in *Martin Luther: Selections from His Writings*, ed. John Dillenberger (New York: Anchor, 1958) 19.

48. Thomas C. Oden, *Life in the Spirit: Systematic Theology*, vol. 3 (New York: HarperSanFrancisco, 1992) 149.

However, as effective as the *sola* principles were, they failed to encapsulate the totality of biblical and historic Christian teachings about religious authority and soteriology. From the luxury of distance in time and space, we now understand that religious authority and soteriology are more complex, dynamic, and holistic than what the Reformers articulated. Historically, the *sola* principles are amazing and foundational to Protestantism. However, for a future, modern, or—perhaps—postmodern understanding of religious authority and soteriology, other principles are necessary. The Christian stories of religious authority and soteriology are too multifaceted and paradoxical to be considered in terms of anything "alone." *Prima scriptura*, *prima gratia*, and *prima fide* may not be the best ways to conceive of Christianity, but they represent an important corrective to the historic *sola* principles of the Reformation, which need to be reconceived and promoted more effectively. The *prima* principles are more promising ways of understanding and promoting the complex, dynamic, and holistic dimensions of Christianity today.

New Perspective on Paul

My argument has been that *prima fide*, rather than *sola fide*, represents a better summarization of scriptural teachings as well as those of Catholic, Orthodox, and even Protestant Reformers. A correlative argument in New Testament scholarship represents an intriguing parallel, albeit notably different, challenge to Paul's doctrine of justification by faith and Protestants" subsequent emphasis upon justification by *sola fide*—faith alone. Although the so-called "new perspective" on Paul has more to do with how Christians view Judaism in New Testament studies, it further challenges *sola fide* as an adequate understanding of what scripture says about grace, faith, and salvation.

Scholars such as E. P. Sanders, James D. G. Dunn, and N. T. Wright have led debate about the appropriate understanding of Judaism at the time of Jesus and of the nature of exclusivity Paul discussed with regard to mercy, faith, and people's salvation.[49] For example, they questioned the degree to which Jews believed that they could accumulate merit before God by their good works, and the degree to which Paul challenged works-righteousness rather than exclusivist reliance by Jews upon national righteousness.

Of course, there has been criticism of the new perspective on Paul. Usually critics fear that Sanders, Dunn, and Wright endanger Paul's trust in God's mercy alone and his rejection of reliance upon obeying the law though the "flesh," and the Reformation principles of *sola gratia* and *sola fide*.[50] Such critics say that it has to do with more than just preserving Lutheran, Calvinist, and Reformed theology, though such theology is thought to represent the best interpretation of scripture.

49. For example, see E. P. Sanders, *Paul and Palestinian Judaism* (Minneapolis: Fortress, 1977); James D. G. Dunn, *Theology of Paul the Apostle* (Grand Rapids: Eerdmans, 1998); N. T. Wright, *What Saint Paul Really Said* (West Bromwich, UK: Lion, 1997); and N. T. Wright, *Paul: In Fresh Perspective* (Minneapolis: Fortress, 2006).

50. For example, see Peter Stuhlmacher and Don Hagner, *Revisiting Paul's Doctrine of Justification: A Challenge to the New Perspective* (Downers Grove, IL: InterVarsity, 2001); Simon Gathercole, "What Did Paul Really Mean?" *Christianity Today* 51.8 (August 2007) 22–28; D. A. Carson, Peter T. O'Brien, and Mark A. Seifrid, eds., *Justification and Variegated Nomism*, 2 vols. (Grand Rapids: Baker, 2001, 2004); and Stephen Westerholm, *Perspectives Old and New on Paul* (Grand Rapids: Eerdmans, 2004).

PART TWO: CONTRIBUTION TO CURRENT THEOLOGICAL PROBLEMS

It goes beyond the parameters of this discussion, at this time, to evaluate the merits of the new perspective on Paul. However, it is instructive that affirmation of the Protestant principles of *sola gratia* and *sola fide* is problematical from more than one perspective. They are debatable from scriptural as well as from theological and ecclesiastical perspectives. In the future, debate about the *sola* principles should and, undoubtedly, will increase. No doubt the principles of *prima gratia*, *prima fide*, and *prima scriptura* will provide constructive alternatives for the growing debate.

CONCLUSION

While *sola scriptura* valuably reminds us of the need for maintaining the primacy of scriptural authority, the quadrilateral and its emphasis upon *prima scriptura* provides a better principle of religious authority because it embodies as well as advocates a complex dynamic of relevant authorities. Likewise, *prima gratia* and *prima fide* retain the Protestant Reformation priority upon the sovereignty of God and divine initiation for the salvation of people. They also convey the essential complexity, dynamic, and holism of salvation described in scripture and affirmed by church history in all its diversity.

Certainly *sola scriptura* and the quadrilateral do not need to be seen as contradictory or competing principles of religious authority. On the contrary, it is best to see them as complementary, properly understanding the historical context and spirit of the two principles. In the same way, *prima gratia* and *prima fide* are not opposed to *sola gratia* and *prima fide* in the sense that they advocate a kind of works righteousness or legalism, contrary to the Protestant Reformation. They are complementary in that the *prima* principles affirm the primacy of grace and the primacy of faith, without diminishing the undeniable human dimensions of salvation and the Christian life.

In our present-day world, the benefits of the *prima principles* become increasingly apparent. Christians would do well to utilize them in their ministry as well as theology in attempting to translate biblical truths in ways that are appealing, persuasive, and effective in lovingly interacting with others. If Christians are to meet the complex needs of the world in a way that is faithful to biblical, historical Christianity, then the *prima* understanding of religious authority and soteriology provides the best principles for representing God and God's reign as well as for serving people in the present age.

15

Theological Intepretation and Wesley

JOEL B. GREEN

THE PAST TWO DECADES have seen a significant shift within biblical studies as once-regnant historical-critical modes of interpretation have had to make room for other approaches to working with biblical texts. The list of these new approaches is long and varied, with most taking with greater seriousness than would be typical of historical criticism the reality that biblical interpreters bring to the task of critical reading both conscious and unconscious commitments and dispositions. And among these commitments and dispositions, some are recognizably theological and ecclesial, giving rise to the renewed phenomenon of "theological interpretation."[1]

In fact, theological interpretation of Scripture is a less a *method* and more a *constellation of commitments and sensibilities* that guide the reading and use of Scripture. Theological interpretation concerns the role of Scripture in the faith and formation of persons and ecclesial communities, the potentially mutual influence of Scripture and doctrine in theological discourse and, then, the role of Scripture in the self-understanding of the church and in critical reflection on the church's practices. This is biblical interpretation that takes the Bible not only as a historical or literary document but as a source of divine revelation and an essential partner in the task of theological reflection.

In modern times, the impulse toward theological interpretation as a mode of critical engagement with Scripture is often identified with Karl Barth's *Der Römerbrief* (1919). As a hermeneutic, though, theological exegesis has a much more hoary pedigree, deeply rooted as it is in Israel's own Scriptures (i.e., inner-biblical exegesis), in the interpretations of those Scriptures by the translators of the LXX in its various renditions, in the Dead Sea Scrolls, in the New Testament, and among both Jews and Christians in the early

---

1. For orientation, see Stephen E. Fowl, *Theological Interpretation of Scripture* (Eugene, OR: Cascade, 2009); Joel B. Green, *Seized by Truth: Reading the Bible as Scripture* (Nashville: Abingdon, 2007); Daniel J. Treier, *Theological Interpretation of Scripture: Recovering a Christian Practice* (Grand Rapids: Baker, 2008). For the smorgasbord of approaches to New Testament interpretation more generally, see Joel B. Green, ed., *Hearing the New Testament: Strategies for Interpretation*, 2nd ed. (Grand Rapids: Eerdmans, 2010).

centuries of the Common Era. It was also practiced by many in the post-Reformation era, not least by John Wesley.

WESLEY AS INTERPRETER

Interest in theological interpretation may seem to some as no more than a throwback to the earlier days of "precritical" exegesis. Reacting against medieval modes of interpretation, Protestant Reformers tended toward an emphasis on the one meaning of Scripture and produced hermeneutical handbooks with criteria for legitimate readings—especially philological, including the historical exigencies governing the meaning of words. At the turn of the nineteenth century, new emphases on historical context led interpreters to stress the distance between text and reader, and to construe this distance primarily in historical terms. Consequently, biblical study began to devote its energies, first, to mapping this distance, and then, in some cases, to discussions about how to traverse this distance. For many, recognition of the historical chasm separating the known world of our contemporaries from the strange world of the Bible had its impetus in a concern to protect the biblical materials from easy conscription in the service of modern concerns, including the church's theology. These emphases have cultivated various forms of "higher criticism" characteristic of the historical-critical paradigm that has until recently gripped the scholarly engagement with the Bible.

What of the hermeneutics of John Wesley? When Wesley is read against the backdrop of these developments, it is no surprise that we find him charged with that most marginalizing of modern epitaphs: uncritical.[2] Such indictments typically bemoan the fact that Wesley gave little notice to the sacred cows of the historical-critical paradigm, especially the original meaning of a biblical text according to the (reconstructed) historical context and/or the (reconstructed) intent of the author. Accordingly, one might imagine that an attempt to take seriously Wesley as a biblical interpreter would be similarly charged with either pursuing an agenda of naive primitivism interested in recovering precritical modes of interpretation or attempting to escape wholesale the alleged perils of higher criticism of the Bible.

Let me offer five grounds for denying that an attempt to learn theological interpretation from Wesley is an escape into precritical exegesis. The first and most obvious is the simple absurdity of assuming that the only style of reading worthy of the designation "critical" is modern historical criticism. The critical tradition is far more inclusive, with a variety of disciplined approaches available to adjudicate among alternative renderings of biblical texts.[3]

---

2. E.g., Wilbur H. Mullen, "John Wesley's Method of Biblical Interpretation," *Religion in Life* 47 (1978) 99–108 (esp. 106–7); Duncan S. Ferguson, "John Wesley on Scripture: The Hermeneutics of Pietism," *Methodist History* 22 (1984) 234–45 (esp. 238, 244); George A. Turner, "John Wesley as an Interpreter of Scripture," in *Inspiration and Interpretation,* ed. John F. Walvoord (Grand Rapids: Eerdmans, 1957) 156–78 (esp. 165–66).

3. See M. H. Abrams, *The Mirror and the Lamp: Romantic Theory and the Critical Tradition* (Oxford: University of Oxford, 1953); Hazard Adams, ed., *Critical Theory since Plato,* rev. ed. (Fort Worth, TX: Harcourt Brace Jovanovich, 1992).

Second, to say that we might learn from Wesley is not the same thing as saying that we must recover, index, and repeat Wesley, as though Wesley's modes of theological exegesis might function as the unchanging Laws of the Medes and Persians. We and Wesley live on opposite ends of the modern era of historical criticism, and we cannot act as though we have nothing to learn from the intervening years. Nor, however, should we imagine that the intervening years have obliterated the significance of Wesley's work with Scripture. Persons in the Wesleyan tradition might consider how best to participate in a discerning *ressourcement*, even if it means that we might struggle with one another in identifying those points at which Wesley needs to be corrected or broadened.

Third, classifying Wesley as "precritical" overlooks the degree to which Wesley himself took seriously the currents of learning in his own day. In his reading of the Gospel of Matthew, for example, questions about science and theology surfaced because of Jesus' miracles. In Matt 4:23–25, the evangelist summarizes the nature of Jesus' ministry throughout Galilee as proclamation and healing, and this combination is continued throughout the Gospel. Thus, immediately following the Sermon on the Mount in Matthew 5–7, Matthew reports a series of miracles concerned with healing (Matthew 8–9) as Matthew depicts Jesus as one who makes available the presence and power of God's kingdom to those dwelling on the margins of society in Galilee—a leper, the slave of a Gentile army officer, an old woman, the demon-possessed, a paralytic, a collector of tolls, a young girl, and the blind. With the seventeenth-century emergence of the "new science," what challenges would face interpreters of such texts as these?

Wesley lived in an age of exciting, unprecedented scientific discovery, when mysteries of all sorts had begun to be explained in terms of natural causes—as one might expect of a world influenced by Newtonian mechanics. So he was aware that some educated people had begun to question Jesus' miracles. Consequently, in his note on Jesus' commission to the disciples that they should "cast out devils" (10:8), Wesley observed that someone had said that diseases ascribed to the devil in the Gospels "have the very same symptoms with the natural diseases of lunacy, epilepsy, or convulsions," leading to the conclusion "that the devil had no hand in them." Wesley continues:

> But it were well to stop and consider a little. Suppose God should allow an evil spirit to usurp the same power over a man's body as the man himself has naturally, and suppose him actually to exercise that power; could we conclude the devil had no hand therein, because his body was bent in the very same manner wherein the man himself bent it naturally?
>
> And suppose God gives an evil spirit a greater power to affect immediately the origin of the nerves in the brain, by irritating them to produce violent motions, or so relaxing them that they can produce little or no motion, still the symptoms will be those of over-tense nerves, as in madness, epilepsies, convulsions, or of relaxed nerves, as in paralytic cases. But could we conclude thence, that the devil had no hand in them?[4]

---

4. John Wesley, *Explanatory Notes upon the New Testament* (London: Epworth, 1975 [1754]) 53. In my citations of Wesley, I have introduced inclusive language for human beings.

PART TWO: CONTRIBUTION TO CURRENT THEOLOGICAL PROBLEMS

Reading Wesley's comments, we might forget that serious study of the central nervous system and its relationship to human behavior was barely a century old. Nevertheless, elsewhere Wesley writes that, "for six or seven and twenty years, I had made anatomy and physic the diversion of my leisure hours...."[5] In this way, he documented for us his interest in the new vistas that science had begun to open and his intent to take seriously the importance of science for biblical interpretation and for Christian mission. At this juncture his solution appears to be openness to the truth of both faith and science; rather than deny the truth of stories of demonized persons in the Gospels or of scientific explanations, he allows that both could be true.

Fourth, we see emerging in Wesley's *Explanatory Notes upon the New Testament* the beginnings of an interest in the sort of historical background about which modern biblical studies is most serious.[6] I say "beginnings" because, in his own description of how he engages with biblical texts, we see a decidedly un-modern approach to dealing with difficult texts. "Does anything appear dark or intricate?" he asks. For most students of the Bible formally trained in our colleges, universities, and seminaries, the key to making sense of difficult passages in the Bible is to seek more background, more historical detail, more insight into ancient patterns of thought and behavior. Wesley's approach takes a different route.

> Does anything appear dark or intricate? I lift up my heart to the Father of lights: "Lord, is it not your Word, 'If any lack wisdom, let them ask of God'? You 'give generously and ungrudgingly.' You have said, 'If any be willing to do your will, they shall know.' I am willing to do, let me know, your will." I then search after and consider parallel passages of Scripture, "comparing spiritual things with spiritual." I meditate thereon, with all the attention and earnestness of which my mind is capable. If any doubt still remains, I consult those who are experienced in the things of God, and then the writings whereby, being dead, they yet speak. And what I thus learn, that I teach.[7]

That is, faced with a biblical text that is unclear, Wesley (1) looks to God for help, (2) compares the text with other biblical passages, (3) meditates, (4) consults with "those who are experienced in the things of God," and (5) looks to commentaries and other published works for assistance.[8] (Note how Wesley presents some of these interpretive procedures in phraseology borrowed from the Bible itself.) This is not to suggest that, for Wesley, historical detail was unimportant. In a stinging reversal of much contemporary biblical interpretation, though, Wesley operates with the assumption that the primary chasm that must be overcome if we are to make sense of Scripture is mapped not in terms of our need for more historical detail but with reference to our need to know God and God's ways. "I lift up my heart to the Father of lights. . . . I am willing to do, let me know, your

---

5. John Wesley, "A Plain Account of the People Called Methodists," §XII.2.
6. For a similar judgment, see Robin Scroggs, "John Wesley as Biblical Scholar," *Journal of Bible and Religion* 28 (1960) 415–22 (418).
7. Wesley, "Preface," *Sermons on Several Occasions*, §5.
8. See Mullen, "John Wesley's Method," 102.

will." Here is a transparent window into the kind of knowledge, the kind of truth, Wesley sought in Scripture.

On the one hand, then, his *Explanatory Notes* and many of his sermons are dotted with historical data. On the other, reading Scripture could never be divorced from the Bible's status as divine word. In the end, Wesley's approach to Scripture can be characterized neither as emphasizing prayer over research, nor as prioritizing research over prayer. He held these together, while obviously prioritizing the significance of Scripture for Christian faith and life over the importance of establishing, say, the first-century meaning of a text in its historical context.

Fifth, in what may be a surprising twist, a careful examination of Wesley's biblical interpretation demonstrates the degree to which Wesley worked *with*, not *against*, the significance of biblical materials understood within their own settings. I say that this may be surprising because Wesley himself does not make this plain—or, at least, he does not make this plain in a way that much of contemporary biblical scholarship might recognize. This is because we do not find in Wesley an explicit interest in the hermeneutical move from "what it meant" to "what it means," nor do we find this movement in his hermeneutical practices. Wesley's sermons on the Corinthian correspondence, for example, do not first establish what Paul must have meant in the first century so that Wesley could then add a section to his sermon entitled "How 1 Corinthians Applies to Us" or "The Relevance of 1 Corinthians for Today." But neither did he imagine that 1 Corinthians had been written in the eighteenth century, as though Paul had set out to address the theological arguments and everyday concerns of the Methodist movement. Instead, Wesley seems to have come to the text aware *both* of his theological questions and commitments *and* of the origins of the Corinthian letters within the ongoing relationship between the apostle Paul and the Corinthian Christians. Instead, Wesley comes to the text with the working assumption that, as Scripture, 1 Corinthians was written not only for a first-century audience but for eighteenth-century Christians as well.

In the remainder of this essay, I want to turn more fully to this fifth point in order to illustrate Wesley's theological interpretation of Scripture. Focusing on 1 Peter, I will show that Wesley's theological concerns are quite different when compared to Peter's own, and yet how closely aligned Wesley's aims are with Peter's own central emphases.

WESLEY, 1 PETER, AND PREDESTINATION

The opening of Peter's letter is important for the way it identifies the character of Peter's model audience. It is also interesting for the space it opens up for Wesley to discuss one of the more debated theological questions of his day. The text reads as follows:

> Peter, apostle of Jesus Christ, to the chosen, strangers in the world of the diaspora in Pontus, Galatia, Cappadocia, Asia, and Bithynia, according to the foreknowledge of God the Father, in the sanctification of the Spirit, because of the obedience and sprinkling of the blood of Jesus Christ: May grace and peace be multiplied to you. (1 Pet 1:1–2)[9]

---

9. Translation from Joel B. Green, *1 Peter*, Two Horizons New Testament Commentary (Grand Rapids: Eerdmans, 2007) 14.

PART TWO: CONTRIBUTION TO CURRENT THEOLOGICAL PROBLEMS

THE AUDIENCE OF 1 PETER

Two observations will give us a sense of the significance of this letter opening for 1 Peter as a whole.

First, Peter's readers are designated as "chosen, strangers in the world"—that is, they are God's elect *and* they are alienated from their own worlds. Their lives are a paradox: honored by God and chosen by God, but dishonored by people and forced to the margins of social life in their own villages and towns. Peter's letter, then, is addressed to folks who are not at home, who do not belong, folks whose lives are lived on the margins of acceptable society, whose deepest allegiances and dispositions do not line up well with what matters most in the world in which they live. Dispersion, exile—here are images of trauma, expulsion from the homeland, violence, life on the move, erosion of identity, movement from the center to the periphery of the comfortable and the valued, loss of social and cultural roots, torn from the nourishment of family and tradition, refugees.[10] First Peter has its own register of phrases by which to portray the setting of Peter's audience: "tested by fire" (1:7), abused (2:23; 3:9), suffering (2:23), reviled (3:16), slandered (3:16), "reproached for the name of Christ" (4:14), and "suffering as a Christian" (4:16).

We can push harder to distinguish what it means that Peter characterizes his audience as strangers in their own land, as exiles. First, exile refers to an in-between time and an in-between place. Exiles live between memories of home and the freedom that comes with stability on the one hand, and hopes of restoration on the other. Second, exile is a time of identity formation. Living at home and among our own people, we think little of what makes us who we are: our idioms, our typical practices, the foods we eat, our habits of work and play, the taken-for-granted conventions by which we know who we are. Living among others, such questions demand fresh attention. Who are *we* in relation to *them*? What is the basis of *our* constitution as a community? What are *our* characteristic practices? By what strategies do we keep faith with who we are? Third, exile is a time of temptation and testing. The experience of exile resides in this: the social and religious threat confronting a people challenged with the perennial possibility and threat of assimilation and defection. Accordingly, the question arises how Christians ought to live in the midst of wider social currents that do not honor Jesus as Lord of the whole of life.

Grasping the oxymoronic nature of the situation faced by Peter's audience is important, since we do not easily correlate rejection within the human family with honorable status before God. Peter writes this letter to address just this sort of problem. Drawing on the experience of Israel in the Old Testament Peter develops the concept of "stranger" in what might be surprising ways, then. He associates being strangers in the world with God's election, and so with such scriptural themes as call and vocation, covenant, and journey. His perspective anticipates the words of the second-century *Epistle to Diognetus*, which develop this idea more fully:

---

10. Cf. Daniel L. Smith-Christopher, *A Biblical Theology of Exile*, Overtures to Biblical Theology (Minneapolis: Fortress, 2002); Jan Felix Gaertner, ed., *Writing Exile: The Discourse of Displacement in Greco-Roman Antiquity and Beyond*, Mnemosyne: Bibliotheca Classica Batava 83 (Leiden: Brill, 2007).

> For Christians are no different from other people in terms of their country, language or customs. Nowhere do they inhabit cities of their own, use a strange dialect, or live life out of the ordinary.... They live in their respective countries, but only as resident aliens; they participate in all things as citizens, and they endure all things as foreigners. Every foreign territory is a homeland for them, every homeland foreign territory. They marry like everyone else and have children, but they do not expose them once they are born. They share their meals but not their sexual partners. They are found in the flesh but do not live according to the flesh. They live on earth but participate in the life of heaven. They are obedient to the laws that have been made, and by their own lives they supersede the laws. They love everyone and are persecuted by all. They are not understood and they are condemned. They are put to death and made alive. They are impoverished and make many rich. They lack all things and abound in everything. They are dishonored and they are exalted in their dishonors. (5:1–14; LCL)

The first observation, then, concerns the plight of Christians: God's chosen ones, scorned by the world at large. Second, Peter uses three parallel phrases to underscore that being rejected by human beings does not entail having been rejected by God. His audience may be strangers in the world, treated like aliens who do not really belong here, but they have been chosen:

- according to the foreknowledge of God the Father,
- in the sanctification of the Spirit,
- because of the obedience and sprinkling of the blood of Jesus Christ.

Peter thus documents, first, that life on the margins of the world is not a denial of one's chosen status before God. Second, and more importantly, he shows that it is precisely because of the work of the Father, Son, and Holy Spirit in the lives of believers that they are being rejected. How could it be otherwise? Did the world not reject Jesus? Should we not anticipate, then, that the world would reject those who have been chosen by God and made holy by God's Spirit?

WESLEY ON GOD'S FOREKNOWLEDGE

I have gone into some detail here in order to show how the phrase "according to the foreknowledge of God the Father" functions within 1 Peter. Divine choice and alien status are deeply rooted in God's purpose as this comes to expression in the Scriptures. Accordingly, the dissonance of present life, chosen by God but held in contempt in society, is neither a surprise to God nor a contradiction of his plan.

Removed from the work this phrase performs in the presentation of Christian life in 1 Peter, though, this reference to God's foreknowledge came to support what Wesley regarded as a problematic, even unbiblical idea of predestination. As a result, in his *Explanatory Notes upon the New Testament*, he departs from his more usual routine of providing a word of historical background here, an explanation of an important term there. Instead, he outlines a full-blown theological essay on foreknowledge and predestination.

What is predestination? It is not easy to give a straightforward answer, since there are varieties of views in the Christian tradition. Wesley's definitions derive from Calvin's writings and from formalized confessions of faith penned in the sixteenth and seventeenth centuries:

> "Out of the general corruption," says the French Church, "he [God] draws those whom he has elected; leaving the others in the same corruption, according to his immovable decree." "By the decree of God," says the Assembly of English and Scotch Divines, "some are predestinated unto everlasting life, others foreordained to everlasting death." "God has once for all," says Mr. Calvin, "appointed, by an eternal and unchangeable decree, to whom he would give salvation, and whom he would devote to destruction." (*Inst.*, cap. 3, sec. 7)[11]

In other words, for Wesley, predestination could be understood thus: "By virtue of an eternal, unchangeable, irresistible decree of God, one part of humankind are infallibly saved, and the rest infallibly damned; it being impossible that any of the former should be damned, or that any of the latter should be saved."[12] This is the view that Wesley encountered—and countered. Predestination was a key theological battleground in Wesley's day, and his engagement in the discussion was motivated in no small part by the influence of Calvinism within the Methodist movement. Thus, in his sermon on Rom 8:32, "Free Grace," Wesley outlined seven arguments against this notion of predestination:

1. Predestination makes preaching unnecessary and thus nullifies one of the ordinances of God.

2. Predestination undermines holiness. After all, "if a sick man knows that he must unavoidably die or unavoidably recover, though he knows not which, it is not reasonable for him to take any medication at all" (§11).

3. Predestination obstructs the work of the Holy Spirit to bring assurance to the believer and so leads to despair.

4. Predestination destroys the zeal of believers toward works of mercy, such as feeding the hungry or clothing the naked.

5. Predestination renders needless the whole Christian revelation.

6. Predestination introduces contradictions into the message of the Bible.

7. Predestination is an insult to God, since it denies God's justice and mercy and portrays God as having done the work of the devil in leading people to the gates of hell.

In the place of this problematic notion of predestination, Wesley substitutes his teaching on free grace. This is that God gives his grace to everyone, even if not everyone chooses to receive and to act on this gift. To everyone the choice is put, to choose life, to repent, to come and taste.

---

11. John Wesley, "Predestination Calmly Considered," §9.
12. John Wesley, "Free Grace," §9.

What, then, of Wesley's reading of 1 Pet 1:1–2: "chosen ... according to the foreknowledge of God the Father"? The context within which Wesley reads this text is the theological controversy in which he is enmeshed in eighteenth-century England. Hence, he concerns himself immediately and at length with anyone who might misunderstand Peter's reference to God's foreknowledge as support for the (erroneous) doctrine of predestination.

Wesley's opening salvo is his denial that God has the kind of foreknowledge that we humans might attribute to God. With the language of "foreknowledge," Wesley writes, God has adopted human vocabulary that is capable of speaking only partially of God's reality. Peter, then, is simply using language that would be understandable to his readers, rather than describing what is more accurately true of God.

> Strictly speaking, there is no foreknowledge, no more than after-knowledge, with God: but all things are known to him as present from eternity to eternity. This is therefore nothing more than an instance of the divine condescension to our lower capacities.[13]

Clearly, what is at stake here is how we view time, and particularly how we understand God's relation to time.

Wesley held a view that is different from what many have assumed about time, though his view was consistent with that of a number of early church fathers, and of an important figure in philosophical and theological discussions about time and eternity, Boethius. Popular views regard time in linear terms, marking the progress of time from the past to the present to the future. For Boethius, eternity both included and transcended time. Since God inhabits eternity, it follows that all of time is present to God at once. It therefore makes no sense to say that God "foreknew" such-and-such an event. We might experience time in terms of the past, present, and future, but this is not God's experience. This is because nothing is earlier or later than eternity, which God inhabits. Wesley himself knew and embraced the work of Boethius, and this is the basis of his claim that it is absurd to use the term "foreknowledge" with reference to God. Wesley goes on to urge that God's knowledge of all things does not cause things to happen.

These two claims are closely related, and it is worth hearing Wesley's words at length. First, let us review Wesley's understanding of time:

> [W]hen we speak of God's *foreknowledge* we do not speak according to the nature of things, but after the manner of humans. For if we speak properly there is no such thing as either *foreknowledge* or *after-knowledge* in God. All time, or rather all eternity (for time is only that small fragment of eternity allotted to human beings) being present to him at once, he does not know one thing before another, or one thing after another, but sees all things in one point of view, from everlasting to everlasting. As all time, with everything that exists therein, is present with him at once, so he sees at once whatever was, is, or will be to the end of time.

God's experience of time is not the same as our own. Instead, for Wesley, God is omniscient in that he knows all things past, present, and future, because what happened

---

13. Wesley, *Explanatory Notes*, 872.

in the past, what is happening in the present, and what will happen in the future—all understood according to the way we mark time—are always present to God. But if God knows all things, does this not mean that God causes all things? Not at all.

> But observe: we must not think they are because he knows them. No; he knows them because they are. Just as I (if one may be allowed to compare the things of humans with the deep things of God) now know the sun shines. Yet the sun does not shine because I know it: but I know it because it shines. My knowledge takes it as true that the sun shines, but does not in any way cause it. In like manner God knows that humanity sins; for he knows all things. Yet we do not sin because he knows it: but he knows it because we sin. And his knowledge takes it as true that we sin, but does not in any way cause it. In a word, God looking on all ages from the creation to the consummation as a moment, and seeing at once whatever is in the hearts of all the people, knows everyone that does or does not believe in every age or nation. Yet what he knows, whether faith or unbelief, is in no way caused by his knowledge. People are as free in believing, or not believing, as if he did not know it at all.[14]

Wesley's view of time is thus key to his understanding of foreknowledge and predestination.

It remains, then, to inquire into the true meaning of predestination—or, more particularly, what it means in the words of 1 Peter that people have been chosen "according to the foreknowledge of God the Father." For Wesley, God's "fore-appointment" consists in this: (1) whoever believes will be saved from the guilt and power of sin; (2) whoever endures until the end shall be saved eternally; and (3) whoever receives the gift of faith thereby becomes the child of God, and receives the gift of the Holy Spirit so that they are enabled to live as Christ lived.

The way Wesley lays out the life of faith might be called "synergistic," meaning that the life of faith requires cooperation between God and the person of faith. As Wesley himself puts it, predestination involves both God and the human being; at every step along the way "[God's] promise and [human] duty go hand in hand. All is a free gift; and yet such is the gift, that the final result depends on our future obedience."[15]

Having followed Wesley through some of the side streets and back alleys of eighteenth-century theological controversy, we may now seem to be far removed from the opening words of 1 Peter. We might even wonder if Peter himself would be amazed at what has become of what must have seemed so simple a phrase, "chosen . . . according to the foreknowledge of God the Father." Or we might wonder how Peter would respond to Wesley's claim, "God looking on all ages from the creation to the consummation as a moment, and seeing at once whatever is in the hearts of all the people, knows everyone that does or does not believe in every age or nation." In reality, though, what is central to Wesley in this whole discussion is not at all alien to Peter's message. Wesley takes a circuitous route to get there, but this is because of the terrain of the theological skirmishes he

---

14. Wesley, "On Predestination," §5.
15. Wesley, *Explanatory Notes*, 872.

was forced to navigate in eighteenth-century Britain. But the synergism for which Wesley argued is no more important to Wesley than it was to Peter.

We may recall that Peter's audience consists of followers of Christ who live paradoxical lives. They are chosen of God but strangers in the world. As strangers in the world, they are the brunt of the world's scorn, insults, and shame. How will they respond? *This is the central matter.* Peter directs them along two paths at once. On the one hand, he affirms in no uncertain terms their having been chosen by God, their having been made holy by the Holy Spirit, and their having been liberated by the atoning death of Jesus. In the world, they are dishonored, but before God they are honored indeed.

On the other hand, from the beginning of this letter to its conclusion, he calls them to certain behaviors in the world. Note, for example, how in 1 Pet 1:3–21 Peter's affirmation of God's graciousness and Peter's analysis of his audience's status before God opens the way for Peter to articulate the nature of their behavior in the world. His message moves from the indicative to the imperative, from "is" to "ought." Thus, on account of God's mercy, believers must *set their hope* completely on the coming grace (v. 13); on account of God's holiness, believers must *become holy in every aspect of life* (vv. 14–16); and, on account of the Father's impartial justice and the liberation effected by Christ's sacrificial death, believers must *live in reverent fear* (vv. 17–21).

Moving further into the letter, we read that they must follow the example of Christ:

> For to this you have been called, because Christ also suffered for you, leaving you an example, so that you should follow in his steps. "He committed no sin, and no deceit was found in his mouth." When he was abused, he did not return abuse; when he suffered, he did not threaten; but he entrusted himself to the one who judges justly. (1 Pet 2:21–23, NRSV)

They are to set aside the immorality of their former lives, they are to forego retaliation for the abuse they suffer, and they are to cultivate such Christian practices as doing good, practicing hospitality, and extending themselves in acts of mutual love and service to one another (e.g., 1:22; 3:8–17; 4:7–11, 15, 19). And if they do, then this is the promise they have: "And after you have suffered for a little while, the God of all grace, who has called you to his eternal glory in Christ, will himself restore, support, strengthen, and establish you" (1 Pet 5:10). Is Wesley's own conclusion—"All is a free gift; and yet such is the gift, that the final result depends on our future obedience"—not fully at home here?

CONCLUSION

Theological interpretation in recent days has drawn its inspiration from Barth. Without denying the significance of his contribution, it remains the case that his work is not the only model we have. Unlike Barth, and unlike more recent participants in the enterprise of theological interpretation, John Wesley's exegetical work is interesting in that he neither tried to make peace with historical criticism while reading Scripture theologically nor engaged in theological interpretation as an alternative to (or as a denial of) historical criticism. This, of course, is a product of his historical moment. Situated as he was on the front end of the historical-critical movement, Wesley's works witness the importance of historical considerations without imagining that historical inquiry might overwhelm the church's need to hear God's voice in Scripture, or that historical inquiry might claim to provide without remainder the "meaning" of a biblical text. Wesley's theological exegesis is interesting in part, then, because he had no need to adopt a defensive stance vis-à-vis historical-critical method.

What, then, was the design of his theological interpretation? In the example from 1 Peter I have sketched, Wesley demonstrates (1) the need for interpretation—that is, the simple reality that the words of Scripture are not self-interpreting—and in this case the way philosophical considerations can bear on how we read a biblical text; (2) the importance of context in interpretation—underscoring in his case the ecclesial and theological contexts within which God's foreknowledge is understood; (3) and the simultaneity of Scripture—that is, the capacity of the biblical text to speak as divine word in the first century as well as the eighteenth. More needs to be said about Wesley's practices of theological interpretation, especially as this is witnessed in his *Explanatory Notes* and sermons, but these are already important hints. Here we find the beginnings of answers to questions about how theological interpretation might take the biblical text seriously without neglecting or prioritizing historical criticism. And here we find evidence that Wesley's theological interpretation, and our own, need not be "uncritical."

16

Preaching and Practicing Wisdom

MICHAEL PASQUARELLO, III

THIS CHAPTER DISCUSSES THE kind of practical wisdom which characterized Wesley's preaching ministry in eighteenth-century England; a ministry which entailed a renewal and reintegration of Christian devotion, doctrine, and discipline. Contrary to much contemporary homiletic wisdom, the truth and goodness of Christian doctrine is irrelevant to neither evangelism nor the building up of Christian communites through the proclamation of the Word. Rather, knowing and loving the Triune God is necessary if the church is to be formed in the pattern of its crucified and risen Lord. In other words, the truth we know, love, and proclaim is embodied by faith in the activity of the Father through the Son who rules and indwells the church through the presence and work of the Holy Spirit. What follows is offered with deep appreciation for Dr. Larry Wood, whose life and work as a Wesleyan theologian and minister has not only exemplified this kind of practical wisdom, but has also encouraged its cultivation in a generation of students.

Although the efficacy of preaching is dependent upon the presence of the risen Christ whose voice is made audible by the work of the Holy Spirit, it also includes the participation of preachers who have been formed by the practical wisdom intrinsic to faith in the Word that works through love. In other words, the practical wisdom of preaching receives its shape in knowing and loving the truth and goodness embodied by Christ and the witness of Scripture, according to "the analogy of faith." This presumes, however, that the source and goal of preaching is love of God and neighbor—or holiness—which is the gift of the indwelling Spirit through which we know and bear witness to Christ and his work in our midst and in the world. As Wesley writes,

> O who is able to describe such a messenger of God, faithfully executing his high office! Working together with God; with the great Author both of the old and the new creation! See his Lord, the eternal Son of God, going forth on that work of omnipotence, and creating heaven and earth by the breath of his mouth! See the

servant whom he delighteth to honour; fulfilling the counsel of his will, and in his name speaking the word whereby is raised a new spiritual creation.¹

For Wesley, "good" preaching is the good work of good preachers which participates in God's goodness by the grace of Jesus Christ through the witness of the Spirit. The source and goal of such "good" news is the Triune God who delights in communicating his goodness through an intensely intimate communion of love to redeem creation.² Moreover, the redemption of God's good creation—viewed theologically as coming from God and returning to God—entails an "ecstatic" participation in Christ who orders the church's life through the Spirit's grace, gifts, blessings, and empowerments.³

Attending to Wesley in this manner will involve us in a conversation beginning with the early church and extending through the sixteenth-century for which theology—*theologia*—was a practical habit, or *habitus*, an aptitude of the intellect and will having the primary characteristic of knowledge seeking wisdom in love. In earlier times some saw this as a directly infused gift of God which was intimately tied to faith, prayer, virtue, and desire for God. Later, with the advent of formal theological investigation, others saw it as a form of wisdom which could also be promoted, deepened, and extended by human study and argument. However, the meaning of theology did not displace the more primary sense of the term; theology as a practical *habitus*, the habit of attending to God's saving wisdom in Christ through the work of the Holy Spirit in the worshiping life of the church.⁴

Theology, then, is a practical way of knowing which directs the mind and heart to God as the end of all human knowledge, desire, and action. This saving wisdom is mediated by the witness of Scripture in the ministry of the church through which the Spirit engenders faith that works through love of God, the neighbor, and all creatures in God. The mission of God is thus acknowledged within a living tradition grounded in, and continuous with, the sending of Christ and the Spirit who call forth and create the church to embody the distinctive habits of "social holiness." Or as Bryan Stone writes,

> My point . . . is that Christian salvation is ecclesial—that its very shape in the world is a participation in Christ through worship, shared practices, disciplines, loyalties, and social patterns of his body, the church. To construe the message of the gospel in such a way as to hide what Christians called ecclesial is to miss the point of what God is up to in history—the calling forth and creation of a people. The most evangelistic thing the church can do, therefore, is to be the church not merely in public but as a new and alternative public; not merely in society but as a new and distinct society, a new and unprecedented social existence . . . "Social holiness," to

1. "An Address to the Clergy," *The Works of John Wesley*, 3rd ed. (Grand Rapids: Baker, 1978) 488.

2. Daniel A. Keating, "Justification, Sanctification, and Divinization in Thomas Aquinas," in *Aquinas on Doctrine*, eds. Thomas G. Weinandy, Daniel A. Keating, and John Y. Yocum (New York: T. & T. Clark, 2004) 152–55; Matthew L. Lamb, "The Eschatology of St. Thomas," in *Aquinas on Doctrine*, 226.

3. Pinckaers, "Reappropriating Aquinas's Account of the Passions," in *The Pinckaers Reader*, 285–86; Lamb, "Eschatology of St. Thomas," 225.

4. Farley, *Theologia*, 33–39; see also the survey and definition of theology in Aidan Nichols, O.P., *The Shape of Catholic Theology: An Introduction to its Sources, Principles, and History* (Collegeville, MN: Liturgical, 1991).

use John Wesley's phrase, is both the aim and the intrinsic logic of evangelism. The practices of the church that embody this social holiness are the witness that becomes evangelism in the hands of the Spirit.[5]

This theological and ecclesial perspective unites Wesley, the Oxford Don, and Welsey, the popular evangelist; two images that, if divided, betray a theory/practice split which perpetuates views of Wesley as either an irrelevant intellectual or anti-intellectual pragmatist. Dividing Christian doctrine and the Christian life, this modern dogma obscures the wisdom of Wesley's "practical divinity" in which the experience and ministry of the church was bound to and shaped by doctrinal convictions, just as theological understanding was grounded in and enriched by participation in the faith and life of the church.

Geoffrey Wainwright summarizes Wesley's integrity of vision and practice in the following manner,

> First, he looked to the Scriptures as the primary and abiding testimony to the redemptive work of God in Christ. Second, he was utterly committed to the ministry of evangelism, where the gospel was to be preached to every creature and needed only to be accepted in faith. Third, he valued with respect to the Christian Tradition and the doctrine of the Church a generous orthodoxy, wherein theological opinions might vary as long as they were consistent with the apostolic teaching. Fourth, he expected sanctification to show itself in the moral earnestness and loving deeds of the believers. Fifth, he manifested and encouraged a social concern that was directed toward the neediest of neighbors. Sixth, he found in the Lord's Supper a sacramental sign of the fellowship graciously bestowed by the Triune God and the responsive praise of those who will glorify God and enjoy him forever.[6]

Wesley approached the interpretation of Scripture as both an act of faith and means of grace through which the understanding and desire are engaged by the Word and the Spirit to induce the knowledge and love of God. He rightly insisted that Methodist preachers engage in daily prayer and study for the purpose of nourishing faith, deepening understanding, and inspiring love—for God and neighbors in God—which enhances one's capacities for thinking, living, and speaking according to the "mind that was in Christ."[7] David Cunningham comments on the loss of such character in our time,

> The persuasive role of character was seriously devalued during the Enlightenment. The rise of experimental science emphasized the goal of neutrality, which was thought to be guaranteed only through radical detachment: subject and object were thus torn asunder. On this view, an experiment needed only to take place under properly controlled conditions; the character of the experimenter was irrelevant. Empirical experimentation tended to focus attention away from how things appear in nature, and toward exceptions to the rule. This narrow focus contributed to the

---

5. Bryan Stone, *Evangelism after Christendom: The Theology and Practice of Christian Witness* (Grand Rapids: Brazos, 2007) 15–16.

6. Geoffrey Wainwright, *Methodists in Dialog* (Nashville: Anbingdon, 1995) 283–84.

7. On Wesleyan spirituality see the essay by Geoffrey Wainwright, "Trinitarian Theology and Wesleyan Holiness" in *Orthodox and Wesleyan Spirituality*, ed. S. T. Kimbrough (Crestwood, NY: St. Vladimir's Seminary Press, 2002) 59–80.

reduction of the meaning of ethos from a complex, holistic *habitus* to a mere series of rules and regulations.[8]

Forgotten in this empirically derived view is that the goal of Christian faith, hope, and love is the restoration of the image of God in human creatures; an image which has been defaced but is now being restored by the Spirit through participation in the fellowship of the Father and the Son. "This renewal into the image of God takes place in the embodiment of a new law, which the Holy Spirit gives internally. This 'new law' is a participation in Christ's human righteousness where the Spirit sanctifies the believer."[9]

The life of Christian people, which includes preachers as exemplary witnesses, is the fruit of the new law of the Gospel ruling the intellect, affect, and will through the grace of the Holy Spirit. Becoming a preacher entails cultivating capacities for discerning the truth and goodness of Christ through the illumination of the Spirit which engenders the knowledge we live by in the intellectual and moral virtues. Wesley writes of this transformation,

> There can be no doubt that with this love to God and man a suitable conversation will follow. His "communication," that is, discourse, will "be always in grace, seasoned with salt," and meet to "minister grace to its hearers." He will always "open his mouth with wisdom," and there will be "in his tongue the law of kindness." Hence his affectionate words will "distil as the dew, and as the rain upon the tender herb." And men will know "it is not" he only "that speaks, but the Spirit of the Father that speaketh in him." His actions will spring from the same source as his words, even from the abundance of a loving heart.[10]

The virtue of practical wisdom is committed to pursuing the good which is rooted in a definite community and tradition with favored character, dispositions, and habits. As a way of "knowing in action," practical wisdom, or prudence, is sustained by good character and habits which enable discernment of the good for the sake of doing good acts that are a source of joy. ". . . . the good practitioner has been formed by a history of participation in the practice itself. His or her experience of serving the end or *telos* of the practice—and recurrently trying to discover what this concretely requires—has laid down certain dispositions of character which, through discipline and direction, enable and energize."[11] Writing in *Back to the Rough Ground*, Joseph Dunne comments,

> For this reason, a practically wise person will possess skills of deliberation, discernment, and decisiveness that make him or her capable of transforming knowledge of reality into virtuous speech and action: "Prudence not only includes making the right decision, but also demands we carry out the decision. In this way prudence links the intellectual and moral virtues (knowing and doing). Moreover, prudence

---

8. David S. Cunningham, *Faithful Persuasion: In Aid of a Rhetoric of Christian Theology* (Notre Dame: University of Notre Dame Press, 1991) 107.

9. D. Stephen Long, *John Wesley's Moral Theology: The Quest for God and Goodness* (Nashville: Abingdon, 2005) 174.

10. *Works*, vol. IV., 70–71.

11. Joseph Dunne, *Back to the Rough Ground: Practical Judgment and the Lure of Technique* (Notre Dame: University of Notre Dame Press, 1993) 378.

shapes the other moral virtues insofar as it enables the just person to act justly, the courageous person to act bravely, and the temperate person to act with self-control."[12]

Dunne's discussion challenges an instrumentalist, "cause and effect" approach to practice which frames objectives in advance, anticipates plans, controls the moves one will make, and then evaluates both the activity and results on terms defined by "effectiveness."[13] Following the moral philosophy of Aristotle, Dunne argues persuasively that practice is irreducible to external techniques or procedures, but requires a non-technical, personal, and participatory way of knowing which cannot be framed in terms of detachment, universality, and utility. This discussion shows that cause and effect utility, while presuming to be only "practical," actually embodies a definite kind of theory which is effectively reduced to mere skill and technique with no larger purpose or end.

Dunne defines this type of activity as a form of "making" which is specified by a maker who determines its end or goal in advance: "*Techne*, then, is the kind of knowledge possessed by an expert maker, it gives him a clear conception of the why and wherefore, the how and with what of the making process and enables him, through the capacity to offer a rational account of it, to preside over his activity with secure mastery."[14] In contrast to the activity of making or producing which proceeds by explanation, prediction, and control for acting externally upon the raw material of one's work, Dunne discusses the social activity of practice. A practice is conducted in public places in cooperation with others and with no ulterior purpose or goals external to sharing in the truth and goodness of the practice itself; and with a view to no other end or outcome than the moral intentions, habits, and qualities exemplified by wise, experienced participants of the practice.

This definition of shared communal activity may arguably be extended to Christian practices such as worship, the intepretation of Scripture and preaching, evangelization, catechesis, training in discipleship and pastoral care. Activities of this nature are carried out in such a way to realize and demonstrate as their true end those virtues, dispositions, and excellences valued by the church as a historical community and constitutive of its life and witness. This will require prudence, as Josef Pieper writes,

> Prudence, then, is the mold and mother of all the virtues, the circumspect and resolute shaping power of our minds which transforms knowledge of reality into realization of the good. It holds within itself the humility of silent; that is to say, of unbiased perception; the trueness-to-being of memory; the art of receiving counsel; alert, composed readiness for the unexpected. Prudence means the studied seriousness and, as it were, the filter of deliberation, and at the same time, the brave boldness to make final decisions. It means purity, straightforwardness, candor, and

---

12. Michael Dauphinias and Mattew Levering, *Knowing the Love of Christ: An Introduction to the Theology of St. Thomas Aquinas* (Notre Dame: University of Notre Dame Press, 2002) 57.

13. Dunne, *Back to the Rough Ground*, 235.

14. Ibid., 319.

simplicity of character; it means standing superior to the utilitarian complexities of mere, "tactics."[15]

Dunne interprets this kind of activity, that is, *phronesis,* or practical knowledge, as a kind of "knowing how" which is historical, traditioned, personal, embodied and shared with others. In other words, the wisdom of practice is as much a matter of who we are and to whom we belong as much as what we know.

> In questioning the attainability of technical mastery over these areas an alternative to the technicist picture has been developed. In this alternative picture, practical knowledge has been shown as a fruit which can grow only in the soul of a person's experience and character; apart from cultivation of this soil, there is no artifice for making it available in a way that would count. In exposing oneself to the kind of experience and acquiring the kind of character that will yield requisite knowledge, one is not the kind of epistemic subject that has been canonized by the modern tradition of philosophy. One is at the same time a feeling, expressing, and acting person; and one's knowledge is inseparable from one as such.[16]

Dunne's description of these two distinct modes of activity can illumine how preaching articulates and embodies the practical wisdom that we are to love God and our neighbor as ourselves. Seen from this perspective, good preaching will be characterized by a particular kind of history, experience, judgment, and influence which, although rooted in the wisdom of Scripture and the Christian past, remains open to gifts, dispositions, and habits appropriate to hearing the Word and responding to the Spirit in the present.

In other words, preaching is a form of "ecstatic" speech which is enabled by the Holy Spirit through ongoing encounter with the living Word in worship, the sacraments, and the other means of grace. On the other hand, when preaching is reduced to following "how to" steps—the procedural application of abstract, disembodied principles—its character is limited to technocratic knowledge possessed by an "expert" belonging to a specialized craft. What this means, however, is that the identity of "preacher" has been defined as a person whose primary form of knowing consists of applying rules to effect results according to external criteria such as "relevance," "effectiveness," or "church growth." Stone comments,

> For if a practice [such as preaching] can be described and understood apart from the specifying ends (in other words, can be described in soley pragmatic terms), then one must ask whether the ends have been made external to the means, thereby disqualifying the practice as *practice*. Excellence is then determined by the efficacy of the activity in achieving or producing an assumed end rather than by the character of the practice itself embodying an end to which it is internally related.[17]

Craig Dykstra has commented extensively on a tendency toward reducing Christian practices to universalistic and abstract "one size fits all" procedures rather than the skills

---

15. Josef Pieper, *The Four Cardinal Virtues: Prudence*, trans. Richard and Clara Winston (Notre Dame: University of Notre Dame Press, 1966) 22.

16. Ibid., 358.

17. Stone, *Evangelism After Christendom*, 33–34.

of living and speaking faithfully according to scriptural wisdom which is embodied by participatory, communal ways of knowing tested by the wisdom of God and the wisdom of the Church. Dykstra's discussion parallels that of Dunne; that when practice is reduced to making something happen—a combination of knowledge, power, and the application of skills and techniques for producing desired outcomes and results—its nature will be understood technologically, individualistically, and a-historically. What matter most in this kind of activity is the merely functional, which operates through cause-and-effect relations and is dependent upon its utility for attaining immediate ends—rather than convictions and virtues intrinsic to the church's faith, identity, tradition, and, wisdom.[18]

Thus what is true or good and what is practical become separate issues; just as the faith of the preacher, the method of preaching, the content and context of preaching, are divided and treated as discrete, unrelated matters for the pursuit of "effectiveness." When this occurs, fidelity between speaker and words, language and truth, and language and deeds, are lost. Dykstra argues that this popular notion of practice, predicated upon effectiveness for production rather than excellence of the whole person, will in the end be left with no practice [and no practicioners]. If what practice that exists is reduced to mere technical routine or process with no point other than effecting change, it will exclude both the practice and participants from an ongoing history of knowledge, understanding, and love in which the distinctive truth, wisdom, and habits of the church and its way of life are handed down, received, and learned.[19]

The indispensability of prudence for the moral life provides an alternative to the popular vision of preacher as "Gnostic technician," since practical wisdom, as the fruit which grows in the soil of one's knowledge and love of God, is inseparable from the whole self as a thinking, feeling, expressing, and acting person. "In the end the guarantee of the trustworthiness of practical judgments and the validity of moral judgments lies not in any code but in the verdict of good, experienced, wise people."[20] Such practiced wisdom cannot be produced by a body of generalized knowledge, a set of principles and procedures, or a "method" which is "applied" according to technical rationality and mastery for the "effective" achievement of pre-determined outcomes. Rather, as Dunne states,

> To speak of "action" as well as (but not separate from) knowledge and expression is to advert to the network of undertakings within one finds oneself—the unpredictability, open-endedness, and to the hazardousness of one's undertakings within this network—the unpredictability of what these undertakings set in train. No one is exempt from action in this sense (a sense which allows that speech often is action); it is through it that one discloses and achieves the unique identity that distinguishes one as a person; and at the same time it reveals the dept of one's interdependence with others . . . When one's actions are not imposed on materials but are directed to-

---

18. Craig Dykstra, *Growing In the Life of Faith: Education in Christian Practices*, 2nd ed. (Louisville: Westminster John Knox, 2005) 53–83.

19. Dykstra, *Growing in the Life of Faith*, 76–77; Dykstra, "Reconceiving Practice in Theological Inquiry and Education" in *Virtues & Practices in the Christian Tradition: Christian Ethics after Mcyntire*, ed. Nancy Murhpy, Brad J. Kallenberg, and Mark Thiessen Nation (Harrisburg: Trinity, 1997) 164–73.

20. Dunne, *Back to the Rough Ground*, 358–59.

ward others persons . . . mastery is not attainable. One cannot determine in advance the efficacy of one's words and deeds.[21]

What we love plays a significant role in shaping our judgments. Loves moves the intellect to engage in the process of practical reasoning and focuses the intellect's attention upon certain objects rather than others because of the intensity of its love.[22] For reason to discover the right act to be done, here and now, love in the will must be ordered wisely toward the practical good that is timely and appropriate. However, love ordered well will be directed toward God as its true end, while disordered love will be directed toward the self, to created things as their own ends, or as means to ends less than God. Prudence is akin to "love discerning well" with the power of the intellect working through practical judgment, counsel, and direction, an insightfulness which directs one's reason, desire, and actions to the end of love for and in God.[23]

Because prudence is "love choosing wisely," it is in the service of human excellence—loving the truth and desiring the good—which renders happy the person who knows, judges, speaks, and acts well.

> . . . prudence is a kind of practical wisdom receiving a new, profound light from faith and a higher strength from charity; which unites it to God and deepens its understanding of the neighbor. Furthermore, it is disposed through the gifts of counsel, understanding, and wisdom to correspond to the movements of the Holy Spirit. Thus enlightened and penetrated, prudence becomes capable of fulfilling its role as director of action according to the designs of God. Its intervention is indispensable, because by means of prudence the theological virtues, like the others, can be embodied in concrete action. Without it, even charity could not discern and follow the right path with precision.[24]

There can be no wisdom or virtue without the gift of charity, since the goal of moral discernment is dependent upon knowing God through faith penetrated by love. Flowing from the will to the intellect, charity transforms prudence for knowing the right end and choosing the right means in conformity to that end. John Mahoney points out that the wisdom of the Gospel and the illumination of the Spirit are the key elements of the New Law which inspired the prophets and apostles and moved the saints to act. Thus in addition to the union of heart and mind with God, the virtue of practical wisdom will require moral skills that enable assessment of specific situations and transformation of knowledge into appropriate action; for speaking or doing the right thing, for the right reason, in the right manner, for the right persons, and in the right circumstances.[25]

The mark of practical wisdom is a life ordered by love for God and the neighbor through prayer and the virtues. The virtue of faith grants knowledge of divine revelation as articulated by the articles of faith (the Creed) engendering the gift of wisdom that

---

21. Ibid., 361.
22. Sherwin, *By Knowledge & By Love*, 102.
23. Ibid., 106–18.
24. Pinckaers, "Conscience and Christian Tradition," in *The Pinckaers Reader*, 332–33.
25. John Mahoney, S.J., *Seeking the Spirit: Essays in Moral and Pastoral Theology* (Denville, NJ: Dimension, 1982) 67–69.

judges their truth according to God's self-giving in Christ. "The unfolding of doctrine in the practices of the church—for it is both a doing and a saying—serves to enfold the church into the very life of God. Thus all theology is finally mystical, a habit or "wisdom" given by the Spirit."[26] Moreover, the end of wisdom, as the gift which unites human being and acting, ". . . is to let the primary action of God to spread out in us the divine being, the divine life."[27]

While the Holy Spirit bestows the gift of wisdom, the virtue of practical wisdom is indispensable for directing virtuous performances of the gospel that participate in, and are improvisations of, God's prior performance of the Word in Jesus Christ. The virtue of prudence thus lies at the heart of the preaching life, since without prudence we cannot speak in ways appropriate to becoming "holy performances." "Good" preaching, then, communicates God's goodness for the common good of the church which is dependent upon ". . . . a wisdom embodied in lives, practices and communities through the continual improvising of life in the Spirit shaped according to the 'mind of Christ.'"[28]

The preaching life, then, is shaped by the gift of wisdom which is received through attentiveness to Christ and the working of the Spirit's grace. "In other words, performance that is truly improvisatory requires the kind of attentiveness, attunement, and alertness traditionally associated with contemplative prayer. All of which is to say that the virtuoso is played even as she plays . . . likewise, language speaks the speaker as much as if not more than the speaker speaks the language."[29] Practicing such wisdom requires ingenuity, flexibility, and reliance upon an insightfulness that is immediate and intuitive, a way of "seeing" that is tested through long experience of patient decision making and good actions within the communion of love that is the church.[30] Fr. Cessario writes,

> Prudence aims at shaping the character of Christian believers so that they can fully participate in the communion of charity that abides in the Church. In the moral life of each person, the virtue of prudence must both conform and be conformed; prudence must be conformed to moral wisdom, i.e., to all the human intelligence can learn about a given subject. Prudence also learns from divine truth. In turn, prudence conforms to human behavior, so that human action lies . . . in accord with right direction that the ends or goods of human nature stipulate. Prudence brings us into right conformity with the "thing" or *res*, with reality as God knows the world to be.[31]

Practical wisdom requires the integration of human wisdom, virtue, and the will of God; the apprehension of an analogy between divine providence and the virtuous acts of

---

26. Gerald Loughlin, "The Basis and Authority of Doctrine," in *The Cambridge Companion to Christian Doctrine*, 57.

27. Aidan Nichols, O.P., *Discovering Aquinas: An Introduction to His Life, Work, and Influence* (Grand Rapids: Eerdmans, 2002) 106.

28. David F. Ford, *Christian Wisdom: Desiring God and Learning in Love* (Cambridge: Cambridge University Press, 2007) 7.

29. Hauerwas and Fodor, "Performing Faith," 81.

30. Romanus Cessario, O.P., *The Virtues, Or the Examined Life* (London/New York: Continuum, 2002) 99–121.

31. Cessario, *Virtues, Or the Examined Life*, 114.

prudent human beings.³² Moreover, because the work of prudence puts right reason into emotion and desire, it is completed by judgment drawing from all the virtues to act as the "eyes and ears" of human excellence.³³ "... the very grammar of faith points up to a vital sense in which theology is intrinsically performative. Word and deed are inseparable in the Christian life and practice; but since word and action will not always or completely coincide, Christians have always been concerned about 'getting it right.'"³⁴ Pervading the whole of one's life, prudence is the capacity which judges rightly in uniting theological knowledge, love, and the activity of preaching, in virtuous performances of the gospel. As Fr. Chenu comments,

> Having these transcendent convictions and being empowered by its hope for eternal happiness, prudence still follows its appropriate means and keeps to its task and its functional orientation. Its efficacy remains bound up with the ways and means of its practical knowledge. Neither divine nor human love dismantles its ways of acting or its resources. The gospel moves through it.³⁵

Thomas Aquinas' description of the relation between wisdom and prudence highlights the importance of the linkage between the Word of God, what is preached, the person who preaches, those to whom we preach, and the end (s) to which we preach.

> Since prudence concerns human affairs and wisdom, by contrast is concerned with the highest cause [God], it is not possible for prudence to be a greater virtue than wisdom.... Likewise Paul says, "The spiritual person judges everything and is judged by no one." So prudence does not get involved in the highest things which are the concern of wisdom, but rather governs matters that are subordinated to wisdom. In this way, prudence ... is the servant of wisdom, because prudence prepares the way for wisdom a lot like the doorkeeper prepares the way for a king.³⁶ (ST, I. II. q. 66. art. 5, resp.1)

Prudence, then, is neither a mechanical art nor a technical skill. Rather, it is a capacity linking the intellectual and moral virtues for choosing good ends that are appropriate to a particular moral activity such as preaching (i.e., receptivity to the Spirit's grace, attentiveness to and the praise of God, the gifts of faith, hope, and love, building up the Body of Christ according to the law of the gospel) rather than external (i.e., cultural relevance, pragmatic effectiveness, institutional self-promotion or preservation, a preacher's program or a particular social agenda). "The intellectual virtue of prudence is concerned with judging well among those means not only as effective for the end but also appropriate to me."³⁷

---

32. Fergus Kerr, O.P., *After Aquinas: Versions of Thomism* (London: Blackwell, 2002) 123.

33. Pinckaers, "Conscience and Christian Tradition" in *The Pinckaers Reader*, 332–33.

34. Hauerwas and Fodor, "Performing Faith," 82.

35. Marie-Dominic Chenu, O.P., *Aquinas and His Role in Theology*, trans. Paul Philibert, O.P. (Collegeville: Liturgical Press, 2002) 111.

36. *Summa Theologica*, I. II q. 66. art 5. resp.1.

37. Herbert McCabe, *The Good Life: Ethics and the Pursuit of Happiness*, ed. Brian Davies, O.P. (London and New York: Continuum, 2005) 91.

"Good" preaching is the practice of knowledge which is cultivated by receptivity to God's incarnate Wisdom revealed in the apostolic witness to Christ; a non-utilitarian way of speaking that awakens the church to faith and love to God in ways that are timely and appropriate to building up the Body of Christ.

> Clearly the horizon of prudence or the Christian conscience is as a broad as the Gospel of the Kingdom of Heaven, which the apostles were commissioned to preach to the whole world. This means, among other things that while being entirely personal, Christian prudence cannot be constrained within the limits of an individual life ... or focused on the self. It is called to open outward and to collaborate with God's plans for the church, to become an ecclesial prudence or conscience, whose work will consist in building up the Body of Christ in great affairs as well as small ...[38]

The collaboration of charity and prudence works to integrate one's thoughts, affections, and actions for imitating the second person of the Trinity, the incarnate Wisdom of God. "Charity unites the virtues by ordering them to God, our ultimate end and our complete beatitude. Prudence ... takes up the other end ... and governs each concrete action and fulfills its function of judging all the other virtues, including the theological ones."[39] Governed by prudence, the knowledge of faith is transformed into fitting performances of the Word through human speech that turns both preacher and listeners to the One who is the source and end of all our actions and words. Thomas Hibbs writes,

> There is an inescapable reciprocity between understanding and loving in the Christian conception of the good life. Although the virtue of faith resides in the intellect, the object of faith is simultaneously the first truth of the good that is the "end of all desires and actions" ... The reciprocity of contemplation and action is also evident in the connection between the theological virtues and the gifts of the Holy Spirit. The goal is union with a personal God ... The intimate connection between charity and the gift of wisdom is instructive. The gift of wisdom is the fruit of charity ... It empowers us to conduct life in light of divine truth ... Like prudence charity efficaciously orders the whole of human life and integrates cognition and affection.[40]

As a Christian practice, preaching is attentive to and affected by the presence of Christ who constitutes the church as his Body through the work of the Holy Spirit. In other words, the practical wisdom of preaching is engendered by divine grace which works through the virtues of faith, hope, and love to enable judgment and discernment for speaking "to the right person, to the right extent, at the right time, with the right aim, and in the right way." Or as Wesley writes: "... the love of God and man not only filling my heart, but shining through my whole conversation."[41] Dunne concludes that such wisdom and virtue requires a form of kenosis, or self-emptying,

---

38. Pinckaers, "Conscience and Christian Tradition," in *Pinckaers Reader*, 333–34.
39. Ibid., 349.
40. Hibbs, *Virtue's Splendor*, 188–89.
41. Wesley, "Address to the Clergy," 485, 499.

.... divesting itself of godlike notions and coming to accept that it cannot have and therefore must no longer aspire to a god's eye view for the human condition. And this movement away from detachment, sovereignty, and imperturbability has at the same time been a movement into and a taking upon itself the burdens of finitude, contingency, and situatedness. In subverting the Cartesian subject, it has been reincarnating the real person in the world of history and language, actions and involvement with other people—and, of course, in his/her own affective and bodily being.[42]

In the sermon "The Circumcision of the Heart," Wesley writes of the particular kind of self-emptying or humility which will be required if we are to see the fullness of reality; with the eyes of the heart and understanding illumined by the "mind of Christ" which was embodied in his obedience of love to the Father.

> In general we may observe it is that habitual disposition of soul which in the Sacred Writings is termed "holiness," and which directly implies the being cleansed from sin, "from all filthiness of both flesh and spirit," and by consequence of being endued with those virtues which were also in Christ Jesus, the being so "renewed in the image of your mind" as to be "perfect, as our Father in heaven is perfect."... This is that lowliness of mind which they have learned of Christ who follow his example and tread in his steps. And this knowledge of their disease, whereby they are more and more cleansed from one part of it, pride and vanity, disposes them to embrace a willing mind the second thing implied in "circumcision of the heart"—that faith which alone is able to make them whole, which is the one medicine given under heaven to heal their sickness.[43]

An example of Wesley's practical wisdom is evinced by a letter he wrote in December 1751, when the spread of evangelical revival was provoking both enthusiasm and resistance. Wesley wrote to an inquirer on the subject of "preaching Christ," presumably after pondering this matter for a period of three months.[44] His description of "preaching Christ" is both theological and pastoral in scope and provides a summary of God's mission —the love of God for sinners demonstrated in the life, death, resurrection, and intercession of Christ and his blessings—and the law—setting forth the commands of Christ, and in particular, the Sermon on the Mount.

This practical vision was cultivated by Wesley's study of Scripture and intimate knowledge of the Christian life. Revealing his theological and pastoral understanding of the relation between the law and Gospel, his comments reflect the practical judgment which is required to address a wide range of spiritual and moral conditions, including that of sinners, the justified, the diligent, the proud, the careless and weak in understanding.[45]

Wesley directs particular attention to Methodist preacher John Wheatley, whom he describes as a "gospel preacher" and "neither clear nor sound in the faith." According to Wesley, Wheatley's sermons had the sound of "an unconnected rhapsody of unmean-

---

42. Ibid., 374.

43. *Works*, Vol. 1, 405.

44. For the following description I am drawing from *The Works of John Wesley*, 3rd ed. (Grand Rapids: Baker, 1978) 11:486–92.

45. Ibid., 488–90.

ing words . . ." and "Verses, smooth and soft as cream, in which was neither depth nor stream." Wesley was concerned with the effects of "gospel" preaching, which despite its rhetorical finesse and popular appeal, lacked both theological coherence and moral wisdom. Long on promises and short on commands, it corrupted hearers, vitiated their taste, ruined their desire for sound teaching, and spoiled their spiritual appetites, feeding them "sweetmeats" until the genuine wine of the kingdom seemed insipid. Wesley concluded that while such popular "gospel preachers" were adept at attracting and pleasing large crowds, their preaching was characterized by "cordial upon cordial" that destroyed listeners' capacities for retaining and digesting the pure milk of the Word.[46]

On the other hand, the Methodist manner of preaching provided a practical wisdom for construing both law and Gospel in light of the truth of Christ through the work of the Spirit who calls and creates a people in the knowledge and love of God. Wesley states,

> At our first beginning to preach at any place, after a general declaration of the love of God to sinners, and his willingness that they should be saved, to preach the law, in the strongest, the closest, the most searching manner possible; only intermixing the gospel here and there, and showing it, as it were, afar off. After more and more persons are convinced of sin, we may mix more and more of the gospel in order to "beget faith," to rein into spiritual life those whom the law hath slain; but is not to be done too hastily either.

Wesley sketches a brief order of salvation in which one is drawn, converted, and led by the teaching of the law to living faith in the saving activity of Christ through which the Spirit bears the fruit of good works and holiness. "God loves you; therefore, love and obey him. Christ died for you; therefore, die to sin. Christ is risen; therefore, rise in the image of God. Christ liveth forevermore; therefore, live to God, till you live with him in glory."[47]

A sermon from the same year, "The Law Established by Faith" II, states this more fully,

> It is our part thus to "preach Christ" by preaching all things whatsoever he hath revealed. We may indeed, without blame, yea, and with a peculiar blessing from God, declare the love of our Lord Jesus Christ. We may speak in a more especial manner, of "the Lord our righteousness" (Jer 23:6), we may expatiate upon the grace of God "reconciling the world unto himself" (2 Cor 5:19); we may, at proper opportunities, dwell upon his praise, as bearing the "iniquities of us all," as "wounded for our transgressions" and "bruised for our iniquities," that "by his stripes we might be healed" (Is 53:4–5). But still we should not preach Christ according to his Word if we would wholly confine ourselves to this. We are not ourselves clear before God, unless we proclaim him in all his offices. To preaching Christ as a workman that needeth not be ashamed (2 Tim 2:15) is to preach him not only as our great "High Priest, taken from among men, and ordained foremen, in things pertaining to God" (Heb 5:1), as such "reconciling us by his blood" (Rom 5:9, 10), and "ever living to make intercession for us" (Heb 7:25), but likewise as the Prophet of the Lord, "who

---

46. Ibid., 489.
47. Ibid., 486, 492.

of God is made unto us wisdom" (1 Cor 1:30), who, by his word and his Spirit, "is with us always, guiding us into all truth" (John 16:13); yea, and as remaining a King for ever, as giving laws to all whom he has bought with his blood, as restoring those to the image of God whom he had first reinstated in his favour, as reigning in all believing hearts until he "subdued all things to himself" (Phil 3:21), until he hath utterly cast out all sin, and "brought in everlasting righteousness" (Dan 9:24).[48]

Wesley's doctrinally informed, evangelically oriented preaching—"plain truth for plain people"—articulated the Gospel as the wisdom and power of God. Such preaching evoked new conversions and fresh re-turnings; penitent responses to the promptings of the Spirit which were communicated by joyful witness to Christ and nurtured into disciplined love for God and neighbor within a common life of grace. The gift of living faith in love and the fruit of good works was evinced in a wide range of circumstances, but especially among the poorest and most humble of circumstances and conditions where God's generous love and abundant goodness were gladly received. Bearing witness to surprising manifestations of divine grace, such communal remembrances of God's redemptive work evoked robust, energetic, outpourings of "wonder, love and praise" that called attention to their source and goal: the praise of the Triune God who forgives, reconciles, and restores human creatures to the divine image.[49]

Such startling acts of conversion, growth, and social witness were not seen as a result of choosing the right homiletic method or using the most effective evangelistic technique; rather, they were viewed as forms of concrete, visible witness—in both their initial workings and maturing fruit—pointing to the joy of knowing and loving God, or "one thing needful." Wesley articulated this practical wisdom in his sermon, "The New Creation," demonstrating a proper relation between the goods of creation and the final good which is God.

> The one perfect good shall be your ultimate end. One thing shall ye desire for its own sake—the fruition of him who that is all in all. One happiness ye shall propose to your souls, even a union with him that made them, the having fellowship with the Father and the Son, the being "joined to the Lord in one Spirit." One design ye are to pursue to the end of time—the enjoyment of God in time and eternity. Desire other things so far as they tend to this. Love the creature—as it leads to the Creator. But in every step you take be this, the glorious point that terminates your view. Let every affection, and desire or fear, whatever ye seek or shun, whatever ye think, speak, or do, be in order to your happiness in God, the sole end as well as the source of your being. Have no end, no ultimate end, but God. Thus our Lord: "One thing needful."[50]

---

48. *Works*, vol. 2, 37–38.

49. Hardy and Ford, *Praising and Knowing God*, 148–52; see the discussion of Wesley, worship, and Methodism in "Worship, Evangelism, Ehics: On Eliminating the "And," in Stanley Hauerwas, *A Better Hope: Resources for a Church Confronting Capitalism, Democracy, and Postmodernity* (Grand Rapids: Brazos, 2000) 155–62; and Horton Davies, *Worship and Theology in England, Vol. II: From Watts and Wesley to Martineau, 1690-1900* (Grand Rapids: Eerdmans, 1996) 184–209.

50. See the sermons "On the Trinity" and "The New Creation" in *The Works of John Wesley*, 2:373–86, 500–510; On Wesley and Christian conversion, see William H. Willimon, "Suddenly a Light from Heaven," in *Conversion and the Wesleyan Tradition*, eds. Kenneth J. Collins and John H. Tyson (Nashville: Abingdon, 2001).

Wesley homiletic wisdom points to a "grammar" of faith which is ordered by knowledge and by love.[51] Such practical wisdom will entail our participation in Christ's human righteousness; having the "mind that was in Christ" through which the Spirit transforms and guides our thinking, living, and speaking by the law of the Gospel ruling in the mind and heart.[52] As Wesley writes,

> Prudence (or practical wisdom), properly so called, is not that offspring of hell which the world calls prudence, which is mere craft, cunning dissimulation; but . . . that "wisdom from above" which our Lord peculiarily recommends to all who would promote his kingdom upon earth. . . . This wisdom wil instruct you how to suit your words and whole behavior to the persons with whom you have to do, to the time, place, and all other circumstances.[53]

In *An Address to the Clergy*, Wesley writes of the need to be zealous in doing good and careful to abstain from evil. He describes the kind of practical wisdom required for guiding others to be discerning in the life of faith.

> Have I any knowledge of the world? Have I studied men (as well as books) and observed their tempers, maxims, and manners? Have I learned to be beware of men; to add the wisdom of the serpent to innocence of the dove? Has God given me by nature, or have I acquired, any measure of the discernment of spirits; or of its near ally, prudence, enabling me on all occasions to consider all circumstances, and to suit and vary my behaviour according to the various combinations of them? . . . And do I omit no means which is in my power, and consistent with my character, of "pleasing all men" with whom I converse, "for their good to edification?"[54]

Preaching the Gospel is inseparable from the sense that a preacher's vocation consists in making the truth and goodness of Christ her own. However, this will not be possible unless the love of God is the controlling passion of one's life and ministry; a desire that the eyes of the heart be purified to see God's truth and goodness in all things. Significantly, Wesley gives this practical wisdom a Christological interpretation.

> Do all who have spiritual discernment take knowledge (judging of the tree by its fruits) that "the life which I now live, I live by faith in the Son of God;" and that in all "simplicity and godly sincerity I have my conversation in the world?" Am I exemplarily pure from all worldly desire, from all vile and vain affections? Is my life one continued labour of love, one tract of praising God and helping man? Do I in everything see "Him who is invisible?" and "beholding with open face the glory of the Lord," am I "changed into the same image from glory to glory, by the Spirit of the Lord?"[55]

---

51. Cf. Maddox, *Responsible Grace*, 26–47.
52. Long, *John Wesley's Moral Theology*, 171–202.
53. *Works*, vol. II, 318.
54. "An Address to the Clergy," 484.
55. Ibid., 499.

17

From Suspicion to Synthesis
Toward A Shared Wesleyan and Pentecostal Theology of Spirituality

TONY RICHIE

INTRODUCTION

I FIRST MET DR. Laurence Wood in the 1980s through his spiritual and theological writings. I knew immediately I had found a friend. Though I saw him a few times during brief visits in the 1990s to Asbury Theological Seminary in the Doctor of Ministry program, we did not actually become personally acquainted. In 2003, at a Tercentennial Wesley Conference hosted at Dutch Valley Church of God in Knoxville, TN, by Pastor "Corky" Alexander, I met Larry Wood in person. I was so excited to be speaking on the same program with someone who had influenced me so much through his published thought. I found him to be all that his reputation and writings suggested—and then some. His presentation and discussions were profound and provocative. Further, a personal testimony he gave in a worship period of that meeting still stirs my soul at the thought of it. Happily, for me, since that time our relationship has blossomed into real friendship. Moreover, he has become an important teacher and mentor, particularly in my pursuit of a second doctorate, a PhD in theology. He has that rare ability to be simultaneously encouraging and challenging. Thank you, Larry, for all you are and do! I am humbled even as I accept the invitation to contribute to a collection of essays aimed at honoring one of the great Wesleyan and Evangelical theologians of the day.

My own spiritual and theological heritage is Pentecostal, and my ecclesial affiliation Church of God (Cleveland, TN), a denomination with a marked Wesleyan orientation, part of a tradition often known as Wesleyan-Pentecostal. Therefore, discussing an element of Wood's thought that specifically addresses the relation of Wesleyans and Pentecostals seems suitable. He has written several volumes relevant to this discussion, including *Pentecostal Grace* and *The Meaning of Pentecost*.[1] However, many of the central

---

1. Laurence W. Wood, *Pentecostal Grace* (Wilmore, KY: Asbury, 1980) and *The Meaning of Pentecost in Early Methodism: Rediscovering John Fletcher as John Wesley's Vindicator and Designated Successor* (Lanham, MD: Scarecrow, 2002).

issues are succinctly listed and elaborated in his contribution to *Christian Spirituality*.[2] This text discussed Reformed, Lutheran, Wesleyan, Pentecostal, and Contemplative views, and included responses from participants to all the presentations. Wood, of course, presented the Wesleyan view. His response to the Pentecostal presentation by Russell Spittler is particularly provocative for me, not only outlining the history of relations between Wesleyan-Holiness groups and Pentecostals, at first characterized by more and then by less suspicion, but also suggesting a way forward toward a feasible synthesis through developing a shared theology of spirituality. Following up on this suggestion is the focal task of the present essay. The approach adopted is to overview pertinent discussion in *Christian Spirituality*, then to offer examples of Pentecostal attitudes on these self-same issues, and finally to engage directly the task of moving forward, giving explicit attention to evidentiary glossolalia.[3] The immediate ground of my work here is strong general agreement with Larry Wood regarding developing a shared Wesleyan and Pentecostal theology of spirituality, but my eventual goal is to move beyond his suggestions through a specifically Wesleyan-Pentecostal perspective.

EXAMINING WESLEYAN AND PENTECOSTAL THEOLOGIES OF SPIRITUALITY

Russell Spittler's chapter in *Christian Spirituality* begins with a demographic account tracing the rapid rise of Pentecostalism.[4] He explains the relevance of spiritual gifts, including speaking in tongues, and that some (but not all) maintain that speaking in tongues is the 'initial physical evidence' of Spirit baptism.[5] Spittler distinguishes between the older, historic Pentecostal denominations, the "classical Pentecostals," which arose around the turn of the twentieth century, and those in mainline Protestantism and in Roman Catholicism who in the mid-twentieth century accepted Pentecostal experience regarding restoration of the gifts of the Spirit, the Neo-Pentecostals or Charismatics.[6] In the latter, there is a great deal of variety. Even in the former, there are important distinctions between major branches, namely between the earlier Wesleyan (Holiness) Pentecostals and the later Baptistic or Reformed Pentecostals. A major distinction is their respective orientation on sanctification.

---

2. *Christian Spirituality: Five Views of Sanctification*, ed. Donald L. Alexander (Downer's Grove, IL: InterVarsity, 1988).

3. As Wood generally agrees with Pentecostals concerning contemporary validity of spiritual gifts, or charismata, refuting typically Reformed teaching (a la, B. B. Warfield) of cessationism, or the restriction of these to the earliest days of the Church, is unnecessary. However, see S. M. Burgess and G. B. McGee, "Signs and Wonders," in *The New International Dictionary of Pentecostal and Charismatic Movements* (*NIDPCM*), eds. Stanley M. Burgess and Eduard M. Van Der Mass, 1063–68 (1068) (Grand Rapids: Zondervan, 2002).

4. Spittler, "The Pentecostal View," *Christian Spirituality*, 133–54 (133–34). See e.g., D. B. Barrett, T. M. Johnson, "Global Statistics," *NIDPCM*, 283–302.

5. Spittler, "Pentecostal View," 134–35. Simply put, the doctrine of "initial evidence" teaches that glossalic utterance accompanies and signifies the experience of Spirit baptism. See G. B. McGee, "Initial Evidence," *NIDPCM*, 784–91.

6. Spittler, "Pentecostal View," 135–40.

PART TWO: CONTRIBUTION TO CURRENT THEOLOGICAL PROBLEMS

Spittler explains that, unlike the usual sociological definition of spirituality, for Pentecostals spirituality typically has an adjectival nuance. Thus, "spiritual" is a personal or individual quality descriptive of a committed, consecrated believer signifying degrees of openness to the things of the Spirit, and includes individual piety. As "spirituality" per se may be a difficult and perhaps a-typical way for Pentecostals to express themselves, Spittler elects to index unique spiritual practices common among Pentecostals.[7] However, before proceeding he explains Pentecostal spirituality in terms of the primary importance of religious experience for adherents. Obedience and orthodoxy are also important, but personal experience is primary.[8] In fact, even speaking in tongues, as well as other demonstrative features of Pentecostal worship, are most valued as intimate, intense spiritual experience.[9]

Prayer, especially glossalic prayer (praying in tongues), holy laughter (almost uncontrollable outbursts of joy), and "pandemonium" (deliverance/exorcism) are some of the features of Pentecostal spirituality which Spittler indexes. He also explains unique terms such as "slain in the Spirit" (falling under the influence of divine power), "prayer language" (praying in tongues), and so on.[10] He closes with some evaluation, highlighting the reality of excesses and inadequacies, even elitist and triumphalist tendencies, with a stern warning that "Charisma must never be divorced from character." For all the "occupational hazards," as Spittler calls them, he concludes that Pentecostal spirituality "offers a simple enrichment to personal faith" and suggests it is a legitimate way to "love God and enjoy him forever."[11]

In response, Wood agrees that viewing speaking in tongues as 'a legitimate, and even necessary, variety of Christian experience' is "the decisive difference" between Pentecostals and Wesleyans. However, he immediately objects to Spittler's failure to give due attention to "the Wesleyan element" in Pentecostalism on sanctification.[12] In Spittler's behalf, he admits discomfort with the category "spirituality" as typically understood and intends rather to give an index of distinctive spiritual practices whereas Wood addresses the need for in depth attention to spirituality per se, wherein sanctification is central. Indeed, Wood's own essay capably addresses holiness and perfect love in terms of the "second blessing" of "entire sanctification" through the biblical models of "exodus and conquest" and the "circumcision of the heart."[13] Spittler and Wood are simply not speaking the same language here.[14] Nevertheless, even so, as stated above, for Spittler the link

---

7. Ibid., 140–41. Alister E. McGrath admits spirituality is difficult to define but concludes it generally means experiencing God and resulting transformation, and argues for the strength of its relation to theology, *Christian Theology: An Introduction* Fourth Edition (Oxford: Blackwell, 2007) 109–11.

8. Spittler, "Pentecostal View," 141–47.

9. Ibid., 146–47.

10. Ibid., 147–52.

11. Ibid., 152-53.

12. Wood, "A Wesleyan Response," *Christian Spirituality*, 162–67 (162).

13. Wood, "The Wesleyan View," *Christian Spirituality*, 95–118.

14. Spittler takes a similar approach in a later publication, but adds more in depth analysis of spirituality as such (e.g., experience, orality, spontaneity, otherworldliness, and biblical authority). See R. Spittler, "Spirituality, Pentecostal and Charismatic," *NIDPCM*, 1096–1102.

between charisma/spiritual gifts and character/spiritual fruit is necessarily inseparable. Yet Wood is certainly correct that these issues are ignored only ill advisedly and that they require direct address for the Wesleyan and Pentecostal conversation to advance.[15]

The Pentecostal and Wesleyan conversation takes a different tone when more directly addressing sanctification, contra the ambiguous, almost amorphous topic of "spirituality." In one such work, the Pentecostal participant, Stanley Horton, dealt extensively with sanctification and its relation to baptism in the Spirit, from the perspectives of both Wesleyan-Holiness and Baptistic/Reformed visions of Pentecostalism, though espousing the latter.[16] The Wesleyan respondent, Melvin Dieter, graciously, and in my opinion, correctly, challenged Pentecostals to be more consistently Wesleyan. Dieter also asserted that both the Wesleyan emphasis on the fruit of the Spirit and the Pentecostal emphasis on the gifts of the Spirit "are essential to the edification and witness of the church."[17] Dieter's acknowledgement is amicable with Wood's analysis as well as with my own understanding that the diminishment of either ethical purity or charismatic empowerment seriously incapacitates the contemporary Church.

Although Wood questions what he sees as Pentecostalism's overemphasis on speaking in tongues, he concludes that the "experimental religion" of John Wesley and Wesleyans and of Pentecostalism, with their shared emphasis on personal awareness of the Holy Spirit, have much in common that can be constructive.[18] Wood suggests the Wesleyan-Holiness Movement is indebted to Pentecostalism for its renewed emphasis on the gifts of the Spirit, and its theological implications for a stronger sense of Christian community and for the meaning of the Church as the Body of Christ. For him, Wesleyan theology and Pentecostal spirituality are "certainly compatible." He suggests Pentecostals would do well to emphasize sanctification more, and that Wesleyans would do well to recognize more the dynamic Pentecostal experience of the Spirit-filled life. He expresses personal hope that Pentecostals and Wesleyans might blend or synthesize their distinctive emphases on gifts and fruit into "a larger understanding of the meaning of Pentecostal reality."[19]

---

15. E. Glenn Hinson also wondered why Spittler failed to address sanctification and how directly this reflects the Pentecostal movement overall, particularly Wesleyan-Pentecostals. See "A Contemplative Response," *Christian Spirituality*, 168–70 (168).

16. Stanley M. Horton, "The Pentecostal Perspective," *Five Views on Sanctification*, Marvin E. Dieter, Stanley M. Horton, et al. (Grand Rapids: Zondervan, 1987) 105–35. Horton also stressed Pentecostal appreciation and dependency on Wesley and Wesleyans, and the imperative of both purity and power, in a later dialogue, "Spirit Baptism: A Pentecostal Perspective," *Perspectives on Spirit Baptism; Five Views*, ed. Chad Owen Brand (Nashville: Broadman & Holman, 2004) 47–94. The Wesleyan participant, H. Ray Dunning, "A Wesleyan Perspective on Spirit Baptism," 181–229, appeared more rigid and less reciprocal, including casual dismissal of charismata, 98–101 and 237–39.

17. Melvin E. Dieter, "Response to Horton," *Five Views on Sanctification*, 136–38 (138). Cf. Donald Gee, *Concerning Spiritual Gifts* (Springfield, MO: Gospel, 1949, 1972, 1980) 91.

18. Wood, "Wesleyan Response," 164–65.

19. Ibid., 165-66. Notably, Cecil M. Robeck Jr., "The Nature of Pentecostal Spirituality," *Pneuma* 14:2 (Fall 1992) 103–6, asserts that Pentecostals aim at the same end as Christians have since the earliest ascetics and monks, love, specifically, the love of God and neighbor (105).

Wood's apt use of the phrase just quoted, "a larger understanding of the meaning of Pentecostal reality," strikes me as significant. I take it to imply, in part, that the Pentecostal reality of the Holy Spirit is broader, deeper, and fuller than either Pentecostalism or Wesleyanism or their distinctive doctrines. In other words, neither movement represents with full voice the forceful vitality of Pentecost. Rather, in blending or synthesizing, in Wood's words, aspects of Pentecostal power applicable to purity, on the one hand, and to empowerment, on the other hand, we come closer to the grander, greater reality of the Spirit of Pentecost. If that is the case, and I think it is in the main, then neither movement can afford to dismiss the special insights and experiences of the other. A choice between tragic impoverishment and mutual enrichment confronts us. Thus, a synthesis of Wesleyan and Pentecostal theologies of spirituality surpasses ordinary ecumenical endeavor, and surpasses the sentimental sharing of movements and persons enjoying commonality; it is, if Wood is right, the only way either can be fuller of the Holy Spirit.

EXEMPLIFYING WESLEYAN-PENTECOSTAL THEOLOGIES OF SPIRITUALITY

Even prior to Wood's essay in *Christian Spirituality,* Hollis Gause, a biblical scholar and Pentecostal theologian, published a definitive book from a Wesleyan-Pentecostal perspective. *Living in the Spirit* expresses the involvement of the Spirit of God in every experience of redemption, including conviction and the call to repentance, as well as regeneration, adoption, sanctification, and baptism of the Holy Spirit. For Gause, "To be saved and live a godly life is to live in and by the agency of the Holy Spirit. The way of salvation is life in the Holy Spirit."[20] Spirit baptism involves both a distinct experience and a manner of life. All of the prior experiences in redemption "anticipate" and "culminate" in the baptism of the Holy Spirit.[21] Thus, Gause stresses the unity of redemptive experiences and resists "a sense of fragmentation" regarding life in the Holy Spirit. He yet expresses his own joint commitment to Wesleyan distinction between regeneration and sanctification and Pentecostal distinction between sanctification and Spirit baptism in the context of "the sense of unification of life in the Holy Spirit."[22]

Gause describes sanctification as redemptive provision and claim of faith and as the provision of Christ's intercession.[23] He defines baptism of the Holy Spirit as an initiating experience for the believer and being filled with the Spirit as a continuous experience.[24] Spirit baptism relates to the order of salvation in that it is the provision of Christ's atonement and intercession, anticipates and gives a foretaste of final glory, is received by and lived out in faith, and has as its agents the Word and the Spirit.[25] Due to the Spirit's

---

20. See R. Hollis Gause, *Living in the Spirit: The Way of Salvation* (Cleveland, TN: Pathway, 1980) Introduction.
21. Ibid.
22. Ibid.
23. Ibid., 39–48 and 49–58.
24. Ibid., 63.
25. Ibid., 68.

sovereignty and holiness, interpersonal relations between the human and divine has far-reaching significance. The Spirit's sovereignty involves complete commitment of the entire person to the Spirit's will in all areas of life and service, including all ministries and manifestations. Perhaps most important for the present discussion, Gause argues that the Spirit's holiness means holiness of life is "the primary manifestation of the Holy Spirit-filled life."[26]

Gause contends the nature of the Spirit determines the conditions under which the baptism of the Spirit is received and its continued enjoyment, and distinguishes between Spirit baptism's outer effects, and its inner effects, specifically commitment to truth and to fellowship and worship.[27] He considers speaking in tongues the "normative" manner in which Spirit baptism is "outwardly signaled" and its "initial externally observable manifestation."[28] He emphasizes the moral and spiritual evidences of the baptism of the Holy Spirit, insisting that, "The primary evidence of the Spirit-filled life is the visibility of Christ in the believer." Clearly, for Gause, "It is the work of the baptism of the Holy Spirit to cultivate these evidences."[29] Further, Gause argues that the Holy Spirit aims to produce unity in the body of Christ, that this occurs through living in the Spirit, and that the gifts of speaking in tongues and prophecy, often controversial and conflictive, are a valuable function as part of the Spirit's ministry in the body of Christ. Finally, he insists that love is the essential personal attribute for the operation and regulation of all spiritual gifts.[30]

Roger Stronstad's landmark work in biblical theology, *The Charismatic Theology of St. Luke*, helpfully informs the Wesleyan and Pentecostal conversation. Stronstad notes that the New Testament reveals "three primary dimensions" of the Holy Spirit's activity: salvation, sanctification, and service. Significantly, these dimensions are "interdependent and complementary." Yet Protestants have tended to emphasize initiation-conversion, Wesleyans holiness and sanctification, and Pentecostals the charismatic activity of the Spirit in worship and service. He opines that the charismatic dimension does not flourish in environments that are not open to it, and challenges the Reformed and Wesleyan traditions to add the charismatic element to existing emphases.[31] In all fairness, we might also suggest that Pentecostals give due attention to the initiation-conversion and holiness and sanctification activity of the Holy Spirit. In part, that is what the present conversation entails. However, in my opinion Pentecostals are certainly correct to insist that full-orbed and robust biblical pneumatology includes charismatic empowerment.

26. Ibid., 72.

27. Ibid., 78, 84, and 92–94.

28. Ibid., 82 and 84.

29. Ibid., 96, 97, and 104 (esp. 104). I confess some confusion at how anyone who affirms (as I also do) Wesley's intricate distinctions between "immediate," "approximate," "direct," "indirect," and "remote" "degrees" of conditionality regarding faith, repentance, and works in justification and sanctification can casually dismiss such Pentecostal explanations of the interrelatedness of ethical and charismatic/glossolalic evidences of Spirit baptism. See "The Scripture Way of Salvation," *Wesley's Works* (Rio, WI: Ages Software, 2002) 6:52–63 (esp. 6:57–61). Might not this represent a point for further discussion?

30. Ibid., 105, 115–24, and 125–36.

31. Roger Stronstad, *The Charismatic Theology of St. Luke* (Peabody, MA: Hendrickson, 1984) 83.

PART TWO: CONTRIBUTION TO CURRENT THEOLOGICAL PROBLEMS

Steven Land's *Pentecostal Spirituality* explicitly relates purity and power. Land argues that, "the unfinished theological task of Pentecostalism is to integrate the language of holiness and the language of power."[32] He undertakes this daunting task through a presentation of sanctification of the affections as part of an eschatological passion for the coming kingdom.[33] Therefore, in a sense, Land revisions Pentecostal spirituality as a foretaste of God's coming kingdom.[34] However, though well received, some suggest Land's effort neglects the full force of Pentecostal distinctiveness regarding baptism of the Spirit.[35] Nevertheless, even these admit Land has helpfully connected personal sanctification and the latter rain (of the Holy Spirit), and that he presents a vibrant, non-fundamentalist vision of Pentecostalism that does not falter on debates of subsequence and initial evidence.[36] Doubtless Land's work splendidly exemplifies a Wesleyan/Holiness-Pentecostal approach to Christian spirituality that consistently takes both purity and power very seriously.

Frank Macchia argues that the "unfinished business of Pentecostal theology" is rather "to cherish the charismatic empowerment and renewal of the church but also to situate this Pentecostal understanding of Spirit baptism within a broader pneumatological setting that accounts for *all* of the nuances of Spirit baptism." He therefore aims at a broader interpretation of Spirit baptism integrating and relating themes of eschatology and pneumatology in terms of the final transformation of all of creation into God's dwelling place (cf. 1 Cor 15:20–28).[37] Although he himself is part of the Baptistic/Reformed branch of Pentecostalism, Macchia's emphasis on the Spirit-baptized life as the life of love has strong Wesleyan overtones.[38]

Amos Yong (Assemblies of God) argues convincingly from Wesley and the Wesleyan tradition for a pneumatological theology of conversion, that is, for a pneumatological soteriology. He thus champions a dynamic and holistic Wesleyan-Pentecostal soteriological pneumatology that seeks to understand crisis and process in Christian experience on that basis.[39] In fact, Yong references Wood in *Pentecostal Grace* regarding "a dynamic soteriology" in Wesleyan thought contra the more rigid Reformed theory.[40] For the present task, note that dynamic versus static approaches to pneumatology and spirituality,

---

32. Steven J. Land, *Pentecostal Spirituality: A Passion for the Kingdom* (Sheffield, UK: Sheffield Academic, 1993) 23.

33. Ibid., 62–63.

34. Cf. Peter Althouse, *Spirit of the Last Days: Pentecostal Eschatology in Conversation with Jürgen Moltmann* (New York: T. & T. Clark, 2003) 61–66.

35. Cf. Frank D. Macchia, *Baptized in the Spirit: A Global Pentecostal Theology* (Grand Rapids: Zondervan, 2006) 41–45.

36. Ibid., 41, 43.

37. Ibid., 257–58. Italics are original.

38. Ibid., 257–82.

39. Amos Yong, *The Spirit Poured Out on All Flesh: Pentecostalism and the Possibility of Global Theology* (Grand Rapids: Baker, 2005) 103–8. For Yong, apparently Wesley and Fletcher offer a great deal to the contemporary Pentecostals in several fields, including theology of religions and theology of creation. See 247–50 and 273–77.

40. Ibid., 104 n. 68.

specifically regarding baptism in the Spirit, perhaps offer much for the contemporary Wesleyan and Pentecostal conversation. Rigidity regarding the experience of Spirit baptism, that is, exclusively interpreting it either as all about only sanctification or all about only empowerment, inevitably forestalls the conversation. Such rigidity is not representative of either the biblical witness or the Wesleyan and Pentecostal way. More biblical, more Wesleyan, and more Pentecostal would be to view, as Wood has suggested, Spirit baptism in terms of "a larger understanding of the meaning of Pentecostal reality."

ENGAGING A WESLEYAN AND PENTECOSTAL THEOLOGY OF SPIRITUALITY

Laurence Wood suggested that for Wesleyans and Pentecostals to realize synthesis a general "spirit of collegiality and amicable dialogue" should prevail in jointly addressing six specific needs.[41] First, he suggested exploring the Anglo-Catholic sacramental tradition of baptism and confirmation for understanding two distinct events in conversion-initiation and the Spirit-filled life. Subsequently, Wood has followed up admirably on his own advice. In *The Meaning of Pentecost* he argues that a liturgical renewal of baptism and confirmation including personal response and appropriation is part of the enduring legacy of Wesleyan theologian John Fletcher, inspiring and influencing both Wesleyan-Holiness and Pentecostal movements. Thus for Wood, "the primary purpose of Pentecost was to make accessible to the world a global baptism of love for God and each other through the gift (and gifts) of the Holy Spirit to the Church."[42] At least in part, this line of reflection is also an ecumenical conversation for Wesleyans and Pentecostals with other Christians in authenticating and explicating their "subsequence" theology of spirituality in the context of the greater liturgical tradition.

In a similar but distinct vein, Pentecostal scholar of Christian spirituality and religious studies Daniel Albrecht has suggestively explored Pentecostal spirituality as ritual. He summarizes that,

> Pentecostal ritual creates a liminal dimension which together with the ritual process helps to produce a uniquely ordered social group, which often has the marks of a communitas. The liminality of the ritual also works toward a "space" for personal and collective reflexivity, which, in turn, provides a basic stimulus toward transformation, namely, personal conversions, healings, empowerments, Spirit baptisms and dedications to missions, consistent with Pentecostals' understanding of the gospel.[43]

Wood's instinct that the liturgical tradition of the ecumenical church holds insights for understanding Wesleyan and Pentecostal spirituality seems on target. I would only add that both the matrix and complex of that spirituality is diverse and dynamic.

---

41. Wood, "Wesleyan Response," 166–67.

42. Wood, *Meaning of Pentecost*, 379. Cf. 357–79.

43. Daniel E. Albrecht, "Pentecostal Spirituality: Looking through the Lens of Ritual," *Pneuma* 14:2 (Fall 1992) 107–25 (125).

Secondly, Wood suggested Wesleyan and Pentecostal dialogue include discussion of the place of spiritual fruit/sanctification and spiritual gifts/edification and their relation in a broad approach to the meaning of Spirit baptism. I intend the preceding section to demonstrate that this discussion is well underway and rapidly developing, not by Wesleyan-Pentecostals only but also by the larger Pentecostal movement, and that it is occurring in terms that perhaps the Wesleyan-Holiness movement will find agreeable or, minimally, inviting. I would also rather suggest that Pentecostals are addressing Wood's third through fifth suggestions in these same examples. His third suggestion involved the relation of the gift of the Spirit and the gifts of the Spirit in terms of the Spirit's sovereignty, his fourth, the outward and inward evidences of the Spirit, and fifth, the intellectual and emotional components necessary for formulating a theology. Gause specifically addresses the Spirit's sovereignty in all the Spirit's gifting and working, as well as the inward and outward evidences of the Spirit's activities, effectively arguing that both fruit and gifts are part of the Spirit's sovereign purpose for believers, including a variety of manifestations, in the context of holy living. Stronstad demonstrates a biblical-theological basis for a full-orbed view of pneumatology incorporating initiation-conversion, sanctification and holiness, and charismatic empowerment. Land, Macchia, and Yong all demonstrate the intellectual-experiential underpinnings of sophisticated eschatological-pneumatological theologies capably charting present belief and practice into the future. This not to say that we could not say much more on the themes under consideration, only that the basic thrust of Wood's suggestions is receiving appropriate attention.

Accordingly, for the purpose of the present essay, I will focus on Wood's sixth suggestion on "the role of tongues-speaking as a valid and necessary gift for the experience of the church in today's world." I choose to focus on speaking in tongues for two specific reasons. One, Wood identifies it as "the decisive difference" between Wesleyans and Pentecostals, "the most troublesome part" of their dialogue, and indicates its discussion is required if "our witness is to be maximally effective" and that both traditions "would profit greatly" thereby.[44] I agree. Thus, it requires more intense attention. Two, in my mind, the traditional, generic critique of tongues speaking on which Wood apparently draws in responding to Spittler invites some specific and sustained elucidation. Discussion about a topic as controversial as speaking in tongues can only advance constructively by a clear and consistent presentation of the subject itself. I understand with Wood that Pentecostal teaching on evidence is derivative though distinct from Wesleyan doctrine of assurance. Therefore, the precise nature of that evidence is a legitimate topic of discussion between the two traditions.[45]

My approach will be twofold. First, I am obliged to offer some mild criticisms of Wood's critique of tongues speaking. My objective here, however, is not polemical but the establishment of a firm starting point for fertile discussion. Second, I will then present a brief theological overview of the subject of tongues speaking in terms of an overture to Wesleyan brothers and sisters. Again, my objective here is not polemical or sectarian.

---

44. Wood, "Wesleyan Response," 167.
45. Ibid., 164–65.

Contrariwise, please note that this sort of give and take is what I intend as a way forward in a "spirit of collegiality and amicable dialogue."

A frequent fallacy of non-Pentecostal observers is assuming that Pentecostalism elevates speaking in tongues as "the prized possession of Christian experience." Given Pentecostalism's distinctive emphasis on speaking in tongues, this is an understandable error. Pentecostal historian Gary McGee identifies the doctrine of speaking in tongues as the initial evidence of Spirit baptism as "the chief doctrinal distinctive of classical Pentecostalism." However, it is important to note the meaning of such statements. McGee, for example, goes on to relate the prominent place the doctrine of initial evidence has played in the historical development of Pentecostalism as a distinctive movement. He does not argue anything like that it is the "prized possession of Christian experience" for Pentecostals.[46] In fact, this is language foreign to normative Pentecostal nomenclature.

Rather, a quite different perspective appears appropriate:

> Pentecostal spirituality emphasizes a deep, sustainable piety that focuses on divine immanence, a reality that can be the experience of every individual, as was witnessed on the first day of Pentecost in the Acts of the Apostles. This spirituality affects the totality of human existence and affects one's beliefs, convictions, emotions, thought life and behavior with regards to God. In Classical Pentecostalism, the emphasis of this spirituality is affirmed through the "giftings of the Spirit" and the subjective religious experience of "Spirit baptism," all experiences which are understood as normative in the life and work of Pentecostal churches.[47]

The article continues by stressing the "personal and direct awareness of the Holy Spirit" in the context of the Christian gospel through Spirit baptism evidenced by speaking in tongues. Spirit baptism is primarily about empowerment for service and edification of the faith community with worship as "the heart of Pentecostal spirituality"—so long as worship includes not only church services but also a way of life. Insistence centers on Spirit baptism as "a doorway into the diverse area of the experience and practice of charismata" followed by the process of a "Spirit-filled life."[48]

Contrary to Pentecostals conceiving speaking in tongues as some kind of "prized possession," more accurate would be a conceptualization considering speaking in tongues as an inseparable part of an intricate complex of authentic spiritual experience

---

46. See G. B. McGee, "Initial Evidence," *NIDPCM*, 784–91 (784).

47. Garnet Parris, "Pentecostal Spirituality," *The New Westminster Dictionary of Christian Spirituality* (*NWDCS*), ed. Philip Sheldrake (Louisville: Westminster John Knox, 2005) 484–86 (484). Cf. Christopher Cocksworth, "Charismatic Spirituality," *NWDCS*, 185–87.

48. Numerous denominational handbooks and study guides strongly support a contention that Classical Pentecostals have a broader and more balanced understanding of Spirit baptism and speaking in tongues than is sometimes attributed to them. E.g., (all Cleveland, TN: Pathway): Charles W. Conn, *A Balanced Church* (1975); Ray H. Hughes, ed., *The Holy Spirit in Perspective: A Study of the Person and Work of the Holy Spirit*, (1981); John Sims, *Power with Purpose: The Holy Spirit in Historical and Contemporary Perspective* (1984) and *Our Pentecostal Heritage; Reclaiming the Priority of the Holy Spirit* (1995); James D. Jenkins, ed., *A Lifestyle to His Glory; Practical Commitments for Christian Living* (1988); T. David Sustar, *A Layman's Guide to the Fruit of the Spirit: A Pentecostal Perspective* (1990); Robert White, *Endued with Power: The Holy Spirit in the Church* (1995); and Homer G. Rhea, compiler, *The Holy Spirit in Action: The Person and Work of the Holy Spirit* (1996).

accentuating the reality and validity of the gospel of Christ for contemporary believers.[49] Obviously, this perspective determines a quite different tone of approach. Yet the intent is not to diminish the importance of speaking in tongues among Pentecostals so much as to set it in proper perspective.

Therefore, similarly astray is assessing speaking in tongues as somehow of little or lesser importance as a spiritual gift or of dismissing distinctions about varieties of gifts. Biblically, these unfortunate tendencies are unsustainable from Paul's Corinthian correspondence. Pentecostal Pauline scholar Gordon Fee notes that for Paul there are varieties of gifts each having edificatory value in its proper time and place with appropriate regulation in its operation.[50] In fact, Fee reasons that the common contrasting of Paul's discussion of love versus gifts (i.e., tongues) is fundamentally wrong. "Thus it is not 'love versus gifts' that Paul has in mind, but 'love as the only context for gifts'; for without the former, the latter have no usefulness at all." Indeed, he adds, but then "neither does much of anything else in the Christian life."[51] By the way, Paul's listing of speaking in tongues last in 1 Corinthians 12:8–10 no more indicates it is least in value than his listing love last in 13:13 suggests love is least. Nor does his not listing speaking in tongues in Ephesians 4:11 any more indicate an indirect diminishment than his not listing apostles in 1 Cor 12:8–10. In 1 Cor 12:27–31 he gives a mixed list mentioning both apostles and tongues speakers as well as others gifted in various ways.[52]

However, inadequate for understanding Spirit baptism and speaking in tongues is any approach that dismisses large chunks of relevant biblical data. Here Chan is certainly correct to argue for consideration of the pneumatological motifs of both Luke and Paul. Though he rightly warns Pentecostals of too exclusive focus on Luke, the same surely applies to Evangelicals regarding Paul—even with his overall integration of soteriological and charismatic elements.[53] Thus, it is required for Wood and other Wesleyans to wrestle with the Lukan idea of evidentiary charismata, including glossolalia. The Acts Prologue (1:1–5) introduces the Book with τεκμηριον (v. 3), signifying, "a compelling sign," and implying "proofs that carried certainty of conviction with them, as contrasted with those that were only probable or circumstantial."[54] Arguably, the strong pneumatological context, explicitly referencing the Holy Spirit and Spirit baptism, suggest application beyond the interim between Jesus' resurrection and ascension to the subsequent Pentecost event

---

49. E.g., Telford Work, "Pentecostal and Charismatic Worship," in *The Oxford History of Christian Worship*, eds. Geoffrey Wainwright and Karen B. Westerfield Tucker (New York: Oxford University Press, 2006) 574–85 (574–75).

50. Gordon D. Fee, *Paul, the Spirit, and the People of God* (Peabody, MA: Hendrickson, 1996, 2006) 163–78.

51. Gordon D. Fee, *God's Empowering Presence: The Holy Spirit in the Letters of Paul* (Peabody, MA: Hendrickson, 1994, 2005) 197.

52. Ibid., 164–75.

53. Simon Chan, *Pentecostal Theology and the Christian Spiritual Tradition* (Sheffield, UK: Sheffield, 2000, 2003) 48–49.

54. F. F. Bruce, *The Acts of the Apostles: Greek Text with Introduction and Commentary* (Grand Rapids: Eerdmans, 1952, 1990) 100, and Charles John Ellicott, *Ellicott's Bible Commentary in One Volume*, condensed and edited by Donald N. Bowdle (Grand Rapids: Zondervan, 1971, 1980) 856.

and experience of the Church as well. Thus, Luke's paradigmatic Prologue implies an emphasis throughout Acts on evidentiary charismata as signs of "Jesus' enduring activity" through the Holy Spirit in his disciples (cf. Acts 2:33).[55] Indeed, Chrysostom argued from Acts 1:3 that continuing apostolic miracles in Acts provided "evidence" and "proof" of Christ's resurrection, and that this in effect "authorized" the Christian religion.[56] In other words, extraordinary demonstrations and manifestations of the Spirit's power have evidentiary value. This evidence includes (but is not limited to) speaking in tongues.

Therefore, generally seeing tongues as evidence is not esoteric or outlandish. However, admittedly the burden of proof lies on Pentecostals to articulate more precisely the nature of that evidence regarding their particular experience in terms of the doctrine of initial evidence. Yet at this point, I only wish to suggest that Wesleyans enter that discussion by exploring together with Pentecostals the evidentiary nature of glossolalia rather than a priori deploring the Pentecostal teaching as altogether inappropriate.

I have already indicated that Pentecostals, not even in the shibboleth of initial evidence, do not simplistically presume that speaking in tongues is "the necessary evidence of spirituality". Further, though I do not deny that it may be now happening among some, and there is admittedly great diversity regarding initial evidence,[57] yet "moderation" (read diminishment) of the place of speaking in tongues among Pentecostals is probably not the basis best for opening or developing relations with Wesleyans. A misleading premise is that Pentecostals are finally letting up on tongues and now can become better conversation partners for those put off by tongues. Better is that as the Pentecostal movement and its proponents mature they defend and discuss the complexity and subtlety of their experience of speaking in tongues with greater theological acumen and nuance. Yet, the older movement, the admittedly more theologically sophisticated Wesleyans, may more readily appreciate their perspective as expressed more precisely and, hopefully, more profoundly.[58]

EXPLICATING A WESLEYAN-PENTECOSTAL THEOLOGY OF SPIRITUALITY ON SPEAKING IN TONGUES

This section takes up the second point in the preceding section: presenting a brief theological overview of the subject of tongues speaking in terms of an overture. Frank Macchia's summary treatment in *NIDPCM* serves to indicate suggestive themes. Macchia

---

55. Bruce, *Acts of the Apostles*, 127.

56. *Ancient Christian Commentary on Scripture: New Testament V: Acts,* eds. Thomas C. Oden and Francis Martin (Downer's Grove, IL: InterVarsity, 2006) 3–4. We distinguish today between pre-scientific and scientific understandings of "evidence" or "proof" but an idea of reasonably persuasive witness to reality is certainly sufficient.

57. E.g., Gary B. McGee, ed., *Initial Evidence: Historical and Biblical Perspectives on the Pentecostal Doctrine of Spirit Baptism* (Peabody, MA: Hendrickson, 1191). Cf. William W. and Robert Menzies, *Spirit and Power: Foundations of Pentecostal Experience* (Grand Rapids: Zondervan, 2000).

58. Cf. John Christopher Thomas, 1998 Presidential Address to Society for Pentecostal Studies, "Pentecostal Theology in the Twenty-First Century," *Pneuma* 20 (Spring 1998) 3–19. This is not to deny speaking in tongues requires moderation in the sense of regulation rather than limitation (cf. 1 Corinthians 12–14).

notes the social and ecumenical role of speaking in tongues as "a unifying force" in the early history of Pentecostalism and its continuing significance relation to prayer.[59] He observes various emphases from distinctive contexts. Black Pentecostal pioneer and administrator Charles Mason taught that the edificatory nature of tongues forms "solidarity with Jesus" for sharing in his mission through the Spirit. Hispanic Pentecostal theologian Samuel Solivan has spoken of tongues speech as "the cry of suffering and complaint" of the oppressed, Harvard theologian Harvey Cox as "primal speech" revealing the limits of human language in expressing the mystery of God's redemptive presence, and biblical scholar Gordon Fee as, contra common criticisms of escapism, "expressions of strength in weakness"[60]

Macchia himself stresses the eschatological context for tongues as a theophany foreshadowing God's future appearance in fullness. Tongues renew a sense of awe and wonder in God's presence, contributing to vital and vibrant worship and personal piety. Accordingly, tongues can involve a challenge the present status quo and stimulate forward movement in openness to "the voices of the powerless and the victims of evil and injustice." For him, speaking in tongues "clearly symbolize the crossing of cultural barriers in the united witness of the people of God."[61] The ambiguity, and even occasional abuse, surrounding the practice of speaking in tongues is part of the psychology and vulnerability of any religious experience but need not detract from its value and validity.[62] He gently warns critics harsh judgments against contemporary tongues speakers can also apply to biblical proponents. As William Samarin has shown, arguments of psychological aberration or specific personality proclivities regarding tongues are weak. As Amos Yong observes, a variety of symbols inspiring truth value for community transformation as living witness of the nature and will of God is congruent with the nature of tongues. Simon Chan has suggested tongues may represent "a playful response to God as loving Father." Again, Macchia argues tongues may have "sacramental" significance in "bringing to verbal expression the grace of God that encounters believers in Spirit baptism."[63]

Certainly significant for the present discussion, Macchia attributes an early loss of theological significance of speaking in tongues, a heightening of the emotional aspect of the experience, and the particularly North American emphasis on the dogma of initial evidence to disappointment over the failure of missionary tongues (xenolalia). This development, Macchia claims, led to problematic presentations of the doctrine and presumptions about its Lukan support and Pauline challenge. However, as Macchia mentions, not even every early North American Pentecostal was rigidly dogmatic about

---

59. Frank D. Macchia, "Theology, Pentecostal," *NIDPCM,* 1120–41 (1132). Macchia also explains early consternation over xenolalia (missionary tongues) for preaching in foreign lands.

60. Ibid: 1132–33.

61. Craig S. Keener, "Why Does Luke Use Tongues as a Sign of the Spirit's Empowerment?" *Journal of Pentecostal Theology* (*JPT*) 15:2 (April 2007) 177–84, argues Luke intentionally uses the sign of speaking in tongues to emphasize baptism in the Spirit as power to testify for Christ cross-culturally.

62. Macchia, "Theology, Pentecostal," 1133.

63. Ibid., 1134. Elsewhere, Macchia draws on biblical images of Babel and Pentecost through themes of threat and promise to suggest the unity in diversity Spirit baptism and speaking in tongues symbolize. See *Baptized in the Spirit,* 212–22.

initial evidence. For example, Joseph Roswell Flower in effect shifted the focus away from tongues as "the necessary accompaniment" of Spirit baptism to "the ideal or full biblical expression of what occurs in Spirit baptism." Macchia maintains that the evident Lukan fascination with miraculous speech may actually entail an ecumenical focus. Thus, people of all denominations might think of speaking in tongues as suggestive of Spirit baptism "uniting the people of God across cultural boundaries in the missionary work of the Spirit of God."[64]

Land prefers to speak of evidentiary aspects of Spirit baptism in terms of "initial evidence," "essential evidence," and "ultimate evidence." The essential evidence of Spirit baptism, that without which it cannot be genuine, is love in manifestation of the character of God. The ultimate evidence, that which is the goal in issuance of the experience, is a life of prayerful service to God in powerful witness of redemptive reality.[65] The initial evidence is speaking in tongues. Land carefully qualifies this role of speaking in tongues, warning against excesses by critics and proponents alike. The Day of Pentecost is the biblical model of the contemporary Pentecostal pattern of Spirit baptism and speaking in tongues. We should keep speaking in tongues in the context of other forms of prayer, of worship, and of the Word of God. Land describes tongues as the distinctive eschatological language of the Kingdom of God through which the Christian community testifies to the advent of the last days with demonstration and power.[66]

Land explicitly denies that Pentecostals claim to be more mature, knowledgeable, or somehow superior to other Christians. Rather, they testify to the beneficial blessings of the Spirit, which they cannot honestly deny. Land warns against allowing being filled with the Spirit to become divisive. He suggests two errors that might have that undesirable result: either forcing out those who are Spirit-filled or those who are Spirit-filled becoming vain about it. For him, Spirit baptism and speaking in tongues are analogous to the intimacy of a marriage relationship and its normative expressions. (Neither stands on legality or logic, but on love.) When as a boy, he heard his mother passionately interceding in tongues, it permanently convinced him of the authentic power of the practice. However, he carefully and concisely explains what he means by speaking in tongues as evidence.

> Speaking in tongues is the evidence of the filling with the Spirit, an eschatological sign of the last days, a source of personal edification to the believer, a gift to be interpreted for the edification of the body of Christ, and a means of underscoring the difference between the church and the world. Speaking in tongues is not law but gospel. It is not the cause of the baptism in the Holy Spirit; it is the evidence. But it

---

64. Macchia, "Theology, Pentecostal," 1134. African American pastor of Azusa Street Mission William J. Seymour understood Spirit baptism and speaking in tongues are essentially ecumenical, primarily evidenced in love and unity. The Holy Spirit unites those full of his presence and power. Speaking in tongues signifies the unification of all peoples surpassing manmade creeds and confessions. See Dale T. Irvin, "Drawing All Together in One Bond of Love," *JPT* 6 (1995) 25–53.

65. Steven J. Land, "The Nature and Evidence of Spiritual Fullness," White, *Endued with Power*, 55–82, esp. 69–78.

66. Ibid., 69–72.

is not the only evidence; and when it is the only evidence, it is not evidence of the filling with the Spirit.[67]

In my own reflections regarding speaking in tongues, I have drawn on insights of ecumenical Anglican apologist C. S. Lewis. Lewis explained the divine-human interface that occurs through the operation of the Holy Spirit in the experience of believers through the principle of "transposition" as exemplified in the practice of speaking in tongues. Simply put, the import of transposition is an adaptation from a higher to a lower medium. Accordingly, one might think of tongues as an adaptation of a supernatural experience of the Holy Spirit to the natural human medium of expression. Speaking in tongues may embarrass our human pride but we still must account for its undeniable biblical precedents. Through the principle of transposition, one transports glossolalia from the realm of the apparently hysterical to that of the profoundly holy. I argue that a transpositional approach suggests tongues speech is an event including supernatural, incarnational, transformational, sacramental, and eschatological nuances.[68] In other words, speaking in tongues involves an authentic encounter with the divine in which the human and divine cooperate and unite in changed human hearts and lives in and by the presence of God the Holy Spirit in view of their full realization in the consummation of God's purpose for time and for eternity.

An explicit theology of spiritual experience undergirded Lewis's theology of transpositional tongues. Aware of and interacting with Freudian (negatively) and Jungian (positively) religious psychology, Lewis agreed with Rudolf Otto that religious experience is essentially mysterious encounter with the Numinous. Arguably, numinous encounter constitutes the seed of all real religious experience. Thus, at its core authentic religious experience is divine encounter characterized by ineffable awe in God's presence. Therefore, I argue, religious experience is ontologically, epistemologically, and anthropologically legitimate.[69] In other words, in authentic religious experiences, such as Spirit baptism and speaking in tongues, an objective reality exists and is encountered, of which experiential knowledge is as necessary as intellectual knowledge, and that human nature is so created and designed as to be joyously responsive to spiritual experience.

For me, transposition provides an apologetic framework for viewing speaking in tongues (and other charismata). It suggests the practice of speaking in tongues entails a multi-tiered, divine-human collaborative partnership observable as and indicative of God's graciously condescending presence in relation and operation. In addition to edifying participants and congregants, it is evidentiary testimony to the possibility and reality of an intimate interaction of the Holy Spirit with the human spirit and the incredibly empowering effects of such an experience.

---

67. Ibid., 72–75 (75). Cf. fn. 29 above.

68. Tony Richie, "Transposition and Tongues: Pentecostalizing an Important Insight of C. S. Lewis," *JPT* 13 (October 2004) 117–37. Cf. C. S. Lewis, "Transposition," in *The Weight of Glory and Other Addresses* (New York: HarperCollins, 2001 [1949]) 91–115.

69. See Tony Richie, "Awe-full Encounters: A Pentecostal Conversation with C. S. Lewis Concerning Spiritual Experience," *JPT* 14 (October 2005) 99–122.

In light of the preceding models, speaking in tongues ought to be thought of as a complex reality congruent with the larger purposes of God in Christ through the power of the Holy Spirit in the Church today as it accomplishes its mission to the world by the proclamation and demonstration of the gospel (cf. 1 Cor 2:4–5). Simplistic assessment resulting in casual dismissal is incongruous with the biblical and theological status of the practice. For me, fecund conversation about tongues between Wesleyans and Pentecostals begins here. Whatever our respective stance, this is a subject we should take seriously.[70]

CONCLUSION

In sum, I suggest Wesleyans and Pentecostals discuss the potentiality of baptism in the Holy Spirit as a multi-dimensional dynamic capable of carrying confidently the themes of sanctification/purity and edification/power, that is, of holiness and charismatic empowerment, without destroying or in any wise diminishing the distinctive significance of either. Furthermore, I suggest that we discuss the role of the fruit of the Spirit and of the gifts of the Spirit as indicative of diverse elements of the Spirit's unified activity, namely, ethical and charismatic, supporting and building up each other rather than undermining or tearing down. Finally, I suggest that we discuss the practice of speaking in tongues at a depth true to the richness of its biblical and theological rationale. This includes evaluating its evidential and functional validity and value. In shorthand form, speaking in tongues is:

> *Edificatory*—builds up participants and congregants,
> *Initiatory*—ushers in the realm of the charismatic,
> *Participatory*—shares in the reality of the Spirit without subsuming it,
> *Revelatory*—discloses the mission of the Spirit and the Church in the world, and
> *Signatory*—points beyond itself in attestation.

As a Wesleyan-Pentecostal Christian, I am deeply grateful for the leadership of Laurence Wood among Wesleyans and Pentecostals. I close with a telling quote from Professor Wood on Fletcher.

> [T]here was a diversity of the Spirit's operation in the lives of different people ... the baptism with the Spirit was an ongoing dynamic event always being updated in one's daily life. It was never a static, absolute attainment, representing final achievement ... today's reception of the Spirit's fullness became tomorrow's promise of greater infillings of the Spirit. This Pentecostal experience was multidimensional in meaning, including: purity of love for God and others, the abiding witness of the Spirit that one's sins were forgiven, the full assurance of faith, peace, joy, spiritual rest, the fruit and gifts of the Spirit, and enjoying a growing relationship with the

---

70. Thus, Clark H. Pinnock, *Flame of Love: A Theology of the Holy Spirit* (Downer's Grove, IL: InterVarsity Press, 1996), argues two extremes on speaking in tongues are exaggerating its importance or refusing to take it seriously. For him, speaking in tongues is "normal" but not "normative" or "the norm." A truly "noble and edifying gift," academics and educated people tend to resist it rationalistically, but the humble receive it in childlike trust, 172–73.

triune God. The baptism with the Spirit also had social implications as well, directed outward toward others in sacrificial living.[71]

To which I only add "Amen!"

---

71. *Meaning of Pentecost*, 366–67.

Afterword

A Response to the Essays

Laurence W. Wood

I WOULD LIKE TO express my appreciation to Nate Crawford for putting this work together. Nate, along with seven of the contributing authors, was a model student in my classes. Nate has become a scholar in his own right and is emerging as one of the most promising scholars on the horizon today. He has already demonstrated his ability to interact with the leading ideas in systematic theology and philosophy of religion. Much of his work has been presented in scholarly societies, ranging from the American Academy of Religion to the Wesleyan Theological Society, which provide an opportunity for his work to be part of the scholarly debate and conversation with subjects across the academic curriculum.

I would like to take this opportunity make a few comments on each of the authors and their essays. Nate Crawford's summary of my views on the importance of Fletcher was helpful as he placed this ongoing conversation in context and summarized some of the variegated views among Wesley scholars. I am keen on Fletcher's importance for Wesleyan theology in connecting with the larger Christian tradition. One example I have seen is the revised baptismal liturgy incorporated by mainline denominations based upon the revisions recommended within *Baptism, Eucharist, and Ministry*, also known as the "Lima text." Some of the same theological issues connected with the meaning of Pentecost in Christian initiation in early Methodism are now being discussed in the liturgical renewal movement, especially in regard to the meaning of water baptism and confirmation.

Christopher Bounds' carefully researched and incisive essay on Augustine reinforces what Wesley believed, namely, voluntary transgressions is the primary definition of sin and "is a definition which has passed uncensored in the Church for at least fifteen hundred years."[1] As Bounds suggests, this distinction between voluntary and involuntary sins is pastorally significant because it provides a basis for understanding Christian ethics and helps one to see the difference between a moral definition of sin and a legal

---

1. John Wesley, *Letters*, edited by John Telford (London: Epworth, 1931) 4:155, "Letter to John Hosmeer, June 7, 1761.

definition. Both definitions are important (as I point in several of my writings), but it is insightful to understand the distinction between them, especially in conversations among Wesleyan and Reformed scholars on the meaning of sanctification. Without this understanding, the Wesleyan view of a holy life would be unintelligible.

Steve O'Malley's essay has broken new ground with his research on the meaning of Pentecost in radical pietism. This essay shows the background of Wesley's views on Pentecost as they were adopted from Christian David while both were present at Herrnhut and how these subsequently became the basis for Fletcher's fuller development. O'Malley's research provides the background for my essay, "The Origin, Development, and Consistency of John Wesley's Theology of Holiness," *The Wesleyan Theological Journal* 43.2 (Fall 2008) 33–55. This new information will become a basis for future PhD theses. O'Malley's research into the original German and French sources is surely one of the most important contributions taking place within Wesley studies. I am sure we will hear more about this ground-breaking research in the near future. O'Malley's research particularly provides a missing piece of historical continuity that goes back beyond Wesley and ultimately to the Eastern Fathers regarding the meaning and significance of Pentecost. O'Malley's research justifies Fletcher's claim that his own theology of Pentecost was derived from Wesley who was influenced by Christian David and who in turn was influenced by radical pietism. Fletcher identified his earliest extra-biblical source with the Early Greek Fathers. This essay should whet one's appetite for O'Malley's forthcoming book on *Pentecost and the New Humanity*.

Barry Callen has been a long time friend whom I have admired over the years as a model of one who possesses an irenic spirit and a creative mind among Wesleyan theologians. His Church of God (Anderson) tradition has been a dynamic and powerful influence within the Wesleyan holiness tradition. As he points out, the Church of God (Anderson) represents the essential spirit of the "come-outers" who refuse to allow denominationalism to become a substitute for the meaning of the universal church of God. Its founder, Daniel Warner, championed a spirit of unity as the basis of the community of believers, downplaying incidental differences that did not cut away the essentials of Christian belief. Those of us who are members of mainline denominations may think this "come-outism" may not be too sophisticated, but its all-inclusive disposition has ministered to many who are looking for a genuine experience of love and acceptance as members of the body of Christ without a divisive spirit of bickering over issues that ultimately do not matter. Theologically, its call for organizational simplicity is a poignant reminder that the body of Christ cannot be equated with human institutions or even doctrinal orthodoxy. Its appeal to simplicity of heart and a simple affirmation of the essentials of biblical teaching should not cause one to overlook the fact that leaders in the Church take theology seriously. Callen himself has been one who dares to think outside the box on matters of opinion such as divine foreknowledge. While I do not share his views on "open theism" (see my *God and History* and also my forthcoming essay "Divine Omniscience: Boethius or Open Theism?" *The Wesleyan Theological Journal* 45.2 [Fall 2010]), it is a sign of vigorous theological creativity when one of its leading theologians proposes a view that is doctrinally outside the mainstream of Wesleyan theology and he does so in a church that favors doctrinal simplicity and a non-divisive spirit. So the ideas of "come-outism" and doctrinal simplicity can be misleading slogans if one is not aware that theology is after all serious business within the (Anderson) Church of God. Callen's essay is in many ways a challenge to those of us who label ourselves Wesleyan not to get bogged down in institutionalism and party politics, while at the same time taking the task of theology seriously.

Bill Faupel's essay on the adaptation of Fletcher's idea of soteriological dispensationalism, as it was transmuted into an eschatological dispensationalism among some late-nineteent-century Methodist authors, is an interesting and helpful contribution for understanding why some Wesleyan writers became Darby dispensationalists, in spite of the fact that Wesleyan theologians like Daniel Steel (an advocate of Fletcher's doctrine of dispensations) strongly warned against it. We are indeed indebted to Bill for sorting this out. Don Dayton and I have exchanged differences of opinion about this connection, but I think Bill has provided a helpful way of viewing this connection that incorporates both our concerns.

Kim Alexander (and her husband, Corky) is a dear friend and greatly respected scholar. She embraces the Wesleyan-holiness tradition faithfully and sincerely, while at the same time incorporating her Pentecostal tradition. She demonstrates in her writings and life that Pentecostals are indeed Wesleyans. Her splendid essay demonstrates that the classical Wesleyan tradition and the classical Pentecostal tradition (stemming from William Seymour) have many points of similarity and congruence, as it can also be seen in my essay, "Biblical Sources of John Fletcher's Theology of Pentecost," *The Wesleyan Theological Journal* 42.2 (Fall 2007) 98–113. Her essay provides an exciting point of dialog for overcoming some of the divisions that have sometimes surfaced between Wesleyans and Pentecostals. Her exposition of the soteriological implications of the baptism with the Spirit was lucid and convincing.

Jonathan Dodrill has contributed an insightful essay on the meaning of the word "Evangelical." I am sympathetic to Dodrill's conclusion that the word Evangelicalism has become confused and should be avoided unless its broader meaning can be recaptured. That is why I have suggested in *Theology as History and Hermeneutic, A Post-Critical Conversation with Contemporary Theology* that the term "post-critical evangelicalism" is a term that could be used to help Wesleyans move beyond this impasse. Post-critical is a term coined by Michael Polanyi to suggest that all knowing is personal, contextual, and embodied knowledge. It recognizes that our language is not literal (as distinct from fundamentalism and neo-Evangelicalism), but is poetic and expressive (as Paul Ricoeur has persuasively argued).

Billy Abraham has always been able to challenge the status quo and turn things upside down. This essay on "The End of Wesleyan Theology" is no exception. With crystal clear logic, he shows that contemporary Wesley scholars (as significant as their research has been) often have fallen into the same trap that was characteristic of the life-of-Jesus biographers of the late nineteenth century, who gave us a portrait of Jesus that reflected more of their own presuppositions and biases than a picture of the Jesus Christ presented in the gospels. The consequence of that movement was largely negative about even trying to recover the so-called real Jesus of history, giving rise to the skeptical conclusion of Bultmann's demythologizing theology. Abraham does not share that same kind of skepticism when he negatively analyzes the current status of Wesleyan theology. Rather, he calls for a re-appraisal of Wesley as one who was a well informed evangelist and whose preaching and writings had more of a pastoral intent than an academic one. His analysis serves as a point of inspiration of exploring all of the rich nuances implicit in his fertile theology. I agree with his comment that a fresh look at John Fletcher would be appropriate as one among other ways of interpreting the relevance of Wesley for today. It is interesting that John Fletcher was lost to Methodism at the close of the 19th century as theological liberalism was sweeping through American Methodism and his writings were removed from the course of study. Wesley's significance was also eclipsed for a time until G. C. Cell's *The Rediscovery of John Wesley* was published in 1935. Fletcher's significance for Methodism and its continuing relevance for today has still not been rediscovered. Some would just as soon that it not be rediscovered for fear of the legalistic and rigid notions of the late 19th century Wesleyan holiness movement that took some of his ideas about Pentecost to an extreme limit. I remain convinced that Fletcher holds great significance for the postmodern world because of the pneumatological focusing of Wesley's theology. I think if we are to understand the dynamics of early American Methodism, we will see how they viewed Wesley through the lens of John Fletcher. That is not to say that Wesley could not have been interpreted in other ways, but at least it is to acknowledge that Fletcher gave an interpretation of Wesley's idea that Wesley himself came to approve of. The contemporary relevance of Fletcher is the reason for my book on *The Meaning of Pentecost in Early Methodism*.

Nate Crawford has given us an important essay on the necessity of developing a fundamental Wesleyan theology that arises primarily from a way of being and thinking rooted in love of God and love of one's neighbor. Fundamental theology can be defined in different ways, but its core task is to correlate the human condition with our basic beliefs about God in a responsible, intellectual manner. The task of fundamental theology that Crawford proposes alters the modernist, rationalistic apologetic (characteristic of liberalism, fundamentalism, and neo-Evangelicalism); instead, Crawford proposes that the character of faith begins with a way of being that is defined in terms of perfect love. Drawing from Augustine, he shows that the ability to see the meaning and relevance of Scripture depends upon a right disposition toward God. Augustine's intention was to develop a right rhetoric and not a system of ideas or a systematic method. Crawford's focus on a hermeneutic of love is a reminder of the continuing relevance of Wesleyan theology as the contemporary theological conversation is rapidly moving away from rationalistic apologetics of modernist thought to a more relational and narrative-based fundamental theology.

I was delighted with Kevin Kinghorn's essay. He is absolutely right that the mystery button can be pushed too easily as an escape from critical, logical thinking about issues. Wesley warned his preachers against speaking disparagingly about reason, and he referred to the discipline of logic as the single most important subject—next only to the study of the Bible. Kinghorn's postgraduate study with Richard Swineburne focused on analytical philosophy of religion, whereas my postgraduate study focused on continental philosophy with John McIntyre (although McIntrye was primarily oriented in the analytical tradition). These two types of philosophy are quite different in orientation, but I believe both traditions are enriched by the other. I believe Kinghorn's analysis of the issues surrounding the logic of space-time relativity and quantum mechanics in reference to the logic of eternity and time was fair-minded and profitable.

Mike Peterson, in his typically balanced and scholarly way, takes on a subject of phenomenal importance for the continuing relevance of Wesleyan theology. Opposition to evolution has done much to undermine the credibility of faith for many university students, and Peterson has provided an instructive essay on why evolution can be affirmed with theological integrity. Drawing from the Early Church Fathers and the history of the church down, Peterson shows that Christian theology has all the necessary resources to engage in constructive conversation with science without falling into obscurantism. The relationship between God and creation is to be taken seriously with a recognition that with the gift of finite existence God works more by process than by episodic interruption. Peterson shows that relationality is characteristic of a Trinitarian-kenotic-perichoretic Christian understanding and that the evolutionary development of creation is an integral part of the Christian view of things.

Bradford McCall continues this evolutionary theme by expanding on Philip Clayton's paradigm of emergence and unpacking some of the metaphysical themes implicit in it. I particularly like the way McCall develops the idea of the Spirit kenotically entering the creative order and redemptive process in history. His theological and biblical exposition of this theme is incisive, and his explication of Clayton's concept of emergence provides a way for appreciating God's free interaction with creation while preserving God's transcendence and human freedom. I am not sure why McCalls thinks the concept of *ex nihilo* is an irrelevant abstraction, except that he is right that God has limited God's self by what God created, but to make God dependent upon the eternal existence of the created order makes God more of a captive than the creator and hence God is indebted to it, which stands in contrast to the biblical meaning of divine grace—that creation and salvation are gracious gifts of divine love. If God is not the author of the material world, then God's limitation is not self-imposed, but it is imposed from without God's life and this can only mean that God is not creator and by implication is finitely limited by what is other than the divine existence. Of course, McCall does not believe God is finite and his insistence upon God's real relationship to the world is incisive. I still think my critique of those process theologians (excluding Philip Clayton) who deny *creatio ex nihilo* in my book *God and History* is valid.

Graham McFarlane is an internationally known and respected theologian with whom I have had enjoyed many conversations. He has provided a fresh reconsideration of the relevance of the theological concept of sin and its solution in reference to the "Day of Atonement," showing how sin is a theological term and not a psychological or sociological one. This is reminiscent of Kierkegaard's claim in *Philosophical Fragments* that the non-biblical religions do not know about the category of sin (although they know about evil) because sin is a personal and relational term in which one stands in opposition to

God's will. McFarlane shows how one's personal identity is shaped by relationships and that sin is a dysfunctioning of relationships; sin is a breakdown of relational expectations that are needed for human wholeness. McFarlane's focus on the possibilities of divine grace to transform human relationships is one of the distinctive features of the continuing relevance of Wesleyan theology.

Aaron Perry provides an insightful interpretation of the concept of violence, shame, atonement, and restoration. His analysis of the function of shame and violence has implications right across life's continuum from discretionary shame to disgrace shame. Particularly impressive is the way that Perry has unpacked the paradoxical effective-ineffective function of shame/violence associated with the sacrificial system of the Old Testament and how Christ is the perfect sacrifice who atoned for shame-producing behavior of humanity. Perry's work on violence provides a basis for understanding why communion is the sacrificial ritual that serves as a means of converting and sanctifying grace, which was integral to Wesley's understanding.

Don Thorsen is the premier theologian of the Wesleyan quadrilateral with his comprehensive grasp of its meaning and significance for today. He offers an illuminating discussion of the Reformers' concepts of *sola gratia, sole fide, sola scriptura*, and he shows that Wesley, drawing from his Anglican sources, understood *sola* as *prima* instead of the literal exclusive meaning of *sola* because church tradition, logical reflection, and personal experience play significant roles in the way Christian truth is interpreted. I appreciated Thorsen's correction of the Protestant frequent misunderstanding of the Roman Catholic notion of grace and good works. It was in part this confusion that was responsible for Wesley's critics to accuse him of being a "papist" by which they meant that Wesley denied justification by faith. At this point both Catholics and Wesley have been badly caricatured by their critics. Thorsen's contribution is to show that Wesley did not hold to a narrow epistemology or methodology. This intellectual openness reinforces why Wesleyan theology will continue to have significance in contemporary theology, and it offers the kind of flexibility that allows theology to stand back and reconsider its views of things as the disciplines across the curriculum continue to inform our minds about the nature of the world in all of its multidimensional aspects.

Joel Green is a preeminent New Testament scholar who has incorporated a postcritical hermeneutic in which modern historical criticism has had to reassess its role in understanding the biblical text—instead of constituting an exclusive and domineering control of what the text is allowed to say. His interpretative approach takes into consideration personal assumptions and interests that permit the interpreter to see what the text is saying as it is understood from the interpreter's own context as he/she confronts the original text. This corresponds with my focus in *Theology as History and Hermeneutics* on the autonomy of the text in contrast to an abstract notion of authorial intent, as if it were the responsibility of the interpreter to try to reach back behind the text to some deeper motivation and intent not immediately given in the text. Green's contribution here and elsewhere has been to allow the interpreter to see the biblical texts as the word of God for all times and places and which can be read and applicable for all cultures and situations. Karl Barth offered a new generation of scholars a fresh and new approach to hearing the text that had been effectively silenced by the assumptions of historicism, which essentially denied the text any contemporary significance unless it could be explained according to the supposedly provable facts of scientific historical criticism. Green has taken this Barthian insight to a new level without resorting to the dualism of fact and meaning that still haunted Barth's method. Drawing from Wesley's practice of theological interpretation of the text, Green illustrates how the original text has an expanse of meaning that is relevant to our world today. This is not a simplistic reader-response hermeneutic, but incorporates "a constellation of commitments and sensibilities" that enables the reader to appreciate the word of God today. Green's use of Wesley as a test case of this post-critical hermeneutic shows the continuing relevance of Wesley for today.

Mike Pasquarello shows that the integration of theory and practice, knowledge and faith, Word and Spirit, constitutes the meaning of "practical divinity" as was practiced by Wesley who was both an evangelist and a scholar. Albert Outler referred to Wesley as a "folk theologian," but Pasquarello perhaps more accurately refers to Wesley as a practical theologian. Pasquarello shows that it is the task of the preacher and theologian to do more than just understand biblical truth in a technical sense but to participate in the truth through faith. Even as the Father loves the Son through the Spirit, this Trinitarian model of participation is the basis for understanding the significance of practical wisdom. Practical wisdom in the Christian tradition entails a shared communal life that includes worship, preaching, Scriptural interpretation, evangelism, catechesis, discipleship training, and pastoral care. If modernist epistemology presupposed absolute proof based on the Cartesian thinking self, as I argue in *Theology as History and Hermeneutics*, Pasquarello shows that practical wisdom is based on the shared experience of the church community—the public sharing of the goodness and truth of God through revelation and the ongoing life of the Spirit within the church. Practical wisdom is not derived from simply a thinking subject, but one exists in a community of like-minded believers who also are persons with feelings and expressions, and who actively are engaged in living out truth. I like his emphasis on the importance of truth as a communal experience of Christian believers who exercise good and wise judgments. The modernist notion of truth as an impersonal, detached grasp of facts has the consequence of bifurcating persons into a schizoid split of fact and value. Pasquarello's plea for a recovery of practical wisdom has enormous implication for doing theology with an emphasis upon the importance of the mature and wise judgments of a Spirit-filled community as opposed to the rationalistic methodologies so dominant in modernist thinking.

Tony Richie recently defended his British PhD thesis, *Speaking by the Spirit: Exploring the Classical Pentecostal Tradition of Testimony in Developing a Pneumatological Theology for Interreligious Encounter and Dialogue*. His examiners praised his work as constituting a "sturdy publishable thesis." His essay here is an illustration of the thoroughness of his research and penetrating insight. He proposes a thoughtful and mediating position that is helping to bring together in fruitful dialog the traditional Wesleyan and Pentecostal overlapping traditions. The once-Wesleyan suspicion of their Pentecostal offspring (including me) has been replaced with a more constructive appreciation and understanding of the way each tradition nuances its understanding of the meaning of Pentecost. The enormous impact for good and righteousness that the Pentecostal tradition has injected into the life of church should cause anyone to temper and to reassess negative criticisms directed at a movement that obviously has been blessed of God. Richie reminds us that Pentecost is a larger umbrella that entails more dimensions than either the Wesleyan or Pentecostal traditions can define or limit to their respective traditions. Pentecost is the day of beginnings when the church was injected with the life of the Spirit. The early Methodist movement in the eigteenth century and the Pentecostal movement in the early twentieth century were decisive moments when the first day of Pentecost in Acts 2 was felt anew in remarkably new and unexpected ways. Nor is there any reason to suppose that there will not be further surprisingly new expressions of Pentecost in the ongoing life of the church. One lesson to be learned from the initial negative reaction of the Wesleyan holiness tradition to Pentecostalism in the twentieth century is that we need to wait and see what the Lord might be doing in the life of church through "earthen vessels" instead of too hastily dismissing a new "wind of the Spirit." We are all flawed and imperfect in our understanding of things as "Now we see through a glass darkly" but then "we shall know even as we are known" because we will see Christ "face to face." What are we to make of the fact when some in the late-nineteenth-century and twentieth-century Wesleyan holiness movement exaggerated the meaning of the baptism with the Spirit as an absolute crisis moment that would resolve one's personal problems, or when some in the Pentecostal movement in the twentieth-century demanded the initial evidence of speaking in tongues in order to be genuinely Christian? I suspect that humans have been more worried about possible harmful consequences from these extremes than God was. Both movements were surely blessed of God and were means of grace for millions of people throughout the world.

 I have come to appreciate theological diversity more and more as I have reflected on my own experience as a professor and have observed the changes in dispositions and thinking of my students over thirty-five years of seminary teaching. I have come to realize that theological views should be evaluated as more or less adequate instead demanding absolute precision in thinking about doctrinal matters. We are human, whereas the fundamentalist pursuit of literal, rational clarity about everything doctrinally is chasing an illusion. Kierkegaard got it right at this point—an approximation to the truth is the most one can hope for in this world, but even so, he notes that objective truth alone is not salvific. Faith is an existential decision enabled by the Spirit as a gift of God. I offer my Pentecostal friends words of thanksgiving for their holy and faithful lives. I would hate to think how impoverished the world would be today without them. I do not discount their theology of Pentecost, and what is clear is that Pentecostals like Tony Richie and Kim Alexander are as truly Wesleyan as anyone whom I know, both in their living and in their theology. I honor and respect both of them, and their theological writings are helping to inform the church in significant ways.

Works by Laurence W. Wood

BOOKS

God and History: The Dialectical Tension of Faith History. Lexington, KY: Emeth, 2005.
Theology As History and Hermeneutics. Lexington, KY: Emeth, 2005.
The Meaning of Pentecost in Early Methodism: Rediscovering John Fletcher As John Wesley's Vindicator and Designated Successor. Lanham, MD: Scarecrow, 2002.
Truly Ourselves, Truly the Spirit's. Grand Rapids: Zondervan, 1989.
Pentecostal Grace. Grand Rapids: Zondervan, 1980.

CHAPTERS IN BOOKS

"John Fletcher as the Theologian of Early American Methodism." In *Religion, Gender, and Industry: Exploring Church and Methodism in a Local Setting*, edited by Geordan Hammond and Peter Forsaith. Eugene, OR: Wipf & Stock, forthcoming.
"From Barth's Christological Trinitarianism to Moltmann's Pneumatological Trinitarianism." In *The Promise of God's Future: Essays on The Thought of Jürgen Moltmann*, edited by Robert Cornelison, 51–67. Fordham University, Special Book Edition of *The Asbury Theological Journal* 55 (Spring 2000).
"The Bible and Truth." In *The Asbury Bible Commentary.* Grand Rapids: Zondervan, 1992.
"Recent Brain Research and the Mind-Body Dilemma." In *The Best in Theology*, edited by James I. Packer and Paul Fromer, 199–241. Carol Stream, IL: Christianity Today, 1988. Winner of *Christianity Today's Best in Theology* series in systematic theology for the year 1988.
"The Wesleyan View of Sanctification." In *Christian Spirituality*, edited by Donald L. Alexander, 96. Wheaton, IL: InterVarsity, 1988.
"Confirmation." In *The Beacon Dictionary of Theology.* Kansas City, MO: Beacon Hill, 1985.
"The Pastor's Ministry to Ill Persons." In *A Celebration of Ministry*, edited by Kenneth Cain Kinghorn, 126–40. Wilmore, KY: Asbury, 1982.

SELECT SCHOLARLY JOURNAL ARTICLES

"Divine Omniscience: Boethius or Open Theism?" *Wesleyan Theological Journal* 45.2 (2010) 41–66.
"The Need to Contextualize Wesley's Sermons." *Wesleyan Theological Journal* 45.1 (2010) 259–67.
"The Origin, Development, and Consistency of John Wesley's Theology of Holiness." *Wesleyan Theological Journal* 43.2 (2008) 33–55.
"Can Pentecostals Be Wesleyan? My Reply to Don Dayton's Rejoinder." *Pneuma: Journal of the Society for Pentecostal Studies* 28 (2006) 120–30.
"Biblical Sources of John Fletcher's Theology of Pentecost." *Wesleyan Theological Journal* 42.2 (2007) 98–113.
"An Appreciative Reply to Donald W. Dayton's Review Essay." *Pneuma: Journal of the Society for Pentecostal Studies* 27 (2005) 163–72.
"Methodism and the Recently Revised Baptismal Liturgy." *Asbury Theological Journal* 59.1–2 (2004) 233–41.

Works by Laurence W. Wood

"John Fletcher's Influence on the Theology of John Wesley." *Bulletin of the John Rylands University Library of Manchester* 85.2-3 (2003) 387-404.

"Does God Know The Future? Can God Be Mistaken? A Reply to Richard Swinburne?" *Asbury Theological Journal* 57 (2002) 5-48.

"Pentecostal Sanctification in John Wesley and Early Methodism," published simultaneously in *Pneuma: Journal of the Society for Pentecostal Studies*, 21.2 (1999) 251-87, and *Wesley Theological Journal* 34 (1999) 24-63.

"Historiographical Criticisms of Randy Maddox Response." *Wesleyan Theological Journal* 34.2 (1999) 111-35.

"Purity and Power: The Pentecostal Experience according to John Wesley and John Fletcher." *Society for Pentecostal Studies, Annual Papers*, vol. 2, 1998.

"The Attainment of Christian Perfection: A Wesleyan Re-interpretation of the Anglican Rite of Confirmation." In *Sanctification in the Benedictine and Methodist Traditions,* a special edition of *The Asbury Theological Journal* 50-51, containing essays given in a world ecumenical conference, sponsored by the World Methodist Historical Society, July 4-10, 1994, in Rome, Italy, 50-51 (1995; 1996) 173-95.

"Third Wave of the Spirit and the Pentecostalization of American Christianity: A Wesleyan Critique." *Wesleyan Theological Journal* 31 (1996) 111-40.

"Above, Within, or Ahead-of? Pannenberg's Eschatologicalism as a Replacement for Supernaturalism." *Asbury Theological Journal* 46 (1991) 43-72.

"From Barth's Trinitarian Christology to Moltmann's Trinitarian Pneumatology: A Methodist Perspective." *Asbury Theological Journal* 48 (1993) 49-80.

"The Miracle of Atheism: A Critique of J. L. Mackie." *Asbury Theological Journal* 47 (1992) 43-78.

"Recent Brain Research and the Mind-Body Dilemma." *Asbury Theological Journal* 41 (1986) 37-78.

"Defining the Modern Concept of Self-Revelation: Toward a Synthesis of Barth and Pannenberg." *Asbury Theological Journal* 41 (1986) 85-105.

"The Panentheism of Charles Hartshorne: A Critique." *Asbury Seminarian* 37 (1982) 20-46.

"The Pursuit of Holiness: Some Thoughts for the Asbury Community Near and Far." *Asbury Seminarian* 37 (1982-1983) 37-44.

"Presidential Address to the Wesleyan Theological Society: History and Hermeneutics: A Pannenbergian Perspective." *Wesleyan Theological Journal* 16 (1981) 7-22.

"Thoughts upon the Wesleyan Doctrine of Entire Sanctification with Special Reference to Some Similarities with the Roman Catholic Doctrine of Confirmation." *Wesleyan Theological Journal* 15 (1980) 88-99.

"Exegetical\Theological Reflections on the Baptism with the Holy Spirit." *Wesleyan Theological Journal* 51 (1979) 51-63.

"Wesley's Epistemology." *Wesleyan Theological Journal* 10 (1975) 70-79.

www.ingramcontent.com/pod-product-compliance
Lightning Source LLC
Chambersburg PA
CBHW081145230426
43664CB00018B/2810